GUN CONTROL

GUN CONTROL

Other books in the Current Controversies Series:

GUN CONTROL

David L. Bender, *Publisher*
Bruno Leone, *Executive Editor*

Bonnie Szumski, *Managing Editor*
Carol Wekesser, *Senior Editor*

Charles P. Cozic, *Book Editor*

CURRENT CONTROVERSIES

Cover photo: AP/Wide World Photo

Library of Congress Cataloging-in Publication Data

Gun control / Charles P. Cozic, book editor ; Carol Wekesser, book editor.
    p. cm. — (Current controversies)
    Includes bibliographical references and index.
    Summary: Presents articles on both sides of the gun control issue, discussing such topics as constitutionality, the effectivenss of guns as a means of self-defense, and reducing gun-related violence.
    ISBN 1-56510-015-8 (lib.) : ISBN 1-56510-014-X (pbk.)
    1. Gun control—United States. [1. Gun control.] I. Cozic, Charles P., 1957-   . II. Wekesser, Carol, 1963-   . III. Series.
HV7436.G86   1992
363.3'3'0973—dc20   92-19875
                                                                   CIP
                                                                    AC

Contents

Chapter 2: Is Gun Control Constitutional?

Yes: Gun Control Is Constitutional

lobbying groups has convinced many Americans that the Second
Amendment prohibits gun control. This is false. Americans must be
told that gun control is both necessary and constitutional.

Chapter 3: Is Gun Ownership an Effective Means of Self-Defense?

Yes: Gun Ownership Is an Effective Means of Self-Defense

Chapter 5: Are Other Nations' Gun Control Measures Effective?

Yes: Other Nations' Gun Control Measures Are Effective

Foreword

By definition, controversies are "discussions of questions in which opposing opinions clash" (Webster's Twentieth Century Dictionary Unabridged). Few would deny that controversies are a pervasive part of the human condition and exist on virtually every level of human enterprise. Controversies transpire between individuals and among groups, within nations and between nations. Controversies supply the grist necessary for progress by providing challenges and challengers to the status quo. They also create atmospheres where strife and warfare can flourish. A world without controversies would be a peaceful world; but it also would be, by and large, static and prosaic.

The Series' Purpose

The purpose of the Current Controversies series is to explore many of the social, political, and economic controversies dominating the national and international scenes today. Titles selected for inclusion in the series are highly focused and specific. For example, from the larger category of criminal justice, Current Controversies deals with specific topics such as police brutality, gun control, white collar crime, and others. The debates in Current Controversies also are presented in a useful, timeless fashion. Articles and book excerpts included in each title are selected if they contribute valuable, long-range ideas to the overall debate. And wherever possible, current information is enhanced with historical documents and other relevant materials. Thus, while individual titles are current in focus, every effort is made to ensure that they will not become quickly outdated. Books in the Current Controversies series will remain important resources for librarians, teachers, and students for many years.

In addition to keeping the titles focused and specific, great care is taken in the editorial format of each book in the series. Book introductions and chapter prefaces are offered to provide background material for readers. Chapters are organized around several key questions that are answered with diverse opinions representing all points on the political spectrum. Materials in each chapter include opinions in which authors clearly disagree as well as alternative opinions in which authors may agree on a broader issue but disagree on the possible solutions. In this way, the content of each volume in Current Controversies mirrors the mosaic of opinions encountered in society. Readers will quickly realize that there are many viable answers to these complex issues. By questioning each author's conclusions, stu-

13

dents and casual readers can begin to develop the critical thinking skills so important to evaluating opinionated material.

Current Controversies is also ideal for controlled research. Each anthology in the series is composed of primary sources taken from a wide gamut of informational categories including periodicals, newspapers, books, United States and foreign government documents, and the publications of private and public organizations. Readers will find factual support for reports, debates, and research papers covering all areas of important issues. In addition, an annotated table of contents, an index, a book and periodical bibliography, and a list of organizations to contact are included in each book to expedite further research.

Perhaps more than ever before in history, people are confronted with diverse and contradictory information. During the Persian Gulf War, for example, the public was not only treated to minute-to-minute coverage of the war, it was also inundated with critiques of the coverage and countless analyses of the factors motivating U.S. involvement. Being able to sort through the plethora of opinions accompanying today's major issues, and to draw one's own conclusions, can be a complicated and frustrating struggle. It is the editors' hope that Current Controversies will help readers with this struggle.

> *"Often, arguments for and against gun control are fueled by the passion of personal experience."*

Introduction

Debates over gun control concern how far the government can and should go in regulating the purchase, sale, and possession of the at least 200 million guns federal officials estimate are in the United States.

Often, arguments for and against gun control are fueled by the passion of personal experience. For example, Sarah Brady became a gun control activist after one tragedy and another near-tragedy in her family. The first was the shooting and permanent disabling of her husband James Brady by John Hinckley in 1981. The second, less well known incident involved her young son, Scott. On vacation at a friend's home in 1984, Scott picked up what appeared to be a toy gun from the seat of a friend's truck and pointed it at his mother. After warning him never to point a gun, even a toy gun, at anyone, she realized that the gun in question was a real, loaded, .22-caliber pistol. After these incidents, Sarah Brady dedicated herself to working for stricter gun control laws.

Similarly, many who violently oppose gun control of any kind have been personally affected by guns. An example is Kate Petit, a Florida woman whose story is recounted in Paxton Quigley's *Armed & Female*. When Petit's car broke down on the highway between Lake Kissimmee and Tampa, Florida, a man stopped, apparently to assist her. Instead, he kidnapped her at knifepoint and forced her into the trunk of his car. After driving to a deserted road, he stopped and opened the trunk. Petit shot him three times with the .38-caliber revolver she had hidden in her purse, killing him. Petit, who had carried a gun for self-defense for years, later learned that the man was a felon who had been convicted of eleven counts of sexual assault, including sodomy, child molestation, and rape.

The personal accounts of Sarah Brady and Kate Petit reveal why the gun control debate often takes on the elements of a crusade. Those who have been victims of gun violence often view guns as threatening, dangerous objects that must be strictly controlled or even banned. People who have used guns for protection or sport, however, view firearms as useful objects that every American has a right to own.

These divergent views are represented by several national organizations. The National Rifle Association (NRA), the primary pro-gun lobby, is a powerful grass-roots organization well-supported by its 2.7 million members. The NRA's political clout comes from its effective marshalling of these members, most of whom are gun owners who oppose all forms of gun control. Through effective direct mail campaigns, the NRA gets its members to write to their congressional representatives to oppose gun control bills. As one of the most powerful lobbying groups in the nation, the NRA compels many senators and representatives to vote against gun control measures.

Gun control advocates are represented by several organizations, including Handgun Control, Inc. and the National Coalition to Ban Handguns (NCBH). Rather than being united behind one goal, like the NRA, these organizations seek different approaches to gun control. For example, Handgun Control, Inc. supported legislation such as the Brady Bill, which would have required a seven-day waiting period for potential gun buyers. The NCBH, however, seeks to ban all handguns. Gun control organizations also lobby state legislatures, often effectively. Frequently these organizations use the personal testimonies of gun violence victims such as Jim Brady to persuade legislators of the need for stricter gun control laws.

Both gun and gun control advocates use statistics on crime and self-defense to bolster their causes. For example, gun control proponents contend that guns in the home are more likely to be used against family members than against criminals. Gun owners, in contrast, cite statistics showing that guns in the home are effective in deterring criminals. These conflicting statistics cloud the issue and make it difficult for most Americans to clearly understand the relationship between guns, gun control, and crime.

In general, most Americans fear crime and simply want to be safe from it. To gain this assurance of safety, some—nearly seventy million—purchase guns. Others refrain from purchasing firearms because they fear that a gun in the home could be used against them or could be the cause of an accident, homicide, or suicide in the family. The emotionalism and rhetoric of the gun and gun control lobbies does little to help Americans make informed decisions about this important issue.

How lobbying groups affect the gun control debate is just one of the issues addressed in *Gun Control: Current Controversies*. Contributors such as Sarah Brady, Warren E. Burger, Franklin E. Zimring, Sanford Levinson, and David B. Kopel also examine the relationship between guns and crime, the constitutionality of gun control, guns and self-defense, measures to reduce gun violence, and how other nations deal with gun violence and gun control.

Chapter 1

How Would Gun Control
Affect Crime?

CURRENT CONTROVERSIES

Gun Control and Crime: An Overview

by Franklin E. Zimring

About the author: *Franklin E. Zimring is a law professor and director of the Earl Warren Legal Institute at the University of California, Berkeley. He is an expert on the relationship between firearms, violence, and gun control, and has directed the U.S. government's Task Force on Firearms of the National Commission on the Causes and Prevention of Violence.*

Americans own a greater number and variety of firearms than do the citizens of any other Western democracy, and they also use their guns against one another much more often. This special significance of firearms in American life has led to a protracted and acrimonious conflict about gun control. Gun control laws in the United States have not achieved the levels of public safety that their supporters had hoped for. Firearms continue to multiply, and deaths from guns have increased since the early 1960's to roughly 30,000 per year. From the failure of existing gun control laws, opponents conclude that controls cannot work, while proponents declare that existing laws must be better enforced or different kinds of controls tried.

The central task of firearms controls through public law is to reduce the hundreds of thousands of occasions each year when guns are used illegitimately without unduly disrupting the millions of occasions when guns are used legitimately—including hunting, target sports, self-defense, and collecting. A perfect gun control law would eliminate the unlawful use of guns and leave all legitimate users undisturbed. Real world choices involve harder tradeoffs.

Guns and Violence

What exactly is the "gun problem"? Advocates of control begin by pointing out that more than 20 percent of all robberies and about 60 percent of all homicides are committed with firearms. Their opponents reply that the vast majority of the country's 130 million firearms are not involved in violence, and that crime rather than firearms is the real problem. "Guns don't kill people," they assert, "people kill people."

Excerpted from Franklin E. Zimring, *Gun Control*, National Institute of Justice Crime File Study Guide, U.S. Department of Justice, 1984.

Serious assault with a gun is, according to the best estimates, three to five times as likely to cause death as a similar attack with a knife, the next most dangerous weapon. And gun robberies are three to four times as likely to result in the death of a victim as are other kinds of robbery.

Firearms are often discussed as a general category, without distinguishing among handguns, rifles, and shotguns. In some respects that approach is appropriate because a rifle or a shotgun, if used in an attack, is at least as dangerous as a handgun. Even a superficial study of statistics on firearms and violence, however, suggests that the handgun presents special problems. The handgun—small, easy to conceal, and relatively unimportant in hunting—accounts for about one-fourth of the privately owned firearms in the country, but it is involved in three-fourths of all gun killings. In the big cities, handguns account for more than 80 percent of gun killings and virtually all gun robberies.

> *"A perfect gun control law would eliminate the unlawful use of guns and leave all legitimate users undisturbed. Real world choices involve harder tradeoffs."*

Even though the most common reason for owning a handgun is for household self-defense, studies suggest that loaded household handguns are more likely to kill family members than to save their lives. A Detroit study found that more people died in 1 year from handgun accidents alone than were killed by home-invading robbers or burglars in 4-1/2 years. The discovery that self-defense handguns are from this standpoint a poor investment suggests that rejecting handgun ownership makes sense from a safety perspective, even if other families retain their guns. But if unilateral disarmament is rational, why do people not give up their guns voluntarily, and why do handguns continue to proliferate in the cities?

Guns Remove Fears of Violence

To some extent, urban gun ownership for self-defense results from misinformation about the risk of accidental death and the usefulness of guns in defense of the home. However, it is foolish to think that millions of American families keep handguns merely because they have not read the statistics, or to suppose that showing them data will change their minds. The risk of accidental or homicidal death from a loaded gun in the home—although greater than the chance that the gun will save lives—is nevertheless small. In the majority of homes with handguns, the only real use of the gun may be to make its owner feel safer. People will reject statistics that show otherwise because, even if their guns do not give them any real measure of protection, they have no other way to deal with their fears.

Simply because the problems are real does not mean that the solutions are easy. Indeed, the extent of the gun problem in the United States should be a warning that reducing gun violence will be difficult and expensive. There are already more than 20,000 gun laws in the Nation to match the thousands of gun killings. Why should gun laws decrease the rate of criminal killings when criminals, by definition, do not obey laws?

Gun Control Strategies

A number of different types of gun control strategies have been attempted and proposed. How are these various laws supposed to work, and is it likely that they will?

1. *Place and manner restrictions.* Most of the gun laws in the United States attempt to separate illegitimate from legitimate gun use by regulating the "place and manner" in which firearms may be used. They prohibit the carrying of firearms within city limits or in a motor vehicle, the carrying of concealed weapons on one's person, or

> *"Reducing gun violence will be difficult and expensive."*

the discharging of a firearm in a populated area. Such laws attempt to reduce firearm violence by authorizing the police to intervene before violence or crime actually takes place. Since there are obvious limits to the ability of police to prevent firearm violence and to discover persons who violate place and manner laws, these laws may deter at most a limited amount of gun violence.

2. *Stiffer penalties for firearm violence.* Members of the National Rifle Association have been among the most vocal supporters of laws that increase prison sentences, or make them mandatory, for persons committing crimes with guns. Such laws do not make it harder for potential criminals, or anyone else, to obtain guns, but they are intended to reduce gun crime by making punishments for crimes with guns so severe that potential criminals either will commit the crime without a gun or will not commit the crime at all. More than half of the States have laws providing for longer sentences for criminals who carry or use a gun while committing a felony.

A Question of Deterrence

In order to reduce the number of gun crimes, such laws would have to deter persons who would not be deterred by the already stiff penalties for gun crimes. Can the threat of additional punishment succeed? Perhaps the robber could be deterred from using a gun if the punishment for gun robbery were several times greater than that for nongun robbery.

The issue is especially complicated for the crime of gun assault, that is, actual shootings; he who attacks with a gun is already risking the law's maximum punishment if his victim dies. How much additional deterrence can come from lesser mandatory penalties for nonfatal attacks? Proponents of this approach suggest that the apparently severe penalties for crime are misleading; in reality light punishments are often given. Of course, the same thing can happen with mandatory sentences; one way or another they may not be imposed.

There may be some hope of reducing gun crime by increasing the gap between the penalty for that crime and the penalty for other crimes. At the same time, there is reason to doubt that such a program will have a major effect on the rates of gun killings and assaults.

3. *Prohibiting high-risk groups from owning guns.* Another strategy is to forbid certain high-risk groups from owning firearms. The groups usually covered include those with serious criminal records, the very young, alcoholics, drug addicts, and mental patients. Nearly every State and the Federal Government prohibit some type of high-risk ownership. However, many of these laws do not require proof of eligibility to own a gun before purchase. Instead, the ineligible person will be subject to criminal penalties if caught possessing a firearm. If such laws could reduce the number of guns owned by people subject to the prohibition, they would indeed reduce gun violence. But enforcing such laws is neither easy nor effective. It is not *easy* because, by not requiring purchasers to prove that they are not in the prohibited class, the law is still trying to use the threat of future punishment as a substitute for making it more difficult for high-risk groups to obtain guns. It is not *effective* since most homicides are committed by persons who would qualify for ownership under any prohibition that operated on only a minority of the population.

4. *Permissive licensing.* Many States try to enforce the ban on gun ownership by high-risk groups by requiring people to qualify themselves before they can buy guns. This type of restriction takes one of two forms: a license to buy a gun, or an application to purchase coupled with a waiting period. Permissive licensing is thought to be an advantage over a simple ban on ownership because it makes persons prove that they are eligible to own a

> *"It is extraordinarily difficult to let the 'good guys' have all the firearms they want and at the same time to keep the 'bad guys' unarmed."*

gun before they can obtain a license. Such a system does not depend solely on the prudence of the people barred from ownership because they are not thought to be good risks. However, adoption of such a system is also precisely where opponents of gun control draw the line because licensing imposes costs and inconveniences on all gun owners.

Considering the Constitution

Finding appropriate gun control strategies also involves constitutional considerations and the balance between Federal and State responsibility for crime control. The second amendment to the United States Constitution provides for a right of the people to bear arms, and many State constitutions contain similar provisions. While there is dispute as to what that provision of the second amendment means, it has never been held to invalidate Federal or State gun control legislation. Nonetheless, the "right to bear arms" is frequently invoked as a reason to avoid restrictions on legitimate gun ownership and use.

Would licensing work, assuming that the opponents could be outvoted? Like ownership prohibitions, it would not prevent the majority of gun killings, which are committed by persons who would qualify for ownership. But would it at least keep guns from high-risk groups?

The problem with permissive licensing is that it leaves some 35 million handguns in circulation. Half of all the handguns in the United States are acquired secondhand, and most of these are purchased from private parties, who may not ask to see licenses. Moreover, there are 35 million handguns available to steal. In short, it is extraordinarily difficult to let the "good guys" have all the firearms they want and at the same time to keep the "bad guys" unarmed. It does not appear that States with permissive licensing systems made much progress in reducing gun violence during the years when the Federal Government failed to control interstate traffic in most firearms. With stronger Federal aid, the potential of such laws is still limited, but it is not known how limited.

5. *Registration.* Under registration laws, every gun is registered as the property of a particular licensed owner. Several States and cities have such laws, often coupled with other types of gun controls. Gun registration thus usually requires owners to provide information about the guns they own, in addition to the information about themselves that is required to obtain a license. An analogy to the registration system for automobiles is often drawn by supporters of such controls.

Effectiveness of Registration Is Questionable

The best argument against registration is clearly its cost, but the debate centers on the purpose of registration. If criminals—who, it must be remembered, do not obey the law—fail to register their guns, how can registration possibly reduce gun crime? The answer usually offered is that registration is designed only as a support to any system that seeks to allow some people, but not others, to own guns. If such a system is to prove workable, then some method must be found to keep guns where they are permitted by making each legitimate gun owner responsi-

> *"The very crime rate that makes many people want gun control also makes gun control extremely difficult to achieve."*

ble for each gun he owns. After all, some of the "good guys" would otherwise transfer guns through the second-hand market to "bad guys" and thus frustrate permissive licensing systems. If registration helped to keep the "good guys" good, it could help prevent gun violence, even if not a single criminal were polite enough to register his gun.

It is also possible that gun registration will deter the qualified owner from misusing his gun since it can be traced to him; yet no one is quite sure how much deterrence would result. All in all, it is difficult to estimate how much additional prevention a licensing system obtains by requiring registration, but it seems self-defeating not to require registration of some kind in any system that seeks to bar certain groups from gun ownership.

6. *Cutting down on the handgun.* The most extreme solution to firearms violence is to reduce substantially the number of handguns owned by civilians. Under this proposal, no one would be permitted to own a handgun unless he had a special need for it. Two approaches have been enacted: restrictive licensing and handgun bans. Under restrictive licensing, persons who want to own a gun must establish their need for one before they can receive a license. Under a handgun ban, certain classes of persons (for example, police officers and members of gun clubs) are exempted from the operation of the law. Thus, a handgun ban is not necessarily a more restrictive control than restrictive licensing: whether it is depends on the classes allowed to possess guns. Moreover, handgun bans usually exert no direct control over those who are exempt from its coverage, whereas a restrictive licensing system licenses those who would probably be exempted under a ban. A significant minority of American cities have experimented with either restrictive licensing or handgun bans.

> *"Any gun control policy will be something of an experiment in the coming years."*

Many gun owners doubt that such plans will work because "when guns are criminal, only criminals will have guns." Moreover, they argue, if handguns are illegal, criminals will switch to other kinds of guns, a development that will not reduce gun crime but will spur efforts to confiscate all kinds of civilian firearms.

Both of these arguments have some force, but they must be balanced against important facts about the relationship between guns and violence in the United States. First, guns are more lethal than other weapons. Thus, substantially reducing the number of handguns should reduce the number of homicides resulting from accidental weapon use and the use of a weapon to settle an argument, even though some criminals will undoubtedly continue to use handguns. Second, it appears to be harder than one might suspect for the handgun robber or attacker to switch to a rifle or other "long" gun. For this reason, the average handgun is many times more likely to kill than the average long gun. States that try to restrict handguns find that their major problem becomes not the long gun but the illegal handgun.

Controlling a Vast Arsenal of Guns

The real difficulty in restricting the handgun is how to reduce the number of such guns in circulation enough to make headway against gun violence, and, if it can be done, how long this will take and what its cost will be. It is possible, by law, to put a stop to the manufacture of handguns at any time, but even if this were done, some of the 35 million handguns in the civilian inventory would still be killing people in the 21st century. Under the best conditions, collecting the vast arsenal of civilian handguns would be neither easy nor swift. Americans do not live under the best of conditions—the very crime rate that makes many people want gun control also makes gun control extremely difficult to achieve. How many citizens would turn in their guns when the law took effect? How long would it take to remove the guns from the streets, where they do the most harm? Should urban households be left fearfully defenseless? Is it desirable to add yet another victimless and unenforcable crime—possession of a handgun—to the depressingly long list of such crimes that have already accumulated? These are not easy questions to answer.

Finding appropriate gun control strategies also involves constitutional considerations and the balance between Federal and State responsibility for crime control. The second amendment to the United States Constitution provides for a right of the people to bear arms, and many State constitutions contain similar provisions. While there is dispute as to what that provision of the second amendment means, it has never been held to invalidate Federal or State gun control legislation. Nonetheless, the "right to bear arms" is frequently invoked as a reason to avoid restrictions on legitimate gun ownership and use.

Federal, State, and Local Responsibilities

The traditional division of authority for crime control between the Federal Government and the States also limits the extent of Federal involvement in gun control. Street police work is the province of local government in the United States. Gun control laws that require police enforcement must be carried out by municipal police.

But whatever gun control strategies are tried, it seems that local initiatives must have State and national support if they hope to achieve their goals. When jurisdictions pass strict laws against certain kinds of gun sales and resales, guns leak in from other jurisdictions that do not have the same controls. Moreover, the existing Federal law designed to assist States and localities has not been adequately enforced.

Any gun control policy will be something of an experiment in the coming years. It is not known how effective any law can be when there are so many guns in circulation and so much pressure to keep them there.

Gun Control Would Reduce Crime

by Jerome P. Kassirer

About the author: *Jerome P. Kassirer is a physician and contributor to the* New England Journal of Medicine.

Firearms and their grisly consequences are so pervasive in our society that they seem to be standard fare. Each day newspapers in major cities report injuries and deaths from guns, frequently among teenagers, and show photographs of their bereaved families. Movie advertisements scream titles that promise plenty of bloodshed, illustrated by guns and the tough characters who flaunt them. And the newest movie innovation: women who sport handguns or automatic rifles and who look as scary as their male counterparts, with new slogans, such as "Killer eyes. Killer legs. Killer instincts." A casual flip through several television channels often reveals a succession of handguns, automatic rifles, and murders. We seem to thrive on violence.

The Toll Mounts

Within this social context, the rate of injuries and deaths from firearms continues to increase. Since 1987 the murder rate reached a new record each year, increasing from almost 18,000 in 1987 to more than 23,000 in 1990. There are approximately 200 million firearms in the United States, of which some 60 million are handguns. Each year 640,000 citizens face offenders armed with handguns in attempted rapes, robberies, and assaults; more than 90,000 of these citizens are injured and nearly 10,000 are killed. Almost 20,000 people die in suicides committed with firearms each year, and in some areas more than half of these deaths are attributable to handguns. In a survey a few years ago, firearm injuries were among the 10 most frequent causes of death in the United States, ranking higher, for example, than perinatal causes and renal disorders. Among young people, they rank even higher, especially among black males. We do not lack legislation: more than 20,000 laws at the federal, state, and local levels deal with the sale, distribution, and use of firearms in the United States. Obvi-

Adapted from Jerome P. Kassirer, "Firearms and the Killing Threshold." The complete article, with references and graphics, can be found in *The New England Journal of Medicine* 325 (Dec. 5, 1991): 1647-49. Reprinted with permission.

ously, these existing laws have not stopped the carnage.

Despite the alarming statistics, the national debate over handgun control is narrowly focused on relatively bureaucratic measures, such as gun registration and waiting periods. Handguns should remain available, according to the debate, but perhaps there should be either a period preceding purchase in which to check a potential owner's record or a national registration system for licensing the guns. Talk of more restrictive measures is political suicide.

A decision about whether such mildly restrictive measures are adequate or whether access to firearms should be more severely restricted is in many respects similar to the medical decisions physicians make every day about disparate choices. Such decisions depend on an objective assessment of the benefits and risks (and costs) of the relevant options and the weighing of these countervailing values. In medicine, this kind of analysis is often applied to decisions about using diagnostic tests, drugs, and other therapeutic approaches. Benefits are assessed in terms of the accuracy of tests and the efficacy of treatments, and risks in terms of morbidity and mortality. When one choice yields benefits that clearly outweigh the risks we embrace it, and when the reverse obtains we reject it. When the comparison of benefits and risks fails to yield an unambiguous choice, we develop either a formal or an informal benchmark, or threshold, based on the benefits and risks, that defines how a procedure or treatment should be used. We would use the procedure or treatment when our suspicion of a certain disease exceeds this threshold, and we would avoid it when it falls short of the threshold.

A similar analysis can be used in deciding whether to restrict private ownership of firearms. Firearms are associated with both benefits and risks, and when we exceed some threshold level of firearm-induced injuries and deaths, we should be willing to restrict their use. This threshold level would be determined by many factors: the benefits of firearms and how we value them; the risks and costs and their magnitude; the balance between benefits and risks; and the efficacy of measures that either increase the benefits, reduce the risks, or both.

> **"We seem to thrive on violence."**

The Benefits of Firearms

Americans ascribe several benefits to the personal ownership of firearms. Many believe they protect us against those who might harm us. They give personal satisfaction to others: pleasure in the sport of target practice and in the hobby of gun collecting, a feeling of control, and perhaps social status. Some believe that possession is guaranteed by the Bill of Rights and regard this "benefit" as an inalienable right. Guns also appeal to our American pride in individuality and independence. Lastly, the manufacture and distribution of firearms by American companies produce economic benefits.

The risks are somewhat more concrete. Firearms are often used impulsively against oneself or others. They produce unintentional or intentional injuries and deaths in people's homes and at various sites of criminal activity. These risks are not equally shared by all classes of society: the young and members of minority groups are affected disproportionately. Medical costs and the grief suffered by families and friends are important added hidden costs.

> *"States with relatively stringent handgun laws have lower suicide rates."*

These benefits and risks have changed with the times. Decades ago, gun-related deaths were not an everyday occurrence, and the balance, most agreed, tilted in favor of private gun ownership. Even today, given the different ways that people perceive the benefits and risks, it is not surprising that the decision to restrict or not to restrict private ownership of firearms varies considerably, even among reasonable people. Yet on the face of it, because the choice today is between personal satisfaction as the principal benefit and thousands of injuries and deaths as the risk, even a small number of injuries and deaths should persuade us to limit private ownership, at least of handguns and assault rifles. Nonetheless, it is apparent that as a nation we have not exceeded the threshold number of deaths—the "killing threshold"— necessary to evoke serious restrictions on firearms, even when only handguns or assault rifles are at issue. Why not? Do we overvalue the benefits? Do we undervalue the risks?

I believe we do both. As a society we value the benefits of firearms too highly. Aside from an obvious overvaluation of firearms for social status, a prime example is the value placed on firearms in the home for purposes of protection. Studies of firearm-related deaths in the home show that suicides, criminal homicides, and accidental deaths outnumber deaths attributed to self-defense by a factor of more than 40. This is a remarkable disproportion. Many who acknowledge this disproportion, however, argue that if we disarmed law-abiding citizens, the criminals would still acquire and use guns, and by inference the risks would not be reduced sufficiently to change the balance in favor of gun control. Other methods of control—such as enforced safety devices on handguns, widespread educational programs on firearm safety, or laws that restrict the use of guns already in circulation or impose stiff penalties on illegal gun use—are rational, but they simply have not affected the rate of death from firearms.

Studies Prove Effectiveness of Gun Control

What was missing in this emotional dispute until recently were objective data on the efficacy of firearm restriction. Over the past several years, a series of important epidemiologic studies have provided evidence of the efficacy of gun control; the paper by Colin Loftin et al. in the December 5, 1991 *New England*

Journal of Medicine describes one such study. These authors found that there was a statistically significant, sustained decline in gun-related homicides and suicides in the District of Columbia after a law was adopted that banned the circulation, purchase, sale, transfer, and possession of handguns. There was no parallel increase in mortality from causes other than guns, suggesting that other lethal weapons were not being used as substitutes. The results of this study are consistent with others published in the *Journal*. Two such studies compared firearm-related homicides and suicides in the adjacent metropolitan areas of Seattle, Washington, and Vancouver, British Columbia. These cities are quite similar in demographic characteristics and criminal activity, but Vancouver has tougher handgun laws and fewer handgun owners. The chance of being murdered with a handgun was nearly five times higher in Seattle than in Vancouver, and the chance of suicide by handgun among young adults was almost six times higher in Seattle. The rates of homicide by methods other than the use of handguns were not substantially different between the two communities, suggesting that restriction of handgun ownership in Seattle might lower the homicide rate. The low rate of handgun-related suicide in Vancouver, however, was offset in the population at large by a higher rate of suicide by other means, but among young adults, who often use guns impulsively in suicide attempts, the suicide rate was nearly 30 percent lower in Vancouver than in Seattle. Other data also suggest that suicide rates depend on the availability of handguns. In particular, states with relatively stringent handgun laws have lower suicide rates.

Thus, several conclusions emerge from the analysis: the benefits of firearm availability are almost entirely intangible, the risks are substantial, and the efficacy of restrictive laws in influencing deaths from firearms seems established. Objective observations such as these would predict that the threshold level of deaths necessary to convince us that we should regulate the private ownership of handguns and automatic rifles tightly should be quite low. I

> *"The task of persuading the public to hand in their guns will not be easy."*

believe we exceeded this threshold long ago. Yet physicians and their medical organizations have not responded adequately. Individual physicians are nearly invisible in campaigns against the private ownership of lethal firearms. The policies of major medical organizations vary considerably: many have no policy on firearm control, and others advocate only registration in one form or another. Only a small number support legislation to ban the private use of handguns.

A Medical Problem

What can physicians do? They can look on gun-related deaths not only as a social problem but also as a medical problem. They should acknowledge that the epidemic of injuries and deaths from firearms consumes their time and expertise, particularly if they practice in the inner cities, and drains resources from other critical health needs. Doctors should examine the benefits and risks of handgun and automatic rifle ownership. They can assess the data themselves, examine all the elements that influence the decision, assign their own personal values to the benefits and risks, and make a judgment. If they concur that we have exceeded the killing threshold, they should speak out and be counted as they did in the campaign against cigarettes. Physicians can pledge to keep handguns out of their own homes, obtain commitments from their patients to eliminate handguns from any household containing children, and become vocal advocates for gun-free households. Because many of us have become so attached to guns, as we were to cigarettes, the task of persuading the public to hand in their guns will not be easy. Results will be measured in years, yet during that time lethal firearms will still be available to many who should not have them. Doctors can address themselves to this problem, too. They can cite evidence of the efficacy of firearm legislation to their patients and to their professional societies. They can persuade these organizations to adopt policies advocating the limitation of private ownership of handguns and automatic rifles. But they must not stop there, because policies are not sufficient; our professional organizations must exert pressure on state and national legislators to act.

The death rate from guns has long been a national disgrace. Now that we have the data, we must have the will.

Gun Control Would Reduce Crime Against Blacks

by Robert Berkley Harper

About the author: *Robert Berkley Harper is a law professor at the University of Pittsburgh School of Law in Pennsylvania. He is a former police legal advisor to the city of Pittsburgh.*

Violence in the form of carnage by firearms continues to be an integral part of the lives of the American people. Since 1900, over 800,000 lives in the nation have been sacrificed as a result of our permissive misuse of guns. The recorded incidence of death shows that gun killings have resulted in a greater death toll than all American deaths from wars dating from the Revolution. . . . Well over one million Americans have been killed by handguns in domestic violence, twice the number killed in the four wars this nation has been involved in during this century. This violence has resulted in citizens securing their homes and being afraid to walk the streets at night. Their fears are grounded in harsh reality, for every twenty-six seconds a violent crime is committed and every twenty-seven minutes someone in the United States is murdered. Added to the murder figures are the nearly 3,000 fatal domestic firearm accidents and 10,500 firearm suicides, making a total gun fatality count in this country of about 23,000 per year.

Young Blacks and Murder

Most murders involve victims and offenders who know one another—an outgrowth of quarrels between spouses, lovers, relatives, neighbors, and friends. However, since the early 1960's, murder by strangers has increased nearly twice as fast as murder by relatives, friends, and acquaintances. The victims of crime and the offenders are surprisingly alike. It has long been known that the race of victims and offenders are likely to be the same. In addition, it has been found that the victims of assaultive violence generally are male, young, poor, black, and unmarried.

Excerpted from Robert Berkley Harper, "Controlling and Regulating Handguns—A Way to Save Black Lives," *National Black Law Journal* 9 (3): 229-51. Reprinted with permission.

According to the National Center for Health Statistics, the murder rate of blacks by blacks for males age 15 to 24 is 73 per 100,000 population—compared with 12.5 per 100,000 for the same age group of white males. In August 1984, the National Institute of Mental Health (NIMH) stated that black-on-black killing has become a national epidemic. According to the Bureau of Justice Statistics, there is one chance in twenty-one that a black American male will be murdered. These odds are about six times greater than those confronting white men.

Stopping the Killing

Dr. James Ralph, a black psychiatrist and chief of NIMH's Center for Minority Group Mental Health said, "The killing has to stop." It is only hoped that this sentiment is shared by all Americans both black and white. Our nation should be stunned by these appalling statistics, and make a national commitment to bring about a significant change.

Measured by any yardstick—law and order, human tragedy, finance—the easy access to private ownership and the use of guns has become a menace to our society. A sampling of the tangible and intangible tragedies interwoven in the handgun menace indicates that over $500 million is spent annually in hospital care nationwide for handgun wounds. Annually, handguns take the lives of over twenty thousand individuals, many of whom are black and have potential average lifetime earnings of $116,000. Thousands of families are thereby reduced to welfare for want of a breadwinner. The needless death of so many black young men has increased the hardships that already face the black community.

> *"Black-on-black killing has become a national epidemic."*

There are numerous reasons for the extremely high murder rate among black Americans, many of which are within the control of the members of the community. Thus it is the purpose of this viewpoint to suggest ways of lowering the murder rate of black victims by black perpetrators. It is not the purpose of this viewpoint to suggest a prohibition of all guns at the state and federal level, but to suggest ways that current gun laws can be enforced so that the number of black Americans killed each year will be drastically reduced. It is the author's view that limiting access to guns combined with affirmative community action, will enable us to follow the admonishment of Dr. Ralph and stop the killings. . . .

Violence Against Black Citizens

Violence in America is an outgrowth of the greatest strengths and virtues of our society (its openness, ethos of equality, and heterogeneity) as well as of its greatest vices (its long heritage of racial hatred and oppression). Slavery began in violence. The uprooting of Africans from their homes and the transportation of them, first to the African coast, then to the New World, was the beginning of a long history of violent acts against blacks. Slaves were transported across the sea at a ghastly cost in human lives. Moreover, slavery was maintained by violence, as was the racial caste system that was erected after Emancipation and which in some forms endures even today. Violence was used after slavery officially ended to keep blacks "in their place."

For most of their history in this country, blacks were victims, not initiators, of violence. In the old South, violence against blacks was omnipresent—sanctioned both by custom and law. Whites were free to use any method, up to and including murder to control "their Negroes." In the late nineteenth century, after federal troops were withdrawn from the South, the white leadership made vigilante violence against blacks an integral part of the system of white supremacy which was erected. Between 1882 and 1903, no fewer than 1,985 blacks were killed by southern lynch mobs. Violence against blacks was not limited to mob action; individual acts of violence and terror became an accepted part of the resulting caste system.

Blacks Were Victimized

America's slavocracy developed a number of methods of control, one of which was to keep guns away from blacks. An intense fear of slave revolts throughout the South resulted in legislation restricting the access by slaves to firearms. In fact, the first recorded legislation concerning blacks in Virginia excluded blacks from owning guns. The political functions of these laws were often indicated in their title, e.g., "an Addition Act for Better Preventing Insurrections by Negroes."

Immediately after the Civil War some southern provisional governments set up militia organizations which not only excluded freedmen but which were used to disarm them. Blacks were generally forbidden to possess firearms and thus were rendered substantially defenseless against assault. This was a way to intimidate blacks into political impotence. From the 1870's until well into this century, many southern gun laws deprived black victims of this means of self-defense, while "cloaking the specially deputized Klansmen in the safety of their monopoly of arms." As Raymond Fosdick learned when he studied American police methods shortly before the country's entry into World War I, southern police departments had three classes of homicide. "If a nigger kills a white man, that's murder," one official told Fosdick. "If a white man kills a nigger, that's justifiable homicide. If a nigger kills another nigger, that's one less nigger." A quarter of a century later, Gunnar Myrdal found little had changed: "Any white man can strike or beat a Negro, steal or destroy his property, cheat him in a transaction and even take his life without fear of legal reprisal."

> *"Current gun laws can be enforced so that the number of black Americans killed each year will be drastically reduced."*

A propensity to violence was not part of the cultural baggage black Americans carried with them from Africa. Indeed, black Americans learned violence in this country. They had many teachers; violence has been an intrinsic part of the black American experience from the outset. Our present state shows that we have learned our lesson well. The perplexing question remains: Why is black violence directed against blacks, thus in many ways accomplishing what the Klan could not accomplish?

Violence in the Black Community

Recognizing the existence of violence as a part of American society affords only a partial understanding of why homicide occurs the way it does within the black community. The perceived oppression by white society and its agents would seem to cause movements like those present in the 1960's—the beginnings of the militant "Black Power" movement and the Black Panther Party. The Black Panther Party sought to obtain firearms as a self-defense action for protection against white society. However, the opposite has occurred; weapons within the black community are not used for self-defense, but for self-destruction.

Research data indicate that the actual risk of criminal victimization is different for blacks than for whites. Blacks are eight times more likely to be victims of homicide and two and one-half times more likely to be victims of rape than are whites. For robbery, the black victimization rate is three times that of whites, and the rate of aggravated assault among blacks is one and one-half times of that among whites. Within the black community, perhaps because of a preoccupation with perceived racism, assaults and homicides on blacks are not widely condemned, but are often given tacit approval. It seems we are within a subculture of society where overt physical violence is the accepted, if not expected, response to certain interpersonal situations.

> *"For most of their history in this country, blacks were victims, not initiators, of violence."*

The significance of a jostle, a slightly derogatory remark, or a weapon in the hands of an adversary are stimuli differentially perceived and interpreted by blacks and whites. A black male is usually expected to defend the name and honor of his mother and the virtue of womanhood in general (even though his female companion for the evening may be an entirely new acquaintance). He is also expected to accept no derogation about his race (even from a member of his own race), his age, or his masculinity. Quick resort to physical combat as a measure of daring, courage, or defense of status appears to be a cultural expectation within the black community.

When such a cultural norm response is elicited from an individual engaged in social interplay with others who harbor the same response mechanism, physical assaults, altercations, and violent domestic quarrels resulting in homicide are likely to be relatively common. The black subculture not only provides values which support violence—by implication, values disregarding the importance of human life—but also generates situations that spark tempers to the point of overt aggression.

Where do black Americans learn such values? Perhaps we teach such value in the early school years when we urge our boys to "hit back." Should we try to teach black children to adhere more to middle class values and use the legal system for redress? It is not the purpose of this viewpoint to impose middle class values on black Americans, but to commend universal values relating to the importance of human life. We do our society and our race a disservice by committing the black-on-black violence which has resulted in so many needless deaths. We must no longer foster behavior which reflects the notions that life is cheap and aggression is acceptable conduct.

> *"Black Americans learned violence in this country."*

Many homicides can be prevented by recognizing causes of the homicidal event and correcting these causes through changes in attitudes, behavior, and environment. Might not some of our resources and energies be better spent in preventing the homicidal event from taking place than in the expense of the criminal justice system imposed after the fact? Education is needed at all levels. We must educate children as to the importance of human life, educate victims as to an awareness of perpetrators and community resources available to handle aggressions, and educate the community as to its responsibility.

Blacks, Whites, and Handguns

Many Americans believe that the possession of handguns is useful for "self-protection." This view is held by black and white men at the same ratio, but to a greater degree by black females than white females. Records show, however, that at best, a handgun creates only an illusion of safety and at worst, it endangers the life of its owner and those around him. . . .

The extent to which whites and blacks either own guns or oppose gun control has long been a matter of controversy, with various polls reporting disparate results. One thing is certain, most blacks support gun control. Paula McClain's extensive and detailed survey of Detroit census tracts found that blacks seem to have more confidence in the capacity of severe gun laws to reduce violence and are more likely to support such laws than are whites. Does this mean that most citizens do not want stricter gun controls? The evidence is that they do, but the lack of such legislation is a classic example of special interest group conflict in which the majority does not necessarily prevail. . . .

Guns and violence have been partners in the tradition of American life. The frontier which required guns has long disappeared, but the American love for guns has remained and even intensified. Violence is clearly rejected by most

Americans as a part of our expressed system of values. But so great has been our involvement with violence over the long sweep of our history that violence has become part of our unacknowledged (or underground) value structure. Too many Americans do not truly realize that guns are designed specifically for one purpose: to kill and maim. Children at an early age are given guns as toys and are permitted to watch hundreds of programs glorifying the use of firearms. The real danger of firearms, as well as the irreversibility of the harm it causes, must be brought to the attention of all Americans.

It would do our society well to follow the advice found in an article in *The New York Times Magazine* which recommended that children visit an emergency ward of a big city hospital. Seeing the results of violence might serve as an antidote for the unreal violence on our television and movie screens. An educational program of this type should not only be directed at children, but adult community education programs should be implemented to emphasize respect for human life.

Recently, community action groups have developed community action programs to make the public aware of this national epidemic. Through these community programs, the black community and the community at large are sensitized to the enormity of the problem. Alternatives to violence are discussed and "love not kill" is being presented as the watchword of the community. Because family homicides are dominant, citizens are instructed as to other community resources available in solving domestic disputes. They learn of more constructive alternatives to gun use. With community awareness and involvement, the number of black-on-black homicides should decrease. The development of programs that address the immediate impact of crime on the black community is an issue of first priority for black citizens.

> *"Quick resort to physical combat as a measure of daring, courage, or defense of status appears to be a cultural expectation within the black community."*

Because of the illusion utility guns have for self-protection in the home, there should be an allocation of resources to improve crime detection equipment. Citizens should be educated in ways of self-protection without arming themselves. People must be made to understand that human life is more important than the value of any personal property.

Enforcement of Current Laws

Research suggests that blacks perceive the police as providing only limited protection to the black community, whereas whites have a more positive perception of police protection. Through effective law enforcement, there may develop a greater respect for police and other authority. Citizens may more readily seek community resources rather than seeking self-help in the form of handguns.

Current laws and regulations relating to firearms must be enforced. The effectiveness of such laws depends greatly upon the actions of the police, prosecutors, and judges. From some reports there is evidence suggesting that police are reluctant to enforce current gun control laws, prosecutors do not always press charges, and judges are

> *"One thing is certain, most blacks support gun control."*

unlikely to fully sentence individuals guilty of such crimes. Laws must be enforced to impress upon our citizens (especially those in the black community) that conduct involving the misuse of firearms will not be tolerated.

Individuals breaking gun control laws must be punished to the full extent of the law. The punishment of such individuals will dissuade others from engaging in this type of conduct. Also, the educational function of punishment will be satisfied in that the need for the public to know and reaffirm that this type of conduct is criminal will be met. Too long have we in the black community condoned this type of behavior.

Police officers should not only diligently enforce gun laws, but all laws, thereby giving the black community some feeling that they are receiving as complete protection as any other community. There should be greater communication between the police and the community. Through community relations units in police departments, contact should be made with community groups to establish crime watch units within the community. If those in the community feel safer, there will be less reason to resort to firearms.

Reducing the Availability of Handguns

Gun prohibition may be unconstitutional; however, gun regulation and control enforcement exists in many sections of our country. Enforcement of current gun laws on our books will reduce the number of guns available for violent use. The debate continues regarding the effectiveness of gun control laws to reduce gun violence, and many say that we may not reach that elusive panacea by this route. However, an affirmative start in enforcement seems a good route.

A current hand gun law in force in all U.S. jurisdictions regulates the carrying of concealed weapons. Since many firearm incidents occur outside of the home and occur with the use of handguns, keeping the streets free from handguns should reduce the homicide rate to a large degree. Since many of these same crimes are crimes of passion or emotion, reducing the availability of weapons should reduce the overall number of homicides.

A strict permit system or a ban on private possession of handguns would significantly alter the firearms habits of law-abiding citizens, who would then turn to safer, long guns for self-protection. Hence, the twenty-five hundred handgun deaths and 100,000 accidental handgun woundings that take place every year cannot be excluded from measurement. Cheap handguns, commonly categorized as a "Saturday night special" should be banned altogether. This would deny many people access to a common source of an instrument of violence, the most common weapon obtained and found in the streets of our community. Cutting off this major supply of handguns should bring about a reduction in the number of gun homicides in our nation.

Enforcing and modifying our current gun laws will not completely alleviate the societal detriment caused by their presence, but it is undoubtedly a viable method destined for use in efforts to rectify the problems permeating our social structure. We must stop the killing, and the banning of cheap guns and the enforcement of current gun laws seems to be an appropriate beginning.

The Black Community Holds the Answers

Columnist William Raspberry succinctly summarized the issue as follows: "It would be nice to live in a society which is both free and gunless, but I'm not sure how you can get there from here." The author does not claim to be any wiser than Mr. Raspberry, but has attempted to suggest several positive steps that we as a society can take to reduce the violence that is caused by black-on-black killings. Most, if not all, of the answers to the problem are within the black community. As Reverend Jesse Jackson, the civil rights leader and recent Democratic Presidential Candidate, has put the matter: "Nobody will save us from us—but us."

The lingering question still arises as to why this violence is so prevalent within the black community. The answer lies not in the genes, but in the nature of the lives we lead and of the communities in which we reside. We are both black and American; we have fused American culture with the culture we brought with us from Africa. We have created "our culture" with our own music and dance, vocabulary and rhythm of speech, religious denominations and life style. But violence was not brought by us to these shores, it is something that has been acquired since our arrival here. And, it is something that we must learn to cast off if we are to continue to exist.

The purpose of this viewpoint is not to paint a grim picture of the state of black America, but to extend a bit of hope for the immediate future. The deaths resulting from black-on-black killings occur in epidemic proportion. United action by all Americans is needed to attempt to implement the meager recommendations stated here. With their implementation, this national problem will be lessened to the status of a lingering disease. It will take many great minds within our society to face and study this problem before a complete cure can be found.

Controlling Assault Weapons Would Reduce Crime

by Gregory Curtis

About the author: *Gregory Curtis is the editor of* Texas Monthly, *a general interest periodical.*

Unfortunately, we couldn't find any pumpkins; they would have shown vividly the violence these guns could do. But we didn't let that slight disappointment stop us. At a remote rifle range, we blasted away. Or, to be precise, I blasted away, as my two friends, a law enforcement officer and a military man, supervised my amateur gunsmanship.

Questions Concerning the Second Amendment

I was here because I wanted to sort out what I thought about guns. The massacre in Killeen, Texas in October 1991, when a man named George Hennard killed 23 people with a semiautomatic pistol, had the effect, almost against my will, of making guns and the horror they can cause a subject of interest, just as Scud missiles suddenly became interesting during the war with Iraq. I didn't think individuals had any more business owning semiautomatic pistols than they did owning Scud missiles, but owning guns is a constitutional right. And in this 200th anniversary year of the Bill of Rights, I believed more strongly than ever in absolute freedom of speech, in trial by jury, in the free exercise of religion, in the right to confront witnesses in court, in the prohibition against unreasonable searches and seizures, and, even after hearing many hoodlums take the Fifth, in the right not to have to testify against yourself. But did those convictions mean that I had to be an absolutist about the Second Amendment as well? Did supporting the Bill of Rights require that I believe that "the right of the people to keep and bear arms shall not be infringed" as strongly as I believed that there should be no law "abridging freedom of speech, or of the press"?

Gregory Curtis, "A Round per Second." Reprinted, with permission, from the December 1991 issue of *Texas Monthly.*

At the shooting range, my two friends explained with great care how each weapon worked and what its proper purpose was. I began with a Smith and Wesson .357, a standard police handgun for many years. It is a six-round revolver with a double-action trigger pull, which means that pulling the trigger first pushes the hammer back and then releases it. After loading .38-caliber bullets, I could fire six rounds fairly quickly with reasonable accuracy, although reloading took precious time. A .357 magnum bullet was so much more powerful that I couldn't shoot it accurately. The kick broke a blood vessel at the base of my thumb. At night the flash from the explosion would have blinded me just as if a flashbulb had gone off in front of my eyes. Even policemen who, for reasons of their own, carry .357 rounds when on duty often don't like to practice with them because of the toll the kick takes on the hands, arms, and nerves. These ferocious rounds are available in most gun shops.

Thirty-Six Rounds in Thirty Seconds

Next, we loaded a 9mm Sig Sauer semiautomatic pistol, a gun very like the Glock pistol that George Hennard used in Killeen. It is a sleek, black, aristocratic-looking weapon that feels very good in the hand. After the first shot, a slight touch on the trigger releases the hammer. With each succeeding shot, the mechanism ejects the spent shell, puts a new round in the chamber, and cocks the hammer again.

> *"Most people think assault rifles should be used in Fort Hood, not on the streets of Killeen."*

The gun has very little kick, so bringing the sights back onto the target after a shot is easily done. The magazines come in two sizes, one that carries fifteen bullets and one that carries twenty. With two magazines and one shell already in the chamber, it's no trick to shoot 36 acceptably accurate rounds in twenty to thirty seconds. Private citizens who feel they need to shoot 36 rounds in less than half a minute can buy a Sig from a gun shop for about $700.

Next was an assault rifle, a Heckler and Koch MP5. It is a compact, surprisingly light weapon that is common among SWAT teams throughout the Western world. It is accurate at one hundred yards or beyond but is best for close-range firing. Its clip carries thirty 9mm rounds, and the standard procedure in an assault is to carry one magazine in the gun and three in your belt. It has virtually no kick, and I was able to fire round after round downrange into a target rather resembling a human torso. The MP5, elegantly black and a marvel of design, materials, and engineering, is extremely useful in making arrests in dangerous circumstances. It has no use as a hunting weapon. Nor does it have much use in law enforcement outside the specific one mentioned above. Yet it is possible to buy this or a similar weapon from a registered dealer or, better still, at a gun show where there may be no record whatsoever of the transaction.

We shot various other weapons. Despite the ominous overtones, it was a pleasant way to spend an afternoon. And if I were certain that these weapons would always be used to keep good people safe and prevent bad people from doing harm, then it would be possible to look at guns with gratitude and almost with affection. And the typical politician's opposition to gun control would make perfect sense.

But of course guns are not always used to help the good, as the Killeen massacre sadly proves. The shock from that tragedy has changed some minds, including that of Chet Edwards, the Democratic congressman from the area. He decided to vote for a bill to ban certain kinds of assault rifles. He is, he told me, "not generally a supporter of gun control. But the emotion of that incident caused me to think rationally and do what I think is right. I represent a district with a long history of gun ownership and the largest military base in the United States. But most people think assault rifles should be used in Fort Hood, not on the streets of Killeen."

> *"Words in the mouth of a madman are an annoyance, but a gun in the hands of a madman is death for anyone within range."*

Political Posturing

That this commonsense view should be the least bit controversial is evidence of how poisoned the public rhetoric about gun control really is. Ask most Texas politicians and you will hear, as I did when I called the office of East Texas congressman Charles Wilson, "The congressman is totally opposed to any form of gun control." But those words do not mean what they appear to mean. Is he for felons being allowed to own guns? Well, no. What about children? Should ten-year-old kids be allowed to buy guns? No. So Wilson *is* in favor of some forms of gun control. But he cannot say, "I am in favor of gun control under certain circumstances"—an accurate statement of his position—because that would be taken to mean that he favors a ban on handguns or something similar. The National Rifle Association would level its forces against him. It's just simpler to stick by the code phrase "totally opposed to all forms of gun control." Thus what goes on in Congress is not political debate about gun control but simple posturing.

Having said that, I have also to say that if asked a question about free speech, I might very well reply, "I am totally opposed to all forms of censorship." And I am. But that statement doesn't quite mean what it says either. There ought to be, and there are, sanctions against publishing fraudulent statements to get money or knowingly publishing falsehoods. The government has certain information—for instance, the exact workings of nuclear weapons, the deployment of troops in wartime, the proceedings of grand juries—that it can rightfully suppress. Free speech does not allow violating a copyright. And there are several other examples of speech that I would say should be prohibited, including shouting "Fire!" in a crowded theater. Though the language of the First Amendment is absolute, there is nevertheless, between suppression of all speech and no suppression whatsoever, a point that divides what is allowed and what is not. The Constitution insists that that point be as close as possible to no suppression and as far as possible from total suppression. We have the right to decide for ourselves—but for no one else—which political commentary is persuasive and which is not, which nude is art and which is something else, which song lyrics are acceptable and which are not, and even whether we want to read or see or hear anything at all.

Similarly, somewhere between water guns and atomic weapons, there is a point that divides what is allowed in private hands and what is not. The language of the Second Amendment about owning firearms is as absolute as the language in the First Amendment about free speech. But I don't think that means that the point that divides what we allow and what we don't should be as close to atomic weapons as possible. The difference is that words in the mouth of a madman are an annoyance, but a gun in the hands of a madman is death for anyone within range. It is both good public policy and consistent with the Constitution to try to keep the point determining what is allowed from moving any closer to atomic weapons than it already has.

Handgun Ban Is Ineffective

Opposing handguns is not the answer. They cannot be banned. Enforced background checks or waiting periods before allowing someone to buy a handgun might do some good but very little. There are already 35 million handguns in private ownership in the United States. It would be impossible to round them up even if that were constitutional, which it isn't. With that many pistols out there, it means that lots of bad people have them and intend to use them; so it isn't irrational for good people to want handguns too, just in case.

But traffic in assault weapons is a relatively new phenomenon. There aren't yet that many assault rifles in private hands. Neither are there that many extended magazines that hold twenty or thirty or even more rounds. It is still possible to restrict such weapons before they proliferate so widely that the public will want to buy them just to keep up. Even licensing them to the degree that we license automobiles would help. Shouldn't the Killeen massacre change more minds than just Chet Edwards'?

Disarming the Police Would Make Gun Control Effective

by James B. Jacobs

About the author: *James B. Jacobs is a law professor and the director of the Center for Research in Crime and Justice at New York University in New York City.*

Current American gun law generally allows most people to own firearms, and there are approximately 140 million guns in private possession. It is estimated that one-third of the privately owned firearms are handguns. Only members of the most unreliable social categories—drug addicts, the mentally ill, convicted felons, juveniles—are denied permission to own firearms. Some who decry this situation advocate "total disarmament," arguing that everyone would be safer if *no one* were permitted to possess a firearm, especially a handgun. They believe that a universal right to own firearms, especially handguns, makes guns more accessible to criminals and more likely to be misused by law abiding citizens; thus, they advocate a program of prohibition.

Disarmament Needs Wide Support

Many gun control skeptics have pointed out the practical difficulties of disarming what might amount to one in four American households and suppressing a black market in new and used guns. It would be impossible to enforce handgun prohibition against a highly resistant public; therefore, a disarmament proposal would have to enjoy widespread support to have even a small chance of success. Without the cooperation of gun owners and would-be owners, gun prohibition would be no more successful than alcohol prohibition, perhaps less so. Reducing the stockpile of firearms in private hands depends upon changing public perceptions about the necessity and desirability of owning and carrying firearms. The thesis of this viewpoint is that gun control proposals that allow for large numbers of individuals and groups to retain their weapons will not encourage voluntary and cooperative disarmament by nonexempt individuals and groups. To the contrary, politically expedient gun control proposals, rife with exemptions, will be viewed cynically and hostilely. In fact, such proposals legitimate the value of gun possession for persons and groups with "good reasons" for possessing firearms. This viewpoints seeks to understand why gun control proposals categorically exempt any groups. Is there more than political expediency at work?

> *"Without the cooperation of gun owners and would-be owners, gun prohibition would be no more successful than alcohol prohibition."*

Most gun control proposals put forward in the last few years are not likely to be perceived as fair because they explicitly and implicitly recognize the value and importance of gun ownership by carving out gaping exceptions to a general gun prohibition. Close examination reveals that many prohibitionists are not advocating "total disarmament." To begin with, practically all "control" scenarios seek to prohibit only "handguns," leaving people free to own rifles, shotguns, and other long guns. Some scenarios would ban only "Saturday Night Specials," leaving people free to own more expensive and powerful handguns as well as long guns. Nor do handgun-only prohibitionists mean to eliminate *all* handgun ownership; exceptions are invariably made for persons judged to have *good reasons* for owning or carrying handguns. Police, private security guards, private investigators, business persons, and selected individuals are typically exempted from handgun bans. . . .

If the police showed leadership in disarming or "de-arming" themselves, more private citizens, including gun owners, might view firearms as unnecessary in their own lives. . . .

The Peace Officer Exception

The exception to general handgun prohibition that enjoys the greatest consensus is the exception made for "the police." Even fervent advocates of handgun control (including police themselves) concede that under stringent handgun control the police will continue to possess and carry handguns. This concession should not go unquestioned. It may well turn out that there is a relationship between arming the police and arming the general citizenry.

Curiously, gun control advocates have not urged the police to give up their handguns in order to achieve a complete prohibition. If *even* the police (or some portion of them) were denied handguns, the force of the prohibitory norm would be very strong indeed. A society that denied, seriously limited, or even seriously questioned the need for police handguns would be unquestionably committed to eliminating this weaponry.

To speak of "disarming" the police of their handguns does not convey any indication as to what weapons the police would be allowed instead. Just like civilians, the police might arm themselves with rifles or shotguns under a hand-gun-only prohibition. Would that be desirable? The answer depends upon the comparative advantages and disadvantages of these high-powered weapons. They might well be too unwieldy for effective deployment in many police encounters; whenever they are fired, the chance of death or serious injury is greater than when handguns are used. It is conceivable, however, that their greater firepower would better deter criminal violence and attacks on police, thus producing fewer fired shots.

Alternatives to Guns

Instead of "trading up," the police could be forced to "trade down," and make do with rubber or plastic bullets, tasers or stun guns, or blackjacks and mace. It seems extraordinary that there has been so little thinking about and experimentation with weapons other than the traditional handgun. Creative experiments in "arming down" might contribute to a social and political environment in which civilian gun ownership would lose some of its attraction.

Whether or not prohibiting police handguns is politically conceivable, virtually all handgun prohibition proposals, like the San Francisco and Morton Grove ordinances, exempt the police. Why? Surprisingly little attention has been given to this question. Illuminating the reasons for the police exemption might be of assistance in discerning the core rationale that justifies or defeats other claims for exemptions from handgun prohibition. In other words, why should the police be armed and the general citizenry or various discrete groups of citizens be disarmed? Four plausible reasons are: 1) personal safety; 2) arrest powers; 3) deterrence of crime; and 4) superior training and judgment.

1. *Personal Safety.* The extent to which personal safety justifies handgun ownership is central to the handgun controversy, since many persons own handguns in order to defend themselves. If self-defense provides the crucial justification for permitting police to carry guns, why does personal security not justify handguns for everyone? Are the police in greater danger than other citizens? Are firearms a more effective and appropriate means of self-defense for police than for other citizens? Are private citizens better situated than police officers to absorb the risks of unarmed self-defense? Are the "costs" of police firearms less than the "costs" of civilian firearms?

> *"If the police showed leadership in disarming or 'de-arming' themselves, more private citizens, including gun owners, might view firearms as unnecessary."*

It is true that an unarmed police officer might be at the mercy of an offender armed with a gun (knife, tire iron, etc.), but so too might an unarmed store owner, apartment dweller, or pedestrian. The police officer is likely to come into contact with dangerous offenders more frequently than most, but not all, private citizens, some of whom live in dangerous neighborhoods (and public housing projects) where they are highly vulnerable to attack. Arguably, the police officer has fewer self-defense options than the private citizen, because the officer cannot avoid dangerous areas, streets, and taverns, and cannot flee from potential assailants. There is some force to this point, but only some. Many private citizens, among them the elderly, poor, weak and powerless, lack realistic options for avoiding attacks and defending themselves. Some of these people could plausibly claim that the state has created their vulnerability by its maladministration of public housing or public transportation and by its ineffective criminal justice system.

Complete Protection Is Impossible

On the other hand, the police officer might argue that his or her claim to bear arms is especially compelling because the state creates the officer's vulnerability by organizing a public agency charged with keeping the peace and enforcing the laws—hazardous activities to be sure. The handgun might be for the police officer what protective goggles are for the welder. Even so, asking police officers to assume greater risks than ordinary citizens is morally permissible. The police cannot be protected against all risks. They cannot be encapsuled in bulletproof bubbles and made invulnerable to snipers, maniacs, and drunk drivers. Fortunately, gun attacks on police officers are still rare, even in big cities. In addition, it is not totally far-fetched to hypothesize that some gun attacks may occur precisely because police project an aggressive armed presence. A significant number of police officers each year mistakenly shoot other police officers, and some are victims of their own gun accidents.

"A society that denied . . . the need for police handguns would be unquestionably committed to eliminating this weaponry."

Prison and jail guards work unarmed every day among men proven to be violent and dangerous, some of whom are either "lifers" or very long-term prisoners with little to fear from new criminal charges. In a typical exercise yard or cell block a guard vastly outnumbered could be stabbed, bludgeoned, strangled, or otherwise eliminated at any time; yet there is no move to arm jail and prison guards. It seems odd that so much attention is paid to minimizing the risk of attacks on police, but not on prison officers.

Police Adept at Self-Defense

The police are surely in a much better position than civilians to develop alternative protective technologies and strategies. While the future of police weaponry is beyond the scope of this viewpoint, the police are well positioned to experiment with all sorts of nonlethal weapons, to outfit themselves in bulletproof clothing, and to train themselves in martial arts. Even without any developments along these lines, an unarmed police officer is probably more adept at self-protection than a private citizen because he or she is likely to be better trained in self-defense, to carry a night stick, chemical mace, and other weapons, to travel with another officer, to have recourse to reinforcements, and to be alert to potential trouble. In deterring assaults, the officer can rely upon the state's moral

> *"Some gun attacks may occur precisely because police project an aggressive armed presence."*

authority and the widely shared knowledge that prosecutors and courts regard assaults on police officers more seriously than assaults on private citizens. Why, then, should the police officer be permitted to carry a handgun, but the private citizen be prohibited, perhaps on pain of imprisonment, from even keeping a handgun in his home?

In sum, advocates of handgun prohibition cannot justify an exception for the police on self-defense or safety grounds without letting loose tremendous pressure to recognize other self-defense and safety claims that could ultimately swallow up the prohibition.

The Ability to Make Arrests

2. *Arrest Powers.* The police are authorized to arrest when they have probable cause to believe an individual has committed an offense. To take an offender into custody the police arguably need special powers. Perhaps the need to make arrests, more than a special need for self-protection, distinguishes the police officer from the private citizen. Does the authority and responsibility to make arrests support a special claim to carry firearms? If so, this is a much narrower justification than safety and security, and one that might distinguish the police from other citizens wishing to possess firearms.

Proof is lacking, however, on the extent to which police officers do need handguns in order to take suspects into custody. Americans, accustomed as they are to a thoroughly and continuously armed police (and to constant television and movie depictions of shootouts), may find it hard to imagine that police could carry out their duties without handguns. In part, this difficulty is because the popular image of "the police" is shaped by those who patrol the toughest areas of America's largest cities, precisely the officers who have the most need to be armed. Tens of thousands of officers work in rural and suburban environments far less dangerous than the violence-ridden neighborhoods of large cities. It is hard to believe that the need to make arrests could justify arming *all* of these personnel at *all* times on *all* assignments. Some officers have duties that never bring them into confrontational situations; for them a holstered handgun is part of the uniform, perhaps indicative of status but not a functional necessity. Their psychological investment in the need to be armed is similar to that of many civilians who feel just the same way.

Whether patrol officers need firearms to make arrests is worth examining. There may be a good deal of exaggeration of such need, especially in suburbs, towns, and villages with low rates of violent crime. Self-defense skills, moral and legal authority, and availability of reinforcements might enable officers to make arrests in most cases, even if they were not armed. Police effect most arrests in Great Britain and Japan without the use of guns. Even in large American cities, police officers very rarely draw their guns, although admittedly the visible presence of a gun might deter the kind of attacks that would make it necessary to draw. . . .

Undeniably, there are situations in which dangerous armed felons must be apprehended who would not acquiesce without the threat of lethal force. Still, this type of situation does not justify arming all police all of the time. Firearms could be assigned selectively, "as needed," to police officers investigating serious offenses or violent offenders, or firearms might be assigned routinely to patrols in certain dangerous neighborhoods or even to all patrols in the largest cities. A police firearms policy that required a showing of need before a firearm was issued would reflect a powerful societal commitment to restrict the use of handguns. . . .

The Drive Toward Increased Weaponry

A further option is the possibility of "de-arming." If it is granted that police officers need handguns, what kind of guns and what kind of bullets are required? Should police officers be "armed to the teeth" in order to maximize the possibility of "neutralizing" any threat, or should they "make do" with the least lethal weaponry they are likely to need? Police weaponry of all kinds has apparently increased in caliber, destructiveness, and "stopping power"

> *"Even in large American cities, police officers very rarely draw their guns."*

over the last several decades. Like the international arms race, there seems to be an inexorable drive to accumulate more powerful weaponry. An issue the Supreme Court did not reach in *Tennessee v. Garner* is the constitutionality of the "dum-dum" bullets used by the Memphis Police Department. A comprehensive "gun control" program would aim to reduce the destructive power of police weaponry as much as possible.

3. *Deterring Crime.* Some people might justify a police-only handgun exemption on the ground that an armed police depresses crime by inhibiting would-be criminals from violating the law. For the deterrence proposition to be true, there would have to be potential offenders who would commit crimes but for fear of being shot by the police or of being arrested by armed (but not unarmed) police. It seems unlikely that the number of such potential offenders is very large, but if it is, is it not also plausible that an armed citizenry, or at least a partially armed citizenry, also serves to deter crime? Potential offenders might

fear being shot or arrested by armed civilians as much as by armed police. Indeed, they might fear an armed citizenry more because it is less identifiable and predictable.

4. *Superior Training.* It will surely occur to some readers that, due to background and training, police officers handle firearms more carefully and responsibly than private citizens. However, this assumption may not be as justified as it might at first seem. Most police officers receive little entry-level weapons training, especially in night firing, and annual requalification requirements are rare. Very few departments have the resources and facilities to provide effective training in confrontational situations. Unnecessary off-duty shooting and accidents are a significant problem, at least in some departments. Even if the police as a group are more competent than private gun owners, however, it begs the question to base a weapons policy on police officers' superior training since current public policy discourages weapons training for civilians. If private citizens were willing to submit to the same training as police, and to abide by the same rules (or even more stringent ones) on the use of deadly force, could the police officer still claim to be more reliable in possessing and carrying a handgun than is the private citizen in keeping a handgun at home?

> *"There seems to be an inexorable drive to accumulate more powerful weaponry."*

Few Checks on Character

As for judgment, reliability, and overall moral character, while a prior felony conviction or mental illness disqualifies applicants for police jobs, recruits must merely pass minimum scrutiny; in no sense are they chosen on the basis of superlative psychological stability or moral character. After joining the force, there are no further background checks and investigations in most departments unless charges of corruption or abuse of force arise.

5. *Summary.* Should the police retain their handguns because the benefits of crime prevention and control outweigh the costs of crimes committed and accidents caused? If so, are the police the only subgroup for which cost-benefit analysis would support gun possession? Other groups or individuals would surely claim that their gun ownership provides a net benefit to society—small shop owners, for example, might be able to show that as a class they deter and thwart more harm with their weapons than they cause. If it is accepted that police need powerful handguns (and dum-dum bullets) on an around-the-clock basis, in all types of departments, and on all assignments, it would not be surprising if large numbers of people concluded that they were unsafe, that guns enhance personal security, and that, like the police, they should be armed. . . .

Men and women desire to possess handguns for many reasons, including safety, security, and self-defense. Many have "learned," from the example set by police, peace officers, and the private security sector (reinforced by the media), that firearms are "necessary" for personal security. The personnel of such agencies may be so accustomed to their handguns that they find alternative weapons and protective devices unimaginable. This attitude may be a major stumbling block to formulating a coherent and successful firearms policy. If the police feel handguns are absolutely necessary, especially for self-defense, and if they refuse to accept the risks that might be entailed in disarmament or de-armament, all sorts of other groups and individuals will inevitably take the same position. Police leadership on the issue of gun control does not guarantee shrinkage of the arms pool, but without police leadership, further arms proliferation and escalation seems inevitable. . . .

A handgun prohibition must be symbolically right as well as politically expedient. A prohibition that accommodates the concerns and influences of all kinds of powerful interests will not be worth the paper on which is is printed. More than legislation is needed to reverse the internal arms race. A *disarmament climate* must be created, and that can best (perhaps only) be accomplished through police leadership and example. The best strategy toward handgun disarmament may not be to chip away at peripheral owners, but to change the attitudes, values, and practices of the core ownership group—the police, other law enforcement personnel, and private security forces.

Gun Control Would Not Reduce Crime

by Robert W. Lee

About the author: *Robert W. Lee is a frequent contributor to the conservative* magazine The New American.

> *Our greatest strength lies in the fact that so many of our people not only possess weapons but also understand their use, and above all, they are prepared to defend themselves against any sudden attack by an enemy. You will remember that we won our freedom because we were armed. We were not a simple peasantry unused to weapons. The men who wrote our Constitution knew our people would be safe as long as they were armed.*
> —Louis L'Amour
> *The Lonesome Gods*

A recent catalogue of exotic paramilitary paraphernalia and literature included plans costing $3.95 for constructing a Mark-1 submachinegun "that can be built at home for less than $20.00." It was indicative of the futility of keeping guns—even machineguns—out of the hands of those determined to obtain (or make) them.

On November 13, 1989 a murder suspect with an extensive criminal record was being driven to New York's Riker's Island jail in the back seat of a car driven by two members of the Queens district attorney's detective squad. He was handcuffed, yet somehow obtained a gun, forced the car to the side of the highway, then shot both detectives to death. According to news reports, both officers carried pistols in ankle holsters, but neither had been fired. The suspect escaped. Once again, it was demonstrated that, despite New York's draconian gun control laws, even a handcuffed prisoner can obtain firearms in circumstances in which only the police are supposed to have them.

Blame People, Not Guns

Meanwhile, advocates of gun control continue to blame guns, rather than the humans who wield them irresponsibly, for gun-related deaths. For example, *Time* magazine declared in its July 17, 1989 issue: "At any one time, the nation

Robert W. Lee, "Going for Our Guns," *The New American*, April 23, 1990. Reprinted with permission.

harbors a large tribe of those crying and struggling with the loss a gun has caused." (Will a future *Time* evaluation of education lament the large tribe of students crying and struggling with the misspelled words their pencils have caused?)

Even some doctors have joined the hue and cry for gun control. Let's hope their evaluation of patients is more on target than their analysis of the gun issue. An article in the *Journal of the American Medical Association* guessed that it costs $1 billion annually to treat gunshot victims; concluded that government must foot most of the bill because most gunshot victims do not have insurance; and prescribed gun control as a remedy to eliminate this drain on the treasury. The article did not mention the 20,000 existing gun control laws that have failed miserably to curb crime (but have harassed and intimidated law-abiding citizens). Nor did it discuss the billions of dollars saved each year when handguns are used in self-defense to prevent or deter hundreds of thousands of crimes.

> *"The 20,000 existing gun control laws . . . have failed miserably to curb crime."*

Flawed Conclusions

An article in the *New England Journal of Medicine* of November 10, 1989 argued that Vancouver, British Columbia has a lower handgun-related homicide rate than does Seattle, Washington due to the 1977 Canadian law that effectively precluded the possession of handguns for self-defense. That flawed conclusion was autopsied by David B. Kopel, former assistant district attorney in Manhattan, in the February 11, 1990 *Human Events*. If a criminologist had analyzed the data cited by the *NEJM*, Kopel speculated,

> he would have noted that the handgun homicide rates among white residents of Seattle and Vancouver were nearly identical. He therefore would have attributed Seattle's higher rate to the greater number of shootings perpetrated by and upon blacks and Hispanics. (Neither ethnic group is present in Vancouver in significant numbers.) . . .
>
> A criminologist would also have noted that Vancouver had a lower handgun homicide rate before Canada's handgun law was enacted. . . .
>
> Data for the rest of Canada indicate that the 1977 law also failed to curb crime nationwide. After the law was enacted, Canada's homicide rate remained the same. Armed robbery soared. Burglary of an occupied residence (the crime most often deterred by gun ownership) also rose sharply and exceeded the American rate.

A competent criminologist would also have noted that the number of knife murders in Vancouver is rising, a phenomenon authorities attribute in part to the gun control law.

In any event, the severe Canadian gun laws (even rifles and shotguns may not be purchased and used for sporting purposes without proper application and a police checkout) did not prevent Marc Lepine from massacring 14 women and wounding 13 other persons at the University of Montreal on December 6, 1989. Indeed, he had obtained his Sturm Ruger .223-caliber semiautomatic rifle at a hunting store on November 21st in full compliance with the nation's gun laws. This despite the fact that he had been rejected by the armed services for behavioral problems.

Cultural, Not Legal, Differences

Regarding the attempt by anti-gun scholars to draw meaningful comparisons between gun-related U.S. crime statistics and those of foreign nations that have even more stringent gun control laws, criminologist Don G. Kates, Jr. asserts that the differences are actually due to basic sociocultural and economic factors that have nothing to do with gun laws. In a February 1990 policy briefing paper, entitled *Guns, Murders, and the Constitution*, published by the Research Institute for Public Policy in San Francisco, Kates notes that, while it is true that Western Europe has less gun violence than does the U.S., it also has less violence of all kinds.

The difference was even greater *before* Western Europe's gun laws were adopted in the 1920s and 1930s. "In such equally crime-free countries as Switzerland, Israel, and New Zealand," Kates reports, "there is even more gun availability than there is in the United States." Ironically, "the two nations that most severely restrict gun ownership (punishing violation with death), Taiwan and South Africa, both have far higher apolitical murder rates than the United States."

The gun laws in New York City, England, Switzerland, and Israel all require permits to own handguns. But, whereas permits for self-defense are routine in the latter two countries, they are discouraged by New York City and nonexistent in England. Despite New York City's harsh laws, police estimate that there are at least 2 to 3 million illegally owned guns in the city. According to Kates, "The rate at which handguns are (illegally) owned for defense in New York City is more than double the rate of defensive ownership in states where it is legal. If people really want a gun for family defense, they will get one, regardless of any law."

> *"While it is true that Western Europe has less gun violence than does the U.S., it also has less violence of all kinds."*

Armed Citizens Fight Terrorists

In April 1984 three terrorists attacked a cafe in Jerusalem with automatic weapons, intending to kill everyone in sight. They were able to claim only one victim before being shot themselves by handgun-armed Israelis. Kates recalls:

"When presented to the press the next day, the surviving terrorist bitterly explained that his group had not realized that Israeli civilians were armed. The terrorists had planned to machine-gun a succession of crowded spots, believing that they would be able to escape before the police or army could arrive to deal with them."

Three months later, in sharp contrast, James Oliver Huberty (a recently fired security guard) killed 21 customers and employees (and wounded 19 others) at a McDonald's restaurant in San Ysidro, California. There was no on-the-spot resistance. He was killed by a police sniper 77 minutes later.

Kates reminds us that the relatively low crime rates in Europe long preceded any anti-gun legislation. In England, crime fell during the 19th Century and reached "it's idyllic low in the early 1900s—yet the only gun control was that police could not carry guns." The motivation for European gun control was not so much crime, but terrorism and political violence, "from which they continued to suffer until today far more than the United States." Also, today's English murder statistics do not include "political" murders, whereas U.S. statistics include every type of murder and manslaughter.

> *"If people really want a gun for family defense, they will get one, regardless of any law."*

The number of guns smuggled into England each year offsets the number confiscated by authorities. "In other words," Kates observes, "70 years of an ever more strictly administered ban has not diminished the illegal gunstock." On August 19, 1987, Michael Ryan shot and killed 16 people (including his mother), then himself, in the town of Hungerford in Berkshire, England. Despite the nation's anti-gun laws, he had been able to obtain with ease both the handgun and the Chinese-made AK-47 semiautomatic rifle used in the massacre. The government responded in knee-jerk fashion by banning the sale of all multiple-fire weapons and short-barreled guns.

Emotionalism Overrides Logic

During his January 24th, 1990 "Peter Jennings Reporting" special on guns, ABC newsman Peter Jennings asserted: "It does seem . . . that gun control only gets our fullest attention when something truly horrible happens." Gun-related massacres truly are the mother's milk that sustains the gun-control lobby, providing the emotionally charged atmosphere that short-circuits rational consideration of the issue. Yet, when incidents of mass murder are closely scrutinized, it becomes obvious that gun control laws could not (and did not) stop them, and that most of the tragedies are largely attributable to a failed criminal justice system that refuses to deal realistically with the criminal element even when it has them in custody. Also, in a shocking number of cases legally prescribed drugs also appear to have been a factor:

• Laurie Dann shot six children, killing one, in a Winnetka, Illinois school-house on May 20, 1988. She had been previously accused of thefts, of trying to stab her ex-husband with an ice pick, and of making threatening phone calls, and had been under psychiatric care (by at least two, and possibly three, psychiatrists). An autopsy found evidence of two doctor-prescribed drugs on the day of the atrocity: lithium (for treating manic-depressives) and Anafrinal (an antidepressant that had not then been approved by the Food and Drug Administration). Dann's supply had come from a pharmacy in Montreal, Canada.

According to Dr. Mark Thoman, a clinical toxicologist in Des Moines, Iowa, combining lithium and Anafrinal could result in "a myriad of reactions, including going completely out of control." The prescribing information for Anafrinal, provided by the manufacturer (Ciba-Geigy), advised that the seriously depressed "should not have easy access to large quantities of clomipramine [Anafrinal]." As noted by the medical newsletter *The Doctor's People*, "Between November 1987 and March 1988, Laurie Dann received 1,000 Anafrinal tablets," an average of more than eight per day. On February 8, 1990, a federal judge in Chicago ruled that the psychiatrist who prescribed the Anafrinal could be sued for negligence by Dann's victims.

Mentally Ill Criminals

• Patrick Edward Purdy, who killed five schoolchildren and wounded 21 others before killing himself in Stockton, California on January 17, 1989, was a product of California's criminal justice system. Between 1979 and 1987 he had been arrested for a plethora of offenses ranging from drug charges and extortion to the receipt of stolen property and attempted robbery. In 1983 he was placed on probation following conviction for possessing a dangerous weapon. A probation report described him as a danger to himself and others. Yet, he was able to legally purchase the weapons used in the massacre because in each instance the charges against him were either dropped or plea-bargained down to misdemeanors. Technically, he had no "criminal record" that would bar him from buying guns.

"When incidents of mass murder are closely scrutinized, it becomes obvious that gun control laws could not (and did not) stop them."

• Emanuel Tsegaye, an Ethiopian immigrant, killed three coworkers and himself at a bank in Chevy Chase, Maryland on February 14, 1989. In 1984 he had been found not guilty by reason of insanity on charges of assault with intent to rob and murder a motorcycle police officer in April of that year. He was committed to a hospital for the criminally insane, but was conditionally released on September 14, 1986 after psychiatrists concluded that he was not a threat to others, including himself. In April 1989 he was hospitalized for depression, for which the drugs Asendin (an antidepressant) and Klonopin (a tranquilizer) were prescribed. Homicide detectives were perplexed as to where he may have obtained the .38-caliber revolver he used. He had, after all, violated the state's gun laws and the terms of his conditional release from the hospital (by failing to keep a therapy appointment in July, an infraction authorities declined to punish).

In his recent research paper, Don Kates reminds us that massacres are "a very small part of the American homicide problem," and that "no confiscation effort (however broad or stringent) will disarm hardened criminals, much less political terrorist or killers, who are so highly motivated for personal reasons that they undertake massacres even though their actions will probably result in their own death." Even "if massacres were a serious threat to life in the United States, the best policy response would probably be that of Israel, which depends on the defensive value of widespread precautionary gun possession among the populace." Kates observes, moreover, that "anti-gun policies not only offer no solution for the massacre situation, but also are detrimental because they preclude whatever chance victims might have to protect themselves in the crucial time before police arrive.". . .

Acquaintance Murders

There is a widespread notion that most murders are of the "acquaintance" sort, involving otherwise law-abiding citizens impulsively embroiled in a domestic squabble and killing a friend or family member. To the contrary, Don Kates found that intra-family homicides are typically just the last episode in long-simmering syndromes of violence. "Intrafamily murderers," he explains, "are especially likely to have engaged in far more previous violent crimes than

> *"Anti-gun policies . . . preclude whatever chance victims might have to protect themselves."*

show up in their arrest records. But because these attacks were on spouses or other family members, they will rarely have resulted in an arrest. So domestic murderers' official records tend not to show their full prior violence, but only their adult arrests for attack on people outside their families."

One review of police records in Detroit and Kansas City revealed that, in 90 percent of domestic homicide cases, police had responded at least once before during the prior two years to a disturbance call, and in 54 percent of the cases had been called five times or more. "Murderers (and fatal gun accident perpetrators)," Kates asserts, "are atypical, highly aberrant individuals whose spectacular indifference to human life, including their own, is evidenced by life histories of substance abuse, automobile accident, felony, and attacks on relatives and acquaintances." Many of the so-called "acquaintance" murders, Kates adds, involve such occurrences as "a drug addict killing his dealer in the course of robbing him; a loan shark or bookie killing a nonpaying customer; or gang members, drug dealers, and members of organized crime 'families' killing each other."

The conclusion that a murderer who knows or is related to his victim must be an ordinary citizen, rather than a long-time criminal, is unjustified. A National Institute of Justice abstract declared as long ago as 1981: "It is commonly hypothesized that much criminal violence, especially homicide, occurs simply because the means of lethal violence (firearms) are readily at hand and, thus, that much homicide would not occur were firearms generally less available. There is no persuasive evidence that supports this view."

Regarding the incidence of gun accidents involving children, Kates found that only 10 to 15 children under age five are killed annually in handgun accidents, while 50 to 55 under age 15 die in accidental shootings. (The National Safety Council's figures of identifiable accidental fatalities from handguns average only 246 people of *all* ages per year.) Those figures are tragic, to be sure, but they pale in comparison to the 380 or so children who drown each year in swimming pools and the 432 who die in residential fires.

Guns Protect Average Citizens

Kates notes that civilian handgun ownership "averts thousands of victim injuries, and even deaths, that would not otherwise have been avoidable, given the manifest physical and tactical advantages that criminals have over unarmed citizens." Applying the accident and murder rates of irresponsible gun users and criminals to gun possession by the average citizen makes no more sense, he contends, than "estimating a citizen's chance of dying from a cut by using death rates among hemophiliacs." Accidents and misuse of firearms are arguments for more safety training and more stringent owner liability for negligence. They are not arguments for a gun ban.

Homicides increased in the U.S. in the 1960s (the anti-gun lobby blamed guns), but the rate stabilized in the 1970s and fell in the 1980s. In 1968 there were an estimated 24 to 29 million handguns in the country; by 1988 there were 65 to 70 million. Yet handgun (and other gun) homicides decreased markedly during that period. Kates cites figures showing that "in 1974, when our population was 211 million, handguns were involved in approximately 11,125 murders (54 percent of all murders). By 1988 the total U.S. population was 245 million and handguns were involved in around 8,275 murders (45 percent of all murders), a 27 percent decline in handgun homicide. . . . In the 20-year period from 1966 to 1985, murders with guns declined from 64.8 percent of the total murder rate to 58.7 percent."

> *"Intra-family homicides are typically just the last episode in long-simmering syndromes of violence."*

In 1974, the American homicide rate was 40 times that of the English. Fifteen years (and 30 million additional handguns) later, the U.S. rate was only ten times greater. Kates reports that "the approximate 100 percent increase in handguns during 1968-1979 was followed by a 26.6 percent decrease in domestic homicide from 1984 on—despite adding another 2 million handguns in 1980 and in each succeeding year.". . .

Police and Self-Defense

Gun control advocates sometimes argue that personal self-defense is obsolete, since we now have professional police forces to protect us. But, Kates points out, numerous court precedents have established the principle that a government and its agents are under no general duty to provide police protection (or, for that matter, other public services) to any individual citizen. That doctrine of sovereign immunity has often been cited to preclude cities from suing citizens for failure to protect them from criminal actions. . . .

There are only about 500,000 police officers throughout the country today. Assuming three eight-hour shifts per day (and taking into account assignments other than patrol, days off, and sick leave) perhaps 125,000 police are on duty at any given time to protect a population of nearly 250,00 million! According to a U.S. Department of Justice study, 83 percent of American children now aged 12 will be victims of some kind of violent felony, 52 percent will suffer two or more such offenses, and 87 percent will have property stolen on three or more occasions. Clearly, individual Americans remain largely responsible for their own personal safety while the police provide what amounts to auxiliary support.

Dr. Gary Kleck, an associate professor at the Florida State University School of Criminology found "about 645,000 defensive uses of handguns against persons per year," compared with approximately 581,000 criminal misuses of handguns. In other words, handguns are used more by law-abiding citizens to repel crime than by criminals to perpetrate crime. (If long guns are included, the number of crimes defensively repelled by firearms each year totals around one million.)

> *"Handguns are used more by law-abiding citizens to repel crime than by criminals to perpetrate crime."*

Handguns are used another 215,000 times each year to defend against dangerous animals (snakes, rabid skunks, etc.). Dr. Kleck also reported that, over a 50-year adult lifespan, at least 98.32 percent of gun owners are not involved in unlawful homicides. . . .

According to Dr. Gary Kleck, citizens acting in legitimate self-defense kill about three times more assailants and robbers than do police. Little wonder, then, that a survey of felons in state prisons across the country, conducted under the auspices of the National Institute of Justice, found that 34 percent, when contemplating crimes, "often" or "regularly" worried that they "might get shot at by the victim," while 57 percent agreed that "most criminals are more worried about meeting an armed victim than they are about running into the police.". . .

Women . . . often require the special protection afforded by a firearm if they are to successfully defend themselves from rape, spouse abuse, and other types of assault. The federal Bureau of Justice Statistics reported in 1984 that, in incidents of *criminal* violence between spouses, 91 percent of the victims are women. . . .

In Orlando, Florida, in the wake of a wave of robberies and rapes, more than 2500 women were trained to use firearms properly. Within nine months, robberies and attacks plummeted 90 percent, forcible rapes dropped 25 percent, and aggravated assaults and burglaries fell 24 percent.

There is the bugaboo that a woman who resists a male attacker may have her gun taken away and used against her. When Don G. Kates, Jr. looked into the matter, he found it to be "only a *theoretical* bugaboo: the rape literature contains no example of such an occurrence. Moreover, police instructors and firearms experts strongly reject its likelihood. Not only do they aver that women are capable of gun-armed defense, they find women much easier to properly train than men. . . ."

Kates cites an instance in which a police academy instructor simultaneously trained a male police academy class and a group of civilian women (most of whom had never held a revolver, much less fired one). The instructor "found that after one hour on the range and two hours of classroom instruction in the Chattanooga Police Academy's combat pistol course, the women consistently outshot police cadets who had just received eight times as much formal instruction and practice."

Other studies have shown that the average woman is actually superior to the average man in many physical and mental traits related to shooting skills. She is, for instance, more patient, has superior hand-eye coordination, excels in the concentration required to perform delicate motor functions time after time, and is not as stubborn in resisting instruction.

Kates notes that most rapes occur in the home, where (except for a few jurisdictions) a woman may legally have a gun, and "that in 83 percent of the cases it will protect her from being raped."

Though having what is arguably the nation's harshest gun control laws, the District of Columbia nevertheless successfully defended its title as murder capital of the nation in 1989 (a record 373 homicides during 1988 was surpassed by the 1989 total of 438—70.9 per 100,000 population, compared to a national average of around 8.4 per 100,000). Another 1500 or so shooting victims in the District did not die. Despite the anti-gun laws, the criminal element is armed to the teeth, while law-abiding citizens, by definition, are disarmed.

Gun Control Would Not Reduce Crime Against the Poor and Minorities

by Stefan B. Tahmassebi

About the author: *Stefan B. Tahmassebi is assistant general counsel for the office of the general council of the National Rifle Association of America.*

That all such free Mulattoes, Negroes and Indians . . . shall appear without arms—Virginia law, 1619.

The history of gun control in America possesses an ugly component: discrimination and oppression of blacks, other racial and ethnic minorities, immigrants, and other "unwanted elements," including union organizers and agrarian reformers. Firearms laws were often enacted to disarm and facilitate repressive action against these groups.

The first gun control laws were enacted in the antebellum South forbidding blacks, whether free or slave, to possess arms, in order to maintain blacks in their servile status. After the Civil War, the South continued to pass restrictive firearms laws in order to deprive the newly freed blacks from exercising their rights of citizenship. During the later part of the 19th century and the early part of the 20th century, gun control laws were passed in the South in order to disarm agrarian reformers and in the North to disarm union organizers. In the North, a strong xenophobic reaction to recent waves of immigrants added further fuel for gun control laws which were used to disarm such persons. Other firearms ownership restrictions were adopted in order to repress the incipient black civil rights movement.

Blacks Harmed by Distrust

Another old American prejudice supported such gun control efforts, then as it does now: the idea that poor people, and especially the black poor, are not to be

Adapted from Stefan B. Tahmassebi, "Gun Control and Racism," *George Mason University Civil Rights Law Journal* 2 (1): 67-99. Reprinted with permission.

trusted with firearms. Even now, in many jurisdictions in which police departments have wide discretion in issuing firearm permits, the effect is that permits are rarely issued to poor or minority citizens.

Blacks, and especially poor blacks, are disproportionately the victims of crime. Yet, these citizens are often not afforded the same police protections that other more affluent and less crime ridden neighborhoods or communities enjoy. This lack of protection is especially so in the inner city urban ghettos. Firearms prohibitions discriminate against those poor and minority citizens who must rely on such arms to defend themselves from criminal activity to a much greater degree than affluent citizens living in safer and better protected communities. . . .

> *"Permits are rarely issued to poor or minority citizens."*

Gun Control Measures Oppress Minorities

The historical purpose of gun control laws in America has been one of discrimination and disenfranchisement of blacks, immigrants, and other minorities. American gun control laws have been enacted to disarm and facilitate repressive actions against union organizers, workers, the foreign-born and racial minorities. Bans on particular types of firearms and firearms registration schemes have been enacted in many American jurisdictions for the alleged purpose of controlling crime. Often, however, the purpose or actual effect of such laws or regulations was to disarm and exert better control over the above-noted groups. As Justice Buford of the Florida Supreme Court noted in his concurring opinion narrowly construing a Florida gun control statute:

> I know something of the history of this legislation. The original Act of 1893 was passed when there was a great influx of negro laborers in this State drawn here for the purpose of working in turpentine and lumber camps. The same condition existed when the Act was amended in 1901 and the Act was passed for the purpose of disarming the negro laborers. . . . The statute was never intended to be applied to the white population and in practice has never been so applied. . . . [T]here has never been, within my knowledge, any effort to enforce the provisions of this statute as to white people, because it has been generally conceded to be in contravention of the Constitution and non-enforceable if contested.

Implicit in the message of such a law was the perceived threat that armed negroes would pose to the white community. As applied, therefore, the statute sent a clear message: only whites could be trusted with guns, while negroes could not.

Gun Control in the South

The development of racially based slavery in the 17th century American colonies was accompanied by the creation of laws meting out separate treatment and granting separate rights on the basis of race. An early sign of such emerging restrictions and one of the most important legal distinctions was the passing of laws denying free blacks the right to keep arms. "In 1640, the first recorded restrictive legislation passed concerning blacks in Virginia excluded them from owning a gun," [according to L. Kennett and J.L. Anderson]. W. Jordan states that:

> Virginia law set Negroes apart from all other groups . . . by denying them the important right and obligation to bear arms. Few restraints could indicate more clearly the denial to Negroes of membership in the White community. This first foreshadowing of the slave codes came in 1640, at just the time when other indications first appeared that Negroes were subject to special treatment.

In the later part of the 17th century fear of slave uprisings in the South accelerated the passage of laws dealing with firearms possessions by blacks. In 1712, for instance, South Carolina passed "An act for the better ordering and governing of Negroes and Slaves" which included two articles particularly relating to firearms ownership and blacks. Virginia passed a similar act entitled "An Act for Preventing Negroes Insurrections."

Thus, in many of the antebellum states, free and/or slave blacks were legally forbidden to possess arms.

> *"The historical purpose of gun control laws in America has been one of discrimination and disenfranchisement of blacks, immigrants, and other minorities."*

State legislation which prohibited the bearing of arms by blacks was held to be constitutional due to the lack of citizen status of the Afro-American slaves. Legislators simply ignored the fact that the United States Constitution and most state constitutions referred to the right to keep and bear arms as a right of the "people" rather than of the "citizen". . . .

Black Codes Denied Rights

After the conclusion of the American Civil War, several Southern legislatures adopted comprehensive regulations, Black Codes, by which the new freedmen were denied many of the rights that white citizens enjoyed. The Special Report of the Anti-Slavery Conference of 1867 noted with particular emphasis that under these Black Codes blacks were "forbidden to own or bear firearms, and thus were rendered defenseless against assaults." Mississippi's Black Code included the following provision:

> Be it enacted . . .[t]hat no freedman, free negro or mulatto, not in the military . . . and not licensed so to do by the board of police of his or her county, shall keep or carry fire-arms of any kind, or any ammunition, . . . and all such arms or ammunition shall be forfeited to the informer. . . ."

The firearms confiscated would often be turned over to the Ku Klux Klan, the local (white) militia or law enforcement authorities which would then, safe in their monopoly of arms and under color of the Black Codes, further oppress and violate the civil rights of the disarmed freedmen.

The United States Congress overrode these Black Codes with the Civil Rights Act and the fourteenth amendment. The legislative histories of both the Civil Rights Act and the fourteenth amendment are replete with denunciations of those statutes denying blacks equal access to firearms for personal self-defense. . . .

Banning Blacks' Handguns

Even after the passage of the Civil Rights Act and the fourteenth amendment, Southern states continued in their effort to disarm blacks. Some Southern states reacted to the federal acts by conceiving a means to the same end: banning a particular class of firearms, in this case cheap handguns, which were the only firearms the poverty-stricken freedmen could afford. [As stated in a December 1985 article in *Reason* magazine,]:

> Small pistols selling for as little as 50 or 60 cents became available in the 1870's and '80's, and since they could be afforded by recently emancipated blacks and poor whites (whom agrarian agitators of the time were encouraging to ally for economic and political purposes), these guns constituted a significant threat to a southern establishment interested in maintaining the traditional class structure. . . .

In Alabama, Texas, and Virginia, exorbitant business or transaction taxes were imposed in order to price handguns out of the reach of blacks and poor whites. An article in Virginia's official university law review called for a "prohibitive tax . . . on the privilege" of selling handguns as a way of disarming "the son of Ham", whose

> cowardly practice of 'toting' guns has been one of the most fruitful sources of crime. . . . Let a Negro board a railroad train with a quart of mean whiskey and a pistol in his grip and the chances are that there will be a murder, or at least a row, before he alights.

Often systems were emplaced where retailers would report to local authorities whenever blacks purchased firearms or ammunition. The sheriff would then arrest the purchaser and confiscate the firearm, which would either be destroyed or turned over to the local Klan or a white militia. Mississippi legislated this system by enacting the first registration law for retailers in 1906, requiring retailers to maintain records of all pistol and pistol ammunition sales, and to make such available for inspection on demand. . . .

"In many of the antebellum states, free and/or slave blacks were legally forbidden to possess arms."

It was not just the newly freed blacks in the South who were disarmed through discriminatory legislation which denied them the ability to defend their life and property, and kept them in a servile position, but also other "undesirable" white elements which were targeted by gun control laws.

At the end of the 19th century, Southern states began formalizing firearms restrictions in response to an increased concern about firearms ownership by certain whites, such as agrarian agitators and labor organizers. In 1893, Alabama, and in 1907, Texas, began imposing extremely heavy business and/or transaction taxes on handgun sales in order to resurrect economic barriers to ownership. South Carolina, in 1902, banned all pistol sales except to sheriffs and their special deputies, which included company strongmen and the KKK. . . .

In the Northeast, the period from the 1870's to the mid-1930's was characterized by strong xenophobic reactions to Eastern and Southern European immigrants. Armed robbery in particular was associated with the racial stereotype in the public mind of the East and South European immigrant as lazy and inclined to violence. Furthermore, these immigrants were associated with the concept of the foreign-born anarchist. The fear and suspicion of these "undesirable" immigrants, together with a desire to disarm labor organizers, led to a concerted campaign by local and national business associations and organizations such as the Immigration Restriction League and the American

> *"Other 'undesirable' white elements . . . were targeted by gun control laws."*

Protective Association, for the enactment of a flat ban on the ownership of firearms, or at least handguns, by aliens. In 1911, New York enacted the Sullivan law. [Don Kates, referring to this law, notes:] "Of proven success in dealing with political dissidents in Central European countries, this system made handgun ownership illegal for anyone without a police permit." The New York City Police Department thereby acquired the official and wholly arbitrary authority to deny or permit the possession of handguns; which the department used in its effort to disarm the city's Italian population. . . .

Gun Control and Native Americans

The history of firearms prohibitions in regard to native Americans presents a parallel example of the use of gun control to oppress and, in this case, to exterminate a non-white ethnic group. Though many legal restrictions against blacks in respect to firearms were abolished, at least facially, during Reconstruction, the sale of firearms to Indians often remained prohibited. Federal law prohibited the sale of arms and munitions to "hostile" Indians. Idaho prohibited the sale or provision of firearms and ammunition to "any Indian."

Usually the disarmament of Indians was quickly followed by the imposition of oppressive measures or even murder and wholesale massacres. "Since the Army had taken from the Sioux their weapons and horses, the alternative to capitulation to the government's demands was starvation," [stated an Indian lawsuit against the government]. A *Washington Post* article related that

On December 28, 1890, the 7th Cavalry was escorting this group [350 Indians] to the government headquarters on the Pine Ridge reservation. After camping overnight along Wounded Knee creek about 15 miles from the headquarters, the Indians were called together on the morning of December 29th, surrounded by troops and told to surrender their rifles. Gun and cannon fire broke out, and many fleeing Indians died huddling in a ravine.

Federal government restrictions on the sale of firearms to Indians were only abolished in 1979.

A Legacy of Racism

Behind current gun control efforts often lurks the remnant of an old American prejudice, that the lower classes and minorities are not to be trusted with firearms. The bias originated in the post-antebellum South for political reasons and may have changed its form, but it still exists. Today the thought remains: if you let the poor, and especially the black poor, have guns, they will commit crimes with them. Even noted anti-gun activists have admitted this. In his book *The Saturday Night Special*, anti-gun journalist Robert Sherrill frankly admitted that the Gun Control Act of 1968 was "passed not to control guns but to control Blacks." Barry Bruce-Briggs, in *The Public Interest*, stated that "it is difficult to escape the conclusion that the 'Saturday Night Special' is emphasized because it is cheap and it is being sold to a particular class of people. The name is sufficient evidence. The reference is to 'Niggertown Saturday Night.'"

Even today firearms regulations target minorities or other unpopular groups. For instance, present Massachusetts law still makes possession of guns by aliens a criminal offense. Present federal statutes make it a felony for one dishonorably discharged, or having renounced American citizenship to purchase or possess a firearm.

"Restrictions on the sale of firearms to Indians were only abolished in 1979."

This federal statute is surely a punitive measure against those who have trespassed certain norms of acceptable behavior even though there is no indication of violent criminal tendencies.

The worst abuses at present occur under the mantle of facially neutral laws that are, however, enforced in a discriminatory manner. In many jurisdictions which require a discretionary gun permit, police departments have wide discretion in issuing a permit, and those departments unfavorable to gun ownership, or to the race, politics, or appearance of a particular applicant frequently maximize obstructions to such persons while favored individuals and groups experience no difficulty in the granting of a permit. In St. Louis, [according to Don B. Kates, Jr.],

> permits are automatically denied . . . to wives who don't have their husband's permission, homosexuals, and non-voters. . . . As one of my students recently learned, a personal 'interview' is not required for every St. Louis application.

After many delays, he finally got to see the sheriff—who looked at him only long enough to see that he wasn't black, yelled 'he's alright' to the permit secretary, and left.

Although legislatures insist that permits are necessary for a variety of reasons, such arbitrary issuance of gun licenses should not be tolerated. . . .

Double Discrimination

The obvious effect of gun bans and prohibitions is to deny law-abiding citizens access to firearms for the defense of themselves and their families. That effect is doubly discriminatory because the poor, and especially the black poor, are the primary victims of crime and in many areas lack the political power to command as much police protection as richer neighborhoods. Of course, present gun prohibitions make possession of firearms illegal in the hands of the entire population of the affected political subdivision, for all races and religions, and the rich and the poor alike. Yes—and the law, in its majestic equality, [as Anatole France stated,] "forbids rich and poor alike to sleep under bridges, to beg in the streets, and to steal bread." Those living in well-off, police protected neighborhoods are less likely to "sleep under bridges, to beg in the streets" or to need a firearm for self-protection.

> *"Today the thought remains: if you let the poor, and especially the black poor, have guns, they will commit crimes with them."*

As noted, blacks, especially poor blacks, are disproportionately the victims of crime, and the situation for households headed by black women is particularly difficult. In 1977, more than half of black families had a woman head of household. A 1983 report by the U.S. Department of Labor states that

> among families maintained by a woman, the poverty rate for blacks was 51%, compared with 24% for their white counterparts in 1977. . . . Families maintained by a woman with no husband present have compromised an increasing proportion of both black families and white families in poverty; however, families maintained by a woman have become an overwhelming majority only among poor black families. . . . About 60% of the 7.7 million blacks below the poverty line in 1977 were living in families maintained by a black woman.

The problems of these women are far more than merely economic. National figures indicate that a black female in the median female age range of 25-34 is about twice as likely to be robbed or raped as her white counterpart. She is also three times as likely to be the victim of an aggravated assault.

In the final analysis, victims must protect themselves and their families or property from criminal attack at the moment the criminal strikes. The need for the ability to defend oneself, family and property, is much more critical in the poor and minority neighborhoods ravaged by crime and without adequate police protection.

However, these citizens who are most likely to be victims have no right to demand or even expect police protection. Courts have consistently ruled "that there is no constitutional right to be protected by the state against being murdered by criminals or madmen," [as determined in *Bowers v. DeVito*, 1982]. Furthermore, courts have ruled that the police have no duty to protect the individual citizen, absent facts establishing a special relationship between the authority and the person assaulted.

The fundamental civil rights regarding the enjoyment of life, liberty and property, the right of self-defense and the right to keep and bear arms, are merely empty promises if a legislature is allowed to restrict the means by which one can protect oneself and one's family. Furthermore, this constitutional deprivation discriminates against the poor and minority citizen who is more exposed to the acts of criminal violence and who is less protected by the state . . . .

Maintaining a Monopoly on Force

The history of gun control in the United States has been one of discrimination, oppression, and arbitrary enforcement. Although the purported legislative intent behind gun control statutes was to decrease crime and violence and thereby ensure public safety, the primary purpose was to keep blacks, immigrants, and native Americans in check. If, as the white establishment believed, blacks and other minorities generally could not be trusted, they certainly could not be trusted with arms and ammunition. Those in power wielded gun control laws in efforts to preserve their monopoly on the instruments of force.

To argue against gun control, such as discriminatory permit schemes, is not to assert that every man and woman should arm themselves before leaving for work in the morning. However, if citizens decide to purchase a gun for whatever reasons and continue to be subjected to permit laws, they have the right to be treated in a non-discriminatory manner.

By prohibiting the possession of firearms, the state discriminates against minority and poor citizens. In the final analysis, citizens must protect themselves and their families and homes. The need for self-defense is far more critical in the poor and minority neighborhoods ravaged by crime and without adequate police protection. Enforcing gun prohibitions, furthermore, will only lead to vast increases in civil liberties violations, including illegal searches and seizures. Unfortunately, the tenants of the Richmond and Chicago housing projects have become second class citizens; their rights to defend themselves and to be free from warrantless searches have been circumscribed. These excesses and other policies and statutes which unduly infringe upon second and fourth amendment rights should not be tolerated by courts or a free citizenry.

Controlling Assault Weapons Would Not Reduce Crime

by Wayne R. Austerman

About the author: *Wayne R. Austerman is a writer who resides in Colorado Springs, Colorado.*

The semiautomatic rifle has been part of the American scene for nearly a century. In 1903 the Winchester Repeating Arms Company marketed the first commercially successful semiautomatic rifle. It was not designed as a military arm, and no sales were made to the US Army. The new rifle was marketed among sportsmen and touted as a great technical improvement over the lever- and bolt-action weapons that had dominated hunting since the post-Civil War period. Only in 1939 did the United States Army begin large-scale issue of a recently adopted semiautomatic rifle (the famous M-1 Garand), and it was not until the mid-1960's that the American military adopted a selective-fire "assault rifle" (the initially problem-plagued M-16) as its new standard small arm.

Misinformation Generates Fear of Guns

Eighty-six years after the first Winchester semiautomatic rifle left the factory and entered a private citizen's hands, the nation has been convulsed by a wave of controversy and deliberately induced hysteria over the alleged menace of the privately-owned "semiautomatic assault rifle." The result has been massive confusion on the part of the nonshooting public, generated in large measure by the ignorance, incompetence, and poorly concealed bias of a national news media working in concert with an alliance of social activists whose ultimate goal is to deny the private citizen any right to own firearms of any description. No one should oppose the free discussion and debate of the potential need for reforms in our gun laws, but lies and willful distortions of the truth employed in the service of a hidden agenda have no legitimate part in such a process. There exists a definite need for someone to dispel some of the prevalent myths about

Wayne R. Austerman, "Those Deadly, Depressing, Syncopated, Semiautomatic Assault Rifle Blues," *Chronicles*, November 1989. Reprinted with permission.

semiautomatic firearms and the uses to which they are put by the people who own them, the overwhelming majority of whom are law-abiding citizens.

What is a semiautomatic rifle? What is an assault rifle? Those two terms are bandied about as synonymous by the news media and anti-gun activists, but their specific meanings elude most of the people who use them so glibly to condemn an entire class of firearms. Simply put, a semiautomatic weapon (handgun or longarm) is one that possesses the capability to fire single shots in quick succession by using the force generated by the explosion of each cartridge in its chamber to set up the next shot. Early repeating rifles utilizing lever- and bolt-action systems required the shooter to manually manipulate a mechanical loading and firing system for each shot. A semiautomatic weapon requires the shooter only to load a quantity of cartridges into its magazine before firing and then to squeeze the trigger for each successive shot. Semiautomatic weapons can be fired very rapidly, but they are not fully automatic, like the machine gun. They do not fire continuously for as long as the trigger is held back or cartridges remain in the magazine.

> *"Even the shooting and killing of a pop icon like John Lennon failed to muster new legions of supporters behind the standards of the gun-haters."*

An assault rifle is a member of a class of weapons first developed for military use by the Germans in World War II. Assault rifles are capable of selective fire—i.e., they can be fired in both semi- and fully-automatic modes as the situation confronting the soldier demands. Assault rifles typically take intermediate-size cartridges that are shorter in length and lack the range and striking power found in the full-size cartridges used in most conventional bolt-action and semiautomatic rifles. The so-called "assault rifles" marketed in this country by both domestic and foreign manufacturers do not have the built-in capability to produce fully-automatic fire. In this they differ from their military-production counterparts. Although most semiautomatic weapons of any type can be altered to be permanently fully automatic, such procedures are strictly illegal. In reality the various "assault rifles" being sold in this country are not assault rifles, for they lack a selective-fire capability. Weapons like the improved AK-47's are simply semiautomatic rifles chambering the same intermediate-size cartridges used by their military cousins. Likewise, the American Colt AR-15 rifle is very much like the M-16, except that the Colt lacks the machine gun-like capability to spray bullets at a single touch of the trigger.

Private Use of Weapons

At the end of World War II semiautomatic rifles like the M-1 Garand became readily available in large numbers to the American public via sales by surplus arms dealers. Fully automatic weapons like machine guns and submachine guns (which fire pistol cartridges) were not easily acquired by private citizens, for since the 1930's such firearms had been subjected to severe licensing and registration requirements that made them expensive and unattractive for the casual shooter or arms collector. The semiautos remained in common possession, however, and few authorities at any level of state or national law enforcement questioned their suitability for private ownership by nonfelons.

By the mid-1960's attitudes had begun to change. Gun control became a major issue and advocates of more restrictive laws governing the acquisition and use of firearms gained support from the public backlash against the Kennedy and King assassinations as well as such tragedies as the 1966 "Texas Tower" shooting spree staged by the brain tumor-maddened Charles Whitman in Austin. The growing revulsion against the war in Vietnam and the taint of all things martial also aided the anti-gun forces. At the same time

> *"The semiautomatic AK-47 and Uzi are in some respects no more lethally effective than such conventional and 'low-tech' weapons as the shotgun."*

a rising tide of social permissiveness and a legal system obsessed with observing procedural minutiae at the expense of dispensing justice contributed to a steady rise in violent crime across the nation. (Remember when Attorney General Nicholas de Belleville Katzenbach declared that he regarded the person who left his ignition keys in a car to be just as guilty of a crime as the worthy who stole the same vehicle?)

Despite their best efforts the hoplophobes [those who fear weapons] failed to win passage of their desired restrictive and/or confiscatory gun legislation by the time the 1980's opened. They were frustrated by a crime-weary public that remained skeptical of their aims and methods, as well as a national leader who cheerfully defended the rights of honest gun-owners while he lay recuperating from an attempt on his own life. Even the shooting and killing of a pop icon like John Lennon failed to muster new legions of supporters behind the standards of the gun-haters. By the time poor Bernie Goetz chose to defy the prevailing liberal orthodoxy by defending himself with a handgun on a New York City subway, many citizens were willing to stand up and cheer his courage.

Massacres Trigger Public Concern

In the latter half of the 80's the anti-gun crowd has had better luck gaining adherents. The "McDonald's Massacre" in California and the string of mass shootings that followed between April 1987 and February 1989 triggered a new wave of public concern about firearms. The January 17, 1989, attack upon a California grade school by an AK-47-wielding psychotic left five children dead and 30 other people wounded in a horrifying act of madness. It also served as the rallying point for an attack upon the ownership of semiautomatic weapons. Patrick Purdy, the suicide-bent assailant in the California killings, was armed with a "street-legal" imported semiautomatic AK-47, as well as a semiautomatic pistol. That much was indisputable. Conveniently suppressed or overlooked in the media stories were the facts of Purdy's lengthy criminal record, which included arrests for extortion, prostitution, possession of narcotics, attempted robbery, receipt of stolen property, criminal conspiracy, and two dangerous-weapons charges. This was a man who had

> *"The anti-gun, anti-Second Amendment message is pervasive in both mass-media entertainment and journalism."*

once been arrested for shooting at trees because, he explained, "I have a duty to overthrow the suppressor." He was subsequently described in his probation officer's report as "a danger to himself and others." Patrick Purdy was cast by the media as a symbol of the tragic laxity of gun laws in America. He was in reality a symbol of the tragic laxity of the criminal justice system, which left him free to walk the streets.

The system of plea bargaining and the apparent indifference of the California legal and public health authorities to Purdy's obviously deranged state put him swiftly back in society following each arrest and left him free to legally purchase firearms. (Purdy's reputed purchase of the AK-47 from an Oregon dealer may have been in violation of the law, although the exact circumstances concerning his acquisition are not yet clear.)

The Purdy killings prompted a spate of municipal bans against the sale of "assault rifles" in California, and a bill was introduced in the state legislature to outlaw numerous semiautomatic firearms. Senator Howard Metzenbaum of Ohio also announced his sponsorship of a federal bill that would place semiautomatic arms in the same legal restrictive category as machine guns and submachine guns.

Obviously there is something wrong with a system that permits the Patrick Purdys of this world to run free and gain access to any sort of weapon. But does the solution to preventing such acts as his lie in outlawing a specific type of firearm and casting ridicule or suspicion upon those who wish to own them? Is the mounting incidence of violence in our society mainly attributable to the presence of semiautomatic weapons, or do other factors encourage the predisposition of certain people to violent crime? Sociologists have debated these issues for decades, without resolution.

The Facts About Semiautomatic Guns

Certain facts are quantifiable and demonstrable, however, and once demonstrated they bring the supposedly criminal and sinister qualities of semiautomatic firearms into clearer perspective. Gun-banners seem incapable (or unwilling) to make any clear distinctions between the legal semiautos like Uzis and AK-47's on the one hand, and genuine "assault rifles" on the other. They further cloud the issue by lumping *all* semiautomatic weapons into the "purely weapons of war" category. The March 15, 1989, US Commerce Department ban on the importation of "AK-47 type weapons" is a case in point. What precisely is the government's interpretation of the phrase "AK-47 type weapons"? Does it refer to all gas-operated semiautomatic rifles (*à la* the American M-1, Belgian FN, and Chinese SKS, among a host of others)? What about those semiautos operating on the blowback principle, like the imported Israeli Uzi carbine? Does the ban cover only those semiautomatic rifles utilizing intermediate-power rifle cartridges like the AK-47? What about (again) the popular Uzi, which chambers nine millimeter pistol ammunition?

A Minor Threat

Although police departments in certain areas where there is heavy drug traffic have testified to the rising criminal use of semiautomatics, just how wide a threat to society does the illicit possession and use of such weapons pose? University of Texas criminologist Sheldon Ekland-Olson estimated that "assault rifle" type firearms figured in less than 1 percent of all homicides committed in the United States, while the cheap "Saturday Night Special" handguns favored by many petty criminals were used in between 30 and 40 percent of such killings.

Leaving aside the actual frequency of their criminal usage, such vaunted and allegedly sinister weapons as the semiautomatic AK-47 and Uzi are in some respects no more lethally effective than such conventional and "low-tech" weapons as the shotgun. The AK will assuredly empty its thirty-round magazine of cartridges within 20 seconds if the shooter has a limber trigger finger and scant regard for the precise placement of his shots. By contrast, a Remington Model 1100 semiautomatic shotgun fitted with a five-round magazine for twelve-gauge cartridges can be fired empty within five seconds or less. A shotgunner using a plastic cartridge-holding tube to speed reloading can easily keep pace with an AK gunner in laying down a curtain of fire. Even an elderly double-barreled shotgun charged with buckshot loads can dispense 18 projectiles in under two seconds and be ready to fire again within five seconds. Compared to such weapons the AK's only advantages are its superior range and accuracy if used in firing slow, aimed shots. A comparison test has even disclosed that in terms of accuracy and striking power the venerable Model 1894 Winchester lever-action deer rifle with its .30-30 cartridge is superior to the AK-47. (The Model 1894 Winchester was the gun used by actor Chuck Connors in *The Rifleman*.)

"Many Americans love firearms for the same reason that they love automobiles."

Given such indisputable technical realities, why do the anti-gun activists have such a zealous hatred for paramilitary-style semiautomatic rifles? It is a matter of popular psychology. Such weapons have a lean, functional look of lethal efficiency that gives them a sinister aspect. Such an appearance plays right into the hands of the hoplophobes. "The weapons' menacing looks, coupled with the public's confusion over fully automatic machine guns versus semiautomatic assault weapons—anything that looks like a machine gun is assumed to be a machine gun—can only increase the chance of public support for restrictions on these weapons," boasts a publication by the Educational Fund to End Handgun Violence.

The anti-gunners and their media allies have no desire to confuse the public with facts. The anti-gun, anti-Second Amendment message is pervasive in both mass-media entertainment and journalism. During the week of March 13-17, 1989, the CBS television network provided repeated grist for the gun-banners' mill. The popular Monday night situation comedy *Designing Women* featured a distortion of fact that could only have stemmed from

> *"The anti-gunners and their media allies have no desire to confuse the public with facts."*

either blatant ignorance or a willful intent to deceive on the part of writer-producer Linda Bloodworth Thompson. In this episode one of the ditzy female characters on the show legally purchased a Colt AR-15 rifle following a series of threats against her and her pet pig. When her friends from work made a surprise midnight call upon her, the nervous Atlanta belle opened up with what was obviously a barrage of *fully-automatic* fire. Actress Dixie Carter then self-righteously delivered a homily on the evils of such weapons and the malign "gun lobby."

Media Distortions

CBS followed this with its evening newscast of March 15. Commentator Dan Rather announced the news of the government ban on importation of "AK-47 type weapons" and then held forth in a prerecorded segment in which he appeared at a police gun range somewhere in New Jersey to interview two alleged experts on the evils of such weapons. The demonstrated expertise of the first "expert" whom Rather interviewed was less than impressive. The government agent proceeded to display an Uzi whose barrel length was plainly below the legally mandated minimum for the semiautomatic versions of the weapon imported into this country from Israel. The audience, of course, was led to believe that they were seeing a weapon that was already in common circulation among the citizenry. He then referred to it as a "rifle," and identified its detachable magazine as a "clip." These were mistakes in technical nomenclature that no truly knowledgeable person would have made. Another law enforcement officer featured in the broadcast referred to those who might wish to use semiautomatic weapons for hunting purposes as "weird." So much for the ethical and objective standards of broadcast journalism.

The Rather broadcast touched upon another distorted issue that constantly surfaces in the debate over semiautomatic arms. Opponents claim that no genuine sportsman would seek to blast Bambi with a thirty-round barrage from a weapon like the AK-47. This ignores the fact that such weapons are legal for hunting purposes in 48 of the 50 states, although in many instances semiautomatics must have their magazines blocked so that they will accept no more than five rounds of ammunition, which is the same number of cartridges carried in most bolt-action sporting rifles. Once again, the opposition ignores reality in its drive to "prove" that semiautomatics are not suitable for sporting purposes and serve only the function of killing people.

If the banners truly want to eliminate all guns capable of rapid-fire or the discharge of multiple projectiles in quick succession, then they will ultimately have to move against all revolvers, all shotguns, and all lever- and bolt-action magazine-fed rifles. . . . The end result of this campaign for public safety would likely be the prohibition of all firearms except muzzleloaders and single-shot breechloading hand and shoulder guns. A ban on all metallic cartridge fixed ammunition might logically follow, since elimination of it would render inoperable any illicit semiautomatic weapons still retained by the rightwing-redneck-diehard element of the population.

A Difference of Values

At its core the crusade against semiautomatic rifles (and by implication all other firearms) reflects a deep split in values between those who honor the traditional warrior virtues and skills as vital necessities for a nation's survival and those who deplore them as being proof of a willing reversion to the bestial. Many Americans love firearms for the same reason that they love automobiles. Both are perceived as guarantors of individual freedom. Both can impart a sense of power to their possessors which serves as a healthy tonic against the myriad petty oppressions of life in a modern mass society. They instinctively know that to be disarmed is to risk subjection to the worst excesses that can be wreaked upon men by the state. They cherish skill with arms for both the intrinsic joy that stems from mastering a powerful instrument and for the assurance it brings that they can still give pause to all Hitlers and Stalins (foreign and domestic). The gun-haters cannot fathom such a people and their feelings. "Our female-dominated, spastic society has been working overtime for a generation to discredit manhood," Bill R. Davidson asserted in *To Keep and Bear Arms*. "People who still like to kill their own snakes bother political leaders in our time. The politicians don't understand and thus vaguely distrust these last traces of self-reliance and do-it-yourself assuredness."

The anti-gun lobby will never realize that an Alvin York will always be more vitally important to the survival of the race than a Dan Rather. For that reason they must not be allowed to prevail, for the triumph of their views will eventually deprive this nation of the essential ability to define its mortal enemies and to unite in arms and oppose them.

Chapter 2

Is Gun Control Constitutional?

The Second Amendment and Gun Control: An Overview

by Sanford Levinson

About the author: *Sanford Levinson is a professor at the University of Texas School of Law in Austin and the author of the book* Constitutional Faith.

One of the best known pieces of American popular art in this century is the *New Yorker* cover by Saul Steinberg presenting a map of the United States as seen by a New Yorker. As most readers can no doubt recall, Manhattan dominates the map; everything west of the Hudson is more or less collapsed together and minimally displayed to the viewer. Steinberg's great cover depends for its force on the reality of what social psychologists call "cognitive maps." If one asks inhabitants ostensibly of the same cities to draw maps of that city, one will quickly discover that the images carried around in people's minds will vary by race, social class, and the like. What is true of maps of places—that they differ according to the perspectives of the mapmakers—is certainly true of all conceptual maps.

A "Map" of the Bill of Rights

To continue the map analogy, consider in this context the Bill of Rights: Is there an agreed upon "projection" of the concept? Is there even a canonical text of the Bill of Rights? Does it include the first eight, nine, or ten Amendments to the Constitution? Imagine two individuals who are asked to draw a "map" of the Bill of Rights. One is a (stereo-) typical member of the American Civil Liberties Union (of which I am a card-carrying member); the other is an equally (stereo-) typical member of the "New Right." The first, I suggest, would feature the First Amendment as Main Street, dominating the map, though more, one suspects, in its role as protector of speech and prohibitor of established religion than as guardian of the rights of religious believers. The other principal avenues would be the criminal procedure aspects of the Constitution drawn from the Fourth, Fifth, Sixth, and Eighth Amendments. Also depicted prominently

Excerpts of Sanford Levinson, "The Embarrassing Second Amendment." Reprinted by permission of The Yale Law Journal Company and Fred B. Rothman & Company from *The Yale Law Journal* 99 (December 1989): 637-59.

would be the Ninth Amendment, although perhaps as in the process of construction. I am confident that the ACLU map would exclude any display of the just compensation clause of the Fifth Amendment or the Tenth Amendment.

The second map, drawn by the New Rightist, would highlight the free exercise clause of the First Amendment, the just compensation clause of the Fifth Amendment, and the Tenth Amendment. Perhaps the most notable difference between the two maps, though, would be in regard to the Second Amendment: "A well regulated Militia being necessary to the security of a free State, the right of the people to keep and bear Arms shall not be infringed."

> *"The second amendment is not taken seriously by most scholars."*

What would be at most only a blind alley for the ACLU mapmaker would, I am confident, be a major boulevard in the map drawn by the New Right adherent. It is this last anomaly that I want to explore in this viewpoint.

The Politics of Interpreting the Second Amendment

To put it mildly, the Second Amendment is not at the forefront of constitutional discussion, at least as registered in what the academy regards as the venues for such discussion—law reviews, casebooks, and other scholarly legal publications. As Professor L.H. Larue has recently written, "the second amendment is not taken seriously by most scholars."

Both Laurence Tribe and the Illinois team of J. Nowak, R. Rotunda, and J. Young at least acknowledge the existence of the Second Amendment in their respective treatises on constitutional law, perhaps because the treatise genre demands more encyclopedic coverage than does the casebook. Neither, however, pays it the compliment of extended analysis. Both marginalize the Amendment by relegating it to footnotes; it becomes what a deconstructionist might call a "supplement" to the ostensibly "real" Constitution that is privileged by discussion in the text. Professor Tribe's footnote appears as part of a general discussion of congressional power. He asserts that the history of the Amendment "indicate[s] that the central concern of [its] framers was to prevent such federal interferences with the state militia as would permit the establishment of a standing national army and the consequent destruction of local autonomy." He does note, however, that "the debates surrounding congressional approval of the Second Amendment do contain references to individual self-protection as well as to states' rights," but he argues that the presence of the preamble to the Amendment, as well as the qualifying phrase "'well regulated' makes any invocation of the amendment as a restriction on state or local gun control measures extremely problematic." Nowak, Rotunda, and Young mention the Amendment in the context of the incorporation controversy, though they discuss its meaning at slightly greater length. They state that "[t]he Supreme Court has not determined, at least not with any clarity, whether the amendment protects only a right of state governments against federal interference with state militia and police forces . . . or a right of individuals against the federal and state government[s]."

Clearly the Second Amendment is not the only ignored patch of text in our constitutional conversations. One will find extraordinarily little discussion about another one of the initial Bill of Rights, the Third Amendment: "No Soldier shall, in time of peace be quartered in any house, without the consent of the Owner, nor in time of war, but in a manner to be prescribed by law." Nor does one hear much about letters of marque and reprisal or the granting of titles of nobility. There are, however, some differences that are worth noting.

The Third Amendment, to take the easiest case, is ignored because it is in fact of no current importance whatsoever (although it did, for obvious reasons, have importance at the time of the founding). It has never, for a single instance, been viewed by any body of modern lawyers or groups of laity as highly relevant to their legal or political concerns. For this reason, there is almost no caselaw on the Amendment. I suspect that few among even the highly sophisticated readers of this [volume] can summon up the Amendment without the aid of the text.

The Importance of the Second Amendment

The Second Amendment, though, is radically different from these other pieces of constitutional text just mentioned, which all share the attribute of being basically irrelevant to any ongoing political struggles. To grasp the difference, one might simply begin by noting that it is not at all unusual for the Second Amendment to show up in letters to the editors of newspapers and magazines. That judges and academic lawyers, including the ones who write casebooks, ignore it is most certainly not evidence for the proposition that no one cares about it. The National Rifle Association, to name the most obvious example, cares deeply about the Amendment, and an apparently serious Senator of the United States averred that the right to keep and bear arms is the "right most valued by free men," [Orrin Hatch, 1982]. Campaigns for Congress in both political parties, and even presidential campaigns, may turn on the apparent commitment of the candidates to a particular view of the Second Amendment. This reality of the political process reflects the fact that millions of Americans, even if (or perhaps *especially* if) they are not academics, can quote the Amendment and would disdain any presentation of the Bill of Rights that did not give it a place of pride.

> *"Millions of Americans . . . can quote the Amendment and would disdain any presentation of the Bill of Rights that did not give it a place of pride."*

I cannot help but suspect that the best explanation for the absence of the Second Amendment from the legal consciousness of the elite bar, including that component found in the legal academy, is derived from a mixture of sheer opposition to the idea of private ownership of guns and the perhaps subconscious fear that altogether plausible, perhaps even "winning," interpretations of the Second Amendment would present real hurdles to those of us supporting pro-hibitory regulation. . . . I want to suggest that the Amendment may be pro-foundly embarrassing to many who both support such regulation and view themselves as committed to zealous adherence to the Bill of Rights (such as most members of the ACLU). In-deed, one sometimes discovers members of the NRA who are equally committed members of the ACLU, differing with the latter only on the issue of the Second Amendment but otherwise genuinely sharing the libertarian viewpoint of the ACLU.

> *"No one has ever described the Constitution as a marvel of clarity."*

It is not my style to offer "correct" or "incorrect" interpretations of the Con-stitution. My major interest is in delineating the rhetorical structures of Ameri-can constitutional argument and elaborating what is sometimes called the "poli-tics of interpretation," that is, the factors that explain why one or another ap-proach will appeal to certain analysts at certain times, while other analysts, or times, will favor quite different approaches. Thus my general tendency to re-gard as wholly untenable any approach to the Constitution that describes itself as obviously correct and condemns its opposition as simply wrong holds for the Second Amendment as well. . . .

Discerning the Amendment's Purpose

Recall the Second Amendment: "A well regulated Militia being necessary to the security of a free State, the right of the people to keep and bear Arms, shall not be infringed." No one has ever described the Constitution as a marvel of clarity, and the Second Amendment is perhaps one of the worst drafted of all its provisions. What is special about the Amendment is the inclusion of an opening clause—a preamble, if you will—that seems to set out its purpose. No similar clause is a part of any other Amendment, though that does not, of course, mean that we do not ascribe purposes to them. It would be impossible to make sense of the Constitution if we did not engage in the ascription of purpose. Indeed, the major debates about the First Amendment arise precisely when one tries to discern a purpose, given that "literalism" is a hopelessly failing approach to in-terpreting it. We usually do not even recognize punishment of fraud—a classic speech act—as a free speech problem because we so sensibly assume that the purpose of the First Amendment could not have been, for example, to protect the circulation of patently deceptive information to potential investors in com-mercial enterprises. The sharp differences that distinguish those who would limit the reach of the First Amendment to "political" speech from those who would extend it much further, encompassing nondeceptive commercial speech, are all derived from different readings of the purpose that underlies the raw text.

A standard move of those legal analysts who wish to limit the Second

Amendment's force is to focus on its "preamble" as setting out a restrictive purpose. Recall Laurence Tribe's assertion that the purpose was to allow the states to keep their militias and to protect them against the possibility that the new national government will use its power to establish a powerful standing army and eliminate the state militias. This purposive reading quickly disposes of any notion that there is an "individual" right to keep and bear arms. The right, if such it be, is only a state's right. The consequence of this reading is obvious: the national government has the power to regulate—to the point of prohibition—private ownership of guns, since that has, by stipulation, nothing to do with preserving state militias. This is, indeed, the position of the ACLU, which reads the Amendment as protecting only the right of "maintaining an effective state militia. . . . [T]he individual's right to bear arms applies only to the preservation or efficiency of a well-regulated [state] militia. Except for lawful police and military purposes, the possession of weapons by individuals is not constitutionally protected."

This is not a wholly implausible reading, but one might ask why the Framers did not simply say something like "Congress shall have no power to prohibit state-organized and directed militias." Perhaps they in fact meant to do something else. Moreover, we might ask if ordinary readers of late eighteenth century legal prose would have interpreted it as meaning something else. The text at best provides only a starting point for a conversation. In this specific instance, it does not come close to resolving the questions posed by federal regulation of arms. Even if we accept the preamble as significant, we must still try to figure out what might be suggested by guaranteeing to "the people the right to keep and bear arms"; moreover, as we shall see presently, even the preamble presents unexpected difficulties in interpretation.

> *"One might ask why the Framers did not simply say something like 'Congress shall have no power to prohibit state-organized and directed militias.'"*

Considering Historical Context

One might argue (and some have) that the substantive right is one pertaining to a collective body—"the people"—rather than to individuals. Professor Cress [in *The Journal of American History*, 1984], for example, argues that state constitutions regularly used the words "man" or "person" in regard to "individual rights such as freedom of conscience," whereas the use in those constitutions of the term "the people" in regard to a right to bear arms is intended to refer to the "sovereign citizenry" collectively organized. Such an argument founders, however, upon examination of the text of the federal Bill of Rights itself and the usage there of the term "the people" in the First, Fourth, Ninth, and Tenth Amendments.

Consider that the Fourth Amendment protects "[t]he right of the people to be secure in their persons," or that the First Amendment refers to the "right of the people peaceably to assemble, and to petition the Government for a redress of grievances." It is difficult to know how one might plausibly read the Fourth Amendment as other than a protection of individual rights, and it would approach the frivolous to read the assembly and petition clause as referring only to the right of state legislatures to meet and pass a remonstrance directed to Congress or the President against some governmental act. The Tenth Amendment is trickier, though it does explicitly differentiate between "states" and "the people" in terms of retained rights. Concededly, it would be possible to read the Tenth Amendment as suggesting only an ultimate right of revolution by the collective people should the "states" stray too far from their designated role of protecting the rights of the people. This reading follows directly from the social contract theory of the state. (But, of course, many of these rights are held by individuals.) . . .

Cress persuasively shows that [none of the Framers] defended universal possession of arms. New Hampshire had no objection to disarming those who "are or have been in actual rebellion," just as Samuel Adams stressed that only "peaceable citizens" should be protected in their right of "keeping their own arms." All these points can be conceded, however, without conceding as well that Congress—or, for that matter, the States—had the power to disarm these "peaceable citizens.". . .

The Costs of Gun Ownership

The arguments on behalf of a "strong" Second Amendment are stronger than many of us might wish were the case. . . . The standard argument in favor of strict control and, ultimately, prohibition of private ownership focuses on the extensive social costs of widespread distribution of firearms. Consider, for example, a speech given by former Justice Lewis Powell to the American Bar Association. He noted that over 40,000 murders were committed in the United States in 1986 and 1987, and that fully sixty percent of them were committed with firearms. England and Wales, however, saw only 662 homicides in 1986, less than eight percent of which were committed with firearms. Justice Powell indicated that, "[w]ith respect to handguns," in contrast "to sporting rifles and shotguns[,] it is not easy to understand why the Second Amendment, or the notion of liberty, should be viewed as creating a right to own and carry a weapon that contributes so directly to the shocking number of murders in our society."

"It seems foolhardy to assume that the armed state will necessarily be benevolent."

It is hard to disagree with Justice Powell; it appears almost crazy to protect as a constitutional right something that so clearly results in extraordinary social costs with little, if any, compensating social advantage. Indeed, since Justice Powell's talk, the subject of assault rifles has become a staple of national discussion, and the opponents of regulation of such weapons have deservedly drawn the censure even of conservative leaders like William Bennett. It is almost impossible to imagine that the judiciary would strike down a determination by Congress that the possession of assault weapons should be denied to private citizens. . . .

The overriding temptation is to say that times and circumstances have changed and that there is simply no reason to continue enforcing an outmoded, and indeed dangerous, understanding of private rights against public order. This criticism is clearest in regard to the so-called individualist argument, for one can argue that the rise of a professional police force to enforce the law has made irrelevant, and perhaps even counterproductive, the continuation of a strong notion of self-help as the remedy for crime.

> *"We ignore at our political peril the good-faith belief of many Americans that they cannot rely on the police for protection against a variety of criminals."*

I am not unsympathetic to such arguments. It is no purpose of this viewpoint to solicit membership for the National Rifle Association or to express any sympathy for what even Don Kates, a strong critic of the conventional dismissal of the Second Amendment, describes as "the gun lobby's obnoxious habit of assailing all forms of regulation on 2nd Amendment grounds." And yet . . . .

Have Circumstances Really Changed?

Circumstances may well have changed in regard to individual defense, although we ignore at our political peril the good-faith belief of many Americans that they cannot rely on the police for protection against a variety of criminals. Still, let us assume that the individualist reading of the Amendment has been vitiated by changing circumstances. Are we quite so confident that circumstances are equally different in regard to the republican rationale outlined earlier?

One would, of course, like to believe that the state, whether at the local or national level, presents no threat to important political values, including liberty. But our propensity to believe that this is the case may be little more than a sign of how truly different we are from our radical forbearers. I do not want to argue that the state is necessarily tyrannical; I am not an anarchist. But it seems foolhardy to assume that the armed state will necessarily be benevolent. The American political tradition is, for good or ill, based in large measure on a healthy mistrust of the state. The development of widespread suffrage and greater majoritarianism in our polity is itself no sure protection, at least within republican theory. The republican theory is predicated on the stark contrast between mere democracy, where people are motivated by selfish personal interest, and a republic, where civic virtue, both in citizens and leadership, tames selfishness on behalf of the common good. In any event, it is hard for me to see how one can argue that circumstances have so changed as to make mass disarmament constitutionally unproblematic. . . .

There is one further problem of no small import: If one does accept the plausibility of any of the arguments on behalf of a strong reading of the Second Amendment, but, nevertheless, rejects them in the name of social prudence and the present-day consequences produced by finicky adherence to early understandings, why do we not apply such consequentialist criteria to each and every part of the Bill of Rights? As Ronald Dworkin has argued, what it means to take rights seriously is that one will honor them even when there is significant social cost in doing so. If protecting freedom of speech, the rights of criminal defendants, or any other part of the Bill of Rights were always (or even most of the time) clearly costless to the society as a whole, it would truly be impossible to understand why they would be as controversial as they are. The very fact that there are often significant costs—criminals going free, oppressed groups having to hear viciously racist speech and so on—helps to account for the observed fact that those who view themselves as defenders of the Bill of Rights are generally antagonistic to prudential arguments. Most often, one finds them embracing versions of textual, historical, or doctrinal argument that dismiss as almost crass and vulgar any insistence that times might have changed and made too "expensive" the continued adherence to a given view. "Cost-benefit" analysis, rightly or wrongly, has come to be viewed as a "conservative" weapon to attack liberal rights. Yet one finds that the tables are strikingly turned when the Second Amendment comes into play. Here it is "conservatives" who argue in effect that social costs are irrelevant and "liberals" who argue for a notion of the "Living Constitution" and "changed circumstances.". . .

A Second Amendment Debate Is Necessary

It is time for the Second Amendment to enter full scale into the consciousness of the legal academy. . . . I am not so naïve as to believe that conversation will overcome the chasm that now separates the sensiblity of, say, Senator Hatch and myself as to what constitutes the "right[s] most valued by free men [and women]." It is important to remember that one will still need to join up sides and engage in vigorous political struggle. But it might at least help to make the political sides appear more human to one another. Perhaps "we" might be led to stop referring casually to "gun nuts" just as, maybe, members of the NRA could be brought to understand the real fear that the currently almost uncontrolled system of gun ownership sparks in the minds of many whom they casually dismiss as "bleeding-heart liberals." Is not, after all, the possibility of serious, engaged discussion about political issues at the heart of what is most attractive in both liberal *and* republican versions of politics?

Gun Control Is Constitutional

by Sarah Brady

About the author: *Sarah Brady heads Handgun Control, Inc., a gun control organization. Her husband is former White House press secretary James Brady, who was severely wounded by John W. Hinckley Jr. in a 1981 attempt to assassinate President Ronald Reagan.*

Like many Americans, I never thought too much about the 2nd Amendment to the Constitution, until I experienced an incidence of handgun violence that changed my life and the lives of my family. As you know, in 1981, my husband, Jim Brady, White House Press Secretary, was shot during the attempted assassination of President Ronald Reagan. That shooting helped propel me into the battle for stronger federal gun laws.

My involvement in the handgun control campaign has encouraged me to examine more closely the 2nd Amendment, which in its entirety reads: "A well regulated Militia, being necessary to the security of a free state, the right of the people to keep and bear Arms, shall not be infringed."

When the Founding Fathers met at the Constitutional Convention in 1787 to create a government that would unite their separate states into a nation, a major issue debated was the extent of the federal government's control of military power. Federalists insisted on the need for a strong standing Army. Anti-federalists argued that individual citizens would continue to serve in state militias, and thus protect and defend the country.

Debate Over Amendment's Meaning

After the Constitution was signed, it was sent to state conventions for ratification, which occurred in 1788. From the debates in these conventions, there emerged a consensus that the Constitution should be amended to include a Bill of Rights. When the Bill of Rights was added in 1791, the 2nd Amendment addressed the issue of who should bear arms and for what purpose.

Over the years, there has been much debate over whether this "right" meant

Sarah Brady, "The Second Amendment: What It Really Means," *San Francisco Barrister*, December 1989. Reprinted by permission of Handgun Control, Inc.

that individuals were guaranteed access to firearms under the Constitution. The National Rifle Association, which has emblazoned only the last fourteen words of the 2nd Amendment across its national headquarters, continues to argue that the 2nd Amendment guarantees the right of any American to own anything from handguns to machine guns.

However much debate there is among the general public, there is little debate in America's courts. In fact, the U.S. Supreme Court has interpreted the 2nd Amendment on five separate occasions. In addition, nearly forty lower court decisions have addressed the Amendment. All have ruled that the 2nd Amendment guarantees a state's right to maintain a militia—not an individual's right to own a handgun.

> *"The 2nd Amendment guarantees a state's right to maintain a militia— not an individual's right to own a handgun."*

Three key cases heard by the Supreme Court were as follows: *U.S. v. Cruikshank*, 92 U.S. 542 (1876). In this case, Ku Klux Klansmen were charged with infringing the constitutional rights of black citizens to assemble and bear arms. Although this was primarily a civil rights case, the Justices did rule on the right of individuals to carry firearms by stating that the 2nd Amendment protects states' rights from the federal government, not individual rights.

Presser v. Illinois, 116 U.S. 252 (1886). Here, the defendant was prosecuted for leading a band of armed men in a parade without a license. The Court reaffirmed Cruikshank's holding that the 2nd Amendment was not a protection of individuals' rights, but instead states' rights.

And in the case of *U.S. v. Miller*, 307 U.S. 174 (1939), Jack Miller and a friend were arrested for violating the National Firearms Act by going from Oklahoma to Arkansas while carrying a double-barreled, sawed-off shotgun. The Supreme Court ruled that the weapon had no "reasonable relationship to the preservation or efficiency of a well-regulated militia" and thus, the laws relating to sawed-off shotguns did not violate the 2nd Amendment to the Constitution.

No Support of Handguns

Former Supreme Court Justice Lewis Powell echoed this view during a speech before the American Bar Association. Arguing that he found no Constitutional support for the private ownership of handguns, Powell said, "With respect to handguns . . . it is not easy to understand why the Second Amendment, or the notion of liberty, should be viewed as creating a right to own and carry a weapon that contributes so directly to the shocking number of murders in the United States." His audience no doubt agreed. The American Bar Association itself has stated: "Neither the United States Constitution nor any of its amendments grant any one the right to keep and bear arms."

Although the NRA continues to fight all forms of gun control measures with the claim that "the Second Amendment is not limited by its language to the type of arms which the people have a right to own," Congress has already legislated some restrictions. In 1986, Congress outlawed the sale and manufacture of new machine guns. Two years later, over the objections of the NRA, President Reagan signed into law a bill preventing the sale of plastic, undetectable handguns.

Regardless of one's interpretation of the 2nd Amendment, the legislation I support would not prevent a law-abiding citizen's access to handguns. But I do not agree with the NRA that the 2nd Amendment guarantees the right of a John Hinckley to purchase a handgun. We at Handgun Control, Inc. do not advocate a handgun ban or handgun confiscation. Rather, we support common-sense measures to ensure that criminals cannot simply walk into gun stores and walk out with the tools of the trade. Our legislative agenda includes a national, seven-day waiting period before the purchase of a handgun, to allow for a criminal records check of the purchasers. We also support law-enforcement backed legislation to take

> *"The legislation I support would not prevent a law-abiding citizen's access to handguns."*

paramilitary assault weapons of war off America's streets. In addition, we favor prohibiting the sale and manufacture of Saturday Night Specials—favored by criminals because of their concealability.

Sensible handgun and assault weapon laws are on the books in cities and states across the country. Currently, 23 states have enacted some form of waiting period legislation. As mentioned above, federal law prohibits the manufacture and sale of new machine guns for civilians. If the gun lobby truly believed that such laws are unconstitutional under the 2nd Amendment, they would have challenged each and every law in the courts.

NRA Failures

In fact, when the NRA has challenged these laws, they have lost. For example, in 1981, the town of Morton Grove, Illinois, passed an ordinance banning handguns. Exclusions were included for police officers, jail and prison authorities, members of the armed forces and licensed gun collectors and gun clubs. The Illinois Supreme Court ruled that the ordinance was a valid exercise of Morton Grove's police power under the Illinois state right to bear arms provision. The U.S. Seventh Circuit Court of Appeals also upheld the ordinance, stating that there is no individual right to keep and bear handguns under the 2nd Amendment. In October 1983, the U.S. Supreme Court declined to hear an appeal of this ruling, allowing the lower court ruling to stand. Clearly, there is little debate about the 2nd Amendment in the courts.

Even those who continue to maintain that the right to own a gun is guaranteed by the 2nd Amendment have to ask themselves how far this "right" goes.

Surely no one would argue that felons, fugitives from justice, drug abusers or the adjudicated mentally incompetent should be given easy access to handguns. Yet that is just the situation we continue to allow in a country that sees 22,000 Americans lose their lives to these weapons each year.

The NRA and others who argue that the 2nd Amendment is limitless in its guarantees are clearly outside accepted constitutional thought and practice. Even they must accept the fact that with every right comes a responsibility. In the case of the 2nd Amendment, reasonable laws to protect the public safety, laws to deny easy access to firearms by those who would misuse them, laws to stop the sale of weapons of war—are obviously constitutional.

Intent of the Founding Fathers

When the Constitution was drafted, our Founding Fathers foresaw a great nation of peace and tranquility. Part of the legacy of that vision is a nation free from violence—where the rights of individuals complement the quest for public safety. The Courts agree that nothing in the Constitution prohibits legislators from enacting common-sense restrictions on firearms. Clearly, our citizens agree. It is up to us to convince more legislators to translate that fact into action and pass a sensible federal gun policy which will make the nation safer for us all.

Gun Control Measures Can Be Constitutional

by Nelson Lund

About the author: *Nelson Lund is associate counsel to President George Bush.*

The Second Amendment to the United States Constitution has become the most embarrassing provision of the Bill of Rights. Although crime, violence, and gun control have been among the hottest topics of political controversy over the past two decades, civil libertarians have generally shown much less enthusiasm about the Second Amendment than about other provisions of the Bill of Rights. The federal courts have also been manifestly uncomfortable with the Second Amendment and, in recent times, have declined every opportunity to give it the same thorough consideration that is automatically given to the other specific guarantees of the first eight amendments. The lower courts generally have either adopted an interpretation that is implausible on its face, inconsistent with Supreme Court precedent, and unsupported by historical evidence about the intention of the Framers, or adhered to ancient precedents that treated the Bill of Rights as being inapplicable to the states. The Supreme Court, moreover, inscrutably denies all petitions for certiorari.

Balancing Act

Despite a growing body of literature examining the original meaning of the Second Amendment and a simmering debate over the desirability and efficacy of gun control legislation, no one has attempted to develop an interpretation of the Second Amendment that fits comfortably within the Supreme Court's modern jurisprudence of individual rights. That jurisprudence can be characterized as an ongoing attempt to reconcile what is known about the original intent underlying the Bill of Rights with the desire of legislatures to respond rationally to modern problems unforeseen at the time it was drafted. Most provisions in the Bill of Rights have been interpreted so as to advance an elaborate effort by the judiciary to act as an umpire between individuals' impulses for freedom and government's concern for the maintenance of order and public safety. And yet,

Excerpted from Nelson Lund, "The Second Amendment, Political Liberty, and the Right to Self-Preservation," *Alabama Law Review* 39 (1987): 103-30. Reprinted with permission.

just when the conflict regarding the Second Amendment is perhaps at its sharpest and most poignant, the Supreme Court has remained strangely silent. Whatever one may think about the motives, character, psychology, or intelligence of those who desire to possess firearms, the principle that those individuals assert is profoundly serious. The claim to the tools needed for exercising one's lawful right to protect himself (and perhaps especially herself) from criminal violence should be given at least as respectful a hearing as the First Amendment claims of Nazis and pornographers or the Fourth Amendment claims of confessed murderers. . . .

The Debate over the Constitution's Meaning

The debate over the original meaning of the Second Amendment has largely focused on the implications of the phrase "[a] well regulated Militia, being necessary to the security of a free State. . . ." One group of commentators treats the phrase simply as a statement of purpose and maintains that the Second Amendment provides individuals the right to keep and bear arms. Another group maintains that the Second Amendment creates an exclusively collective right—the right of the states to maintain organized military forces.

The "collective right" interpretation has become dominant among the courts and academics, while laypersons have generally favored the "individual right" interpretation. The former interpretation deprives the amendment of any application to existing or proposed forms of gun control legislation. Perhaps that is why the "collective right" interpretation is dominant among leaders of the legal profession, where restrictive regulations on the ownership and use of firearms are widely favored as a matter of social policy.

> *"No one has attempted to develop an interpretation of the Second Amendment that fits comfortably within the Supreme Court's modern jurisprudence of individual rights."*

Whatever the explanation, however, the popularity of the "collective right" interpretation should be surprising, since it is virtually baseless.

Advocates of the collective right interpretation focus almost exclusively on the textual reference to a "well regulated Militia." They argue that the introductory phrase of the amendment implies that the right to keep and bear arms is restricted to officially organized military units, such as the National Guard. The language of the Constitution, however, actually refutes this claim. In the eighteenth century, the term "militia" was rarely used to refer to organized military units, and, indeed, eighteenth century *legal* usage seems never to have adopted that meaning. Rather, the "militia" included all citizens who qualified for military service (*i.e.*, most adult males). This definition continues to be included in the United States Code today. There is thus no apparent reason for supposing that the term "militia" in the Constitution refers solely or even primarily to organized military units. Indeed, article I, section 8 of the Constitution clearly assumes the existence of the "Militia" in the states, but article I, section 10 *forbids* the states to "keep Troops" without the consent of Congress.

A Clear Protection of Individuals' Rights

The fact that the Framers referred to a "well regulated" militia lends apparent support to the collective right interpretation, but the reference indicates only that the Framers intended for the militia to be regulated in some way, as for example, by being organized into formal military units *or* by being comprised of individuals already familiar with the principal instruments of military combat. In any case, the Second Amendment does not even mention the right of the states to regulate the militia. Rather, it protects the "right of the people" to keep and bear arms. This is exactly the same phrase used in the First Amendment and in the Fourth Amendment—in both cases the phrase clearly protects individuals',

> *"The Framers' intent to distinguish the rights of the people from those of the states is expressly manifested in the language of the Tenth Amendment."*

not states', rights. Furthermore, the Framers' intent to distinguish the rights of the people from those of the states is expressly manifested in the language of the Tenth Amendment. To conclude that the "right of the people" is synonymous with the phrase "the right of the states" requires one to torture the text of the Constitution so badly that the document's obvious meaning is violated.

Because the text of the Constitution offers little support for the collective right interpretation, proponents of that interpretation focus their attention on evidence indicating that the Framers were especially concerned about standing federal armies, which might have been a threat to political liberty if the citizenry were disarmed. Using this evidence to confirm the collective right interpretation is untenable for two reasons. First, the fact that the supporters of the Bill of Rights probably had as *one* of their foremost concerns the dangers of a federal standing army does not imply that this was their *only* fear. And it certainly does not permit an interpreter of the Constitution to ignore its plain language, which contains no such limitation. Second, even if it is assumed that the Framers were exclusively concerned with the danger of federal despotism, overwhelming textual and historical evidence indicates that they chose to guard against that danger by securing the people's private right to arms.

Establishing that the Second Amendment protects an individual's right to keep and bear arms, however, is only one small step toward developing a sound interpretation of the constitutional guarantee. The exact scope of the individual right is not expressly defined in the Constitution and is not self-evident. Is the right absolute, so that it extends to all devices that might be characterized as "arms," up to and including nuclear warheads and ICBMs [intercontinental ballistic missile]? Are *all* citizens, including convicted murderers and lunatics, free to own and carry lethal weapons? If not, what restrictions are constitutionally permissible, and on what principles may those restrictions be justified? . . .

The Second Amendment and Political Freedom

The language of the Second Amendment protects an individual's right to keep and bear arms. The language also indicates, however, that this private right is protected for the sake of a public good. It follows that the private right of access to firearms is constitutionally protected, at least to the extent that it reasonably contributes to political freedom.

Available evidence of the Framers' intent supports this general proposition. The specific concern foremost in the minds of the proponents of the Second Amendment was almost certainly the dangers associated with standing armies. Europe had a long history, with which the Framers were familiar, of efforts by ambitious monarchs to strengthen their political position by achieving monopolies of the instruments of force; standing armies and gun control laws were used to this end. Like modern gun control laws, these restrictions were ostensibly for such other purposes as game conservation and crime prevention. Along with many others, however, William Blackstone recognized that "prevention of popular insurrections and resistance to the government, by disarming the bulk of the people . . . is a reason oftener meant than avowed."

> *"The exact scope of the individual right is not expressly defined in the Constitution and is not self-evident."*

Subsequent events have weakened, without entirely eliminating, the protection against political oppression afforded by the right to keep and bear arms. Part of the reason for the weakening of this protection is that the Framers prudently declined to put direct constitutional restrictions on the federal government's power to maintain standing armies. Many in the founding generation undoubtedly hoped and expected that the federal army would remain small during peacetime, as in fact it did for a century and a half thereafter. Political events and technological advances, however, have combined to render today's federal military establishment the second strongest in the world, and our military is far more powerful than the Founders could possibly have imagined. At the same time, domestic political and cultural changes beginning with the War Between the States have greatly weakened loyalties to the individual states; this has removed the most likely cause of a major military conflict between American citizens and federal troops. . . .

The Second Amendment at least gives individuals a constitutional right to keep such private arms as will enable them to constitute a reasonable deterrent against government attempts to institute a repressive political regime. It would be hard to define exactly what constitutes a "reasonable deterrent," but it should be obvious that it must be more than a token. Under modern conditions, knives and slingshots are not enough; at the very least, some small and relatively inexpensive firearms, rifles and shot-guns, must be allowed. Similarly, the principal purpose of the Second Amendment requires that arms be reasonably available; a system arbi-trarily limiting the number of weapons in circulation to the equivalent of two percent of the population, for ex-ample, would defeat the main purpose of the constitutional right.

> *"Many in the founding generation undoubtedly hoped and expected that the federal army would remain small during peacetime."*

Draconian gun control measures, such as a total ban on the private possession of firearms, would therefore be unconstitutional. In fact, however, neither the national government nor any state has entertained such a scheme and is not likely to do so any time soon. The more pressing questions have to do with government regulations of certain types of small arms, especially handguns. . . .

A reasonable analysis of the handgun problem should begin by recognizing that there are three distinct groups of people that are affected by government regulation of this area. First, there are people who desire to use firearms in the commission of crimes. Since firearms are useful for this purpose, these people are unlikely to be discouraged by the relatively mild sanctions that are imposed for the mere illegal possession of guns. The only way to deter those people from using guns for criminal purposes is by punishing them for the underlying crime and perhaps imposing additional penalties for using firearms in the commission of a crime. These firearm penalties would pose no Second Amendment problems. At the other extreme are responsible citizens who wish to possess guns for legitimate purposes and who carefully guard against accidents or other misuse. The government has no defensible interest in prohibiting this group of people from possessing arms. The third group comprises people who are without settled criminal designs, but who are prone to carelessness or fits of temper that result in unplanned injuries to innocent persons.

Requiring Insurance Is the Key

Restrictions on the private possession and use of handguns are properly aimed at the first and third groups, and should be narrowly tailored to avoid unnecessary infringements of the rights of those in the second group. Fortunately for the analysis, the American legal system has developed a standard mechanism for dealing with the same kind of problem in other areas of social life. That mechanism is personal liability for tortious conduct combined with mandatory insurance or bonding for people who desire to use unusually hazardous devices. Automobile regulations provide one example, but there is an even closer analogy in the regulations applied to private security guard services.

Instead of presuming that security guards have no legitimate reasons for carrying guns, or erecting extremely burdensome obstacles to their doing so, reasonable licensing requirements for individual guards are typically combined with tort law rules and mandatory insurance requirements.

Requiring Firearm Insurance

The same system could easily be applied to other individuals who want or need to possess firearms. If this were done, the private insurance market would quickly and efficiently make it prohibitively expensive for people with a record of irresponsible ownership of guns to possess them legally, but would not impose unreasonable burdens on those who have the self-discipline to exercise their liberty in a responsible fashion. Furthermore, the insurance market could effectively account for many indirect indicia of irresponsibility that would be problematic if addressed by government regulation. For example, just as young males and persons who live in neighborhoods with high accident rates have traditionally paid higher automobile insurance premiums, one would expect similar classes of persons who represent higher risks to pay more for firearms liability insurance and thus have a more difficult time obtaining it. An added benefit of the insurance requirement is that it would help curb the tendency of some people to obtain arms for insubstantial reasons. Yet another advantage of private ordering would be its capacity to distinguish rationally between "high use" and "low use" firearms owners. Thus, for example, the law could be written to require relatively small amounts of insurance, say 100,000 dollars, for those who wish only to keep weapons in their homes, larger amounts, say 500,000 dollars, for those who plan to use weapons for hunting or target practice, and high requirements, perhaps 2,000,000 dollars or more, for those who feel a need to carry weapons in day-to-day life. Even if the law did not provide this kind of multi-level scheme, the insurance companies would have an incentive to make similar distinctions in the rates charged for whatever flat level of liability insurance the law required.

> *"The private insurance market would quickly and efficiently make it prohibitively expensive for people with a record of irresponsible ownership of guns to possess them legally."*

Turning over the "regulation" of firearms to the private market in this way would ensure that those who most directly benefit from the legitimate use of guns assume, to the extent humanly possible, the inevitable risks that are inherently associated with such devices. Such an arrangement would lead to an optimal level of gun ownership and use, while taking due account of both the Second Amendment's fundamental goal of preserving a reasonable deterrent against political oppression and the natural and constitutional interests in personal security.

The Second Amendment, which protects the individual's right to keep and bear arms, is widely regarded as either an outmoded threat to the public safety or as a narrow provision with little or no relevance to modern problems. Both views are incorrect, and they distract attention from the real challenge, which is to devise an interpretation of the Second Amendment that could be adopted by the Supreme Court in light of its modern approach to individual liberties. The Second Amendment helps to protect both political freedom and the most fundamental individual right, the right of self-defense. Using the basic principles that animate the Supreme Court's civil liberties jurisprudence, reasonable government regulation of firearms is compatible with the language and intent of the Second Amendment. In contrast to the hysterical pronouncements that are often heard on both sides of the modern gun control debate, a proper interpretation of the Second Amendment would protect the legitimate uses of firearms without making the possession of guns a sacrosanct and inviolable privilege. Once the Supreme Court focuses its attention on the Second Amendment, as eventually it must, it should have less difficulty devising a reasonable approach than one might expect given the polemics that have so far dominated public discussion of the issue.

U.S. Court Decisions Support the Constitutionality of Gun Control

by Daniel Abrams

About the author: *Daniel Abrams was a Columbia Law School student in New York when this article was written. He has written several articles on the meaning of the Second Amendment.*

We see it on television, read it in the newspaper, and find it in our mail. The seemingly omnipresent National Rifle Association (NRA) informs the citizens of the U.S. of their "constitutional right" to bear arms. Advertisements by the NRA depicting beaten Chinese students in Tiananmen Square go even further. Offered to demonstrate the importance of the supposed right to bear arms granted by the Second Amendment of the Constitution, the advertisement begins with the powerful observation: "The students of Beijing did not have a Second Amendment right to defend themselves when the soldiers came." *The Washington Post* and *The Wall Street Journal*, among others, ran this full-page advertisement and consequently received a plethora of letters outraged at their publication of such a tasteless ad. *The Washington Post* responded in an editorial two days later, criticizing the ad: "The NRA has surpassed its own record for world-class lunacy in its latest advertising message." These advertisements once again have centered attention on the Second Amendment. Yet, the NRA continues to escape the most crippling criticism of all: the Second Amendment is, like the rest of the Constitution, a law, and that law is plain that there is *no* constitutional right for the individual citizen to bear arms.

Amendment Protects Militias

It will come as a surprise to many people that our courts have heard numerous cases in which individuals have cited the Second Amendment to defend

Daniel Abrams, "The 'Right' to Bear Arms in America," *USA Today*, May 1990, © 1990 by the Society for the Advancement of Education. Reprinted with permission.

their right to bear firearms and that, time and again, the courts have interpreted the amendment to protect *only* the rights of citizens serving as part of an organized militia. Reading the amendment clearly supports this interpretation: "A well regulated militia, being necessary to the security of a free state, the right of the people to keep and bear arms shall not be infringed." The Second Amendment, by its own terms, relates to the militia; it is only because a "well regulated militia" is necessary that the amendment exists at all.

Scholars often debate what the framers' intentions were when they drafted the U.S. Constitution. The Second Amendment is no exception to these debates. Some have argued that the "militia" includes "every able-bodied male" and, therefore, that everyone has the right to bear arms. Clearly, in the late 18th century, the framers feared another all-powerful government like that of the British, whom they had just defeated in war. Thus, in an effort to protect the states from a too-powerful Federal government, the Second Amendment guaranteed the states the right to form their own militia to call upon if necessary. Many citizens kept guns in their homes for this purpose.

> *"The courts have interpreted the amendment to protect* **only** *the rights of citizens serving as part of an organized militia."*

Furthermore, some cite the debates surrounding the creation of the Second Amendment to lend support to the view that individuals have a constitutional right to bear arms. The debates over Congressional approval of the amendment include some references not only to states' rights, but to individuals' rights as well. Does all of this mean that people today who have no affiliation to a "well organized militia" still have the right to bear arms? Was the final outcome of the framers' debates a decision to protect individuals' rights and not just the rights of the states?

Courts' Rejection

Throughout the 19th and 20th centuries, our judges have answered these questions in cases where individuals have attempted to defend their right to carry a wide variety of weapons by citing the Second Amendment. *Every* Federal court and almost every state court has rejected this defense.

In *Eckert v. City of Philadelphia*, the U.S. Court of Appeals answered the question: Can an individual successfully challenge a city regulation over the purchase and transfer of firearms by citing his Second Amendment right to bear arms? The court wrote that Eckert was "completely wrong" in arguing that the city ordinance violated his Second Amendment right. The court went on to say, "it must be remembered that the right to keep and bear arms is not a right given by the United States Constitution."

Stevens v. U.S., another U.S. Court of Appeals case from 1971, addressed another question: Does Congress have the power to prohibit the possession of a firearm by a convicted felon? The court concluded: "Since the Second Amendment right to 'keep and bear arms' applies only to the right of the state to maintain a militia and not to the individual's right to bear arms, there can be no serious claim to any express constitutional right of an individual to possess a firearm."

In 1942, in *Cases v. United States*, the U.S. Court of Appeals addressed the purpose of the Second Amendment: "The right to keep and bear arms is not a right conferred on the people by the federal constitution, and the only function of the Second Amendment precluding infringement of the right of the people to keep and bear arms is to prevent the federal government, and the federal government only, from infringing that right." Furthermore, "The Second Amendment was designed to foster a well-regulated militia as necessary to the security of a free state."

Since the purpose of the amendment was to protect the states from the Federal government, does this preclude Congress from regulating firearms? According to *Cody v. U.S.*, a Court of Appeals case from 1972, "it has been settled that the Second Amendment is not an absolute bar to Congressional regulation of the use or possession of firearms."

Few Supreme Court Cases

I have quoted extensively from the U.S. Court of Appeals because the Supreme Court so rarely has found it necessary to hear these cases on appeal. In fact, the only Supreme Court case directly addressing the rights granted by the Second Amendment is *U.S. v. Miller*, a 1939 ruling. Jack Miller and a friend attempted to transport an unregistered double-barreled shotgun from Oklahoma to Arkansas. Miller claimed that the Federal act which he had violated was unconstitutional in light of the Second Amendment. Justice James C. McReynolds wrote, in a unanimous opinion rejecting Miller's defense, that the Second Amendment does not grant the right to bear arms that do not have "some reasonable relationship to the preservation or efficiency of a well regulated militia." He went on to write, "Certainly it is not within judicial notice that this weapon ['s]. . . use could contribute to the common defense."

"The right to keep and bear arms is not a right given by the United States Constitution."

Even though Miller lost the case, some have claimed that other language in the opinion makes it less than definitive. However, numerous Court of Appeals cases have cited *Miller* to demonstrate that the Second Amendment does not grant any individual the right to bear arms; not one has used it to the contrary. The Supreme Court has cited *Miller* as legal precedent only once. Justice Harry C. Blackmun, writing for the Court in 1980 (along with all the conservative members of the Court) in *Lewis v. United States*, quoted *Miller*'s most significant phrase: "These legislative restrictions on the use of firearms are neither based upon constitutionally suspect criteria, nor do they trench upon any constitutionally protected liberties. See *U.S. v. Miller.* (The Second Amendment guarantees no right to keep and bear a firearm that does not have 'some reasonable relationship to the preservation or efficiency of a well regulated militia.')" Blackmun then went on to cite three Court of Appeals cases, including *Cody v. U.S.,* to support this point.

The only other Supreme Court case that addressed the issue was its 1875 ruling in *U.S. v. Cruikshank.* While this case did not interpret the Second Amendment directly, Chief Justice Morrison R. Waite asserted that "'bearing arms for a lawful purpose'. . . is not a right granted by the Constitution. Neither is it in any manner dependent upon that instrument for its existence." He went on to say of the Second Amendment, "This is one of the Amendments that has no other effect than to restrict the powers of the national government. . . ."

Interpreting States' Constitutions

While the law on this topic is clear and unarguable, one could become confused by looking at some of the state cases from the 19th century. First, there were a number that granted the individual the right to bear an arm under the state's constitution. This must not be misunderstood. Most of these cases were not making comment on the rights granted by the Second Amendment. Rather, they were interpreting their own state's constitution—laws which bind only that state's legislature. No one denies that each state should be permitted to include provisions about firearms in its constitution.

Even though some of the state cases make reference to the Second Amendment, all but two interpret the

> *"No one denies that each state should be permitted to include provisions about firearms in its constitution."*

amendment to be a restriction on the Federal government and not an individual right. The most recent of these was a 1902 Idaho case (*In Re Brickey*), which used language from both the Second Amendment and the state constitution to hold that, while the Idaho State Legislature could regulate firearms, they could not prohibit them altogether: "The second amendment to the Federal constitution is in the following language. . . . The language of section 11 article 1 of the constitution of Idaho is as follows. . . . Under these constitutional provisions, the legislature has no power to prohibit a citizen from bearing arms in any portion of the state of Idaho, whether within or without the corporate limits of cities, towns, and villages."

The Georgia case of *Nunn v. State* (1846) is really the only one to state squarely that, under the Second Amendment, an individual has a right to bear arms. The court wrote: "The language of the Second Amendment is broad enough to embrace both Federal and state governments," and states that the right to bear arms was "the right of the whole people, old, young, men, women, and boys, and not militia only." Being the only one of its kind, this case is note-worthy primarily as a historical aberration.

Most state courts, even if they held that a statute banning firearms was uncon-stitutional under their state constitution, either did not mention the Second Amendment or conceded that it did not apply. In *State v. Kerner* (1921), a North Carolina court held that, under the state's constitution, the legislature only could prohibit concealed weapons. A statute banning any weapon without a permit was held unconstitutional. However, the first sentence of the opinion reads, "The Second Amendment to the U.S. Constitution which provides that 'the right of the people to keep and bear arms shall not be infringed' does not apply, for it has been repeatedly held by the United States Supreme Court and by this court, and, indeed, by all courts, that the first ten amendments to the U.S. Constitution are restrictions upon Federal authority and not upon the states." If anything, this reasoning, which is used in many other state cases as well, makes the Federal cases more pertinent.

Our courts' function is, among other things, to interpret the Constitution. One can argue that they have been wrong, but no one can claim realistically that the legal precedent is not crystal clear on the Second Amendment. Even if in agree-ment with the NRA as to what the law should be, one can not argue seriously about what it consistently has been held to be. Justice William O. Douglas wrote in 1971: "A powerful lobby dins into the ears of our citizenry that these gun pur-chases are constitutional rights protected by the Second Amendment," but, he added, the Second Amendment simply was "designed to keep alive the militia."

NRA Misinformation

Legal precedent should matter, particularly on an issue as publicized as this one. Unfortunately, the primary source of information to the public on this topic has been misleading advertising by the NRA. There is no constitutional right for an individual to bear arms. If the NRA wants to change that, it either should attempt to amend the Constitution or bring a new case in hope of persuading the courts to reverse more than 150 years of legal precedent.

To say that the Second Amendment does not provide an individual with the right to bear arms does not mean that gun control should or should not be adopted. That is for the people to decide through their elected representatives. However, as they decide, they deserve to be told the truth about the Second Amendment.

The Second Amendment Does Not Guarantee the Right to Own a Gun

by Warren E. Burger

About the author: *Warren E. Burger was chief justice of the U.S. Supreme Court from 1969 to 1986. He is the chairman of the Commission on the Bicentennial of the United States Constitution.*

Our metropolitan centers, and some suburban communities of America, are setting new records for homicides by handguns. Many of our large centers have up to 10 times the murder rate of all of Western Europe. In 1988, there were 9000 handgun murders in America. In 1989, Washington, D.C., alone had more than 400 homicides—setting a new record for our capital.

The Constitution of the United States, in its Second Amendment, guarantees a "right of the people to keep and bear arms." However, the meaning of this clause cannot be understood except by looking to the purpose, the setting and the objectives of the draftsmen. The first 10 amendments—the Bill of Rights— were not drafted at Philadelphia in 1787; that document came two years later than the Constitution. Most of the states already had bills of rights, but the Constitution might not have been ratified in 1788 if the states had not had assurances that a national Bill of Rights would soon be added.

Fear of a National Army

People of that day were apprehensive about the new "monster" national government presented to them, and this helps explain the language and purpose of the Second Amendment. A few lines after the First Amendment's guarantees— against "establishment of religion," "free exercise" of religion, free speech and free press—came a guarantee that grew out of the deep-seated fear of a "national" or "standing" army. The same First Congress that approved the right to keep and bear arms also limited the national army to 840 men; Congress in the Second Amendment then provided:

A well regulated Militia, being necessary to the security of a free State, the right of the people to keep and bear Arms, shall not be infringed.

In the 1789 debate in Congress on James Madison's proposed Bill of Rights, Elbridge Gerry argued that a state militia was necessary:

to prevent the establishment of a standing army, the bane of liberty . . . Whenever governments mean to invade the rights and liberties of the people, they always attempt to destroy the militia in order to raise an army upon their ruins.

We see that the need for a state militia was the predicate of the "right" guaranteed; in short, it was declared "necessary" in order to have a state military force to protect the security of the state. That Second Amendment clause must be read as though the word "because" was the opening word of the guarantee. Today, of course, the "state militia" serves a very different purpose. A huge national defense establishment has taken over the role of the militia of 200 years ago.

Confusing the Debate

Some have exploited these ancient concerns, blurring sporting guns—rifles, shotguns and even machine pistols—with all firearms, including what are now called "Saturday night specials." There is, of course, a great difference between sporting guns and handguns. Some regulation of handguns has long been accepted as imperative; laws relating to "concealed weapons" are common. That we may be "over-regulated" in some areas of life has never held us back from more regulation of automobiles, airplanes, motorboats and "concealed weapons."

Let's look at the history.

First, many of the 3.5 million people living in the 13 original colonies depended on wild game for food, and a good many of them required firearms for their defense from marauding Indians—and later from the French and English. Underlying all these needs was an important concept that each able-bodied man in each of the 13 independent states had to help or defend his state.

The early opposition to the idea of national or standing armies was maintained under the Articles of Confederation; that confederation had no standing army and wanted none. The state militia—essentially a part-time citizen army, as in Switzerland today— was the only kind of "army" they wanted. From the time of the Declaration of Independence through the victory at Yorktown in 1781, George Washington, as the commander-in-chief of these volunteer-militia armies, had to depend upon the states to send those volunteers.

> *"People of that day were apprehensive about the new 'monster' national government presented to them."*

When a company of New Jersey militia volunteers reported for duty to Washington at Valley Forge, the men initially declined to take an oath to "the United States," maintaining, "Our country is New Jersey." Massachusetts Bay men, Virginians and others felt the same way. To the American of the 18th century, his state was his country, and his freedom was defended by his militia.

The victory at Yorktown—and the ratification of the Bill of Rights a decade later—did not change people's attitudes about a national army. They had lived for years under the notion that each state would maintain its own military establishment, and the seaboard states had their own navies as well. These people, and their fathers and grandfathers before them, remembered how monarchs had used standing armies to oppress their ancestors in Europe. Americans wanted no part of this. A state militia, like a rifle and powder horn, was as much a part of life as the automobile is today; pistols were largely for officers, aristocrats—and dueling.

Against this background, it was not surprising that the provision concerning firearms emerged in very simple terms with the significant predicate—basing the right on the *necessity* for a "well regulated militia," a state army.

In the two centuries since then—with two world wars and some lesser ones—it has become clear, sadly, that we have no choice but to maintain a standing national army while still maintaining a "militia" by way of the National Guard, which can be swiftly integrated into the national defense forces.

Americans also have a right to defend their homes, and we need not challenge that. Nor does anyone seriously question that the Constitution protects the right of hunters to own and keep sporting guns for hunting game any more than anyone would challenge the right to own and keep fishing rods and other equipment for fishing—or to own automobiles. To "keep and bear arms" for hunting today is essentially a recreational activity and not an imperative of survival, as it was 200

> *"A huge national defense establishment has taken over the role of the militia of 200 years ago."*

years ago; "Saturday night specials" and machine guns are not recreational weapons and surely are as much in need of regulation as motor vehicles.

Reasonable Regulations

Americans should ask themselves a few questions. The Constitution does not mention automobiles or motorboats, but the right to keep and own an automobile is beyond question; equally beyond question is the power of the state to regulate the purchase or the transfer of such a vehicle and the right to license the vehicle and the driver with reasonable standards. In some places, even a bicycle must be registered, as must some household dogs.

If we are to stop this mindless homicidal carnage, is it unreasonable:

1) to provide that, to acquire a firearm, an application be made reciting age, residence, employment and any prior criminal convictions?

2) to require that this application lie on the table for 10 days (absent a showing for urgent need) before the license would be issued?

3) that the transfer of a firearm be made essentially as with that of a motor vehicle?

4) to have a "ballistic fingerprint" of the firearm made by the manufacturer and filed with the license record so that, if a bullet is found in a victim's body, law enforcement might be helped in finding the culprit?

These are the kind of questions the American people must answer if we are to preserve the "domestic tranquility" promised in the Constitution.

The Second Amendment Does Not Prohibit Gun Control

by Michael K. Beard and Kristin M. Rand

About the authors: *Michael K. Beard is the executive director of the National Coalition to Ban Handguns in Washington, D.C. Kristin M. Rand, formerly an attorney with the coalition, is now with Consumer Union, a consumer advocacy group in Washington, D.C.*

The National Rifle Association is the only lobbying organization in Washington with half an amendment emblazoned across the front of its building. The NRA systematically deletes the phrase "A well regulated militia being necessary to the security of a free state," from the oft quoted second phrase, "the right of the people to keep and bear arms shall not be infringed."

The Second Amendment is the most misunderstood of the amendments to the United States Constitution. There exists an extensive body of authority supporting the interpretation that the amendment protects a collective right of the states rather than an individual right to own guns. However, the gun lobby, particularly the NRA, persists in propagating the myth that the amendment guarantees an individual right.

A review of the history and decisions relating to the Second Amendment will explain why those who benefit from the current misinterpretation will not likely choose to make their arguments in court.

States Can Regulate Guns

The Second Amendment was included in the U.S. Constitution to enable the states to maintain a militia composed of civilians who would become soldiers should the security of the nation be threatened. The amendment was generated by a deep distrust of standing armies and not out of any desire to protect the right of an individual to own a firearm for self defense or other proper purpose.

The U.S. Supreme Court has addressed the issue in several cases. In 1886, the

Michael K. Beard and Kristin M. Rand, "Article II," *The Bill of Rights Journal* 20 (December 1987). Reprinted by permission of the National Emergency Civil Liberties Committee.

court ruled in *Presser v. Illinois* that the Second Amendment does not apply to the states and acts only as a check on the power of the federal government. The argument that the Second Amendment is incorporated against the states through the 14th Amendment has been rejected repeatedly. States therefore are free to regulate private ownership of handguns and other firearms in any way they see fit. The issue then becomes to what extent the federal government may regulate the ownership of firearms by private citizens.

The U.S. Supreme Court dealt directly with the scope of the Second Amendment in a 1939 decision. In *United States v. Miller*, the court upheld a federal law making it a crime to ship a sawed-off shotgun in interstate commerce. The court refused to strike down the law as violative of the Second Amendment because there was no evidence that a sawed-off shotgun had "some reasonable relationship to the preservation or efficiency of a well regulated militia." The court held that the Second Amendment "must be interpreted and applied" keeping in mind the obvious intention of the continuation and effectiveness of a militia.

The Supreme Court has not recently had occasion to speak directly on the Second Amendment. However, Justice William O. Douglas addressed the subject in a powerful dissent, joined by Justice Thurgood Marshall, in a case extending police ability to stop and frisk suspects. Justice Douglas pointed out that part of the damage wrought by popular misinterpretation of the Second Amendment is a diminution in Fourth Amendment

> **"The amendment was generated by a deep distrust of standing armies."**

protections against search and seizure. Disagreeing with the majority opinion expanding police power he argued, "The police problem is an acute one not because of the Fourth Amendment, but because of the ease with which anyone can acquire a pistol. A powerful lobby dins into the ears of our citizenry that these gun purchases are constitutional rights protected by the Second Amendment. . . . There is no reason why all pistols should not be barred to everyone except the police."

Federal Cases

The federal courts, in accordance with the Supreme Court precedents, consistently hold that there is no individual right to own a firearm.

In *United States v. Warin*, the Sixth Circuit Court of Appeals expressed exasperation with the misguided arguments made by the defendant in attempting to persuade the court that a federal law prohibiting the possession of an unregistered machine gun violated his Second Amendment rights. In upholding the defendant's conviction under the federal law, the court stated, "It would unduly extend this opinion to attempt to deal with every argument made by defendant and amicus curiae, Second Amendment Foundation, all of which are based on the erroneous supposition that the Second Amendment is concerned with the rights of individuals rather than those of the States."

In a decision upholding a ban on the possession of handguns in the Illinois town of Morton Grove, the Seventh Circuit stated flatly, "possession of handguns by individuals is not part of the right to keep and bear arms." The U.S. Supreme Court refused to review this decision.

The same court upheld an ordinance freezing the number of handguns in Chicago when it was challenged as a violation of the equal protection clause. The court ruled that the ordinance need only be rationally related to a legitimate state interest. Since the legislation did "not impinge upon the exercise of a fundamental personal right," a higher level of scrutiny was not mandated.

In short, every federal court decision that has considered the issue has given the Second Amendment a collective, militia interpretation. Moreover, no gun control measure has ever been struck down as unconstitutional under the Second Amendment. Clearly, the federal government is free to regulate or prohibit the possession and transfer of firearms in order to promote the general welfare of the public.

Public Confusion

Despite the volume of evidence to the contrary, Americans continue to believe the Second Amendment is concerned with individual rights. The extent of the confusion is apparent from the results of a recent Hearst Corp. poll which found that half of those surveyed believed the Constitution guarantees every citizen the right to own a handgun. Why the misinterpretation?

It is primarily the result of an extremely successful propaganda campaign carried out by the gun lobby. At the forefront of the disinformation effort is the NRA. The NRA, and other pro-gun groups, regularly mobilize members' ingrained fear of infringement of a perceived individual right to bear arms for fundraising purposes and constantly reinforce the idea that the

> *"There is no reason why all pistols should not be barred to everyone except the police."*

Constitution guarantees all Americans the right to keep and bear firearms for home and self protection. An NRA ad campaign admonishes, "Don't own a firearm if you choose not to. But never let anyone deny or delay your constitutional freedom to make that choice." Implicit in this message is the suggestion that even a waiting period imposed before a firearm purchase somehow would impinge on rights guaranteed by the Second Amendment.

The NRA and other pro-gun groups get a lot of mileage out of the Second Amendment and have succeeded in convincing most Americans that banning individual ownership of firearms would be unconstitutional. The problem is, the gun lobby doesn't believe their own argument.

The firearm lobby has been presented with the perfect opportunity to prove the Second Amendment was intended to guarantee an individual right. In 1986,

Congress passed the first federal ban on any type of firearm when it banned the sale to private persons of machine guns manufactured after May 19, 1986. This new law represents the first opportunity to challenge the concept of a federally imposed ban on a class of firearm.

If the gun lobby had confidence in the arguments they offer in support of their interpretation of the Second Amendment they would have filed suit on May 20, 1986 challenging the ban as a direct violation of individual Second Amendment rights. The gun control movement realizes that there could be no greater public relations coup than a modern U.S. Supreme Court decision affirming the fact that the Second Amendment guarantees not an individual right to have firearms but a right of the states to arm a militia for the collective defense of the nation. Unfortunately, the gun lobby knows that this indeed would be the result if the Supreme Court were to consider the Second Amendment. They therefore are not anxious to pursue such a case.

The Slaughter Must End

It is time the gun lobby be forced to address the issue of gun control on the merits. Handguns are undoubtedly the murder weapon of choice, accounting for nearly half of all homicides in this country. Almost half of those 9,000 were simply a quick end to an argument. Another 12,000 people commit suicide with handguns each year. Mental health professionals agree that up to 60 percent of handgun suicides would not have occurred were it not for the immediate presence of a lethal weapon. Finally, there is little argument that the 1,000 unintentional fatal injuries would not have happened if a handgun had not been accessible.

However, measures of handgun control, registration, licensing, and even mandatory sentencing may have limited success reducing felony related incidents. Nothing short of a total ban on private possession can make a dramatic impact on the enormous toll this one class of weapon has taken on the citizens of this country. There is certainly no constitutional barrier to laws designed to end the slaughter.

Gun Control Is Unconstitutional

by Richard E. Gardiner

About the author: *Richard E. Gardiner is the director of state and local affairs for the National Rifle Association.*

In the last several decades, a vocal minority, popular with the major news media, has put forth a distorted interpretation of the second amendment to the United States Constitution for the avowed political purpose of removing an obstacle from the path leading toward their goal of depriving private citizens of some or all of their firearms. And, as with virtually all attempts to minimize those precious freedoms guaranteed each American by the Bill of Rights, that minority has twisted the original and plain meaning of the right to keep and bear arms. . . . I will attempt to set out the historical development of the right to keep and bear arms so as to clarify the intentions of the Framers of the second amendment and will discuss and critically comment upon some of the more significant cases decided pursuant to that amendment.

By way of introduction to this discussion, it should be kept in mind that, in construing the Constitution, it is particularly important that the values of its Framers, and of those who ratified it, be applied, and that inferences from the text and historical background of the Constitution be given great weight. Thus, the precedential value of cases and the light shed by commentators with respect to any particular provision of the Constitution tends to increase in proportion to their temporal proximity to the adoption of the main body of the Constitution, the Bill of Rights, or any other amendments. That being so, it is appropriate first to examine the development of the right to keep and bear arms prior to the adoption of the second amendment.

Common Law Development of the Right to Bear Arms

The right to keep and bear arms, like the other rights guaranteed by the Bill of Rights, was not created or granted by the second amendment. Rather, this fundamental, individual right, largely developed in English jurisprudence prior to the formation of the American Republic, pre-dates the adoption of the Constitu-

Excerpted from Richard E. Gardiner, "To Preserve Liberty—A Look at the Right to Keep and Bear Arms," *Northern Kentucky Law Review* 10 (1982): 63-96. Reprinted with permission.

tion and was part of the common law heritage of the original colonies. It is thus to this common law heritage that one must look to begin to understand the right to keep and bear arms. In doing so, it is, however, important to remember that the doctrine which justifies recourse to the common law in order to better understand the guarantees of the Constitution "is subject to the qualification that the common law rule invoked shall be one not rejected by our ancestors as unsuited to their civil or political conditions," [as determined in *Grosjean v. American Press Co.*, 1936]. Thus, although a constitutional guarantee's "historic roots are in English history, it must be interpreted in light of the American experience, and in the context of the American constitutional scheme of government rather than the English parliamentary system," [as determined in *United States v. Brewster*, 1972]. . . .

Guns Help Protect Civil Rights

One of the clearest expositions of the common law, as it had developed by the mid-eighteenth century, came from Sir William Blackstone who, because he was an authoritive source of the common law, was a dominant influence on the Framers of the Constitution. He set forth the absolute rights of individuals, "those which are so in their primary and strictest sense; such as would belong to their persons merely in a state of nature, and which every man is entitled to enjoy," as personal security, personal liberty, and possession of private property. These absolute rights were ultimately protected by the individual's right to have and use arms for self-preservation and defense. As Blackstone observed, individual citizens were entitled to exercise their "natural right of resistance and self-preservation, when the sanctions of society and laws are found insufficient to restrain the violence of oppression."

Blackstone was not alone in this view. In his *Pleas of the Crown*, Hawkins noted that "every private person seems to be authorized by the law to arm himself for [various] purposes." Sir Edward Coke likewise wrote that "the laws permit the taking up of arms against armed persons." This absolute and inalienable right of self-defense, so clearly recognized by the common law, stemmed from the natural law which permits legitimate defense of life and rights equivalent thereto, including the slaying of an unjust aggressor by the use of the force necessary to repel the danger. The natural law permitted such defense not only because, in the conflict of rights, the right of the innocent party should prevail, but because the common social good would also suffer if the right were not recognized.

> *"In construing the Constitution, it is particularly important that the values of its Framers, and of those who ratified it, be applied."*

Cicero, the great legal philosopher of republican Rome and a source for the Framers' understanding of the natural law, recognized the right to be armed to resist violent attacks and robbery:

> And indeed, gentlemen, there exists a law, not written down anywhere but inborn in our hearts; a law which comes to us not by training or custom or reading but by derivation and absorption and adoption from nature itself; a law which has come to us not from theory but from practice, not by instruction but by natural intuition. I refer to the law which lays it down that, if our lives are endangered by plots or violence or armed robbers or enemies, any and every method of protecting ourselves is morally right. When weapons reduce them to silence, the laws no longer expect one to await their pronouncements. For people who decide to wait for these will have to wait for justice, too—and meanwhile they must suffer injustice first. Indeed, even the wisdom of the law itself, by a sort of tacit implication, permits self-defense, because it does not actually forbid men to kill; what it does, instead, is to forbid the bearing of a weapon with the intention to kill.

John Locke, too, upheld the right of potential victims to resist deadly attack with force when he observed that "the law could not restore life to my dead carcass."

In addition to the right of self-defense, a right which would be meaningless for most people without the right to use arms, there also existed in English law, prior to the formation of the American Republic, a positive *duty* of most able-bodied freemen to keep, and be prepared to bear and use, arms both for military and law enforcement purposes. Such a duty was deeply imbedded in English and Germanic history and indeed antedates the invention of firearms. . . .

Early Arms Control

In later years, the Tudor kings began the first attempts to impose limits upon the use and possession of weapons; in particular, crossbows and the then-new firearms. These measures were not, however, intended to disarm the citizenry (who made up the bulk of the military forces) but rather to prevent their being diverted from practice with the long-bow (the primary English military weapon since it could be fired relatively rapidly and penetrate chain mail at as much as 400 yards) by sport with crossbows and firearms which, at the time, were less effective

> *"Individual citizens were entitled to exercise their 'natural right of resistance and self-preservation.'"*

for military purposes. Such laws were also intended to restrict the hunting of game to the king and the landed gentry. . . .

In 1670, after centuries of *requiring* citizens to possess and be exercised in the use of arms so as to vitiate the necessity for both a standing army and a police force, Charles II (1660-1685) instituted the Act for the Better Preservation of the Game, which prohibited the possession of guns and bows and thus, *for the first time in English history*, denied most citizens the common law right to possess arms other than knives and swords. This statute, which followed earlier actions by Charles disarming the remnants of Cromwell's republican army as well as any other persons suspected of not being loyal to the crown, and which ran directly contrary to the common law, were a means of consolidating Charles' power by removing from the citizenry their ability to oppose his tyranny. As Blackstone observed of the purpose of the Game Acts: "For prevention of popular insurrections and resistance to the government, by disarming the bulk of the people; which last is a reason oftener meant, than avowed, by the makers of forest or game laws.". . .

> *"There also existed in English law, prior to the formation of the American Republic, a positive* **duty** *of most able-bodied freemen to keep, and be prepared to bear and use, arms."*

Succeeding Charles II was James II (1685-1688) who attempted to expand the royal standing army and continued many of the repressive policies of Charles; moreover, because he was a devout Catholic, such policies were directed primarily against Protestants. James' brief rule ended, however, with the Glorious Revolution of 1688 and James' abdication.

Since one of the goals of the Glorious Revolution was to reinstate the right of Protestants to have arms, a right of which they had been deprived to prevent resistance to James' repressive policies, when the throne was offered to William and Mary, it was offered subject to their acceptance of the rights, including the right of Protestants to have arms, laid down in a Declaration of Rights. After they ascended the throne and Parliament was formally convened, the Declaration was enacted into law. . . .

In sum, by the time of the American Revolution, English law had developed a tradition of keeping and bearing arms which stretched back almost a millenium, a tradition which was retained and protected by the courts even during the brief eighteen-year period in which the common law right of most citizens to possess and use arms other than knives and swords was extinguished by statute. And it was within this tradition of the individual's right to have and use arms for his own defense, as well as to enable him to contribute to the defense of the nation, that the spark which ignited the American Revolution was struck when the British, by attempting to seize stores of powder and shot in Concord and seeking to disarm the inhabitants of Boston, sought to deny the Masssachusetts colonists the ability to protect their rights.

The History of the Second Amendment

The history of the second amendment indicates that its purpose was to secure to each individual the right to keep and bear arms so that he could protect his absolute individual rights as well as carry out his obligation to assist in the common defense. The Framers did not intend to limit the right to keep and bear arms to members of a formal military body, but rather intended to ensure the continued existence of an "unorganized" armed citizenry prepared to assist in the common defense against a foreign invader or a domestic tyrant.

Subsequent to the American Revolution, which had, to a large extent, been fought by citizen soldiers, it was agreed that the Articles of Confederation were in need of revision to strengthen the structure of the new nation. Once assembled in Philadelphia to write what ultimately became the Constitution, one of the gravest problems faced by the Framers was whether the federal government should be permitted to maintain a standing army. Because of the lessons of history (particularly the reigns of Charles II and James II) and their personal experiences in and prior to the Revolution, the Framers realized that although useful for national defense, the standing army was particularly inimical to the continued safe existence of those absolute rights recognized by Blackstone and generally inimical to personal freedom and liberty.

> *"By the time of the American Revolution, English law had developed a tradition of keeping and bearing arms which stretched back almost a millenium."*

The Unregulated Militia

Unwilling, however, to forgo completely the national defense benefits of a standing army, the Framers developed a compromise position, wherein the federal government was granted the authority to "raise and support" an army, subject to the restrictions that no appropriation of money for the army would be for more than two years and that civilian control over the army would be maintained. Furthermore, knowing that the militiaman or citizen soldier had made possible the success of the American Revolution, and recognizing that the militia would be the final bulwark against both domestic tyranny and foreign invasion, the Framers divided authority over the militia, empowering Congress to "govern . . . [only] *such part of them* [the militia] as may be employed in the Service of the United States . . . ," and leaving to the states "the Appointment of the Officers, and the Authority of training the militia. . . ." It is thus evident, from the underscored language of Clause 16, that, in addition to that part of the militia over which the Constitution granted Congress authority, there exists a residual, unorganized militia that is not subject to congressional control.

This distinction was first codified, to some degree, in the Militia Act of 1792 which defined both an "organized" militia and an "enrolled" militia. (It also required officers and dragoons to be armed with "a pair of pistols.") The "unorganized" or "enrolled" militia, whose members were expected to be familiar with the use of firearms and to appear *bearing their own arms*, were not actually in service, but were nonetheless available to assist in the common defense should conditions necessitate either support of the organized militia or possibly defense against a standing army or even the organized militia.

When the proposed Constitution was sent to the states for ratification, Antifederalists (the popular name for those opposing the Constitution) were concerned that in spite of the restrictions in the Constitution, a federal standing army which would threaten the hard-won liberties of the people, might still exist. . . .

In response to the concerns of the Antifederalists regarding the standing army, the division of power over the militia, and [what R. Rutland referred to as] "the demand for a bill of rights [which] constituted a common ground on which citizens from every section of the Republic could take a stand," a political compromise developed in the course of the ratification process in which the Federalists agreed (at no political cost given the popular sentiment) to support amendments to the Constitution in the First Congress declaring "the great rights of mankind" in exchange for the Antifederalists dropping their demands for changes to the basic framework of the federal government as then outlined in the Constitution. Consequently, when the First Congress met, Madison (who, to win election to the House had become a supporter of a Bill of Rights), drew up proposed amendments based upon proposals made by the state ratifying conventions (proposals which found their source in the state declarations of rights) and submitted them to the First Congress. When he submitted them, as his notes make clear, he intended that the amendments "relate 1st to *private* rights."

> *"The standing army was . . . inimical to personal freedom and liberty."*

His notes also make clear (in that they contain a list of objections to the English Bill of Rights of 1689: "1. Mere act of parlt. 2. No freedom of press—Conscience [.] G1. Warrants Habs. corpus [.] Jury in Civil Causes—criml. [] attainders—*arms to Protessts*."), that he viewed the English Bill of Rights as too narrow.

Proposed Versions of the Amendment

One of the proposed amendments concerned the right to keep and bear arms. In its original form, as proposed by Madison, the second amendment (the fourth proposed amendment) read: "The right of the people to keep and bear arms shall not be infringed; a well-regulated militia being the best security of a free country; but no person religiously scrupulous of bearing arms shall be compelled to render military service in person."

Significantly, when considering the proposed amendment, the First Senate soundly rejected a proposal to insert the phrase "for the common defense" after the words "bear arms," thereby emphasizing that the purpose of the second amendment was not primarily to provide for the common defense, but to protect the individual's right to keep and bear arms for his own defense. . . . Moreover, Madison's plan for amending the Constitution was "calculated to secure the *personal rights* of the people." (Comments of contemporary writers make this point crystal clear. For example: "Last Monday a string of amendments were presented to the lower House; these altogether respected *personal liberty. . . .*" Letter from William Grayson to Patrick Henry, June 12, 1784. Patrick Henry (emphasis added): "[The Amendments] will effectually secure *private rights. . . .*" William L. Smith to Edward Rutledge, Aug. 9, 1789, Letters of William L. Smith to Edward Rutledge: "The whole of the Bill [of Rights] is a declaration of the right of the people at large or considered as individuals . . . [i]t establishes some *rights of the individual* as unalienable and which consequently, no majority has a right to deprive them of." Albert Gallatin to Alexander Addison, Albert Gallatin Papers, Oct. 7, 1789.). . .

Defining a "Regulated" Militia

Adding further weight to the proposition that the second amendment guaranteed an individual right is the fact that appearing in the final version of the second amendment was the term "well-regulated." Contrary to modern usage, wherein regulated is generally understood to mean "controlled" or "governed by rule," in its obsolete form pertaining to troops, "regulated is defined as 'properly disciplined.'" When it is understood that "discipline" refers to the "training effect of experience," it is plain that by using the term "well-regulated" the Framers had in mind not only the individual ownership and possession of firearms, but also practice and training with such firearms so that each person could become experienced and competent in their use.

This conclusion is in complete accord with comments on the rights protected by the Constitution made by a leading constitutional commentator.

The Right is General. It may be supposed from the phraseology of this provision that the right to keep and bear arms was only guaranteed to the militia; but this would be an interpretation not warranted by the intent. The militia, as has been elsewhere explained, consists of those persons who, under the law, are liable to the performance of military duty, and are officered and enrolled for service when called upon. But the law may make provision for the enrollment of all who are fit to perform military duty or of a small number only, or it may wholly omit to make any provision at all; and if the right were limited to those enrolled, the purpose of this guarantee might be defeated altogether by the action or neglect to act of the government it was meant to hold in check. *The meaning of the provision undoubtedly is, that the people, from whom the militia must be taken, shall have the right to keep and bear arms, and they need no permission or regulation of law for that purpose.* But this enables the government to have a well-regulated militia; for to bear arms implies something more than the mere keeping; it implies the learning to handle and use them in a way that makes those who keep them ready for their efficient use; in

> *"The purpose of the second amendment was . . . to protect the individual's right to keep and bear arms for his own defense."*

other words, it implies a right to meet for voluntary discipline in arms, observing in doing so the laws of public order. [T. Cooley, *General Principles of Constitutional Law in the United States of America*, 1898.]

Likewise, in an opinion by one state's Chief Justice, it was held: "The right of the whole people, old and young, men, women and boys, and not militia only, to keep and bear *arms* of every description, and not *such* merely as are used by the *militia*, shall not be *infringed*, curtailed or broken in upon, in the smallest."

[Nunn V. State, Georgia, 1846].

In Massachusetts, Samuel Adams proposed an amendment requiring that the "Constitution be never construed to authorize Congress to . . . prevent the people of the United States, who are peaceable citizens, from keeping their own arms." In New Hampshire the ratifying convention advanced a proposal which provided that "Congress shall never disarm *any citizen* unless such as are or have been in Actual Rebellion." Judge Robert Sprecher has thus aptly noted that "history does not warrant concluding . . . that a person has a right to bear arms solely in his function as a member of the militia."

Need for Guns Is Unchanged

The passage of time has not altered the need for individuals to exercise their right to keep and bear arms, even in the context of the common defense. Indeed, one court has observed that individual marksmanship is an important skill even in the nuclear age. In the Second World War, moreover, the unorganized militia proved a successful substitute for the National Guard, which was federalized and activated for overseas duty. Members of the unorganized militia, many of whom belonged to gun clubs and whose ages varied from 16 to 65, served without pay and provided their own arms. In fact, it was necessary for the members of the unorganized militia to provide their own arms since the U.S. government not only could not supply sufficient arms to the militia but "turned out to be an Indian giver" by recalling rifles. The 15,000 volunteer Maryland Minute Men brought their own rifles, shotguns,

> *"The right to keep and bear arms cannot be interpreted into nonexistence."*

and pistols to musters. And all over the country individuals armed themselves in anticipation of threatened invasion. Thus, a manual distributed *en masse* by the War Department, recommended the keeping of "weapons which a guerrilla in civilian clothes can carry without attracting attention. They must be easily portable and easily concealed. First among these is the pistol." Likewise, in Europe, when the Germans were attempting to occupy Warsaw, the commander of the Jewish Fighting Organization noted, "Our weapons consisted of revolvers (one revolver for every man)." Another partisan in the same resistance movement wrote of "the first weapon shipment—about ten pistols—received from the Polish underground. . . ."

As a final note on the history of the second amendment, it should be observed that the fact that the right to keep and bear arms is joined with language expressing one of its purposes in no way permits a construction which limits or confines the exercise of that right. Like the first amendment right of free assembly, which has as its stated purpose "petition[ing] the Government for a redress of

> *"The right of the people to keep and bear arms was a right which existed prior to the Constitution."*

grievances," and which the Supreme Court has used to invalidate statutes requiring disclosure of organization membership lists, whether or not the organization intends to petition the Government, the right to keep and bear arms cannot be interpreted into nonexistence by limiting it to one of its purposes. To hold otherwise is to violate the principle that "[c]onstitutional provisions for the security of a person and property should be liberally construed. A close and literal construction deprives them of half their efficacy, and leads to gradual depreciation of the right, as if it consisted more in sound than in substance." The Supreme Court of Oregon recognized this principle by stating:

> We are not unmindful that there is current controversy over the wisdom of a right to bear arms, and that the original motivations for such a provision might not seem compelling if debated as a new issue. Our task, however, in construing a constitutional provision is to respect the principles given the status of constitutional guarantees and limitations by the drafters; it is not to abandon these principles when this fits the needs of the moment. . . .

In the *United States v. Cruikshank*, the first case in which the Supreme Court had the opportunity to interpret the second amendment, the Court plainly recognized that the right of the people to keep and bear arms was a right which existed prior to the Constitution when it stated that such a right "is not a right granted by the Constitution . . . *(n)either is it any manner dependent upon that instrument for its existence.* . . .

States Lack Authority

In *Presser v. Illinois*, although the Supreme Court affirmed the holding in *Cruikshank* that the second amendment, standing alone, applied only to action by the federal government, it nonetheless found the states without power to infringe upon the right to keep and bear arms.

> It is undoubtedly true that all citizens capable of bearing arms constitute the reserved military force or reserve militia of the United States as well as of the States, and in view of this prerogative of the general government, as well as of its general powers, *the States cannot, even laying the constitutional provision in question out of view, prohibit the people from keeping and bearing arms, so as to deprive the United States of their rightful resource for maintaining the public security and disable the people from performing their duty to the general government.* . . .

115

In *United States v. Miller*, the only case in which the Supreme Court has had the opportunity to apply the second amendment to a federal firearms statute, the Court carefully avoided making an unconditional finding of the statute's constitutionality; it instead devised a test by which to measure the constitutionality of statutes relating to firearms. The holding of the Court in *Miller*, however, should be viewed as only a partial guide to the meaning of the second amendment, primarily because neither defense counsel nor defendants appeared before the Supreme Court, and no brief was filed on their behalf giving the Court the benefit of argument supporting the trial court's holding that Section 11 of the National Firearms Act was unconstitutional.

The Court's Interpretation

The heart of the Court's decision is found in the following statement:

> *In the absence of any evidence* tending to show that possession or use of a "shotgun having a barrel of less than eighteen inches in length" at this time has some reasonable relationship to the preservation or efficiency of a well regulated militia, we cannot say that the Second Amendment guarantees the right to keep and bear such an instrument. Certainly it is not within judicial notice that this weapon is any part of the ordinary military equipment or that its use could contribute to the common defense. . . .

One of the chief values of *Miller* is its discussion of the development and structure of the militia which, the Court pointed out, consisted of "all males physically capable of acting in concert for the common defense" and that "when called for service these men were expected to appear bearing arms *supplied by themselves* and of the kind in common use at the time." *Miller* is also significant for its implicit rejection of the view that the second amendment, in addition to guaranteeing the right to keep and bear only certain types of arms, also guarantees the right only to those individuals who are members of the militia. Had the Court viewed the second amendment as guaranteeing the right to keep and bear arms only to "all males physically capable of acting in concert for the common defense," it would certainly have discussed whether *Miller* met the qualifications for inclusion in the militia, much as it did with regard to the military value of a short-barrelled shotgun. That it did not discuss this point indicates the Court's acceptance of the fact that the right to keep and bear arms is guaranteed to each individual without regard to his relationship with the militia. . . .

> *"The right to keep and bear arms may not be undercut simply because that right may at the moment be unpopular to some."*

The right to keep and bear arms may not be undercut simply because that right may at the moment be unpopular to some. The Supreme Court has held time and again that "constitutional rights may not be denied simply because of hostility to their assertion or exercise."

Nor can constitutional rights be made dependent upon a popular consensus that there is a continued need for them. [As determined in *Martin v. Hunter's Lessee,*] "The Constitution of the United States was not intended to provide merely for the exigencies of a few years but was to endure through a long lapse of ages. . . ."

Indeed, it is precisely because the courts do not allow any contraction of the Bill of Rights that the evils contemplated by the Framers now seem so removed. As Justice Hugo Black stated:

> Its [the Bill of Rights'] provisions may be thought outdated abstractions by some. And it is true that they were designed to meet ancient evils. But they are the same kind of human evils that have emerged from century to century wherever excessive power is sought by the few at the expense of the many.

From the above discussion, it should be readily apparent that the right to keep and bear arms, as guaranteed by the second amendment, is indeed a fundamental individual right which no amount of historical revisionism can deny. Thus, along with all other rights found in the Bill of Rights, it should be accorded a significant place in American jurisprudence.

The Constitutional Right to Bear Arms Must Be Unlimited

by Robert Dowlut

About the author: *Robert Dowlut is deputy general counsel for the National Rifle Association.*

The second amendment to the United States Constitution guarantees that "[a] well regulated Militia, being necessary to the security of a free State, the right of the people to keep and bear Arms, shall not be infringed." In addition, the constitutions of all but seven states guarantee a right to bear arms. This enumerated and explicit right has generated public attention and controversy over its meaning and scope.

Rights Are Sacrosanct

The purpose of the Bill of Rights guarantees was to enunciate a set of fixed rights that may not be trespassed upon by any branch of government. A constitutional right differs from a right conferred by the common law or by statute in that it is guarded from infringement by any branch of government. The Constitution was not adopted as a means of enhancing the efficiency with which government officials conduct their affairs. Rather, it was meant to provide a bulwark against infringements that might otherwise be justified as necessary expedients of governing. While a court must give due consideration to the needs of the other branches of government, the court's role is to ensure that restraints on governmental power are enforced. Establishing the protected boundaries of a right, by analyzing the four corners of the guarantee, becomes indispensable. While bright boundary lines cannot always be drawn, this is a more principled approach to constitutional interpretation than merely paying no attention to plain words or history and applying elastic labels of "valid exercise of the police power" or "reasonable regulation" whenever a constitutional challenge is made, or even denying the existence of a right by interpret-

Excerpted from Robert Dowlut, "Federal and State Constitutional Guarantees to Arms," *University of Dayton Law Review* 15 (Fall 1989): 59-90. Reprinted with permission.

ing it in such a fashion that it becomes an intangible abstraction. . . .

The Bill of Rights is a catalog of indispensable liberties. Constitutional rights are to be honored equally. Fundamental rights enjoy explicit guarantee in the Bill of Rights. In addition, a constitutional right must be broadly interpreted. Neither oppressive taxes or fees nor waiting periods may be imposed on the exercise of a right. Furthermore, government may not require registration and licensing of persons who exercise constitutional rights nor chill the exercise of a constitutional right.

Balancing Rights

The second amendment should be interpreted according to well-established rules governing interpretation of constitutional guarantees when determining if a particular statute is unconstitutional. Reasonable time, place, and manner restrictions may be imposed on the exercise of fundamental rights, provided the restrictions are narrowly tailored. Courts must balance the justification put forward by the state against the character and magnitude of the asserted injury to the constitutionally protected right.

The state will always argue that a compelling state interest exists for the enactment of legislation. This may tempt courts to reflexively bow to the interests of the state. The erosion of rights must be avoided by recognizing that the keeping of arms in the home must be given special protection to preserve personal autonomy. This expectation is buttressed by the rule that the state can take no action which will unnecessarily chill or penalize the assertion of a constitutional right, and the state may not draw adverse inferences from the exercise of a constitutional right.

The bearing of arms in a public place is different from the keeping of arms in the home on account of the home's special zone of privacy. Reasonable time, place, and manner regulations may be placed on bearing arms in a public place. For example, people may be prevented from bringing arms into court. However, the peaceful bearing of arms in a motor vehicle or on a street could not be prohibited. A constitutional right may not be curtailed simply because some people find its exercise disagreeable or offensive.

"The court's role is to ensure that restraints on governmental power are enforced."

The framing of the right to arms reveals an awareness of crime. Nevertheless, the guarantee promises that the right "shall not be infringed." The Framers also knew the obvious: certain persons have always been treated differently and do not enjoy the full array of rights. In accord with this understanding are decisions holding that a convicted felon may be prevented from voting or holding office in a union. The collateral consequences of a felony conviction go beyond deprivation of the right to keep and bear arms. Infants are also treated differently because the state has a compelling interest in protecting their physical and psychological well-being. Nevertheless, while courts adhere to these well-known exceptions in construing other constitutional guarantees, the right to arms has often been treated with disfavor. The command that the people have a right to keep and bear arms is simply ignored. Courts simply look at the preamble or precatory language of the second amendment, ignore the rest of the language, and interpret it to guarantee the right of a state to have a military force. However, the right of a state to have and train military or constabulary forces does not depend on the second amendment right of the people to keep and bear arms....

> *"The erosion of rights must be avoided by recognizing that the keeping of arms in the home must be given special protection to preserve personal autonomy."*

Court Opposition

Some judges have displayed an open animosity for the right to arms. For example, Chief Justice Earl Warren dissented from a holding that a firearm registration statute offended the fifth amendment privilege against self-incrimination because "[t]he impact of that decision on the efforts of Congress to enact much-needed federal gun control laws is not consistent with national safety." Justice William O. Douglas, joined by Justice Thurgood Marshall, called for the "watering down" of the second amendment in his dissenting opinion in *Adams v. Williams*. This unfortunately demonstrates that at times the prediliction of judges reigns rather than the Bill of Rights. Some courts simply overlook history. Justice Neely of the West Virginia Supreme Court quipped that "Lawyers, certainly, who take seriously recent U.S. Supreme Court historical scholarship as applied to the Constitution also probably believe in the Tooth Fairy and the Easter Bunny."

The second amendment need not be rendered moribund because some courts have ignored its command and the political and social ideas that prevailed at the time of its framing.... Courts are obligated to overrule erroneous precedent. Even a line of cases covering nearly a century has been branded as "an unconstitutional assumption of powers by courts of the United States which no lapse of time or respectable array of opinion should make us hesitate to correct," [as determined in *United States v. Scott*, 1978]....

Which Arms Are Protected?

It is well known that colonial militia statutes required the keeping of firearms, shot, powder, and edged arms. They help determine what the Framers meant by the term *arms*. Cases of old, when interpreting the second amendment or a state constitutional guarantee with a militia or common defense purpose, took either an expansive view of the term "arms" or a narrow view. The broad view held that basically all arms are constitutionally protected. The narrow view held that only arms suitable for civilized warfare are protected. Under the narrow view, large pistols are constitutionally protected but pocket pistols do not enjoy constitutional protection. Accordingly, [as determined in *State v. Bias*, 1885], "[w]hen we see a man with musket to shoulder, or carbine slung on back, or pistol belted to his side, or such like, he is bearing arms in the constitutional sense."

Constitutionally protected arms under the modern view are not limited to those of a militia. They include hand-carried defensive arms and the modern equivalents of arms possessed by colonial militiamen. While semi-automatic firearms are protected, arms of mass destruction used exclusively by the military are not. . . .

Practical Considerations

The solid majority of gun owners are noncriminal, and their guns create no social problems. [According to J. Wright and P. Rossie,] "It is commonly hypothesized that much criminal violence, especially homicide, occurs simply because the means of lethal violence (firearms) are readily at hand, and thus, that much homicide would not occur were firearms generally less available. There is no persuasive evidence that supports this view." Hence, fairness demands that gun owners not be used as scapegoats for society's shortcomings. Reliance on the state for protection is an illusory remedy. Neither the police nor the state has a duty to protect the individual citizen. The burden falls on the citizen to defend himself and his family. The Framers intended that the citizen be armed and not be left defenseless. An armed people also serve as a deterrent against crime.

Gun control laws have at least five political functions: (1) increase citizen reliance on government and tolerance of increased police powers and abuse; (2) facilitate repressive action by government; (3) help prevent opposition to government; (4) lessen pressure for major or radical reform; (5) allow selective enforcement against dissidents. In our imperfect world the servants of the state have committed outrages. Nevertheless, they are always exempted from gun laws designed to disarm the people. Crime, regardless of who commits it, "must be prevented by the penitentiary and gallows, and not by a general deprivation of a constitutional privilege," [as determined in *Wilson v. State*, 1878].

> *"The right to arms has often been treated with disfavor."*

The State Is Untrustworthy

Mankind's oldest right is personal and communal defense. A written constitution was deemed necessary because experience demonstrated that the state cannot always be trusted to exercise power in a reasonable manner. Gandhi's nonviolent methods would fail against the likes of a Nicolae Ceausescu, Hitler,

Stalin, or Pol Pot. The second amendment and its state analogues guarantee that the state would not have a monopoly on arms. The constitutions consistently promise to the *people* a right to bear arms. Judges know this, but some have a deep personal dislike of this right. If a guarantee's text and original intent are no longer controlling, what is controlling? The Constitution is a reminder that judges must be restrained by something more than their own predilections. Legislative bodies also have an obligation to defend constitutional rights. However, ultimately the Constitution retrains them, too. The majority of commentators support the individual rights view on arms. The courts are required to follow it. Laws seeking to disarm the people must be declared unconstitutional. At one time the fourteenth and fifteenth amendments were mainly ignored. Finally, courts started protecting those rights. Responsible judges will make certain that all constitutional rights are protected, regardless of personal feelings. Casting pejorative labels at those who view the arms right as genuine and fundamental will not change history; it only demonstrates the dismal intellectual discourse of some opponents. The Constitution contains a mechanism for change should any provision be deemed worthy of change. The process is involved so that change is accomplished only after suitable deliberation. If the integrity of the process for change is not followed, no right is safe.

Limits on Gun Ownership May Result in Tyranny

by Alan M. Gottlieb

About the author: *Alan M. Gottlieb is president of the Second Amendment Foundation and chairman of the Citizens Committee for the Right to Keep and Bear Arms. He is the author of* The Rights of Gun Owners.

For an area of constitutional law which has received so little modern judicial analysis, the second amendment has evoked a remarkable amount of law review commentary. Undoubtedly this is because of its relevance to the longstanding and virulent national debate on gun prohibition. The Founding Fathers' attitudes on the rights of gun ownership, though readily available, are rarely mentioned in most law review treatments. It is interesting that every one of the Founders who discussed arms emphatically endorsed their possession as a fundamental individual right.

Beyond the refusal of modern commentators to examine relevant materials, the original meaning of the amendment is obscured by the vast gulf of time and perspective which separate us from the Founders—and our greater distance yet from the history and historians, the philosophy and philosophers who shaped the Founders' thought. The function of individuals being armed in order to preserve their liberties and the republican form of government is not a theme in modern political philosophy. But it was supremely important to all the political theorists, [and] valued by the Founders. . . .

Taking the Amendment at Face Value

On its face, the second amendment's language, "A well regulated militia, being necessary to the security of a free state, the right of the people to keep and bear arms shall not be infringed," suggests an intent to guarantee a right which people can effectively enforce. This was invariably what the Founders described on the numerous occasions in which they indicated what they meant by "militia," and that is how the identical "right of the people" language which appears in the first and fourth amendments has always been construed. The following points are offered to support the contention that the language of the sec-

Excerpted from Alan M. Gottlieb, "Gun Ownership: A Constitutional Right," *Northern Kentucky Law Review* 10 (1982): 113-40. Reprinted with permission.

ond amendment must be taken at face value:

1. The Founding Fathers praised the individual ownership of firearms in terms that would seem extravagant even from today's pro-gun organizations, and thus there is no reason for assuming that individuals were excluded from the right to arms the Founders wrote into the Constitution.

2. There is no support for the assumption that the right is only a collective one because all the political philosophers cited by the Founders affirmed that the individual's right to possess arms is his ultimate guarantee against tyranny.

3. By "militia," the Founders meant "all (militarily capable) males . . . bearing arms supplied by themselves."

4. When what was guaranteed by English common law (and confirmed by the English Bill of Rights of 1689) was unequivocally an individual right to keep and bear arms, there is no cause for assuming that its American successor guarantees only an exclusively "collective right"—something that did not exist in any legal system with which the Founding Fathers were familiar.

5. Last, if the Founding Fathers had intended to guarantee an exclusively "collective right," they would not have done so in language which (in light of the English and American legal background) their contemporaries could only— and uniformly did—construe as preserving an individual right.

The evidence for the individual right interpretation is so overwhelming that the existence of an argument which (by studiously ignoring that evidence) degrades the second amendment into a meaningless "collective right" is inexplicable. . . .

The Collective Right Position

The exclusive states' right position urged by many gun control advocates sees the amendment as a modification of Art. 1 & 8, cl. 16 of the original Constitution which gives Congress the power "[t]o provide for organizing, arming and disciplining the militia," over which the states have power. The amendment is characterized as no more than a provision against Congressional misuse of its Art. 1 & 8 powers. Erroneously claiming that this was its only purpose, they assert that the amendment guarantees nothing to individuals. Instead, they picture the second amendment as a "collective right" of the entire people—a right that cannot be invoked by anyone either in his own behalf or on behalf of the people as a whole. As employed in this sense, the concept "collective right" falls victim to the most elementary principle of constitutional construction.

> *"Every one of the Founders who discussed arms emphatically endorsed their possession as a fundamental individual right."*

The second amendment secures individuals the right to possess arms to defend their persons and to protect against attack (whether private or governmental), and a collective right (assertable by individuals) to possess arms for the purpose of militia service. This position is not at all inconsistent with a states' right interpretation of the amend-

> *"The individual's right to possess arms is his ultimate guarantee against tyranny."*

ment, but only with the *exclusive* states' right interpretation. The nature of the Founders' response to these concerns becomes evident when it is realized that the Founders defined the militia as "all males physically capable [and] . . . bearing arms supplied by themselves." The amendment's prohibition against disarming the people was simultaneously a prohibition against disarming the militia because the people and the militia were one and the same.

Once the false dichotomy created between the Founders' concern for the individual and for the states has been stripped away, the exclusive states' right position is devoid of historical support. In sum, while more than ample evidence supports the individual right position, there is not one bit of evidence that the amendment was intended exclusively for the protection of the states and not the individual citizenry. . . .

Thus neither the text nor the direct legislative history provides a scintilla of evidence for the exclusive states' right or "collective right" theory. In the absence of direct legislative history to support that position, the next best evidence would be general statements or writings which reflect the Founders' attitudes toward the individual ownership and possession of firearms and governmental regulation thereof. Though such materials are copiously available—most of them from the original debates on ratifying the Constitution to which the second amendment was immediately added—they are never referred to by those who take an anti-individual right position. Instead, the advocates of that position simply seem to project their own attitudes onto the Founders.

The Attitude of the Framers

"One loves to possess arms," Thomas Jefferson, the premier intellectual of his day, wrote of June 19, 1796 to George Washington. We may presume that Washington agreed for his armory was reputed to have contained as many as 50 guns, of which at least 10 were handguns, and his own writings are full of laudatory references to various firearms he owned or examined. With regards to Jefferson, one of his nephews tells us that he believed that every boy should be given a gun at age ten as Jefferson himself had been. In a letter to another nephew, Jefferson offered the following advice:

> A strong body makes the mind strong. As to the species of exercises, I advise the gun. While this gives a moderate exercise to the Body, it gives boldness, enterprise and independence to the mind. Games played with the ball, and others of that nature, are too violent for the body and stamp no character on the mind. Let your gun therefore be the constant companion of your walks.

In the month before he penned the Declaration of Independence, Jefferson wrote a model state constitution for Virginia which included the guarantee that "no free man shall be debarred the use of arms in his own lands." . . .

Virginia ratified the Constitution only after appointing a committee, headed by Patrick Henry and George Mason, to draft a bill of rights and lobby for its adoption by the new Congress. Mason also had attacked the Constitution's failure to protect the right to arms. Reminding the Virginia delegates that the Revolutionary War had been sparked by the British attempt to confiscate the patriots' arms at Lexington and Concord, Mason characterized the British strategy as an attempt "to disarm the people; that it was the

> *"There is not one bit of evidence that the amendment was intended exclusively for the protection of the states and not the individual citizenry."*

best and most effectual way to enslave them." Together, Mason and Richard Henry Lee have been given preponderant credit for the compromise under which the Constitution was ratified, subject to an understanding that it would immediately be augmented by the enactment of a bill of rights. In his commentary on the Constitution, LETTERS FROM THE FEDERALIST FARMER, Lee discussed the right at length, stating that "to preserve liberty, it is essential that the whole body of the people always possess arms and be taught alike, especially when young, how to use them."

The Necessity of an Armed Populace

The ever-antagonistic Adams cousins, Sam and John, were on opposite sides of the ratification controversy. But on the subject of an individual right to keep arms, they were fully in accord. In the Massachusetts convention, Sam Adams opposed ratification unless accompanied by a provision "that the said Constitution be never construed . . . to prevent the people of the United States, who are peaceable citizens, from keeping their own arms." In a book published the year before, John Adams had enthused that "arms in the hands of citizens may be used at individual discretion," for the defense of the nation, the overthrow of tyranny or "private self-defense."

The fact is that the necessity of an armed populace was so unanimously advocated in the early Republic that it played a central part in the arguments of both sides in the debate over the Constitution. As the Senate Committee on the Judiciary, Subcommittee on the Constitution notes, the anti-federalists opposed ratification because of the lack of a bill of rights, while the Constitution's supporters frequently argued to the people that the universal armament of Americans made such limitations unnecessary. A pamphlet written by Noah Webster, aimed at swaying Pennyslvania toward ratification, observed:

> Before a standing army can rule, the people must be disarmed; as they are in almost every kingdom in Europe. The supreme Power in America cannot en-

force unjust laws by the sword, because the whole body of the people are armed, and constitute a force superior to any and of regular troops that can be, on any pretence, raised in the United States. . . .

The points already made converge on a final refutation of the exclusive "collective right" position. Assume, *arguendo*, that the Founders had decided that the second amendment should *not* express their belief in the individual's right to arms, but only protect those arms actually owned by the states. How would they have expressed such an intention in light of their knowledge of their generation's manner of speaking and philosophical predispositions? The amendment might have read something like, "the right of the states to keep, and of their militias to bear, arms shall not be infringed." But, it seems logical, they would never have chosen the language which actually appears in the amendment to express such an intention—because their contemporaries would necessarily have misunderstood their intent. They could have read the phrase "the right of the people" to keep and bear arms in light of the "absolute right of individuals" to do so as described by William Blackstone and celebrated in the combined Anglo-American common law and republican philosophical traditions most familiar to them.

> [The Founders] were born and brought up in the atmosphere of the common law, and thought and spoke in its vocabulary . . . (W)hen they came to put their conclusions into the form of fundamental law in a compact draft, they expressed them in terms of the common law, *confident that they could be shortly and easily understood.*

Significantly "right of the people" is precisely how their contemporaries and the next several generations of American legal scholars understood the amendment. It bears particular emphasis that the growth of the idea that the second amendment enunciated an exclusively states' right has solely occurred in the twentieth century. Neither Madison's contemporaries nor the next several generations of legal scholars had the slightest inkling of any such concept. The earliest commentary, appearing almost contemporaneously with the amendment, was a feature article in which a friend of Madison's interpreted the meaning of the proposed Bill of Rights to the people:

"It is essential that the whole body of the people always possess arms and be taught alike, especially when young, how to use them."

> As civil rulers, not having their duty to the people duly before them, may attempt to tyrannize, and as the military forces which must be occasionally raised to defend our country, might pervert their power to the injury of their fellow-citizens, the people are confirmed by the next article in their right to keep and bear their private arms.

In 1803, an American edition of BLACKSTONE was published with annotations by St. George Tucker. We may assume that Tucker was learned in American common law since he was the Chief Justice of the most distinguished court of his day, the Virginia Supreme Court. Likewise we may assume his authoritative familiarity with the thought underlying the American Bill of Rights. He was not only an important member of the generation which produced it, but also an intimate of

"Civil rulers, not having their duty to the people duly before them, may attempt to tyrannize."

Jefferson and Madison (and his brother and his best friend were both members of the First Congress which enacted the amendment). Tucker added to Blackstone's description of the common law right the observation that it was incorporated in the second amendment—"And this without any qualification as to their condition or degree as is the case in the British government."

In 1825, yet another commentary of the new federal Constitution was published by William Rawle, to whom Washington had offered the first Attorney Generalship (notwithstanding the fact that, as a Quaker, Rawle had refused to fight in the Revolution). So detached was Rawle from the states' right concept, that he flatly declared that the second amendment prohibited state as well as federal laws disarming individuals. Likewise Hamilton, in THE FEDERALIST, viewed the people's possession of arms as guaranteeing freedom from tyranny by a state as much as by the proposed federal government: the armed people "by throwing themselves into either scale, would infallibly make it preponderate" against either a federal or a state invasion of popular rights. . . .

The Second Amendment Is Relevant Today

Opponents of the individual right interpretation argue that the second amendment may simply be ignored because technological changes since 1791 have rendered an armed citizenry irrelevant for either national defense or resistance to domestic tyranny. Even if this were true, the obvious answer is that the Constitution comes with its own designated mechanism for deleting obsolescence— the amendatory process. It is simply impermissible for government to substitute for the process of constitutional amendment its own self-serving conclusion that rights guaranteed to the people are no longer relevant.

Moreover, it does not follow from the fact we now have a large standing army and an equally large National Guard, that no conceivable military emergency could require mustering the individually armed citizenry. Indeed, as late as Pearl Harbor, a military emergency was deemed to require mustering individually armed citizens. Because available military personnel were insufficient to repel the Japanese invasion that seemed imminent, the governor of Hawaii called upon citizens to man check points and patrol remote beach areas. On the other side of the country, 15,000 volunteer Maryland Minute Men brought their own weapons to muster. Virginia militiamen relied perforce on their own weapons since the federal government was not only unable to supply the state arsenal, but had actually recalled the guns it had previously donated. A manual distributed *en masse* by the War Department recommended the keeping of weapons which a guerilla in civilian clothes could carry without attracting attention, were affordable and could be easily concealed. First among these was, and still is, the pistol.

Even less credible is the oft-made assertion that the amendment's central purpose has no meaning today since a citizenry possessing only small arms would inevitably be defeated by a despotism possessing tanks, aircraft, etc. But the military experience of our century shows many cases in which a revolutionary people having only small arms have defeated a modern army. This is how the Shah came to be expelled from Iran, General Somoza from Nicaragua and the British from Palestine and Ireland. Moreover, if a revolutionary people start out with small arms, they can obtain more sophisticated weaponry if they need it—by capture, from parties outside the country, or by maintaining the struggle to the point at which sympathetic segments of the opposing military break off and join the revolution. Anyone who claims that popular struggles are inevitably doomed to defeat by the military technology of our century must find it literally incredible that France and the United States suffered defeat in Vietnam; that the Shah no longer rules Iran or Battista, Cuba; that Portugal was expelled from Angola and Mozambique; and France from Algeria. It is quite irrelevant for our purposes whether each of these struggles was justified or the people benefited therefrom. However one may appraise these victories, the fact remains that they were achieved against regimes equipped with all the military technology which it is asserted inevitably dooms popular revolt.

> *"The right of citizens to bear arms is just one more . . . safe-guard against a tyranny which . . . historically had proved to be always possible."*

Anticipating a Coup

Even more important for a free country is that the citizenry's possession of arms serves to actively deter any general who might consider substituting his own rule for that of the popular government. To persuade his army to follow him, the general must convince them that his rule can meet the crises confronting the nation better than a democratic government which requires a consensus within a widely divergent citizenry before it can act decisively. But when that widely divergent citizenry possesses upwards of 160 million firearms, the outcome of any coup is likely to be a savage and prolonged civil war, rather than benevolent dictatorship. David Hardy's analysis cannot be improved upon:

> A general may have pipe dreams of a sudden and peaceful takeover and a nation moving confidently forward, united under his direction. But the realistic

general will remember the actual fruits of civil war—shattered cities like Hue, Beirut, and Belfast, devastated countrysides like the Mekong Delta, Cyprus and southern Lebanon. At such cost, will his officers and men accept it? Moreover, he and they must also evaluate its effect in leaving the country vulnerable to foreign invasion. Because it leads any prospective dictator to think through such questions, the individual, anonymous ownership of firearms is still a deterrent today to the despotism it was originally intended to obviate. [While our government has a] quite good record of exerting power without abusing it . . . the deterrent effect of an armed citizenry is one little recognized factor that may have contributed to this. In the words of the late Senator Hubert Humphrey: "The right of citizens to bear arms is just one more guarantee against arbitrary government, one more safe-guard against a tyranny which now appears remote in America, but which historically had proved to be always possible."

Banning Assault Weapons Would Be Unconstitutional

by Eric C. Morgan

About the author: *Eric C. Morgan is an attorney in Winston-Salem, North Carolina, and frequently writes on the topic of gun control.*

In the wake of tragic shooting incidents involving semiautomatic rifles, the media has discovered an "assault weapon" problem in the United States. *Time* magazine subtitled its February 6, 1989, cover story, "America's streets become free-fire zones as police, criminals, and terrified citizens wield more and ever deadlier guns." The story included pictures of the coffins of the victims of the Stockton "massacre," as well as a timeline chart entitled, "Calendar of senseless shootings." As a dramatic climax, the article reproduced a photograph of a police officer holding up the "assault rifle" used by Patrick Purdy to fire into the yard of a Stockton, California school. The *Time* reporters, caught in the emotion of the Stockton shootings, promptly set out their agenda of "what should be done" about the "assault weapon" problem. Their first proposal was, of course, that "[t]he Federal Government should ban outright the import or sale of paramilitary weapons to civilians."

Blame the Man, Not the Gun

Reporters covering the Stockton shootings placed the blame for this tragic event on the semiautomatic weapons misused during the course of the shootings. Patrick Purdy killed himself, and it remains far easier to damn the inanimate objects that he left behind than to cope with the general social problems surrounding such incidents or the more specific criminality of a disturbed individual. However, understandable media and public sympathies have generated an unwise legislative response to the alleged "assault weapon" problem. On the federal, state, and local levels, legislators have hastily drafted and passed bills concerning "assault weapons," particularly when such efforts have been cast as being "anti-drug."

Excerpted from Eric C. Morgan, "Assault Rifle Legislation: Unwise and Unconstitutional," *American Journal of Criminal Law* 17 (Winter 1990): 143-74. Reprinted with permission.

It is the purpose of this viewpoint to show that legislation of this "anti-assault weapon" genre is unnecessary and . . . will be unconstitutional. . . .

The second amendment of the United States Constitution states:

> A well regulated Militia, being necessary to the security of a free State, the right of the people to keep and bear Arms, shall not be infringed.

The debate over current gun control proposals has generated different theories about the meaning of this amendment. Advocates of gun control legislation often espouse a "collective right" interpretation of the second amendment, while opponents of gun control legislation adhere to an "individual rights" theory.

Under the collective rights interpretation, only a state's well-regulated militia possesses any right to bear arms. "Militia" is usually defined as state police and national guard units. Therefore, no individual citizen has a constitutional right to own a firearm. The second amendment prohibits only the federal government from unduly burdening a state's effort to arm its national guard units or its police forces. A 1989 American Journal of Criminal Law article highlighted the net effects of the collective rights approach. It stated that "[t]echnically, . . . Congress could prohibit private ownership of all firearms without violating the second amendment."

"Understandable media and public sympathies have generated an unwise legislative response to the alleged 'assault weapon' problem."

The "individual rights" theory of the second amendment grants each citizen of the United States the right to keep and bear arms. Under this interpretation, federal or state governments would violate the second amendment by unduly burdening an individual's right to possess a firearm. This viewpoint argues that the "right to bear arms" is an individual right and that this right extends to possessing military-style semiautomatics. Current "assault rifle" legislation unduly burdens this right and is, therefore, unconstitutional. . . .

Assault Rifles Are Protected Arms

Proponents of current "assault rifle" legislation have argued that even if one recognizes an individual right to bear arms, military-style semiautomatics are not the type of arms that individuals have a right to bear. Although the framers might have intended that citizens have a right to possess the single-shot rifles, shotguns, and pistols of their day, proponents of assault rifle legislation argue that the second amendment never intended to give citizens the right to own modern small arms such as military-style semiautomatics.

Judges that must interpret the second amendment, like those that must interpret the first and fourth amendments, must consider the implications of new technology. The framers of the Constitution could not foresee surface-to-air missiles, just as they may not have foreseen television, radio, or wiretapping. Courts have reassessed rights under the first and fourth amendments in light of the new technology, and found that new technology has not eliminated the rights protected by those amendments. Under the second amendment, courts have created standards to address the development of new weapons technology and continued to protect the individual right to bear arms.

1. *The Reasonable Relationship Test*—In *Miller*, the United States Supreme Court recognized an individual right to bear arms, but also stated that this right extends to those arms with "some reasonable relationship to the preservation or efficiency of a well-regulated militia." However, *Miller* does not specify the types of modern arms that would satisfy this standard. Fortunately, other courts have provided a framework for deciding which modern "arms" bear "some reasonable relationship to a well regulated militia."

The Oregon Supreme Court noted that "the term 'arms' as used by the drafters of the Constitution probably was intended to include those weapons used by settlers for both personal and military defense. . . . The term 'arms' would not have included cannon or other heavy ordnance not kept by militiamen or private citizens." As personal sidearms, the framers used single-shot rifles, shotguns, and pistols; and they intended, no doubt, that the second amendment would protect the individual ownership of those types of firearms. During the years that immediately followed the drafting of the Constitution, when single-shot sidearms still predominated, courts protected absolutely the private possession of these sidearms without any qualification whatever as to their kind or nature.

Courts Defended Use of New Weapons

After the Civil War, courts addressed the implications of a developing weapons technology. The Civil War firmly established the popular use of repeating rifles and pistols as personal sidearms, and the Tennessee Supreme Court addressed this development. In the 1871 case *Andrews v. State*, the court held that, although the Tennessee Constitution did not protect "every thing that may be useful for offense or defense," the Constitution did protect "the rifle of all description,

> *"The 'right to bear arms' is an individual right and . . . extends to possessing military-style semiautomatics."*

the shotgun, the musket, and repeater." In 1876, the Arkansas Supreme Court stated that protected "arms" included "the usual arms of the citizen of the country." The court agreed with the Tennessee court's listing of these arms and noted the addition of the "army and navy repeaters, which, in recent warfare, have very generally superceded the old-fashioned holster, used as a weapon in the battles of our forefathers." These early courts—without using the exact wording of the later *Miller* test—found that personal sidearms, including new repeating firearms, fell within the reach of constitutional provisions drafted in times of more simplistic weapons technology.

In 1980, the Oregon Supreme Court approached more modern weapons developments in a similar manner. The court noted that since the era of the Civil War, "[t]he development of powerful explosives, . . . combined with the development of mass produced metal parts, made possible the automatic weapons, explosives, and chemicals of modern warfare." It concluded that such modern heavy ordnance, used exclusively by the military, would not be considered individual "arms" deserving of constitutional protection. To the Oregon Supreme Court, citizens possessed a right to own personal arms "commonly used" for individual defense or militia service.

Weapons and Regulations

Miller and these state cases provide some guidance from which to ascertain what "arms" individuals have a right to bear. Clearly these protected personal "arms" are not a category that froze during the 1780's. Courts may constitutionally protect modern military-style semiautomatics just as they protected "repeating" rifles after the Civil War. As *Miller* implied, modern weapons that bear "some reasonable relationship to a well-regulated militia" merit constitutional protection. Relevant considerations for modern or old designs seem to include the following: (1) whether a type of firearm is a personal sidearm and not heavy ordnance used exclusively by the military, and (2) whether a type of firearm is commonly possessed by individuals as a sidearm for purposes of personal defense or potential militia service. These considerations provide guidance to courts in order to preserve individual rights while preventing modern-day heavy ordnance from threatening the public safety.

> *"Judges that must interpret the second amendment . . . must consider the implications of new technology"*

2. *"Assault Rifles" Satisfy the* Miller *Test*—Military-style semiautomatic rifles are personal sidearms, and not "heavy ordnance" used exclusively by the military. These so-called "assault rifles" assess the capability of semiautomatic fire, and they remain functionally indistinguishable from more traditionally-styled semiautomatic sidearms. The military does not exclusively use either modern or traditionally-styled semiautomatics. American civilians have owned semiautomatics since the early 1900s, and currently an estimated twenty to thirty million own these firearms. Modern, military-style semiautomatics are no more dangerous than many non-semiautomatics currently available. Empirical evidence and the experience of urban police indicate that these rifles do not have the serious consequences of military "heavy-ordnance" because they are not the weapons of choice of criminals or drug dealers. Though these rifles may look sinister, "assault rifles" are merely the latest technology in personal sidearms,

just as repeating rifles and pistols were the latest technology during the 1870s.

Many Americans own "assault-rifles" as sidearms for either personal defense or possible militia service. An estimated 600,000 firearms fall under the S. 747 definition of "assault weapon." Whether for use by Gulf-Coast yacht owners or citizens defending the home, these military-style semiautomatic rifles are highly reliable defensive arms. The same characteristics make military-style semiautomatic firearms ideal for militia training and use as well.

Semiautomatics Deserve Constitutional Protection

Of all the firearms on the market today, military-style semiautomatic firearms appear to be the individual "arms" with the clearest claim to protection under the second amendment. These firearms offer all of the advantages of modern, reliable military design, without the public safety threat of fully-automatic capability. So-called "assault rifles" satisfy the *Miller* test by bearing "some reasonable relationship to the preservation of a well-regulated militia."

Current legislative proposals unconstitutionally burden the individual constitutional right to own military-style semiautomatic rifles. S. 747, for example, prohibits the "transfer, importation, or possession" of any "assault weapon." Those who lawfully owned these "assault weapons" before the effective date of the law must go through further registration requirements that may be difficult for them and many legitimate firearms dealers. The severe restrictions, and outright bans, employed in bills like S. 747 clearly impose an undue burden on constitutional rights.

No compelling state interest exists that justifies such violations of individual rights. "Assault weapons" are not a peculiarly dangerous class of firearms, and are not frequently used in modern violent crime. Given the evidence available, "assault rifle" legislation will have no effect beyond the infringement of the rights of law-abiding citizens. The denial of these constitutional rights remains unacceptable, given the availability of less restrictive legislative alternatives.

Chapter 3

Is Gun Ownership an Effective Means of Self-Defense?

Gun Ownership and Self-Defense: An Overview

by Brendan F.J. Furnish

About the author: *Brendan F.J. Furnish is chairman of the sociology depart-* *ment at Westmont College in Santa Barbara, California, and is the author of* The Mounting Threat of Home Intruders: Deciding on Armed Self-Defense as a Moral Option.

Like the abortion controversy, the arguments concerning gun control and firearms policy appear to be inherently polarizing—there appears to be very little opportunity to find a middle ground within the areas of contention. Although many varied issues get bandied about in the heat of the gun-control debate, one enduring and hotly argued theme concerns whether or not firearm ownership for self-defense can be both safe and effective in terms of protecting a gun owner and those in his or her household. The 1992 civil unrest in Los Angeles has added a new depth of intensity to this controversy. Some contend that private weaponry can be highly efficacious for self-defense while others argue that the possession of firearms intended for home defense is not only impractical but inherently dangerous for both the individual gun owner and for society as a whole.

Views from Opposing Sides

Although a variety of organizations are involved in the often shrill public debate over the issue of citizen ownership of firearms for self-defense, two national organizations lead the pack in terms of being spokesmen for the opposing sides in this dispute. On the one hand we have the National Rifle Association [NRA] a venerable organization that traces its beginnings to the U.S. Civil War. Within the last three decades, the NRA has modified its original mission of promoting shooting activities to that of becoming the leading defender of the individual citizen's right to own firearms. The NRA claims to have over three million members nationwide. Depending on one's view of gun control, people tend to either admire or disdain the NRA.

On the other hand, there is Handgun Control Incorporated, founded by Pete

Brendan F.J. Furnish, "The Self-Defense Firearm: Menace or Protector?" Position paper written expressly for inclusion in this anthology, May 1992.

Shields (whose son was killed with a handgun, by a fanatical terrorist who was a participant in the infamous San Francisco Zebra slayings). Handgun Control Inc. is presently headed by Sarah Brady (whose husband James Brady was shot and permanently disabled during the assassination attempt on Ronald Reagan's life). Mrs. Brady has maintained a high visibility in the national media and is very active in promoting the "Brady Bill" national legislation that would mandate, among other things, a mandatory fifteen-day waiting period for the purchase of firearms. Although ostensibly organized to limit the availability of handguns to the public, the organization has also supported attempts to ban certain types of semi-automatic rifles: in general its stance appears to be one of restricting most types of firearms. HCI claims to have over one million members, including many well-known Hollywood figures.

> *"Some contend that private weaponry can be highly efficacious for self-defense while others argue that the possession of firearms is . . . inherently dangerous."*

The Effectiveness of Firearms for Self-Defense

The national debate over the citizen's right to own firearms for self-defense is pretty much framed by these two opposing organizations. Thus, we find Pete Shields arguing that:

> . . . as research in the area of self-defense has borne out . . . a handgun does not protect the American home very well. . . . The home handgun is far more likely to kill or injure family members and friends than anyone who breaks in, and is especially harmful to young adults and children.

Echoing this theme, but from a more reasoned and better qualified academic position, Franklin E. Zimring and Gordon Hawkins claim that while it might be "possible" that the widespread ownership of firearms for self-defense may diminish certain types of crime, there is no empirical evidence to demonstrate that this is true. Rather, self-defensive firearms provide the owner with an emotionally comforting illusion of safety. These writers agree with Shields that, ". . . the handgun in your house is more likely to kill you or a member of your family than to save your life."

Holding to an altogether opposite view, we have the National Rifle Association which claims that home-defense firearms ownership can indeed be a safe and effective way to thwart crime. The NRA holds that the "Mere presence of a firearm, without a shot being fired, prevents crime in many instances. . ." To demonstrate the validity of this assertion, the NRA has, for more than three decades, published a column, entitled "The Armed Citizen" in its monthly membership magazine, *The American Rifleman*. The former editor of this column claims that in the last 30 years almost 3,500 cases were cited where armed citizens successfully prevented a crime. This represents a total of 5,285 individual lawbreakers, of which 19% were killed, 22% wounded, 34% arrested and 25% forced to flee the crime scene by armed citizens.

Although the NRA's crime deterrent data is largely anecdotal, other researchers in the areas of sociology and criminology tend to support their contention, albeit at various levels of agreement. Of particular significance in this area are the works of Gary Kleck, James Wright and Peter Rossi.

Although the effectiveness of citizen possession of firearms as a method of private crime deterrence is a hotly debated topic, several other issues appear to be equally important and provide us with a series of perpetually contested themes by the opposing sides in this controversy. These subjects include the moral and ethical implications of armed self-defense; safety issues involved with the ownership of firearms; and the actual ability of the police to protect individual citizens from crime. Naturally, there are a host of other related issues, particularly concerning the legal aspects of armed self-defense. However, space limitations force us to address just these three significant issues: let's briefly consider each in turn.

Psychological, Ethical, and Moral Intent

First let's look at the psychological, moral and ethical problems involved in deciding to obtain and possess a firearm for self-defensive purposes. The NRA Armed Citizen column masthead caveat says, "Shooting usually can be justified only where crime constitutes an immediate, imminent threat to life or limb or, in some circumstances property." Many people are reluctant to face up to the fact that ownership of defensive weapons implies the very real possibility that the weapon may have to be used; and in using it the defender faces the likelihood of killing or seriously injuring his or her adversary.

> *"The owner may find him or herself unable to use the firearm ... and may be disarmed and have the weapon used against themselves."*

Even though our culture is becoming increasingly violent, many people who are willing to own a firearm for defensive reasons are reluctant to emotionally commit themselves to using it because the thought of doing so is repulsive and barbaric to them.

Beyond a doubt, this is one of the major difficulties involved in the defensive use of firearms by citizens. Many people buy a firearm "to protect themselves," load it and simply place it in a bureau drawer or other hiding place. As Massad Ayoob has warned, the gun is not a "magic talisman" that will ward off evil in itself. Simply buying and retaining a gun with no further commitment makes for the kind of situation in which the weapon may indeed be involved in an accident. Worse yet, if actually needed in a defensive situation, the owner may find him or herself unable to use the firearm for either physical or psychological reasons and may be disarmed and have the weapon used against themselves.

The firearm is a sophisticated device, which requires training and practice in order to successfully—and safely—operate it. Some firearms, such as semi-automatic pistols and pump or semi-automatic shotguns are rather complex mechanisms which require frequent training in order to successfully use them in a possible high stress encounter with a household intruder.

Additionally, and of crucial importance, a person who owns a weapon for defensive purposes must psychologically commit themselves—far in advance of using the gun—to the possibility that they will kill another person if the circumstances warrant such action. This means that long before action is required, the individual has grappled with the ethical and moral implications of taking a life. If this is not dealt with in advance, the individual may well emotionally "freeze" up at the crises moment, leaving them vulnerable to being disarmed and injured

> *"Deaths from gun accidents are relatively rare ... compared to other accidents, particularly those involving swimming pools and motor vehicles."*

or killed by an emotionally stressed intruder-assailant. Such an ethical and psychological commitment to killing—whether or not the action is justified—is abhorrent to many people, making the use of defensive firearms a moral impossibility for them.

Safety Issues

Deaths and injuries from accidental discharge of firearms are also a major source of contention in the firearms debate. Shields claims that "There are far more accidents and acts of passion with one's own handgun than there are either criminal murders or prevention of criminal attack." In a similar vein, Michael Nagler claims that, "if you keep a gun in your home, you are five times more likely to harm someone in your own family than an intruder." Several recent empirical studies, such as one conducted in King's County, Washington, tend to support these assertions.

Contrary to this widely believed view is another that claims that gun related accidents are in fact surprisingly low. It is common to include suicide in with gun accidents, thus significantly inflating the figures.

Despite all this, there is fairly reliable information on accidental death. The National Safety Council reports that in 1989 (the last year complete data was available), 250 children age 1 to 14 died from a firearm accident. Gun accidents among children age 5-14 occur at a rate of 7 per 100,000. Among 15- to 25-year-olds the rate climbs to 12 per 100,000. All sensitive people decry the accidental death of even one child; however, put in objective perspective, deaths from gun accidents are relatively rare, particularly when compared to other accidents, particularly those involving swimming pools and motor vehicles. More to the point, fewer than 2% of fatal gun accidents (excluding police negligence) involve a person accidently shooting someone mistaken for an intruder. Actually, on average, fewer than 28 such incidents of this sort occur annually, compared to an estimated 700,000 defensive gun uses.

The Question of Police Protection

The TV images of Korean merchants protecting their shops with semi-automatic Uzis during the Los Angeles disorder sent a powerful self-defense message to the American public. This message was all the more forceful in light of the disorganization and apparent impotency of the Los Angeles Police to quell large scale anarchy for almost 24 hours—and then only with help from the military. This situation again raises the question with many people as to whether or not police can effectively protect the average citizen.

Conventional wisdom assumes that the police will protect and defend individual citizens whenever we are in need of assistance. Self-defense experts such as Massad Ayoob argue that armed civilians have no business attempting to confront household intruders. Rather, whenever possible, a threatened householder should either flee the scene or barricade themselves in a safe room and call for assistance. In this regard, both sides of the controversy are in agreement.

However, the pro-gun defense side will then ask, what about those times when such strategies are simply not available to the homeowner or apartment dweller? What about confrontational situations when the intended victim cannot flee? This makes for a difficult situation for the average person to contemplate, even if the possibility of such an event is very rare. For the person who lacks the resources to access private security systems, the answer is often the acquisition of a defensive firearm. This answer becomes even more compelling when one begins to examine the true situation regarding police protection in many locations.

The idea of having to defend oneself from a potentially violent intruder seems appalling to most normal folks, particularly if such a defense bears the implication of taking a life. On the other hand, being self-sufficient and providing security—of various forms—for self and family strikes a resonant chord in many Americans. Given the circumstances of life in the contemporary U.S., it seems unlikely that the fear of crime will be alleviated in the near future. If this be so, it also appears unlikely that the controversy over private ownership of firearms for self-defense purposes will be resolved in the immediate future.

Gun Ownership Provides Effective Self-Defense

by National Rifle Association Institute for Legislative Action

About the author: *The National Rifle Association (NRA) is an organization of target shooters, hunters, gun collectors, and others interested in firearms. The NRA Institute for Legislative Action lobbies against gun control laws in order to protect gun owners' rights.*

On February 18, 1982, the Court of Appeals for the State of New York handed down a decision that chilled New York's subway passengers.

Two suits against the New York City Transit Authority charged the agency with negligence for not taking steps to correct conditions it, the Authority, knew presented a clear danger to passengers. In one incident, a woman was raped in a subway station that was the scene of four separate rapes over a span of a few months. The second involved a retired school board official who was robbed and injured by knife-wielding thugs at a stop where 13 separate robberies (eight with knives) occurred over a ten-month period.

The court dismissed both.

The court ruled that the Transit Authority was free from liability just as was any municipality or governmental agency. The Transit Authority had no responsibility *"to protect a person on its premises from assault by a third person"* nor did it have an obligation to increase police protection for well-documented high crime areas within the subway systemording to the court.

The cold, harsh legal facts are that by statute and court decree, local and state governments and "their agents," the police, have no obligation to provide protection for the individual.

Civilians Armed for Self-Defense

The concept of self-defense strikes at the heart of the debate, pro and con, over the private ownership of firearms.

Today, in particular, the focus of the controversy has been primarily on handguns. Each argument, each consideration seems to raise yet another question.

Government research indicates that the majority of firearms owned by Americans are owned for sport and recreational purposes rather than for self-protection, by a rate of three-to-one. The increase in gun sales seems to be people who already own one or more guns rather than among non-gun owning families. *However, among the 10 to 15 million women handgun owners, the figures favor self-protection as the main reason for owning a gun in urban areas.*

What thoughts run through a woman's mind, particularly after an assault or attempted assault, when she considers owning or using a gun for protection?

Do they differ from those of a male?

Does a handgun provide real or imagined security for the woman living alone . . . for the merchant in a high crime area . . . for families with small children?

Are handguns more of a danger to their owners than to criminals?

Are they "accidents waiting to happen"?

Protection: The Root of Gun Ownership

On the negative side is the notion that handguns should be banned to the average citizen. Proponents of this position may concede restricted use of handguns by on-duty military, police and private security personnel, but handguns for protection would not be allowed.

Ironically, police and military views of handguns are 180 degrees opposite to the rhetoric of such prohibitionists. The official view by police and the military is that their on- and off-duty handguns are strictly "defensive" arms. Rifles and shotguns are considered "offensive" implements.

Unresolved, too, is an apparent contradiction in the prohibitionists' line of argument. On one hand, they argue that the handgun, particularly when used by the criminal or the enraged family member, is the most lethal of instruments. On the other, they discount its protective value to the honest citizen because of what they describe as a handgun's "inherent inaccuracy."

"Handguns [are] critical tools that might spell the difference between becoming the victim of a crime or the victor in a confrontation."

Literally tens of millions of Americans disagree with the prohibitionist position. They see their handguns as critical tools that might spell the difference between becoming the victim of a crime or the victor in a confrontation with a criminal predator. Just what does the record show?

Protection of self, of one's loved ones, of one's home and community is the root of the American tradition of gun ownership. It is a concept cherished from the beginning of time and preserved most democratically within the English common law heritage where the defense of home, community and kingdom rested upon an armed and ready populace. This was a distinct divergence from the Continental practice of a disarmed peasantry "protected" by the armed knights of the nobility.

Sir William Blackstone's "Commentaries," upon which the American legal system is based, described "the right of having and using arms for self-preservation and defense" as among the "Absolute Rights of Individuals."

Self-defense, said Sir William, was "justly called the primary law of nature, so it is not, neither can it be in fact, taken away by the laws of society."

What the Law Says

Gun ownership by convicted felons, drug addicts and court-ruled mental defectives is currently forbidden by federal law. That law and more than 20,000 state and local laws not only forbid criminal purchase of, possession of and use of all rifles, handguns, and shotguns by these people, but they also levy prison and/or monetary penalties against anyone misusing firearms in any manner. These laws are in addition to laws against murder, robbery, rape, etc.

> *"For both robbery and assault, victims who used guns for protection were less likely either to be attacked or injured than victims who responded in any other way."*

Nevertheless, the push for yet more layers of federal, state, and local law continues. With virtually every imaginable criminal act covered by existing law, the new suggestions invariably focus on restricting the non-criminal acquisition, possession, and use of firearms, handguns in particular. Toward this end, the idea of handgun use for self-protection is continually dismissed.

Shortly after her husband left for work, a Waco, Texas, housewife heard the front door window break. A strange man reached in, unlocked the door, and entered the front room.

The housewife ran to the bedroom. She locked the door and grabbed a handgun kept beneath the mattress. The intruder kicked in the door. He saw the gun aimed at him. He left.

Twice a 51-year-old Los Angeles, California, woman had been raped by the same man. He had not yet been apprehended. After the second assault, she purchased a handgun. The man returned a third time. His criminal career came to an abrupt end.

Masquerading as a police officer, a man raped a Baltimore, Maryland, woman in front of her two children, ages one and two. When he threatened the oldest child, the woman lunged for a hidden revolver. It was the last thing the rapist saw.

When Phoenix, Arizona, authorities responded to a breaking-and-entering call, they found a 77-year-old woman gently rocking in her favorite chair. Her favorite .38 revolver was pointed at a man obediently lying half in and half out of her "pet door."

Those four incidents are not uncommon.

Based on several public opinion surveys, especially a Peter Hart survey commissioned by a handgun-ban organization, Florida State University Professor

Gary Kleck has estimated that "there were about 645,000 defensive uses of handguns against persons per year, excluding police or military uses." Kleck also found that "guns of all types are used substantially more often defensively than criminally," and that "gun-wielding civilians in self-defense or some other legally justified cause" kill between 1,500 and 2,800 felons annually.

Since the night two decades ago when more than a score of neighbors watched as New York crime victim Kitty Genovese was slashed to death, headlines across the nation appear to be charting a new trend. Apathy and the attitude that the safety of neighbors and one's neighborhood is the job of the police and not of the community *together with the police* seems to be giving ground to a resurgence of community involvement.

In fact, criminologists and police nationwide credit crime drops in the 1980s to increased community involvement.

In Baltimore, a 1979 EVENING SUN headline ran: "Lady D.A. Outshoots Thugs." Chicago's TRIBUNE chronicled one "Gunman Becomes The Victim" to an armed homeowner in 1982. Georgia's ATLANTA CONSTITUTION/ JOURNAL ran the headline "Burglaries Fall in DeKalb (County) as Victims Take Aim" in 1982.

ESQUIRE magazine ran two articles in defense of handgun ownership in 1981. And, the trend toward citizens armed for defense was cover story materials in WOMAN'S DAY (1983), BOSTON MAGAZINE (1982), Philadelphia's TODAY MAGAZINE (1982) and in SAVVY MAGAZINE (1981).

> *"Fears that handguns are somehow home accident or 'crime of passion' catalysts are unfounded in view of research into both areas."*

Television's popular talkshow host Phil Donahue was surprised at the audience's reaction to his attempt to discount handguns as useful self-defense aids. He was hooted by his largely female audience with taunts that he had "never been raped."

Had Donahue read GLAMOUR magazine's readership survey in May of 1981 he would have known that 65 percent of GLAMOUR readers said they own guns; 66 percent of those owned primarily for self-defense. Sixty-eight percent opposed banning handguns.

Risk of Injury

The idea that a potential crime victim runs a greater risk of injury if he or she is armed has been proven groundless.

According to U.S. Justice Department victimization studies analyzed by Prof. Kleck, "for both robbery and assault, victims who used guns for protection were less likely either to be attacked or injured than victims who responded in any other way, including those who did not resist at all" and "victims who resisted robbers with guns . . . were less likely to lose their property. . . . When victims use guns to resist crimes, the crimes usually are disrupted and the victims are not injured."

A follow-up study of rape found that using a gun or knife for protection reduced the likelihood of a completed rape, and using a gun reduces the likelihood of injury to near zero. Such resistance also reduces the likelihood of psychological trauma.

More incidents of victims' successful use of guns would occur, and would be reported to the police, if there were fewer laws against carrying firearms.

> *"The armed citizen or the threat of the armed citizen [is] possibly the most effective crime deterrent in the nation."*

Criminals face greater risk of injury from armed citizens than police, according to available Justice Department data.

One glaring statistic is that burglars who choose, either unintentionally or otherwise, to ply their trade in occupied homes are twice as likely to be shot or killed as they are to be caught, convicted and imprisoned by the U.S. criminal justice system.

Armed citizens kill two to seven times the number of criminals killed each year by law enforcement. Additionally, Prof. Kleck estimates that annually "there were about 8,700-16,600 non-fatal, legally permissible woundings of criminals by gun-armed civilians," with no estimates available on the number held for authorities.

None of this has been lost on the typical criminal.

Research gathered by Professors James Wright and Peter Rossi, co-authors of the U.S. Justice Department's benchmark three-year study of weapons and criminal violence in America, points to the armed citizen or the threat of the armed citizen as possibly the most effective crime deterrent in the nation.

Criminals Fear Armed Citizens

Wright and Rossi questioned over 1,800 prisoners serving time in prisons across the nation. They found:

• 85 percent agreed that the "smart criminal" will attempt to find out if a potential victim is armed.

• 75 percent felt that burglars avoided occupied dwellings for fear of being shot.

• 60 percent felt that the typical criminal feared being shot by citizens more than he feared being shot by police.

• 80 percent of "handgun predators" had encountered armed citizens.

• 53 percent did not commit a specific crime for fear that the victim was armed.

• 57 percent of "handgun predators" were scared off or shot at by armed victims.

The classic example of the threat of armed citizens to criminals and the corresponding effect on an area's crime rate remains Orlando, Florida.

In 1966, rape in that city skyrocketed from 12.8 per 100,000 citizens in 1965 to 35.9 per 100,000. The Orlando police organized a handgun training program for women. The program ran from October 1966 through April 1967. The media gave extraordinary coverage to the fact that Orlando's female population was armed and more than willing to resist criminal attack.

One year later, Orlando's rape rate plummetted to 4.1 per 100,000. Elsewhere in the state (excluding Orlando) rape rates increased that year.

> *"The American public should be commended for its long record of safe firearms handling."*

Other areas which saw similar crime drops for armed robbery or rape after instituting well-publicized firearm training programs for merchants or women were Detroit and Highland Park, Michigan, and Montgomery, Alabama.

Fears that handguns are somehow home accident or "crime of passion" catalysts are unfounded in view of research into both areas.

Criminologist James Wright described the typical incident of family violence as "that mythical crime of passion" on a television documentary, "Gunfight, USA" aired over the Public Broadcasting System in 1983.

Wright denied that the typical "crime of passion" was an isolated incident by otherwise normally placid and loving individuals. The available research showed that it was in fact "the culminating event in a long history of interpersonal violence between the parties."

Wright further noted that handguns did not play the aggressive role most often attributed to them.

"The common pattern, the more common pattern, is for wives to shoot their husbands. Proportionately, men kill their women by other means, more brutal means, more degrading means. To deny that woman the right to own the firearms is in some sense to guarantee in perpetuity to her husband the right to beat her at will," said Wright.

It should be repeated that these men who kill their spouses are not "nice" folks.

Many of the homicides listed by the FBI as occurring between relatives, neighbors and acquaintances are not simple domestic squabbles.

Inflated Homicide Statistics

Homicide by street gang members of rival gang members, homicide between drug traffickers, organized crime "hits," slayings of neighbors by the neighborhood criminal predator are all listed as "non-felony homicides." They are included in the "relative, friend, acquaintance, neighbor" categories that are used by handgun prohibitionists to inflate "crime of passion" statistics.

As "accidents waiting to happen" handguns once again appear to bear the

147

brunt of unfair and unwarranted rhetoric.

The National Safety Council *does not* break down incidents of handgun versus rifle or shotgun-related accidental deaths. Research now underway at Florida State University suggests long guns are involved in a majority of the 1,800 accidental firearm-related deaths logged in the U.S. annually. That research also indicates that a sizeable number of those deaths are, in fact, not accidents but well-disguised homicides or suicides. Alcohol also seems to play a disproportionately large factor in the overall accidental death toll (50 percent).

Since Prohibition, the rate of firearm-related accidental deaths in the U.S. has been reduced by two-thirds according to the Centers for Disease Control (U.S. Public Health Service).

At its highest (during Prohibition) the rate was 2.5 per 100,000 citizens. It leveled out at 0.8 per 100,000 since 1978 before falling to 0.6 from 1987 to 1990.

The American public should be commended for its long record of safe firearms handling. Credit, too, should be given to training programs such as those offered by the National Rifle Association, an organization which has pioneered the field of safe firearms handling and training for more than a century.

> *"The purpose of the self-defense handgun is to preserve life and to discourage criminal violence. It may well prove to be the most immediate means of thwarting criminal activity."*

The first hunter safety program was introduced by the NRA in 1949. The accidental hunting firearms death rate has dropped to 0.9 per 100,000 hunting licenses. Hunter safety is now taught by the fish and wildlife departments of all 50 states. The result of such training is evident.

The most recent program introduced by the NRA is the Personal Protection Program. This program, taught by NRA certified instructors nationwide, is aimed at individuals, women in particular, who feel they want a handgun for self-protection.

An Individual Choice

NRA instructors teach the principles of safe firearms handling and marksmanship excellence to hundreds of thousands of civilians and police each year.

It is not the intention of the NRA to suggest that handguns are the only means of self-defense. Nor is it the NRA's intention to suggest that handguns should be purchased for this purpose.

The question of handgun ownership is one that is highly personal. It is a choice that should be made by the individual. It is a choice that should not be forbidden to the honest citizen by an overprotective government, particularly one which has no responsibility to provide real protection when one's life is threatened. It is a choice that should be approached with information and not emotion.

The purpose of the self-defense handgun is to preserve life and to discourage criminal violence. It may well prove to be the most immediate means of thwarting criminal activity. In that sense, it serves to provide security in a manner similar to health or life insurance. If ever there arises that time when it is needed, no substitute will do.

Editor's note: Sources of facts presented in the pamphlet from which this viewpoint is taken are fully documented in the pamphlet's appendix. Due to space limitations, the appendix has not been included. Interested readers are referred to the original pamphlet, available from the National Rifle Association Institute for Legislative Action, 1600 Rhode Island Ave. NW, Washington, DC 20036.

Gun Owners Protect Themselves from Crime

by Edward F. Leddy

About the author: *Edward F. Leddy, director of the criminal justice program at St. Leo's College in Norfolk, Virginia, is editor of the annual* Journal on Firearms and Public Policy.

It is widely accepted that the ownership and carrying of pistols and revolvers by anyone except the police and those whom they choose to permit is a cause of violent crime. We know this without having to prove it, because it is so obviously reasonable to assume so. Indeed, until recently, in academic circles one would be accused of being radical or at least slightly eccentric to assert that this might not be true. Most of the governments of both Eastern and Western Europe have justified their laws and policies on this belief. Yet there is another side to the issue. . . .

A Duty to Protect Oneself

Historically, keeping the peace and suppressing rebellion were considered the duty of the state in most of Europe. There was little effort made in the past to track down criminals or to protect individuals. People were expected to protect themselves. Until the early decades of this century, the average citizen was permitted and often encouraged to own and carry guns freely. Travelers routinely went armed and in groups. [According to Colin Greenwood in *Firearms Control*:]

> . . . the Common Law right to keep arms and the tradition of owning arms for protection, was built up [in England] during a period when there was no effective police when the individual was compelled to see to his own protection.

Prohibiting the private ownership and carrying of guns is often justified by the assertion that the modern state is now able to provide all the protection a person can reasonably need. Armed self-protection is derided as vigilantism. However, as we all know, crime rates have risen in the last twenty years to the point that it is four times more likely that we shall be the victims of violence today than in 1963. Accordingly, this claim rings rather hollow. The ability of the state to protect us from personal violence is limited by resources, legal restraints, and personnel shortages.

Most of all, the state is usually unable to know that we need protection from attack until it is too late. By the time that the police can be notified and then arrive at the scene the violent criminal has ample opportunity to do you serious harm. I once waited twenty minutes for the New York City Police to respond to an "officer needs assistance" call which has their highest priority. On the other hand a gun provides immediate protection. Even where the police are prompt and efficient, the gun is speedier.

Handgun Ownership

In the United States, the people living in forty-four of the fifty states can legally own and purchase pistols without obtaining a police permit for ownership. Laws do prohibit possession of handguns by felons, and other undesirables. There has been much more research on the issue of handgun ownership than on carrying. There are extensive studies in this area which I will not touch on here except to note that it has not been established that crime is increased by widespread gun ownership. I wish to address the specific problem of legal gun carrying as a crime preventive program.

> *"Until the early decades of this century, the average citizen was permitted and often encouraged to own and carry guns freely."*

Carrying concealed weapons is much more regulated than ownership, requiring permits in most states. I find this rather odd because it would seem that if one has a gun there is little practical obstacle to prevent putting it on and carrying it. I found in many years of gun carrying when I was a Parole Officer that people do not notice.

However, there are many more laws regulating carrying than ownership. Many people who own pistols cannot legally carry them. Yet it is generally accepted that there is a need for *some* people to carry guns for protection. In almost all states procedures are established to license selected people to legally carry concealed weapons. . . .

Because of its diverse laws, the U.S.A. can be regarded as a "vast sociological laboratory." In some parts of the nation, guns are almost banned by strict regulations. In others gun possession in the home or business is not restricted except that persons with records of crime or insanity, minors, and certain other categories may not have guns. Carrying concealed weapons is regulated by both mandatory and discretionary permit systems.

One can compare the results of different gun law strategies because of the variety of laws. These, in effect, have been informal experiments in the use of guns by civilians. While they have not been formal controlled experiments, the results have been so dramatic that the relatively small experimental errors which may have occurred are probably of no real significance.

In Detroit, Michigan, grocery robberies declined 90% after a firearms training program for grocers was instituted by a grocers association.

Highland Park, Michigan, police trained storekeepers to shoot producing a dramatic decrease in store robberies from 80 in the previous four months to none in the subsequent four-month period.

In New Orleans, Louisiana, pharmacy robberies dropped from three per week to three in six months.

In Kennesaw, Georgia, all households have been required by law to keep a firearm since 1982. Serious crime dropped 74.4% in the year after the passage of the law and has remained low.

On the other hand the town of Morton Grove, Illinois, adopted a ban on handguns. Rates of armed crime increased dramatically in comparison with neighboring communities.

Nearby Oak Park, Illinois, passed a similar law in 1984. Burglary rose 35% in the following year.

According to a 1985 NBC News survey, about one in twenty (7,500,000) Americans carry a firearm for self-defense. If the fears of anti-gun advocates were of substance this would produce millions of gun murders instead of the total of about five thousand actually committed in the U.S.A. Crimes of any kind committed by citizens having gun licenses are so rare that the police do not even bother to keep statistics. Few murders are committed by people without prior criminal records. Of course people with criminal histories should not be licensed.

What If Everyone Carried a Gun?

Opponents of allowing citizens to be armed often present this "what if?" argument. They imply that the removal of the discretionary restrictions that they believe in would result in catastrophe. Gun carrying would become universal and we would re-enter "the wild west" with everyone going armed. Aside from its historical inaccuracy, this is pure speculation. Where gun licensing is mandatory no such thing has happened. Instead researchers have found that when a mandatory permit system is implemented, only three to eight percent (four percent is the most frequent) of the population apply for a license. These are largely individuals who are in real danger from crime. Many of these people only carry guns on dangerous occasions, e.g., when they are carrying large sums of money or traveling in bad neighborhoods. Some others apply because they wish the convenience of a carry license to transport guns for sport without legal concerns. Far from becoming universal, gun carrying increases by

"In Detroit, Michigan, grocery robberies declined 90% after a firearms training program for grocers was instituted by a grocers association."

only a few percentage points. The main difference is that many people without criminal records who were carrying illegally regularize their activity.

The 4% figure, however, would project nationwide to a potential carrying population of 8-10 million, [out of 225,000,000] a figure higher than that for those who carry regularly now, but lower than that for those who carry handguns for protection some of the time. With regard to most of the population, widespread issuance of permits to carry to those who wish them, or allowing concealed carrying without a permit, would result in legalizing the technically unlawful activities of a few million Americans and in causing an additional percentage or two of the population to carry protective handguns.

> *"Fourteen percent of the gun owning households in the U.S. (about 14,000,000 people) report that they have used a gun for protection."*

The writer lived for six years in Laramie, Wyoming, where gun carrying openly is legal. I never saw anyone carry except during "Jubilee Days" when we were asked to dress "Western.". . .

The Criminal's View

In 1985, the United States Department of Justice conducted a study of criminal behavior. Convicted criminals were asked a series of questions on their behavior. Thirty-four percent reported that they had been scared off, shot at, wounded or captured by an armed victim. Forty percent reported that they had decided not to commit a crime because they thought the victim was armed:

> The first example in the sequence asked the sample to agree or disagree that "a criminal is not going to mess around with a victim he knows is armed with a gun." About three-fifths (56%) agreed. Another item read, "A smart criminal always tries to find out if a potential victim is armed." More than four-fifths agreed with that. Yet another item read, "Most criminals are more worried about meeting an armed victim than they are about running into the police." About three-fifths (57%) also agreed with that.

The actual frequency of gun use for self-protection varies widely depending on the local laws. (In the United States most gun laws are made by the fifty states. They differ widely in severity, from almost complete prohibition to easy availability.) Accordingly, [as stated in *Attitudes of the American Electorate Toward Gun Control*, 1978], one can compare the results of different levels of control:

> Use of guns in defense of person and property is most common where "controls" on guns are fewest and having needed but not had, a gun for self-defense is most common in big cities where "controls" on gun ownership are generally most stringent.

Rates of those crimes which are deterrable by guns vary with the strictness of gun laws. Robbery (theft by violence) is highest in those states with the lowest gun ownership. It is lowest where private citizens own many guns. This seems reasonable since robbery tends to be a crime committed by repeat offenders. As one Wyoming police official said, "Where citizens have no guns, robbers commit long strings of crimes before the police catch them. Here a storekeeper shoots them on the second or third robbery." This prevents future crimes and thus protects many who are unaware that they would otherwise have become victims.

> *"Experience indicates that the ownership and carrying of guns by potential victims reduces victimization both for the individual and for other potential victims."*

The Extent of Self-Defense

Fourteen percent of the gun owning households in the U.S. (about 14,000,000 people) report that they have used a gun for protection of person or property exclusive of military or police work. In 60% of these cases, the gun was not fired and was used only as a threat. In only 9% of the instances was anyone injured or killed. Only 31% of instances were reported to the police. Accordingly officials tend to be unaware of the extent of citizen self-defense. Armed citizens in the U.S. protect themselves from criminals at least 380,000 times a year. [According to Gary Kleck and David J. Bordua, in *Law and Policy Quarterly*, 1983:]

> Given the data on private citizens' use of firearms against criminals and evidence on the slight risks of legal punishment associated with most crimes, it is a perfectly plausible hypothesis that private gun ownership currently exerts as much or more deterrent effect on criminals as do the activities of the criminal justice system. The gun owning citizenry is certainly more omnipresent than the police, and the potential severity of private justice is at least as severe as more formal legal justice, given the frequency of citizen shootings of criminals and the de facto near abolition of capital punishment by the federal judiciary.

While the value to the potential victim of a gun for self-protection may be admitted, officials might well be concerned about the danger that citizens would misuse their weapons injuring innocent people, committing crimes, and violating the laws on use of deadly force. Research in the United States [by David Conover, in *The American Rifleman*, September 1985] indicates that this problem is more theoretical than real. A comparison was made between errors made by the police and those made by private citizens:

> . . . police were successful in shooting or driving off criminals 68% of the time, private citizens were successful in 83% of their encounters. While 11% of the individuals involved in police shootings were later found to be innocents misidentified as criminals, only 2% of those in civilian shootings were so misidentified.

154

Private citizens encounter and kill about three times as many criminals each year as do law enforcement officials.

It appears, from the writer's experience, that citizens commit fewer errors in the use of force than the police because the police often enter dangerous situations with little information. They arrive on a crime scene often not knowing who is the victim and who is the criminal. In contrast, the citizen almost always uses a weapon in response to attack. Thus the citizen can generally be sure of the criminal's identity.

The reason that few crimes are committed by licensed citizens is that criminals tend to commit crimes and acquire criminal records early in their lives. In a properly operating mandatory system, criminals cannot get licenses and seldom seek them. The chance that a citizen without any record will commit a crime is small. Giving him a gun license does not change this. . . .

Criminalization of the Victim

In New York City, which has had extremely strict gun laws for eighty years, there is widespread disregard for the law on the part of honest citizens. A perennial news story in that city is the honest citizen who is attacked by criminals, wards them off with a gun and is then arrested for violation of the gun law. The internationally reported Bernard Goetz case is only a recent example, [Reported by David Conover, in *The American Rifleman*, September 1985:]

> In the City of New York alone, about 6% of the population admits to owning a firearm for protection. This figure represents about 450,000 gun owners in the Big Apple or seven times the number of citizens granted permits to legally own, carry or transport their personal firearms. In other words, about 85% of those people honest enough to admit owning a gun are technical criminals under the laws of New York. But these New Yorkers have made the choice. They would rather be "criminals" under a bad law than bodies in a police morgue.

According to a 1985 survey by NBC News, about one American in twenty (7,500,000) carries a gun for self-protection. (If such carrying was legal everywhere under a mandatory permit system the figure would probably rise to 8,800,000.) In many areas this carrying is illegal. This brings up the consideration that the vast majority of these "law breakers" are ordinary citizens without any record of criminal behavior. They are merely seeking to protect themselves from the violent criminals who prey on them.

"According to a 1985 survey by NBC News, about one American in twenty (7,500,000) carries a gun for self-protection."

Discretionary licensing systems which refuse to grant licenses to these people are being disregarded. Instead they follow the old police maxim "It is better to be tried by twelve than carried by six."

Judge David J. Shields of Chicago, who tries many such illegal gun carrying cases wrote:

> Probably the most striking experience that one takes away from Gun Court is awareness of the kinds of people who appear there as defendants. For most it is their first arrest; many are old people. Shopkeepers, persons who have been victims of violent crimes and others who carry their guns because of a sincere belief in their need for protection—these constitute the greatest part of the call. . . .

The National Rifle Association of America has proposed and a number of American states have adopted a model law regulating carrying concealed weapons. This law contains the following principles.

1. A permit to carry concealed weapons is required.

2. A character investigation is conducted. The person must supply identifying information.

3. It is presumed that the person has a right to a license unless there is cause for denial. The license must be issued unless there is a record of past violent crimes, pending charges, narcotic use, alien or fugitive status. Commitment to a mental institution or drug/alcohol treatment center is also cause for denial unless a physician certifies that there is no danger to the public.

4. As in other American laws, there is a presumption of innocent intent. If the person is found suitable to carry a gun, evaluation of his or her reason for going armed is not considered the business of the state.

The most significant elements of this law are the refusal to allow police to arbitrarily deny licenses and restriction of their inquiry to clearly defined considerations of personal suitability. These are important limitations because they are designed to prevent personal prejudices from affecting the decision and to prevent social standing, race, wealth or other extraneous factors from being considered.

A Clear Deterrence

Experience indicates that the ownership and carrying of guns by potential victims reduces victimization both for the individual and for other potential victims. The deterrence of such crimes as robbery, assault, rape, and home invasion (illegal entry into occupied dwellings) is clear and dramatic. The hazards of citizen use have been greatly exaggerated because of theoretical fears not actual evidence. Therefore a revision of firearms laws in the direction of the mandatory model appears both prudent and desirable from the viewpoint of potential victims. This would benefit those who do not choose to carry guns as well as those who do so, since, when many people are armed, the criminal cannot be sure that any potential victim is unarmed. This measure would both provide protection to the potential victim and pose a significant threat to the violent criminal.

Gun Owners Can Protect Themselves Against Assault

by John R. Salter Jr.

About the author: *John R. Salter Jr., a social activist and grassroots organizer, is a professor of Indian studies at the University of North Dakota in Grand Forks. He is the author of* Jackson, Mississippi *and many magazine and newspaper articles.*

Community organizing for social justice purposes is, by its very nature, controversial—frequently drawing violent attacks from adversaries and hostility or cold indifference from law-enforcement and other governmental agencies. This paper will discuss the necessity of personal firearms protection in the organizing context, and will cite a number of representative, first-hand examples.

In the mid-1960s, I was a full-time grassroots civil-rights organizer for the radical Southern Conference Educational Fund. I directed a large-scale and ultimately quite successful community organizing project in the extremely recalcitrant, poverty-stricken, and intractable segregated northeastern North Carolina Black belt.

The Terrorist Atmosphere

The multi-county setting was Klan-ridden and night-time terrorism was common: cross burnings, armed motorcades, arson, shootings. Local law enforcement was almost completely dominated by the United Klans of America in some of the counties and at least strongly Klan-influenced in others.

Halifax County, in which our project started and where our central base existed in the town of Enfield, was the toughest. (Klan dues were collected in the Enfield police station!) Thoroughly hated by the segregationists, I was—as I had been for several years in the hard-core South—on several death lists and received many death threats. And, as I had for years, I carried a .38-caliber Special Smith & Wesson, generally in my attache case.

Late one fall night in 1964, I left a Halifax County civil rights rally at Weldon and drove back toward Enfield, twenty-odd miles away. Normally because of the terroristic atmosphere, we traveled two or three vehicles together at night but, on this occasion, I was the only person heading to Enfield.

At this late hour, the road was almost always deserted; two miles out of Weldon, however, a large white car came up behind me—showing no inclination to pass. In the bright moonlight I could see several persons therein and knew these were Klansmen.

Capable and Willing to Shoot

Although there was no question but that they were quite open to shooting me, I was not surprised that they did not. Months before, we had diffused word on the local grapevines that we, and certainly myself, were armed. They knew full well that I was capable to returning fire—and willing indeed to do so.

Hence they settled for futile efforts to force me into a high-speed chase situation—"revving" their motor practically bumper-to-bumper with mine. But I continued to drive sedately, mile after mile. When I finally stopped in Enfield, with my revolver in my hand, they drove past me, obviously frustrated and cursing. But that was *that* evening.

One night not long thereafter, a local civil-rights stalwart, Mrs. Alice Evans of Enfield, opened fire with her double-barreled 12-gauge shotgun, sprinkling several KKKers with birdshot as they endeavored to burn a cross in her driveway and, simultaneously, were approaching her house with buckets of gasoline.

When we arrived after hearing the nearby shots, Mrs. Evans had matters well in hand. The Klansmen were gone—to a hospital, we later learned. We gave the cross to the Smithsonian. These are but two instances in a period of time that includes many direct personal examples.

A half-breed Indian, I grew up in the West, principally in Northern Arizona, and in a hunting family. I had my first rifle when I was seven years old and, by the time I was eighteen, I had owned sixty-seven different firearms.

In my early twenties, as I was embarking on my principal life-long career—that of a social-justice organizer—I was strongly influenced by old-time Wobblies (members of the Industrial Workers of the World) and by organizers of the always radical

> *"Thoroughly hated by the segregationists, I was—as I had been for several years in the hard-core South—on several death lists and received many death threats."*

and militant International Union of Mine, Mill and Smelter Workers (Mine-Mill). Although committed to tactical nonviolence, these men were also, in the quasi-frontier traditions of our section, equally committed to the use of firearms for personal protection in the face of attacks by company thugs.

In the later 1950s, as I became deeply involved in controversial labor unionism in the rough-and-tumble Southwest, I frequently and routinely traveled armed. And this was certainly my approach in such murderous crucibles as Mississippi, eastern North Carolina and other Deep South citadels in the 1960s and in the South/Southwest Side of Chicago in the 1970s. I am convinced that I'm alive today because I traveled with firearms—and that this fact was generally known.

There is no question but that the known existence of pervasive firearms ownership in Southern Black communities prevented much (though not all) massively violent racist retaliation. This was certainly true in the northeastern North Carolina Black belt, and it was true across the South generally.

In a few instances, there were formally organized Black self-defense groups—for example, the Louisiana-based Deacons for Defense. Mostly, though, armed self-defense appeared in innumerable ad-hoc and individual examples.

Beginning in 1961, I taught for several years at Tougaloo College, a private Black school on the outskirts of Jackson, Mississippi, right in the heart of the blood-drenched, closed society. I served as advisor to the Jackson Youth Council of the NAACP [National Association for the Advancement of Colored People] and as chief organizer and strategy-committee chair of the Jackson Movement, which developed in 1962 and 1963 into the most massive grassroots upheaval in Mississippi's history and one of the major efforts in the United States of the 1960s.

> *"Men with knives in their hands came to my home; their intent was quite clear but a vigilant next-door neighbor with a revolver frightened them away."*

Along with many others, I was often beaten and arrested in Mississippi but, as the primary civil-rights organizer in the Jackson area, I was a special target. During the Christmas season of 1962, soon after we had begun active and open Jackson Movement development, night-riders attacked my home on the Tougaloo campus. One of the shots they fired into our house passed just above the crib in which my infant daughter, Maria, slept.

No Law Enforcement Support

If anything, local law officials were strongly supportive of the night-riders; the U.S. Justice Department and the FBI had no interest in enforcing the Constitution in cases such as ours. Those of us on campus at that point then began standing an organized, armed guard at several strategic locations and let this be known to the news media. The attacks ceased for a long time; when they resumed, the guard resumed, and the vigilante moves against Tougaloo subsided.

In North Carolina, in February 1965, I had become so much a target that even the far-from-friendly FBI and Justice Department became somewhat concerned. An agent came to our home in Raleigh and, indicating an informer in a United

Klans "klavern" had reported a conspiracy to bomb our house, concluded by saying the federal government could do nothing about it. Local law enforcement was not reliable.

Fortunately, we lived in the middle of a heavily armed Black community, with neighbors—obviously supportive of my civil-rights work in North Carolina and across the South—who were protective, especially when I was away in the field for long periods of time. We immediately apprised them of the FBI warning, barricaded our windows, and fed our "preparedness" to several grapevines. We were not surprised when the bombing effort never materialized.

How Guns Overcame Death Threats

Years later in Chicago, in the summer of 1970, I was Southside director of the Chicago Commons Association. This private social-service organization was coordinating a large-scale grassroots community organizing project involving mostly Black, Puerto Rican and Chicano people in racially changing sections of the turbulent South/Southwest Side.

White attitudes and practices frequently exemplified a racism often more violent and sanguinary than in the deep South of the previous decade. The Richard Daley machine was openly antagonistic to us and the Chicago police in some (though not all) of the local districts were frequently in league with the racists.

Again, as the prime organizer and the project director, I was a special target. Police harassment and death threats were common, increasing in direct proportion to the growing power and militancy of our grassroots organization.

One afternoon while I was at work, men with knives in their hands came to my home; their intent was quite clear but a vigilant next-door neighbor with a revolver frightened them away. In three days time, I performed more "home improvement" services than the total of everything I've done before or since: barring and boarding windows, chaining doors, changing locks.

But my basic reliance lay in my several firearms. When death threats came over the telephone, I now began telling the callers, somewhat to the discomfiture of my gentle wife, that I had a ticket for them, a pass to permanent eternity via my Marlin .444. No men returned to my home and the death threats tapered off.

In the late fall of 1964, in response to the increasing successes of our northeastern North Carolina Black-belt project, the United Klans of America scheduled a large-scale, state-wide rally in Halifax County—

> *"The number of fatalities would have been, and will be, much smaller if organizers and their grassroots groups had been, and are, sensibly armed for self-defense."*

very close to a Black residential area. Not surprisingly, posters advertising the affair were conspicuously displayed, among other places, in most law-enforcement offices in the county.

We knew the Justice Department and the FBI would be no help and, early on, we petitioned the state government for state police. This request was not even acknowledged and, with the approval of our local grassroots leaders, I went to Governor Terry Sanford's office at Raleigh. He declined to meet with me directly but did send in his chief aide.

"In the South/Southwest Side of Chicago, the known armed state of grassroots people deterred both conventional criminal elements and white racist gangs."

I was very blunt. I told this person in a cold and angry fashion that either the state would send a large contingent of police into Halifax County a day before the Klan rally, to remain through the affair and at least a day afterward—or our people, armed to the hilt, would have no hesitation about utilizing armed self-defense in the event of Klan violence.

Visibly shaken, the aide left me and conferred with Sanford. He returned quickly to promise the state police. The day before the rally, many state police cars rolled into Halifax County and remained there two days after the event. For our part, we actively and successfully encouraged tactical nonviolence but, of course, we and our constituency continued to keep arms handy. There was no violence except a brutal fight among several Klansmen.

For months afterward, the United Klans continued to hold rallies near Black neighborhoods in Halifax County, and we continued the same effective formula—pressuring the state (later under Governor Dan K. Moore), with our people armed and watchful. Eventually, the Klan rallies ceased in northeastern North Carolina and the local Klans faded.

In the South/Southwest Side of Chicago, the known armed state of grassroots people deterred both conventional criminal elements and white racist gangs. In our far-flung community organizational project (almost 300 multi-issue block clubs and related groups organized by the summer of 1973), in a setting where honest police were tired and overworked and the others downright hostile, we set up public citizen "watch-dog" patrols.

Although generally unarmed, these had—regardless of police attitudes one way or the other—primary backup from a network of armed citizenry in the neighborhoods with which the patrols maintained close and constant communication through citizens' band radios, volunteer dispatchers and telephone linkups.

Effective Crime Deterrent

The effect of this well-known campaign in reducing crime and deterring white racial violence was substantial. Before long, frightened politicians forced through increasingly responsible and egalitarian law-enforcement practices. But the patrols and the vigilance of armed neighborhoods continued.

I am not taking the position that there would have been no fatalities in social-justice organizing, and that none will occur, if organizers and constituents were and are armed. A close friend and colleague, Medgar W. Evers, was shot to death in front of his home one night in June 1963, in the Jackson Movement campaign. But the heavily armed—and known to be heavily armed—Medgar lived for nine effective years after he became Mississippi NAACP field secretary—about nine years longer than most friends and enemies felt he would.

A few days after his death, I was seriously injured—almost killed—in a rigged auto wreck. But I had survived to that point, weathered the injuries, and have endured pretty effectively ever since. And all of our community organizational campaigns over the years have been essentially quite successful.

I am stating categorically that the number of fatalities would have been, and will be, much smaller if organizers and their grassroots groups had been, and are, sensibly armed for self-defense. And the success of the campaigns and the projects themselves have been and will be greatly enhanced.

Handguns Are an Effective Form of Self-Defense for Women

by Paxton Quigley

About the author: *Paxton Quigley teaches women how to use handguns and other self-defense methods. Quigley, president of Personal Protection Strategies in Beverly Hills, California, is the author of* Armed and Female, *from which this viewpoint is excerpted.*

If you are over the age of twelve and female, be prepared to be criminally assaulted some time in your life. If you are about thirty years old now, there's a fifty-fifty chance of your being raped, robbed, or attacked.

The odds are reduced as you get older, and are different in various parts of our country. Chances of being raped at any age in New York are one in eight; Los Angeles, one in seven; Atlanta, one in five; Detroit, one in four. Across our nation, one out of every four families will be victims of serious crimes like burglary, rape, robbery, or murder. Our cities are citadels of crime. And there is no such thing anymore as safe rural America.

Criminal Statistics

The statistics are more than frightening. Only four criminals go to prison for every hundred reported crimes. And the FBI estimates that 60 percent of all crimes are not even reported.

For every hundred prisoners with life sentences, twenty-five are freed before their third year; forty-two are out by their seventh year; and people acquitted of murder by reason of insanity spend an average of only five hundred days in mental hospitals before being released.

The nation's prison population increases at a breathtaking pace each year. There are now more than 550,000 behind bars. Nearly six out of ten have been there before, and more than half have been there four or more times.

If you are concerned, fearful about your safety, you are not alone. A Gallup poll finds that six out of ten women in this country are afraid to walk at night in their own neighborhoods.

America is experiencing an epidemic of crime and criminal violence with no immediate or long-range cure in sight. Many people continue to ignore the far-reaching threat and deny their vulnerability, betting that violence will not reach them. For some, it is not truth but hope that matters most.

If crime happens, however, know beforehand that in almost every instance no one will be there to protect you but yourself. Police will not be there unless officers are accidentally nearby, and witnesses can be counted on not to interfere.

A Case of Rape

One example among thousands occurred on the Thursday evening of July 22, 1988. A woman was severely beaten and raped in the parking lot of her apartment in suburban Los Angeles. Not an uncommon event these days certainly, but the story illustrates how the war on women has escalated, and how the victimized are beginning to try to change the odds.

Suzanne MacDonnell is a young attractive professional woman. She works out four times a week and takes a karate class on Tuesday nights. On July 22 Suzanne was walking from her car to her apartment when she heard moaning coming from the garbage bin in her parking lot.

"It was dark, and at first I couldn't see who was there." She approached the container cautiously and suddenly noticed a woman lying on the ground, crying and pleading for help. "Please, someone, help me, I've been raped, I'm hurt," the woman's voice whispered.

Instinctively Suzanne went to the woman's aid, kneeling beside her, trying to comfort her as best she could. Then the woman smashed her in the face.

"I saw a flash and felt a burning sensation across my nose and eyes. I fell backward and my head hit the pavement. It wasn't a woman at all, it was a man who had set a trap. He hit me again." Her eyes blazing with anger, she continued, "I must have been out for a few seconds, because the next thing I remember was my skirt over my head and his hand pushed against my blood-filled mouth. I never really got a good look at his face."

"Chances of being raped at any age in New York are one in eight; Los Angeles, one in seven; Atlanta, one in five; Detroit, one in four."

All Suzanne remembers is that the man wore a red dress and had long blond hair, probably a wig. He raped her and then dumped her in the trash bin. In the darkness, Suzanne cried for help. No one came. She didn't have the strength to lift the lid, so she waited, and moaned for help with the little energy she had. Found almost unconscious six hours later, Suzanne was taken to the hospital and treated for injuries that would heal in time. Treatment of her anger, fear, and distrust of men is ongoing, and to counter her fright and to feel safe again, Suzanne now owns a gun.

"What happened to me is bizarre, there is no question about that. But even though it is not an ordinary kind of crime, it made me extremely aware of my vulnerability. If this could happen to me—to me!—then I have to be on guard about the everyday dangers that we all know exist but ignore as happening to someone else. Now I fasten my seat belt in the car, replace batteries in my smoke detectors, have a fire extinguisher in the kitchen, and carry a handgun. I may be dumb, but I'm not stupid."

Facing an Intruder

Another incident that was told to me involved two young women who avoided assault and rape. Meg Stoddard and Gretchen Winters met during their first week of residency at a hospital in Boston. They quickly discovered many coincidences: both were born in neighboring states in the Northwest, were raised on a farm, played tennis and golf, and each attended a medical school that the other had been rejected from. And so they decided to share a small flat in the Brookline section of Boston.

One cold snowy night in December, after a long and arduous shift at the hospital, they decided to call out for a pizza delivery and spend the evening watching television. As Gretchen was putting on her "couch potato" clothes, the outer door bell rang. Meg buzzed the front door and yelled to Gretchen that the pizza had arrived.

The young delivery man greeted Meg with an affable smile, but as she paid him something about him disturbed her, and she deliberately kept him from entering the apartment. When she started to shut the door, he suddenly seized her arm and pressed a six-inch hunting knife to her throat. He slapped his hand over her mouth when she attempted to cry out. He forced her into the apartment and kicked the door shut. In the kitchen, Gretchen was listening to the seven

"Gretchen reached for the revolver, stood up, and said firmly, 'Let go of her.' The man swirled and faced a .357 Magnum revolver aimed at the center of his chest."

o'clock news and putting the final touches on the salad. Impatient for the pizza, she walked into the living room and saw the attacker holding Meg at knife point. She screamed.

"Shut up, bitch. You want me to cut her throat?" he growled. "Sit down."

The crazed look in his eyes warned Gretchen that he was on drugs and clearly capable of hurting them. She purposely sat down on the left side of the sofa. The attacker rambled on, threatening to have "real fun" with both of them. Meg and Gretchen looked at each other for a moment, aware that a woman in the neighborhood had recently been murdered under similar circumstances.

Breathing hard, the man grabbed Meg's long blond hair and sliced open her nightgown. Gretchen nervously slid her shaking hand toward a hollowed-out book that sat on an end table. The book contained her loaded gun.

"Stop, you bitch!" She froze. "Watch what I'm doing because you're next," he said, laughing.

Gripping Meg's hair with his left hand, he pulled the knife away from her throat and began unzipping his fly. He turned away briefly, and Gretchen reached for the revolver, stood up, and said firmly, "Let go of her." The man swirled and faced a .357 Magnum revolver aimed at the center of his chest.

"He was absolutely paralyzed," Gretchen recounted, "just like a deer caught in the beam of headlights. Meg was screaming and crying as I cursed at him to drop the knife. He obeyed and I kicked the knife out of his reach. He pleaded with me not to shoot him."

She ordered the assailant to lie flat on his stomach with his hands behind his back and told Meg to call the police. As she stood over him, he shouted obscenities at her and an odd thought struck her. If she had to shoot him, would she doctor him?

Although it seemed like an eternity, eight minutes later the police arrived, took the attacker away, spent some time taking a report, and left.

Meg and Gretchen's story was told to me years after it occurred. Each is now married and living in separate cities, but both women own handguns and, needless to say, they hope they will never have to use them. They lived through a nightmare, but Gretchen is proud that she was able to defend her friend and herself against an incident that she never thought would happen.

Women, Guns, and Self-Defense

There are many other women who, like Meg and Gretchen, are armed. They represent a growing movement. In fact, it is a quiet drive that began in the late 1960s, with more women living alone and working outside of the home and having more disposable income. In turn, women have become accessible targets, not only for rape, but for robbery and assault, and the need for personal protection has become more acute.

"Between 1983 and 1986 gun ownership among women jumped 53 percent, to more than twelve million."

The inner cities have always been rife with violence, and black women were one of the first groups of females to purchase guns for self-defense. As crime extended to the suburbs and small towns, white middle-class women began owning guns, and now a large cross section of women are learning to shoot.

No one really knows how many women own guns, or have access to guns and know how to shoot them. According to a 1988 Gallup poll commissioned by gun maker Smith & Wesson, between 1983 and 1986 gun ownership among women jumped 53 percent, to more than twelve million. The poll also found that the number of women who were considering buying a weapon quadrupled to nearly two million. And a 1986 survey done by the Department of Sociology at Louisiana State University finds a handgun in 40 percent of Louisiana *female-headed households*. The National Research Opinion Center claims that 44 percent of adult women own or have access to firearms. That's forty-two million, and of those, Dr. Paul H. Blackman, research coordinator for the Institute for Legislative Action of the National Rifle Association, estimates that twenty-two million own their own guns.

More than 50 percent of the 104,000 women who responded to a March 1987 *Ladies' Home Journal* survey say they have guns in their homes, with 40 percent of them reporting that the firearms are owned strictly for protection. Forty-two percent of the respondents also report that they have been victims of crime when they answered the magazine's special survey, "The Private Life of the American Woman."

That same month *McCall's* did a similar but less extensive survey, with one-third of the respondents saying they or a member of their household owned a handgun for protection. Of those, more than two-thirds said they would use the weapons to defend themselves at home. . . .

Although a large percentage of violent crimes do occur in the streets and, as you will read, some women *carry* guns out of fear of being attacked in the streets, I do not recommend it—not unless you have acquired a license to *carry* a concealed weapon in those states that require it, are very well trained in street defense, and practice frequently on a combat course. There are too many women (as well as

> *"To my surprise, I learned that some of my associates . . . have guns and practice shooting regularly."*

men) who carry guns without knowing combat shooting. Competency with a gun is extremely important and especially crucial in a public place where bystanders may be present.

A woman who carries a gun on the street should not think that its mere possession will dispel the dangers that made her buy it. She may feel less fearful and more confident, but just because she carries a gun doesn't mean it is safer for her to walk the streets.

Discreetness and Competence

If a woman chooses to carry a gun after being thoroughly trained in shooting, she should carry it discreetly, neither displaying nor mentioning it to friends or associates. As gun-defense expert Massad Ayoob says in his book *In the Gravest Extreme*, "The license to carry concealed deadly weapons in public is not a right but a privilege. To be worthy of this privilege, one must be both discreet and competent with the weapon."

Owning a weapon is a private matter; before beginning research on this subject, I thought I knew no women gun owners. To my surprise, I learned that some of my associates and acquaintances have guns and practice shooting regularly.

One such woman was Judy Miller, who was seated next to me at a university alumni luncheon. After the introductions and the fund-raising appeals were over, we naturally talked to each other. It's funny that after a few minutes you can learn so much about a person. Judy is divorced, lives with her sixteen-year-old son, and is a professor of business management at a Chicago-area university. When I told her I was doing research on women and crime, this mild-mannered, very attractive, slight woman who looks far younger than her forty-nine years astounded me by saying that she owned not one but two guns, and has for the last twenty years.

She then confided in me that she keeps a loaded pistol by her bedside and always carries a gun in her briefcase. Moreover, she will take out the pistol and hold it if she walks alone in a subterranean parking lot or unaccompanied at night on a deserted street. She knows it is against the law in Chicago to carry a concealed weapon without a permit, but she chooses to disobey the law. She spoke seriously and with a firmness and confidence I have not heard from many women.

For Judy, the immediate concern in everyday existence is being prepared to face a city that is filled with so much danger. Questioned whether she is overly distrustful, she replied that she feels neither paranoid nor especially fearful.

Rather, at an early age Judy developed a philosophy of what she calls self-sufficiency. A very thoughtful woman, Judy explained that, when she was young, her father always enjoyed going to the lake and walking on the beach. Then one day he was threatened by a couple of kids, and some months later he was mugged. The police came to the house to ask her father questions about his assailants, but the family never knew if the boys were apprehended. Although her father continued walking on the beach, he became suspicious and untrusting. "He really didn't enjoy himself anymore, because he became fearful. From then on, when my sister and I wanted to go to the beach, he insisted that he come with us. I grew angrier and angrier at what they had done to him."

> *"I am willing to use my weapon, ready to kill, rather than be a victim."*

Self-Sufficiency from Within

It was in her early twenties that Judy worked through the concept of protecting herself and taking charge of her life, and not relying on anyone else, like the police, a boyfriend, or friends of the family. Her solution was a gun. When she was twenty-five, she went by herself to a gun range, tried a number of different handguns, and learned how to shoot. To this day, Judy practices once or twice a month.

168

"For me, the concept of self-sufficiency comes from within, and physically protecting myself is part of it," Judy explained. "Am I willing to commit myself totally? Yes—a hundred percent, absolutely. In other words, the issue of carrying a weapon, be it a knitting needle, a hat pin, a concealed knife, a gun, or even a hand grenade—I would rather go to jail than have to see my loved ones, including myself, killed or injured unnecessarily."

Judy does not like carrying a gun illegally, but it is almost impossible to obtain a permit to carry a concealed weapon of any kind in Chicago. She, like so many other women I spoke to, realizes that the police cannot be expected to protect everyone. "So, you use your head and work out the problem of doing something that's illegal," she quietly said. "Then you work through your head, as well as your stomach, the fact that you may hurt or kill someone. I have worked this all through. I am willing to use my weapon, ready to kill, rather than be a victim. There is no argument. This is how I feel, and I have felt this way for more than twenty years. I don't care what anybody thinks of it."

> *"The threat of assault against women continues at an alarming rate . . . and women are arming themselves in self-defense."*

Unlike many other women, Judy has never been victimized, although she has been in a situation where she was prepared to use her gun. It was ten o'clock one cold winter evening in 1984, when she and her son, Mark, were watching television in the living room and heard someone trying to force open a locked kitchen window. The window wouldn't open, and the person quickly moved to pry open the lock on a side door.

Judy and her son didn't say a word to each other; they each knew what to do. Judy went to get her gun, Mark to call the police. Judy stood on the side of the door and yelled, "Go away, don't try and get in." They didn't hear a thing, but whoever it was went away. The police arrived twenty minutes later, asked them some questions, and left, presumably to scour the neighborhood.

Confident and Ready

Would she have shot? She quickly answered yes. "The gun was loaded, but I didn't say that I had a loaded gun, for the simple reason that I'm afraid of the person who is crazy enough to take that as a challenge. I tried to sound very forceful and I felt confident, but my adrenaline was pumping a mile a minute!" She laughed for an instant to ease the tension, but then was serious again. "He wasn't going to hurt us. I don't intend for that to ever happen," she said adamantly.

Judy cannot understand why it has taken women so long to turn to guns for self-defense.

"Speculation tells me that the classic reason is that too many women think that an assault would not happen to them. They're dependent upon a man to lead them or to protect them, or they haven't thought through the risks thoroughly," she said. "There are a lot of women who think that, if they don't think about the possibility of being attacked, they won't be attacked. That's statistically ignorant, and I believe that attitude is changing."

"Again," Judy reiterated to me, "the base issue goes back to self-worth, and whether or not you're totally committed to leading a good strong life and taking charge of your own destiny."

Is a gun a good deterrent against a crime? Judy thinks so. Deterrence refers not to the actual firing of guns in stopping crimes, but to the nonoccurrence of crimes when those who contemplate them are deterred by the potential victims' actual or assumed possession of arms.

A Proven Deterrent

The newest statistics indicate that a gun is a formidable deterrent. Gary Kleck, a distinguished scholar of criminology and a professor at Florida State University, produced a study based exclusively on surveys by anti-gun groups that concluded that guns are used in defending against 645,000 crimes every year, with only one-third of the guns actually being fired.

Don B. Kates, Jr., a leading constitutional attorney and criminologist, studied 150 cases of armed resistance by citizens against criminal attackers. His findings are similar to Kleck's overall results. Criminals were captured or driven off without a shot being fired in 50 percent of the instances, and wounded or killed in 43 percent of the instances. In the remaining 7 percent, assailants, wounded or not, escaped. . . .

After talking with these women, as well as many others, I realized that there is a quiet but definite trend among women to shoulder the responsibility for their personal safety. They feel that they have been made fools of by the experts who advise the use of "personal weapons" for protection against vicious assault and are buying guns in astounding numbers.

Many women are open about their gun ownership, and more than willing to discuss with anyone their reasons for having a gun and their methods of using it should the time come. Yet many women gun owners consider the subject intimate and personal, and refuse to talk about it or be associated with any trend or gun culture. But the evidence is inescapable: the threat of assault against women continues at an alarming rate; law enforcement is virtually incapable of preventing such assault; and women are arming themselves in self-defense.

Gun Ownership Is Not an Effective Means of Self-Defense

by Arthur L. Kellerman and Donald T. Reay

About the authors: Arthur L. Kellerman is an associate professor of medicine at the University of Tennessee in Memphis. Donald T. Reay is chief medical examiner at the King County Medical Examiner's Office in Seattle, Washington.

There are approximately 120 million guns in private hands in the United States. About half of all the homes in America contain one or more firearms. Although most persons who own guns keep them primarily for hunting or sport, three-quarters of gun owners keep them at least partly for protection. One-fifth of gun owners identify "self-defense at home" as their most important reason for having a gun.

Risks of Guns in the Home

Keeping firearms in the home carries associated risks. These include injury or death from unintentional gunshot wounds, homicide during domestic quarrels, and the ready availability of an immediate, highly lethal means of suicide. To understand better the epidemiology of firearm-related deaths in the home, we studied all the gunshot deaths that occurred in King County, Washington, between 1978 and 1983. We were especially interested in characterizing the gunshot deaths that occurred in the residence where the firearm involved was kept.

King County, Washington (1980 census population 1,270,000), contains the cities of Seattle (population 494,000) and Bellevue (population 74,000), as well as a number of smaller communities. The county population is predominantly urban (92 percent) and white (88.4 percent), with smaller black (4.4 percent) and Asian (4.3 percent) minorities. All violent deaths in King County are investigated by the office of the medical examiner.

We systematically reviewed the medical examiner's case files to identify every firearm-related death that occurred in the county between January 1, 1978, and

Adapted from Arthur L. Kellerman and Donald T. Reay, "Protection or Peril? An Analysis of Firearm-Related Deaths in the Home." The complete article, with references and graphics, can be found in *The New England Journal of Medicine* 314 (24): 1557-60. Reprinted with permission.

December 31, 1983. In addition to general demographic information, we obtained specific data regarding the manner of death, the scene of the incident, the circumstances, the relationship of the suspect to the victim, the type of firearm involved, and the blood alcohol level of the victim at the time of autopsy. When records were incomplete, corroborating information was obtained from police case files and direct interviews with the original investigating officers.

Types of Gunshot Deaths

Gunshot deaths involving the intentional shooting of one person by another were considered homicides. Self-protection homicides were considered "justifiable" if they involved the killing of a felon during the commission of a crime; they were considered "self-defense" if that was the determination of the investigating police department and the King County prosecutor's office. All homicides resulting in criminal charges and all unsolved homicides were considered criminal homicides.

The circumstances of all homicides were also noted. Homicides committed in association with another felony (e.g., robbery) were identified as "felony homicides." Homicides committed during an argument or fight were considered "altercation homicides." Those committed in the absence of either set of circumstances were termed "primary homicides."

Deaths from self-inflicted gunshot wounds were considered suicides if they were officially certified as such by Donald T. Reay, who is the medical examiner. Unintentional self-inflicted gunshot wounds were classified as accidental. Although the medical examiner's office considers deaths involving the unintentional shooting of one person by another as homicide, we classified these deaths as accidental for our analysis. Deaths in which there was uncertainty about the circumstances or motive were identified as "undetermined."

Over the six-year interval, the medical examiner's office investigated 743 deaths from firearms (9.75 deaths per 100,000 person-years). This total represented 22.7 percent of all violent deaths occurring in King County during this period, excluding

> *"Although most persons who own guns keep them primarily for hunting or sport, three-quarters of gun owners keep them at least partly for protection."*

traffic deaths. Firearms were involved in 45 percent of all homicides and 49 percent of all suicides in King County—proportions lower than the national averages of 61 and 57 percent, respectively. Guns accounted for less than 1 percent of accidental deaths and 5.7 percent of deaths in which the circumstances were undetermined.

Of the 743 deaths from firearms noted during this six-year period, 473 (63.7 percent) occurred inside a house or dwelling, and 398 (53.6 percent) occurred in the home where the firearm involved was kept. Of these 398 firearm deaths,

333 (83.7 percent) were suicides, 50 (12.6 percent) were homicides, and 12 (3 percent) were accidental gunshot deaths. The precise manner of death was undetermined in three additional cases involving self-inflicted gunshot wounds.

> *"For every time a gun in the home was involved in a 'self-protection' homicide, we noted 1.3 accidental gunshot deaths, 4.6 criminal homicides, and 37 firearm-related suicides."*

In 265 of the 333 cases of suicide (80 percent), the victim was male. A blood ethanol test was positive in 86 of the 245 suicide victims tested (35 percent) and showed a blood ethanol level of 100 mg per deciliter or more in 60 of the 245 (24.5 percent). Sixty-eight percent of the suicides involved handguns. In eight cases, the medical examiner's case files specifically noted that the victim had acquired the firearm within two days of committing suicide.

The victim was male in 30 of the 50 homicide deaths (60 percent). A blood ethanol test was positive in 27 of 47 homicide victims tested (5 percent) and showed a blood ethanol level of 100 mg per deciliter or more in 10 of the victims (21 percent). Handguns were involved in 34 of these deaths (68 percent).

Forty-two homicides (84 percent) occurred during altercations in the home, including seven that were later determined to have been committed in self-defense. Two additional homicides involving the shooting of burglars by residents were considered legally "justifiable." Forty-one homicides (82 percent) resulted in criminal charges against a resident of the house or apartment in which the shooting occurred.

Four of the 12 accidental deaths involved self-inflicted gunshot wounds. All 12 victims were male. A blood ethanol test in the victims was positive in only two cases. Eleven of these accidental deaths involved handguns.

Excluding firearm-related suicides, 65 deaths occurred in the house where the firearm involved was kept. In two of these cases, the victim was a stranger to the persons living in the house, whereas in 24 cases (37 percent), the victim was an acquaintance or friend. Thirty-six gunshot victims (55 percent) were residents of the house in which the shooting occurred, including 29 who were victims of homicide. Residents were most often shot by a relative or family member (11 cases), their spouse (9 cases), a roommate (6 cases), or themselves (7 cases).

Household Members at Risk

Guns kept in King County homes were involved in the deaths of friends or acquaintances 12 times as often as in those of strangers. Even after the exclusion of firearm-related suicides, guns kept at home were involved in the death of a member of the household 18 times more often than in the death of a stranger. For every time a gun in the home was involved in a "self-protection" homicide, we noted 1.3 accidental gunshot deaths, 4.6 criminal homicides, and

37 firearm-related suicides.

We found the home to be a common location for deaths related to firearms. During our study period, almost two-thirds of the gunshot deaths in King County occurred inside a house or other dwelling. Over half these incidents occurred in the residence in which the firearm involved was kept. Few involved acts of self-protection.

Less than 2 percent of homicides nationally are considered legally justifiable. Although justifiable homicides do not include homicides committed in self-defense, the combined total of both in our study was still less than one-fourth the number of criminal homicides involving a gun kept in the home. A majority of these homicide victims were residents of the house or apartment in which the shooting occurred.

Over 80 percent of the homicides noted during our study occurred during arguments or altercations. Susan Baker has observed that in cases of assault, people tend to reach for the most lethal weapon readily available. Easy access to firearms may therefore be particularly dangerous in households prone to domestic violence.

Guns and Suicide

We found the most common form of firearm-related death in the home to be suicide. Although previous authors have correlated regional suicide rates with estimates of firearm density, the precise nature of the relation between gun availability and suicide is unclear. The choice of a gun for suicide may involve a combination of impulse and the close proximity of a firearm. Conversely, the choice of a gun may simply reflect the seriousness of a person's intent. If suicides involving firearms are more a product of the easy availability of weapons than of the strength of intent, limiting access

> *"It may reasonably be asked whether keeping firearms in the home increases a family's protection or places it in greater danger."*

to firearms will decrease the rate of suicide. If the opposite is true, suicidal persons will only work harder to acquire a gun or kill themselves by other means. For example, although the elimination of toxic coal gas from domestic gas supplies in Great Britain resulted in a decrease in successful suicide attempts, a similar measure in Australia was associated with increasing rates of suicide by other methods.

A study of 30 survivors of attempts to commit suicide with firearms suggests that many of them acted on impulse. Whether this observation applies to non-survivors as well is unknown. The recent acquisition of a firearm was noted in only eight of our cases, and we do not know how long before death any suicide victim planned his or her attempt. However, given the high case-fatality rate associated with suicide attempts involving firearms, it seems likely that easy access to guns increases the probability that an impulsive suicide attempt will end in death.

Detectable concentrations of ethanol were found in the blood of a substantial proportion of the victims tested. This suggests that ethanol may be an independent risk factor for gunshot death. Although this hypothesis is compatible with the known behavioral and physiologic effect of ethanol, the strength of this association remains to be defined.

There are many reasons that people own guns. Unfortunately, our case files rarely identified why the firearm involved had been kept in the home. We cannot determine, therefore, whether guns kept for protection were more or less hazardous than guns kept for other reasons.

Self-Defense Handguns Outnumber Long Guns

We did note, however, that handguns were far more commonly involved in gunshot deaths in the home than shotguns or rifles. The single most common reason for keeping firearms given by owners of handguns, unlike owners of shoulder weapons, is "self-defense at home." About 45 percent of the gun-owning households nationally own handguns. If the proportion of homes containing handguns in King County is similar to this national average, then these weapons were 2.6 times more likely to be involved in a gunshot death in the home than were shotguns and rifles combined.

Several limitations of this type of analysis must be recognized. Our observations are based on a largely urban population and may not be applicable to more rural communities. Also, various rates of suicide and homicide have been noted in other metropolitan counties. These differences may reflect variations in social and demographic composition as well as different patterns of firearm ownership.

Mortality studies such as ours do not include cases in which burglars or intruders are wounded or frightened away by the use or display of a firearm. Cases in which would-be intruders may have purposely avoided a house known to be armed are also not identified. We did not report the total number or extent of nonlethal firearm injuries involving guns kept in the home. A complete determination of firearm risks versus benefits would require that these figures be known.

The home can be a dangerous place. We noted 43 suicides, criminal homicides, or accidental gunshot deaths involving a gun kept in the home for every case of homicide for self-protection. In the light of these findings, it may reasonably be asked whether keeping firearms in the home increases a family's protection or places it in greater danger. Given the unique status of firearms in American society and the national toll of gunshot deaths, it is imperative that we answer this question.

The Danger Posed by Handguns Outweighs Their Effectiveness

by Andrew Jay McClurg

About the author: *Andrew Jay McClurg is an associate professor at the School of Law at the University of Arkansas in Little Rock.*

Handguns are perhaps the paradigmatic case of a product unreasonably dangerous per se. As discussed below, they present tremendous risk and have low utility. Accordingly, manufacturers should be strictly liable for handgun inflicted deaths and injuries.

The Risk of Handguns

The risk to human life presented by handguns in terms of both the severity of the risk and the probability of it occurring is almost unparalleled. Of all the millions of products marketed in the United States, only automobiles surpass handguns as a cause of unnatural death. Handguns kill 22,000 people each year and injure probably another 100,000.

A telling contrast in how our society treats dangerous products can be found by examining the case of lawn darts. In 1990, the Consumer Product Safety Commission banned the sale of lawn darts based upon a finding that they "present an unreasonable risk of injury." The commission arrived at this conclusion by applying a risk-utility analysis quite similar to that which would be used to determine whether lawn darts are an unreasonably dangerous product for purposes of strict products liability.

The commission described the degree and nature of the risk as being the "puncture of the skulls of children caused by lawn darts being used by children," but mentioned that the total ban on lawn darts would also eliminate other types of puncture wounds, lacerations, fractures, and other injuries associated with the use of lawn darts. With respect to the probability of the risk occurring, the commission estimated that 670 lawn dart injuries occurred each year and

Excerpted from Andrew J. McClurg, "Handguns as Products Unreasonably Dangerous Per Se," *University of Arkansas at Little Rock Law Journal* 13 (Summer 1991): 599-619. Reprinted with permission.

found that three children had been killed by lawn darts since 1970.

This risk was seen as outweighing the utility of lawn darts: *i.e.*, the "recreational enjoyment" they provided to the more than one million consumers who purchased lawn darts annually. This conclusion was bolstered by the commission's determination that substitute recreational enjoyment can be obtained from other products.

> *"The utility of handguns is outweighed by the tremendous risk they pose to society."*

The commission did not specify any particular type of recreational product which would replace the enjoyment of launching steel tipped missiles across the yard into a hoop. Apparently, the commission deemed recreational products to be fungible. Horseshoes, for example, might be deemed an adequate substitute for lawn darts.

A child being killed or seriously injured by a lawn dart puncturing his skull is a scene almost too horrible to imagine, but certainly no more horrible than a bullet penetrating the child's skull. Compare the three children killed in twenty years by lawn darts to the 22,000 annual handgun deaths, or even to the 365 children under age fifteen killed in accidental handgun shootings every year. Compare the 670 lawn dart injuries that the commission estimated were occurring each year to the estimated 100,000 yearly handgun injuries. Then ask: what is wrong with this picture?

The Utility of Handguns

The answer lies in the exaggerated utility attached to handguns. Our culture glorifies guns. They are elevated to the level of God by one gun magazine, whose motto is: "For Americans who believe that God, Guns & Guts Made US Great." Guns are symbols of manhood, machismo, and power. They are inextricably identified with the courage, ruggedness, and spirit of the American frontiersman.

Handguns have a cult of personality all their own. How many times have we seen the movie or television actor tenderly pat his shoulder holster while making some reference to "my friend here" or "this little baby"? Handguns are likely to be described by adjectives more appropriate for a thoroughbred racing horse—sleek, pretty, awesome—than an ugly instrument designed principally for the purpose of killing human beings.

Our romantic attraction to guns has honorable enough roots. There was a time in this country when guns were a virtual necessity, fulfilling vital needs for early pioneers and settlers. They put food on the table and protected against attack from hostile natives. But that was at least a century ago.

The utility of handguns in modern society is twofold: (1) they have recreational utility in the form of hunting and target shooting; and (2) they have the utility of self-protection. While I do not attach as much importance to these utilities as do gun owners, I do not reject them as insignificant. I appreciate that many people get substantial enjoyment from hunting and target shooting, and also that many people believe handguns afford them effective protection from criminals.

However, the utility of handguns is outweighed by the tremendous risk they pose to society, particularly in light of the availability of a substitute product which serves the same needs as a handgun: *i.e.,* a long gun. It is curious that all of the debate about risk-utility balancing with respect to handguns has ignored this obvious and critical element of the equation. The availability of rifles and shotguns substantially dilutes the utility of handguns. Long guns have almost the same utility and present less risk because they are not easily concealable.

Long Guns Versus Handguns

As to recreational use, long guns are obviously superior in their utility for hunting because of their greater accuracy. This would seem to make them superior for target shooting as well. Some sportsmen might insist that they are fond of shooting at targets with rifles *and* pistols, but this is where risk-utility balancing comes into play. The marginal utility in the smidgeon of extra pleasure derived from plinking a target with a handgun as opposed to a rifle is outweighed by the greatly increased risk of handguns.

With regard to self-defense, it must first be noted that our faith in guns as insurers of personal security is vastly out of proportion to reality. Statistics show that the bumper sticker tribute to guns that "they can take my gun when they pry it from my cold, dead fingers" is likely to be self-fulfilling. The fact is that one who resists a criminal is eight times more likely to be killed than one who does not. It is more probable that the handgun kept in the bedside table drawer for self-protection will be used to shoot a relative or acquaintance than to successfully repel a criminal. More probable still is that the handgun will be stolen by a burglar, increasing the risk that it will be used against an innocent person.

However, accepting that in some cases a gun offers an effective means of defending one's self, long guns fulfill that purpose almost as well. If a homeowner feels more secure with a loaded gun in the house while he sleeps, he should not feel any less secure because the weapon is a long gun rather than a handgun. Indeed, I would think that confronting a burglar with a 12-gauge shotgun would be much more intimidating and effective than a handgun. A large, visible weapon is

> *"It is more probable that the handgun kept for self-protection will be used to shoot a relative or acquaintance than to successfully repel a criminal."*

more likely to deter the criminal, thereby eliminating the need to actually use deadly force. If the use of such force becomes necessary, accuracy counts. However, most people are not expert pistol shooters, particularly in a dark house when they are under tremendous stress. With a shotgun, simply firing the weapon in the general direction of the target offers a reasonable chance of making contact. Moreover, shotgun pellets which miss their target are not likely to penetrate the walls of a dwelling and kill innocent persons outside. That possibility exists as to missed shots fired from a high-powered handgun.

I concede there are situations where a long gun, because it is not small and easily concealable, will not be as effective as a handgun in defending persons or property. A liquor store owner, for example, may have a hard time withdrawing a long gun from beneath the counter to defend against a robber. However, this is another instance where risk-utility balancing dictates that long guns be viewed as an adequate substitute product. This marginal degree of enhanced utility of handguns attributable to their small size is outweighed by the vastly greater risk presented by handguns because of the same feature.

Unreasonably Dangerous Handguns

It is the easy concealability of handguns which makes them unreasonably dangerous as compared with long guns. Roughly seventy-five percent of all firearm homicides are committed with handguns. Handguns are what our children are carrying to school, not hunting rifles. Handguns are what armed robbers use to gun down store clerks. Handguns are what felons use to shoot police officers during routine traffic stops. While rifles and shotguns are very dangerous, they are not unreasonably dangerous because their greater utility for most legitimate purposes outweighs their reduced risk as compared to handguns.

To appreciate the distorted way society has until now applied risk-utility balancing to handguns, it might be helpful to divorce the analysis from a product so steeped in tradition and adoration and cast it upon a different, hypothetical product. Suppose a manufacturer marketed a drug as a remedy for morning sickness.

> *"I oppose the policy in this country which favors ready access to this weapon of destruction which . . . inflicts untold misery and suffering upon many."*

I assume many women who are or have been pregnant would attest that such a drug has significant social utility. But suppose this particular drug, while effective for combatting morning sickness, killed 22,000 women each year and seriously injured 100,000 others. Assume also that the manufacturer was aware of this risk at the time it manufactured and marketed the drug. Finally, assume that substitute products existed which were almost as effective in relieving morning sickness. There can be no doubt that: (a) the Food and Drug Administration would order the drug removed from the market; and (b) the manufacturer would be held strictly liable for manufacturing a defective product.

Some may argue that handguns have more social utility than a morning sickness drug and, therefore, the comparison is not an apt one. I disagree, but even accepting that as true, surely even the most ardent handgun enthusiast could imagine *some* drug with greater social utility than a handgun. Yet I submit that *any* drug—even a miracle cure for cancer or AIDS—which killed 22,000 people each year and seriously injured 100,000 others would be considered unreasonably dangerous, particularly if a substitute medication existed which had almost the same utility. This suggests that handguns have avoided being branded as unreasonably dangerous products not so much as a result of the faithful application of modern tort principles but because of a warped social policy. . . .

Far Too Many Handguns

My agenda regarding handguns is not a hidden one. I oppose the policy in this country which favors ready access to this weapon of destruction which, while it may provide solace and recreation for many people, inflicts untold misery and suffering upon many others. Consequently, it is true that I would not be disappointed if all the handgun companies suddenly decided to devote their resources to making kinder, gentler products.

However, shutting down the nation's handgun industry is not the inevitable consequence of imposing strict liability upon handgun manufacturers. Strict liability would not mean that manufacturers are precluded from making handguns. It would mean only that they, like all other manufacturers of unreasonably dangerous products, must bear the cost of injuries their products cause. The result would be that the price of handguns would rise

> *"There are already sixty to seventy million handguns in this country. That seems to be about fifty-nine to sixty-nine million too many."*

to reflect their true cost to society. Once that price is reached, the free market would determine whether the product is worth that cost to society. If manufacturers can continue to make a profit by marketing handguns at this higher price, all is well and good from a tort perspective. If not, then handguns will be removed from the market.

Under present law, the price of handguns is heavily subsidized by the victims of handgun violence. The estimated direct cost to the economy of the lost lives and resources devoted to treating handgun injuries exceeds $20 billion annually. The manufacturers of handguns should bear, or at least share, this cost. I feel quite confident that, given the fervent devotion of gun enthusiasts, handguns would continue to sell at even ten times their current prices. They undoubtedly would sell at a slower rate, but that is not a bad result. There are already sixty to seventy million handguns in this country. That seems to be about fifty-nine to sixty-nine million too many.

Let me close with a proud parent story. My favorite fodder for constructing classroom hypotheticals is, paradoxically, an Uzi machine gun. In 1990, my daughter, then four years old, picked up the toy Uzi which my Torts students gave me as a Christmas present and pointed it at me. I admonished her never to point a gun at anyone. She asked why and I told her that real guns kill and hurt people. Invoking wisdom only a four-year-old could possess, she asked: "Then how come they make them?" "Astute question," I said. Then, not wanting to brainwash the child, I started to explain the perceived utility of firearms, but she was not listening. She had gone back to watching Elmer Fudd blow Bugs Bunny's head off with a shotgun.

Guns in the Home Endanger Children's Lives

by Katherine Kaufer Christoffel

About the author: *Katherine Kaufer Christoffel is a professor of pediatrics at Northwestern University School of Medicine and a pediatrician at Children's Memorial Hospital in Chicago.*

Just as children share in the strengths and weaknesses of the families they live in, so do they share in the strengths and weaknesses of the societies in which their families live. One of the weaknesses of contemporary U.S. society is its preoccupation with violence in general, and firearms in particular. For U.S. children, the consequence of this is a level of firearm mortality and morbidity that is far higher than anywhere else in the world.

As child health care providers and child advocates, pediatricians are, increasingly, called upon to step in to treat and protect children who find themselves in the crossfire. Therefore, pediatricians must be as knowledgeable about this problem as they were about polio a generation or two ago. There has been a rapid expansion of interest in and knowledge about U.S. pediatric firearm injuries. Pediatricians can utilize that knowledge to help protect their patients . . . and their children. This viewpoint will review what is known about the magnitude of the problem of firearm injury in the U.S., risk factors for injury, and available prevention approaches. . . .

Magnitude of the Problem

Three different circumstances of injury. Any discussion of firearm injuries must discuss each of the major injury circumstances: assault/homicide, suicide, and unintentional injury. The distinction is important because prevention must address risk factors for each of these. Firearm deaths become substantial in early adolescence, and peak in early adult life. Homicide is the most common circumstance for fatal injury, followed by suicide; unintentional injuries, which often command the greatest media attention, are horrible but comparatively infrequent at all ages.

The relative frequency of the different circumstances of firearm injury varies

Reprinted with permission from Katherine Kaufer Christoffel, "Pediatric Firearm Injuries: Time to Target a Growing Problem," *Pediatric Annals*, vol. 21, no. 7, July 1992.

with the age of the victim. Among 1-9 year-olds, homicides are most frequent, followed by unintentional injuries. Among 10-14 year-olds, homicide and unintentional injuries are about equally frequent, and account for three quarters of the deaths; the rest are due to suicide. Among 15-34 year-olds, homicides account for the majority of the deaths (just over half overall, and 80-90% among blacks), and suicides account for the majority of the rest (38-45% overall, about 60% among whites).

Table 1. Firearm Mortality Among Children and Teens

A. Number of Deaths

Age (Years)	Homicide 1985	Homicide 1988	Suicide 1985	Suicide 1988	Unintentional 1985	Unintentional 1988	All Three 1985	All Three 1988
1-4	53	50			41	41	94	91
5-9	58	71			58	51	116	122
10-14	141	182	139	125	177	185	457	492
15-19	1064	1641	1117	1261	241	266	2422	3168
1-19	1316	1944	1256	1386	517	543	3089	3873

B. Fatality Rate/100,000

Age (Years)	Homicide 1985	Homicide 1988	Suicide 1985	Suicide 1988	Unintentional 1985	Unintentional 1988	All Three 1985	All Three 1988
1-4	0.4	0.3			0.3	0.3	0.7	0.6
5-9	0.3	0.4			0.3	0.3	0.6	0.7
10-14	0.8	1.1	0.8	0.8	1.0	1.1	2.6	3.0
15-19	5.7	9.0	6.0	6.9	1.3	1.5	13.0	17.4

Source: LA Fingerhut, JC Kleinman, E Godfrey, and H. Rosenberg. Firearm mortality among children, youth and young adults 1-34 years of age, trends and current status: United States, 1979-88. *Monthly Vital Statistics Report* 1991; 39(11, Supplement).

Rapidly rising fatalities. Table 1 shows the alarming increase in firearm deaths that has occurred in recent years. Data from 1988, the last year fully analyzed in federal publications, are compared with 1985, the year contained in the

CDC's [Centers for Disease Control] 1990 report to Congress on childhood injuries. For all circumstances, the number of deaths increased from 3089 for 1-19 year-olds in 1985 to 3873 in 1988, a 25% increase. The greatest rises were in the number of homicides, which went up 22% in 5-9 year-olds, 29% in 10-14 year-olds, and 54% in 15-19 year-olds. Rates also rose most for homicide, up 33% for 5-9 year-olds, 38% for 10-14 year-olds, and 65% for 15-19 year-olds. For black males aged 15-19 years, firearm deaths more than doubled from 1984-1988. In 1988, firearm death rates were comparable in number to the sum of all natural causes death rates for white males aged 15-19, and 1.5 times the natural causes deaths for black males 15-19 years old.

> *"The most important risk factor involved in all circumstances of firearm death and injury is the accessibility of the firearms themselves."*

International context. The scale of pediatric firearm injuries in the U.S. is unique in the international community. A comparison of homicide deaths among males aged 15-19 years indicated the extent of this discrepancy. In 1987, there were 3187 firearm homicides in the U.S. (75% of all homicides in the age group), as compared with 90 firearm homicides in 14 other developed countries combined (accounting for a mean of 23% of all homicides in those countries). The U.S. rate was 21.9 per 100,000; among 20 other developed countries, the next highest rate was 5.0 (Scotland), and 13 countries had rates below 2.0.

Gun Fatality Risk Factors

Geographic region. Firearm deaths for all ages vary by region within the U.S., with death rates highest in the south and west. Rates also vary substantially within states. Pediatric firearm deaths have been reported to be highest in rural areas. This is presumed to be due to effects of the accessibility of firearms (more firearms in rural areas raising injury rates) and emergency medical services (less e.m.s. in rural areas resulting in lower survival), but this has not been quantitated.

Demography. Age and gender are the strongest demographic risk factors for firearm fatality. As noted earlier, the problem is greatest for teens and young adults. Further, the problem is overwhelmingly one of males, and particularly severe for black males. For example, among 15-19 year-olds, the black male firearm homicide rate in 1988 was 67.9, compared with 7.1 in black females; among white males, the rate was 6.0, compared with 1.3 in females. Among black teen and young adult males, firearm homicide is, very simply, the leading cause of death. Race is almost certainly a proxy for low socioeconomic status in all of these epidemiologic patterns.

The importance of males in the epidemiology of firearm injury is emphasized by findings in recent studies that the presence of firearms in the homes of children and adolescents is correlated with the presence of adult males in the homes. The strong male predominance is apparent even at the low rates of unintentional firearm injuries.

Access to firearms. Many bits of information argue that the most important risk factor involved in all circumstances of firearm death and injury is the accessibility of the firearms themselves.

Firearms are more lethal than the usual alternatives: in one study, 60% of gun assaults were fatal, compared with 4% of knife assaults and <1% of blows and kicks. As a result, the same circumstances are presumed to be less lethal in the absence of firearms than when firearms are present.

Firearm homicides generally affect teenagers, who become involved in arguments that escalate into fights. The assaults become homicides when a firearm, usually a handgun, appears. Recent surveys make it clear that teens have an easy time getting firearms. In a Seattle survey, one-third of male high school juniors said they could easily obtain a handgun. In a national sample of high school students, 20% reported having carried a weapon in the previous 30 days, and 21% of these had carried a gun. Growing numbers of children are reported to carry weapons, including firearms, to school; the available evidence suggests that these weapons often come from home. Other likely sources of the weapons include theft from homes, and federally licensed firearm dealers (some of whom have been known to distribute firearms to "the street").

Suicide and Guns in the Home

The concept that accessibility of firearms is critical to injury occurrence patterns is supported by a recent study of adolescent suicide victims, which demonstrated that suicide was more likely when firearms were present in the home. Presumably because adolescents have excellent fine motor skills, it did not seem to matter how the weapons were stored: locked and unloaded weapons as well as unlocked and loaded ones were used in suicides. While other methods appear to substitute for firearms among suicides of older individuals, this does not appear to be true for youthful suicides; it is inferred that youthful suicides are more impulsive, and so more dependent on immediate availability of lethal means.

"Handguns are the logical focus for efforts to reduce the majority of fatal and life-threatening firearm injuries."

Unintentional injuries generally occur in the homes of the victims, or of relatives or friends, generally during boyish play. It is reasonable to assume that such play would not be lethal in the absence of firearms. The weapons involved are generally handguns, which are the type of weapon most often kept accessible and loaded: because they are in the home as an (illusory) means of self-protection against feared crime and intruders. A 1991 survey suggests that only a

185

relatively small proportion of the homes of children contain loaded handguns; the attributable risk associated with them must therefore be extremely large.

Whether or not it is the most decisive, the presence of the firearms in the environment is surely the most modifiable risk factor for firearm injury of children and adolescents. Prevention efforts must therefore focus on getting the guns out of the environments of children and adolescents.

Which firearms? In the United States, the vast majority of firearm injuries are caused by handguns, although more long guns are owned. This reflects the portability of handguns, and the fact that many are kept or carried for protection, i.e., ready to fire. Although in some circumstances long guns appear to be as dangerous as handguns, handguns are the logical focus for efforts to reduce the majority of fatal and life-threatening firearm injuries.

The Lethality of Semiautomatic Weapons

Another logical focus is on weapons which allow many shots to be fired in a very short period of time. In prior centuries, firearms were extremely cumbersome to use. Over time, multiple-fire weapons and prefabricated bullets have facilitated firearm use for many purposes. However, until fairly recently, it was still necessary to reload weapons frequently, and to depress the firearm trigger periodically for each firing. Fully automatic firearms, which continue to fire self-feeding ammunition as long as the trigger is held down, have been banned in the U.S. for several decades. However, semiautomatic weapons, which accommodate moderately large self-feeding bullet supplies and which fire each time the trigger is pulled at momentary intervals, are increasingly available, as both rifles and handguns. Much political controversy in the early 1990s has involved "semiautomatic assault rifles," which are favored by urban gangs, and which have been killing an increasing number of victims over the years. Most recently, semiautomatic pistols have been reported by urban trauma rooms to be causing injuries with increasing frequency. Semiautomatic weapons merit particular attention because their operating characteristics allow them to cause exceptional lethality.

> *"Interventions that impede bullet acquisition or affect bullet design will more quickly affect injury patterns than similar steps involving the firearms themselves."*

Ammunition. Each type of bullet has its own unique type of path through tissue, e.g., with more or less tumbling, and these affect the extent of the ultimate injury. By international convention, bullets that can be used in war must be full metal jacketed, because this type of bullet construction maximizes the chances that the bullet will exit the victim; therefore, victims who have not suffered fatal injury on impact are likely to be salvageable. Many bullets that are available for civilian use are not of this construction, and are marketed to emphasize the features they contain that maximize the tissue damage that victims suffer (e.g., magnum quantities of gun powder, or soft deformable mushroom tips).

An important consideration in prevention planning is that bullets are consumables, so that regulatory or other interventions that impede bullet acquisition or affect bullet design will more quickly affect injury patterns than similar steps involving the firearms themselves.

Primary Prevention Is Crucial

Prevention approaches. Because of the high lethality of firearm injuries, primary prevention is the only logical approach. Efforts are warranted to reduce the frequency of violent interactions. Several pilot methods for training children and adolescents in non-violent conflict resolution are now undergoing evaluation. At the same time, it is crucial to reduce the lethality of violent interactions that do occur, and also of play and self-destructive behavior: by reducing the use of firearms.

The American Academy of Pediatrics [AAP] has reviewed the epidemiology of pediatric firearm injuries, the prevention options, and the pros and cons of each option. Based on this review, it has developed a policy to guide pediatric efforts to reduce firearm injuries. The guiding goal of the AAP policy is the removal of handguns from private homes, to protect both the children who may live or visit those homes and the children's adults. The AAP is working with the Center for the Prevention of Handgun Violence in the development of educational materials for parents concerning the risks of handgun ownership, and to dispel common fallacies: e.g., that handguns protect families, which they do not, and that gun control is unconstitutional, which it is not. Further, the AAP has approved model state legislation to ban the manufacture, sale, and possession of handguns. This makes the AAP the only public health organization to call for such strong handgun control.

> *"It is particularly important to educate parents of the extreme danger of having a gun in the home."*

The AAP's emphasis on restrictive legislation is based on several considerations. First, there is evidence that legal restraint on handgun access lowers both homicide and suicide rates. Second, experience with other types of injury control has taught us that education alone does not suffice to optimize prevention strategies. Third, the longevity and lethal purpose of handguns will limit the potential for weapon design improvements to have a substantial impact on injury rates in the short term. Finally, the interests of children demand that the most effective approach be taken as quickly as possible. The AAP is hopeful that its emphasis on the need of children will help to focus the populace on public health—rather than political—issues related to firearms.

Pediatricians can contribute to the public health effort that is needed to reduce pediatric firearm injury in several ways. Primary care physicians can help families to understand the dangers of handguns in the home, and can urge their patients' families to reduce or eliminate that danger. It is particularly important to educate parents of the extreme danger of having a gun in the home when someone in the household is at high risk for firearm use and injury. High-risk individuals include preadolescents and adolescents (especially boys), substance abusers, and those who are impulsive, prone to violent outbursts, or depressed.

Pediatricians can act as political advocates, initiating or supporting legislative efforts at local, state, and national levels. We can also continue to record the details of this latest epidemic, bearing witness to its devastation, clarifying its characteristics, and, perhaps within a generation, documenting its control.

Chapter 4

What Measures Would Reduce Gun Violence?

CURRENT CONTROVERSIES

Gun Violence:
An Overview

by Erik Eckholm

About the author: *Erik Eckholm is a projects editor for the* New York Times.

The gun controls most likely to be adopted in the near future would cause only modest inconvenience for legal gun buyers. But the controls, like the Brady Bill, which mandates a waiting period for handgun purchases, would also mean small gains at best against the murderous violence that is increasingly traumatizing an entire nation.

Even a little progress would be welcome. A 1 percent drop in firearm deaths—which totalled 35,000 in 1989, including 18,000 suicides, 15,000 homicides, 1,500 accidents and others unspecified—would mean hundreds of lives saved.

Questions to Consider

But real debate about the role of guns in society has scarcely begun. A central issue is this: Should new laws simply aim to do a better job of keeping firearms away from criminals, the main goal of the Brady Bill and most of the thousands of federal, state and local laws already on the books?

Or should they cut more deeply into legal gun ownership, too—limiting guns in rural hunting regions as well as cities, for example, and preventing frightened people from buying handguns to keep at the bedside? In other words, slashing the number of guns in public hands—but at a cost of crossing what tens of millions of people believe are their hallowed rights.

"I don't think there are easy or cheap gun controls that take us as far down the road, in terms of reducing violence, as a lot of people want to go," said Franklin E. Zimring, a law professor at the University of California at Berkeley known for his advocacy of handgun restrictions. "There are some fundamental questions waiting for us."

The Brady Bill, which has the public's blessing, has been supported by a majority in Congress but is now caught up in a broader battle over crime legislation. Calling for a waiting period on handgun purchases and a background check to weed out felons and others proscribed from gun ownership, it aims to slow the flow of guns into illegal hands, and from lax states to those with tighter controls. While it should help, huge leaks would remain.

Bans on assault weapons that have recently been adopted or considered in several states may reduce the presence of some of these high-capacity, fast-shooting firearms that have provoked special outrage among the police. If it did nothing else, banning them might be worthwhile as a statement of cultural goals. But these weapons are uncommon, and no one thinks that the drug gangs who favor them will go wanting for firepower.

Millions Oppose Gun Laws

More sweeping and stringent gun controls remain well out of political reach. That is not just because of the plotting of the gun lobby. Measures like a general ban on the sale of handguns would face the defiant opposition of millions of law-abiding gun owners—people who want these weapons for target shooting, self-protection or just on principle, and who think that limiting their choices would do nothing to ease the bloodshed on urban streets.

"The Holy Grail of gun control has been to find some way to keep guns out of the hands of the bad guys, yet leave the legitimate firearms-owning population alone," said James D. Wright, a criminologist at Tulane University who thinks that goal is an impossible one.

Alone in the industrial world, the United States has had a firearms "democracy"—some say free-for-all—in which nearly any kind of gun is legally available to nearly anyone without a criminal record. Now, with

> *"The Holy Grail of gun control has been to find some way to keep guns out of the hands of the bad guys, yet leave the legitimate firearms-owning population alone."*

some 200 million firearms in circulation, and at least four million new guns, including two million handguns, added to the supply each year, no one should expect miracles of even the strictest controls.

Dr. Zimring optimistically draws a comparison with automobile injuries, which have been fought with everything from higher safety standards to crackdowns on drunken driving. "There, we've made a whole series of adjustments over time, chipping away at the problem, and deaths are down," he said.

Brady Bill Seeks Middle Ground

Though she is vilified and mistrusted by gun defenders, Sarah Brady, chairwoman of Handgun Control Inc., the largest gun-control advocacy group, has tried to occupy a middle ground. "We're not proposing banning weapons, but passing laws that will help the system do what it's already supposed to do," Mrs. Brady said.

The main bill, which would impose a waiting period of five working days and a background check for handgun purchases, is named after her husband, James S. Brady, who was wounded by a bullet meant for President Ronald Reagan. The goal is to deter felons and gun runners from buying guns, and give hotheads and suicidal people some time to cool off.

At least half the states already have some form of background check or waiting period for handgun purchases. Some cities, including Chicago, New York and Washington, have stringent limits on who may buy or own a handgun. Whether homicide rates would be even higher than they are without those controls is a subject of endless debate. Clearly, though, the restrictions imposed by some places are undercut by the lack of them elsewhere.

Of 19,000 guns seized by law officials in New York City in 1991, for example, more than nine out of 10 were purchased over the counter in states where sales are easier, according to the Bureau of Alcohol, Tobacco and Firearms. Virginia, Florida, Ohio, Texas and Georgia were the leaders. The sales were usually made to local "straw purchasers," or gun runners with phony local identification.

Should States Do More?

Mrs. Brady is the first to say that the Brady Bill alone cannot choke off the supply of guns to criminals. She says states must do more to check out the identification of buyers—a problem in Virginia which, despite requiring a quick computer check to see if buyers have criminal records, remains a major source of smuggled guns. The exemption of private gun transfers from the waiting period is a major loophole. And closer regulation of sales will not help prevent gun thefts, which are a major source of illegal guns in much of the country.

The National Rifle Association has said it would support instant, computerized background checks of handgun buyers, something only feasible in some states for now. But it says a waiting period would be useless, and it still hopes to kill the Brady Bill. It rejects proposals to regulate private gun sales and other measures aimed at increasing the accountability of gun owners.

> *"Closer regulation of sales will not help prevent gun thefts, which are a major source of illegal guns in much of the country."*

"Instead of asking law-abiding people to change what they are doing, why not keep the people that are committing the crimes in jail?" asks James Jay Baker, chief lobbyist with the N.R.A.

California's experience with a waiting period suggests the possible benefits but also shows how hard it is to evaluate them. Going well beyond what would be required by the Brady Bill, California has a 15-day waiting period for the purchase of any gun, including rifles and shotguns, and it covers private sales as well as those through stores.

In 1991, of almost 500,000 requests for gun purchases, the state stopped just under 6,000, including 3,000 involving buyers with assault records and 34 with homicide records. What no one knows, however, is how many of the buyers who were turned down got someone else to buy a gun for them, or turned to the black market. Nor is there a way to know how much violence was prevented.

How Strict a Ban?

A large minority of shell-shocked Americans are ready to go further, restricting legally owned guns, too, in the hope it will curb violence. In a variety of surveys over the years, close to 40 percent of the public has supported a ban on even possessing handguns, let alone selling them.

Though it would stop short of confiscation, the Coalition to Stop Gun Violence, which represents several national religious and other groups, wants to end new handgun sales. "We believe that anything less than a ban on handgun sales, while maybe helpful, is not going to lead to a meaningful reduction in gun violence," said Jeffrey Y. Muchnick, legislative director of the coalition. He said the desires of gun owners may have to give way: "There will always be people who disagree, but for the greater good of the community we will have to pass a ban against their wishes."

> *"I haven't seen a gun proposal . . . that had any potential for reducing the homicide rate."*

Dr. Zimring prefers the term "restrictive licensing" to "ban," but in any case the idea is to limit handgun sales to those who show a strong need, mainly those in law enforcement. Target shooters could buy guns but would have to keep them locked at shooting ranges. Given up would be recreational "plinking" in the countryside and, in the most controversial effect, the ability of most people to buy handguns for self-protection.

The Views of Gun Owners

Any such talk makes many gun owners livid. "When millions of firearms owners say 'You can have my gun when you pry it from my dead hand,' they are not kidding," said Andrew Molchan, president of the National Association of Federally Licensed Firearms Dealers, which represents gun shops. Many gun owners claim that the Second Amendment prohibits any gun ban, although courts have repeatedly upheld strong local restrictions.

"I haven't seen a gun proposal in the 13 years that I've been here that had any potential for reducing the homicide rate," said Mr. Baker of the rifle association. "The law-abiding people will obey the law, and the criminals will not."

In truth, there is serious disagreement among scholars who study guns and violence about how effective even the more sweeping measures might be.

"What I believe in my heart of hearts is that if we ban guns, all the people who want to own one for some nefarious reason will still find a way to get one," Dr. Wright said.

Another skeptic, Gary Kleck, professor of criminology at Florida State University, argues that stringent controls "will have an impact on a relatively slight, marginally involved part of the crime population"—people who are willing to obey gun laws but who are also willing to commit violent acts.

Dr. Kleck does support background checks for gun purchasers and would extend them to private transfers, for the limited good that that would do. But he also says that restricting selective classes of weapons might backfire. Outlawing small, cheap "Saturday night specials," he says, would not only discriminate against poor people who want to buy guns for protection, but also force criminals to use more accurate, higher-caliber weapons—and the ultimate death toll from shootings might rise. Likewise, if frightened homeowners are forced to buy rifles or shotguns rather than handguns, which tend to be less lethal, accidents and so-called crimes of passion would be more likely to cause death rather than injury.

People "On the Edge"

But other experts think that much tighter control over the sale of weapons and especially a reduction in the number of handguns, which are overwhelmingly the kind used in crimes, will surely pay off.

"I'm willing to grant that someone who's determined to have a gun and has the resources will be able to get one under foreseeable regulations," said Philip J. Cook, a professor of public policy and economics at Duke University who advocates measures to drive up the price of black-market guns. "But I don't think that most robbers, rapists and assailants are that determined or clever or systematic in their

> *"Whatever the facts, tens of millions of people evidently think they are more secure with a firearm in the home."*

affairs. These are people who live on the edge financially, and if the gun is worth $300 instead of $100, they are more likely to need that money for something else."

Making handguns scarcer, in this view, might also curb the alarming increase in the number of urban teen-agers and others who carry weapons for vaguely "defensive" reasons—resulting in an escalating arms race that allows petty disputes to erupt into deadly gun battles.

In response to those who say there are enough guns already around to supply criminals for centuries, experts like Dr. Zimring point to evidence that guns used in crimes tend to be relatively new, and that guns tend to have a limited life on the streets before being seized or abandoned.

In New York City, for example, about three-fourths of the guns seized by the police were produced since 1987, said John A. O'Brien of the Federal Bureau of Alcohol, Tobacco and Firearms.

If criminal access to new guns were crimped, thefts of firearms from homes and stores would presumably increase, partly offsetting the benefit. Still, to the extent that the black market depends on a steady infusion of newly produced guns, the problem of control seems more manageable.

Just getting the numbers down would help. "If we really had a stream of 400,000 new handguns a year instead of two million, you'd be surprised how much easier it would be to create a system of accountability," Dr. Zimring said.

Debating Wisdom of Bedside Guns

A large share of the boom in handguns in the last 30 years has involved people buying guns for self-protection. This trend continues despite the incantations of gun-control advocates and some police officials, who say that guns bring a false sense of security and are more likely to mean the death of loved ones than protection from crime.

Their argument is seemingly buttressed by studies of firearms deaths in homes, which show that accidents, murders and especially suicides are far more numerous than killings of intruders.

Whatever the facts, tens of millions of people evidently think they are more secure with a firearm in the home, a feeling that must be reckoned with politically. And recently the common wisdom has been challenged by Dr. Kleck and others. Gun accidents, they say, are concentrated among a small, reckless subset of gun owners. Many of the murders and suicides

"Personal defense is the central question of handgun ownership in American life."

would certainly have occurred whether or not the homeowner kept a gun for protection.

Above all, Dr. Kleck argues, a body count of shot intruders grossly understates the successful defensive uses of guns, which often require merely a threat to shoot. He says there is evidence to suggest that gunwielding homeowners ward off criminals several hundred thousand times a year.

Weighing the Risks

Other scholars accuse Dr. Kleck of gross exaggeration. Dr. Cook, for example, citing what he calls more reliable data, says the number of defensive uses is far lower. He says the slight chance a gun will prove useful in self-defense must be weighed against risks that will vary according to family circumstances, such as how safely weapons are stored and whether any members are suicide-prone. "A public benefit of having a heavily armed citizenry remains to be demonstrated," he adds.

Dr. Zimring believes that widespread gun ownership causes more problems than it solves. But he pleads urgently for more research on the self-protection issue. "Personal defense is the central question of handgun ownership in American life," he acknowledged. "If it were truly shown that self-defense was a good reason to own a gun, that would strike a death blow to a restrictive policy.

"It would have to be defense not obtainable with lesser means, and for protection of life rather than TV sets. But if we're living in that world, then we couldn't justify the limits I have proposed," he said.

Federal Gun Control Laws Would Reduce Violence

by Mark Udulutch

About the author: *Mark Udulutch is a 1990 graduate of Marquette Law School in Milwaukee, Wisconsin. He now serves in the Peace Corps in Morocco.*

The public is polarized on the issue of gun control. Anti-gun control activists believe that it is each and every American's individual right to bear arms. Various pro-gun control organizations disagree and propose different methods of gun control. For example, there are individuals who would ban all handguns; as well as those who take a less radical stand and who would simply increase the controls on firearms. Moderate gun control groups propose measures such as requiring an individual to successfully complete a firearms safety course before possession of a gun is allowed, or to wait for a mandatory period of time before taking possession of a gun.

Today, there are approximately 20,000 different gun control laws in existence, ranging from those enacted by municipalities and states, to those enacted by the federal government. Individuals opposed to gun control point to this fact, and assert that gun control is a failure. The truth is that, for the most part, these laws are ineffective because they lack scope, breadth and enforcement. . . .

Should There Be Gun Control?

In a democratic society, such as the United States, two things need consideration prior to the enactment of legislation for the purpose of solving a social problem. The first concern is whether there is a problem that can, in fact, be controlled through legislation. The second is whether the majority of Americans would support governmental intervention to provide a solution to that problem. Both of these questions must be answered affirmatively or further discussion of gun control legislation would be senseless.

Firearms are used to murder nearly 12,000 people annually; another 1,750 persons suffer death by accident; and an estimated 200,000 people are injured. In addition, more than 16,000 people use firearms to take their own lives each year. Although they constitute only a third of all firearms, handguns are used in

Excerpted from Mark Udulutch, "The Constitutional Implications of Gun Control and Several Realistic Gun Control Proposals," *American Journal of Criminal Law* 17 (1): 19-54. Reprinted with permission.

three-fourths of all firearm murders and one-half of all murders. Even in light of these statistics, the pro-gun advocates continue to herald the "virtues" of gun ownership.

Over the years, both sides of the gun control debate have used statistics in attempts to make their arguments. Statisticians, however, point out that the persuasiveness of a statistic lies in its ability to be factually verified. Here, the pro-gun control forces have had an advantage over the anti-gun control activists. They present the corpses and shattered limbs that result from the misuse of firearms as the evidence needed to successfully state their position. The pro-gun activists, however, argue that firearms actually prevent murders, rapes and burglaries. The problem with this argument is that it lacks credible statistical verification.

No Need for Individuals to Own Guns

Returning to the central question, should additional legislative action be taken to regulate the nearly 70,000,000 handguns and 140,000,000 long guns now in the United States? The answer is yes. Firearms are certainly needed for national defense and law enforcement, but they are not needed by individual citizens to serve as the tools for social violence. Rational, workable federal legislation is the appropriate means to stop the misuse of firearms.

More aggressive gun control laws are needed to reduce the problem. However, legislative measures will work only to the extent they are supported by the majority of the people. While the public has not given its support to every form of increased gun control legislation, it has supported the less intrusive proposals. . . .

Several Realistic Gun Control Proposals

When more than 30,000 people are killed annually by firearms and another 200,000 are injured, it is clear to most individuals that a serious problem exists. Recognizing the problem is the first step toward a solution. Finding a solution is not easy, nor is it achieved quickly, but this should not obviate gun control.

Given American society and its attraction to firearms, legislation must not be so restrictive that, at its outset, it fails to enlist the cooperation of the American public. At this time, it would be unrealistic to ban all firearms from the private sector. Many pro-gun activists try to attack the pro-control position by arguing that one control will lead to another, and eventually guns will be outlawed altogether. Although such a result is conceivable, a complete ban will never be successful unless it is supported by the people. Only public disinterest in firearms would truly result in eliminating them from the social environment.

> *"Should additional legislative action be taken to regulate the nearly 70,000,000 handguns and 140,000,000 long guns now in the United States? The answer is yes."*

Neither the approach of a total ban on firearms, as some gun control advocates propose, nor the do-nothing attitude of the anti-gun control activists, are realistic at this time. Yet firearms are a serious problem to the Amerian society. Their destructive misuse cannot be allowed to continue. Some increases in regulations are definitely needed. These regulations will require a realistic compromise between the two extremes in the gun control debate.

When constructing these controls, two goals must remain constant. First, and most importantly, it is necessary to decrease as much as possible the victimization of individuals through the misuse of firearms. Second, it is important to structure legislation in ways that accomplish the intended purposes while not being overly intrusive upon the individual. In essence, a utilitarian approach must be taken toward gun control. The benefits to society must be maximized, while the possible intrusions to individuals must be minimized.

Federal Legislation: The Only Realistic Answer

Even with 20,000 gun control laws already in existence, the serious problems due to firearm misuse continue. Obviously, the controls that have been designed have not been sufficiently effective. There are three identifiable reasons for this problem: 1) the lack of uniform legislation; 2) the fact that most controls do not go far enough in their attempt to prevent the problems of firearm misuse; and 3) the controls in place are not effectively enforced.

Sweeping federal legislation would go a long way toward resolving all three of these problems. Such legislation could offer a coherent, orderly means of addressing the gun problem, unlike the present hodgepodge of local, state and federal legislation.

One of the most significant problems resulting from the discrepancy in local, state and federal firearm laws is the transportation of firearms from one state to another. If every state had uniformly strict firearm control laws, interstate transport would not be a major problem. No longer would an individual like John Hinckley be able to purchase a firearm in a state with weak gun control laws, transport his weapon across state lines, and then use it to shoot the President of the United States. However, going to the legislatures of the fifty states to achieve uniformly strict firearm controls is not the most efficient course of action. The failure of even one state to adopt the uniform controls would severely weaken the entire chain of controls. Federal legislation would be far more effective; only one body of lawmakers would have to deal with the increased controls instead of fifty. Furthermore, once established, the controls could not be weakened by the efforts of one state legislature.

> *"Legislation could offer a coherent, orderly means of addressing the gun problem, unlike the present hodgepodge of local, state and federal legislation."*

Having concluded that federal legislation is the best way to effectively control firearm possession and use, the next question is what kind of legislation? Some intelligently drafted controls are already in place, but they have not proven sufficient. Controls that go further than present federal legislation in preventing the problems of firearm misuse and that are more rigorously enforced are needed.

1. *Licensing and Education*—A nationwide licensing program would be an effective first step. Such a program already exists for sellers, manufacturers and importers of firearms, but it does not extend to private citizens who buy and use the guns. Not every person who wants to own a firearm should be trusted with it.

To obtain a license, a person would have to meet three criteria. First, he or she could not belong to any of the classes of persons denied the privilege of possessing firearms. Section 922 of the Firearms Owners' Protection Act denies felons, fugitives from justice, drug addicts, illegal aliens, individuals dishonorably discharged from the military, individuals who have renounced their United States citizenship and mental incompetents the privilege of owning guns. It would be wise to add to this list persons under eighteen years of age. A second criteria for obtaining a firearm license would be to pass a firearm safety course. Drivers are required to pass a drivers' training course, so why shouldn't a comparable test be administered to license potential gun owners? A firearm safety course would reinforce student awareness of the danger involved in firearm use and misuse. A course of this nature could, at a minimum, be expected to decrease the number of accidental killings and injuries occurring from gun misuse.

> *"A firearm safety course would . . . decrease the number of accidental killings and injuries occurring from gun misuse."*

The third criteria would require an extensive background check on a prospective licensee to make sure he or she did not belong to one of the classes of persons prohibited from owning firearms. This check would be made by the police department where the applicant resided. Additionally, this investigative program would be overseen by the Bureau of Alcohol, Tobacco and Firearms. . . .

All Firearms Must Be Registered

2. *Firearm Registration*—With nearly 210,000,000 firearms already present in the United States it is foolish to believe that a licensing program by itself will keep firearms out of the hands of people who should not have them. Another step toward keeping firearms from untrustworthy people is to require that all firearms be registered. Federal law already requires that "each manufacturer, importer and maker shall register each firearm that he manufactures, imports, or makes." However, because of the proposed licensing requirements and the uncertainty of who currently owns what firearm, all firearms in the United States

must be registered by their current owners. Each licensed firearm owner would pay for the costs involved in registering his or her own firearms. . . .

Realistically, not every individual now owning a firearm will comply with this firearm control. Some criminals will still have guns; this cannot be denied. However, with every gun removed from the hands of unqualified possessors, it is expected that the misuse of firearms will decrease.

3. *Mandatory Investigation of All Firearm Transferees*—A system whereby transferees are automatically investigated for fitness as a gun owner prior to any actual transfer of the weapon is needed to keep track of firearm ownership. . . .

Because the only lawful transferee of a firearm is one who possesses a valid firearm license, the investigation required need not be extensive. The person would already have been investigated prior to obtaining his or her firearm license. The transferee's history, dating from the time the license was received or from the time a firearm was last transferred to the transferee, is all that must be investigated. . . .

4. *A Waiting Period*—Intricately related to the formalities of a firearm transfer is a mandatory waiting period. Though the idea of a waiting period is not new it is critical that it be established on the federal level. In 1988 Congress considered the "Brady Amendment," which required a one-week waiting period before a transferee could possess a transferred handgun. During this time the police could conduct a thorough background check of the transferee. In the scheme presented here, the transfer investigation would take place during the waiting period. . . .

Worth the Inconvenience

A waiting period would not only allow time for the police to verify a prospective transferee's status, but it would also serve as a "cooling off" period. The otherwise reasonable person who, in the heat of the moment, wants to buy a gun to commit a crime will have to wait to get it. The expectation is that such a person will reconsider his or her plans while waiting.

Anti-gun control organizations are quick to point out that the majority of persons going through the legal channels to purchase a firearm are not in need of any "cooling off" period. Furthermore, they say that anyone who wants a gun badly enough can find a way around the law. These arguments are valid in many situations, but not in all. It is doubtful that a waiting period would stop a hard-core criminal in the quest for a gun. However, some individuals with criminal aspirations or designs will be thwarted. The inconvenience to prospective gun owners of waiting one, two or three weeks to obtain a firearm is minor when compared to the significance of the tragedies that could be avoided. A waiting period is needed.

> *"Some people believe that if they have a firearm they will be able to ward off anyone wishing to do them harm."*

5. *Taxing Measure for Keeping Firearms Out of City Limits*—It seems unlikely that most Americans would accept a ban on all firearms within the limits of their communities. This, together with the fact that most cases of firearm misuse occur in heavily populated areas, produces a serious dilemma. One of the principal reasons for owning a firearm within a city is for self-protection. Some people believe that if they have a firearm they will be able to ward off anyone wishing to do them harm. Although this reasoning is questionable, it has many adherents. The proposed solution is a combination tax burden-tax incentive scheme.

Those persons licensed to own guns and living in a city may still keep their guns at home, but will be subject to a federal tax for doing so. This tax should be progressive to avoid inflicting a disproportionate hardship on those least capable of paying. Even so, the tax would apply to everyone wishing to keep firearms at a private residence within city limits, and it must be relatively high in order to discourage people from exercising this privilege. Furthermore, the tax would double for every firearm over the first one kept at a private residence. All collected

> *"The time to pass increased firearm controls is now. Too many lives have been lost because of firearm misuse."*

taxes would be used for increased law enforcement. Although the federal government would allow licensed individuals to keep their guns in their city residences, there is nothing that would prevent a community from banning firearm possession within its city limits.

The Role of Gun Clubs

Those persons licensed to possess a firearm who do not wish to keep them at their city residence may store their guns under lock and key at a gun club. The adoption of such proposals would no doubt encourage the growth of gun clubs. Guns stored at these clubs would not be subject to the federal taxes imposed on privately housed guns. Only club membership fees would have to be paid. This plan should create a migration of firearms from city residences. Gun clubs could be located either in the country or within city limits. Their main purpose would be to create a centralized secure place where firearms could be kept.

For enforcement purposes, guns would have to be returned nightly to the gun club. Exceptions would be made for hunters wishing to take their guns on hunting trips. To take their guns with them, the hunters would register removal with the club, which, in turn, would report those firearms not returned on time. To ensure that each gun club complies with the law, it would be subject to periodic, unannounced investigations by the Bureau of Alcohol, Tobacco and Firearms or the Internal Revenue Service. It would be presumed that those licensed gun owners not returning their guns to the gun clubs had opted to keep their guns at home, and would, therefore, be subject to the gun tax.

6. *Banning All Automatic and Military Style Semi-Automatic Weapons*—A semi-automatic weapon is one which requires a separate pull of the trigger for each shot. The weapons differ from automatic weapons which fire more than one shot at the pull of the trigger. . . . These weapons were designed for one primary reason, to kill people quickly and in large numbers.

While Americans do not seem willing to accept a total ban on firearms, they might accept a ban on automatic and military style semi-automatic weapons. There will be some resistance to a ban on automatic and military style semi-automatic weapons, but its enforcement will be relatively easy compared to a ban on all firearms, or a ban just on handguns, in that there are far fewer of these weapons in the marketplace. . . .

The Weapons Preferred by Drug Gangs

The average owner of a military style semi-automatic weapon, or an automatic weapon, is not a criminal, and substantial compliance with a ban on these weapons could be expected. This would be especially true if the federal government offered to buy these weapons. After a reasonable period of time given to comply, persons still in possession of automatic and military style semi-automatic weapons would be subject to harsh penalties. A ban on military style semi-automatic and automatic weapons is especially needed now, because these weapons have become the weapons of choice for the drug gangs in the United States. Congress made a good start when it required an additional mandatory ten-year imprisonment for those individuals involved in a violent or drug trafficking crime in which an automatic weapon was used. Nevertheless, the law, as applied to automatic weapons, is not yet broad enough, and it does not address the problem of military style semi-automatic weapons. The ten-year mandatory penalty is sufficiently stern, but it should be extended to all persons in possession of an automatic or a military style semi-automatic weapon after the expiration of a buy back date. The potential for disaster that these weapons present is simply too great to allow them in the hands of the general public.

The need for strong, realistic gun control legislation becomes obvious whenever another life is taken or an injury inflicted as the result of the misuse of a firearm. This viewpoint has presented a number of proposals for increasing gun control nationwide. To be most effective, these proposals should be adopted together and they should be addressed by the federal government. The time to pass increased firearm controls is now. Too many lives have been lost because of firearm misuse.

Increasing Penalties for Gun-Related Crimes Would Reduce Violence

by Richard Cook

About the author: *Richard Cook is the chief of the firearms division of the Bureau of Alcohol, Tobacco, and Firearms.*

We wake up in the morning to headlines about triple murders in the Nation's Capital, large-scale firearms thefts, or of two promising boys—ages 11 and 15—shot to death while playing outside a Boston home—just 5 minutes before the 11-year-old was supposed to go inside.

Targeting vicious criminals and putting them behind bars is the number one priority of the Bureau of Alcohol, Tobacco and Firearms [ATF]. Equally important is shutting down the source of illegal firearms that are fueling the rising homicide rate across the Nation.

We believe the armed career criminal laws passed by Congress in recent years are having an effect on the violent repeat offender. But let me dispel any questions that the war against street crime and drug-related violence will be won as swiftly as Operation Desert Storm.

Our troops who fought in the Persian Gulf to uphold the rule of law have come home to gang-plagued neighborhoods where the semiautomatic pistol and the pipe bomb have replaced the toy guns that they grew up with.

Must Close Revolving Door

Enhanced firearms penalties provide law enforcement with long-term solutions to reduce street crime and drug-related violence, but they will not reduce overnight the level of violence.

In order to give the most to the American taxpayer, we need to incarcerate the armed, career criminal and close down the so-called revolving door where felons are released early. Mandatory sentences reduce crime because they get the violent criminal off the streets for long periods of time.

From Richard Cook's statement to the U.S. House of Representatives' Judiciary Committee, Subcommittee on Crime and Criminal Justice, May 23, 1991.

ATF enforces 18 U.S.C. 924(c) and (e). These laws are aimed directly at the career criminal who commits a disproportionate number of violent crimes. Section 924(c) mandates 5 years imprisonment for the first offense and 20 years for the second, with no parole, no probation, for persons convicted of committing a violent or drug trafficking crime while carrying or using firearms.

Section 924(e) sets a 15-year, no parole, no probation, sentence for anyone found in possession of a firearm who has three convictions for violent felony or drug-related crimes.

> *"Mandatory sentences reduce crime because they get the violent criminal off the streets for long periods of time."*

In 1986, ATF initiated Project Achilles, a nationwide program directed at the armed violent criminal. Project Achilles strikes at the criminal's most vulnerable point—carrying a firearm.

Achilles is directed at targeting, investigating, and prosecuting criminals who qualify for mandatory and enhanced sentencing under the armed career criminal statutes.

Consider the potential of these laws—since enactment in 1987, 1,864 criminals have been put away for a total of 17,680 years plus 10 life sentences.

Currently, all of ATF's 22 districts are participating in Project Achilles. Several districts have formal and informal task forces comprised of local, State and other Federal law enforcement agencies.

In addition, Achilles task forces have been established in 16 major cities with rising crime rates—New York, Dallas, Houston, Boston, San Francisco, Philadelphia, Omaha, Washington, Chicago, Phoenix, Los Angeles, Miami, Detroit, Atlanta, Baltimore and Albuquerque.

The task forces work with local police in targeting specific high-crime areas within a city; and successfully prosecuting the armed convicted felon or drug trafficker and the suppliers of their firearms.

Because of the tremendous success ATF has had with these types of cases, the Attorney General announced Project Triggerlock, a new Department of Justice prosecutive initiative.

[Former] Attorney General Richard Thornburgh has directed all 93 U.S. attorneys to step up prosecution of crimes involving firearms. The key to Project Achilles and Project Triggerlock is to identify the most violent criminals using firearms and to bring Federal gun charges against them.

We are working with the Justice Department to effectively integrate the Achilles initiative with Triggerlock so there is no duplication of effort.

Insight into the Career Criminal's Mind

ATF's firearms enforcement program is directed at the violent criminal. In 1990, we recommended 7,955 criminals for prosecution. Their profile revealed that 47 percent had prior felonies, 56 percent were narcotics violators and 23 percent had a history of violence.

A study begun in May 1990 by ATF on the effectiveness of the Federal armed career criminal statutes gives us valuable insight into the behavior of the criminal and the effects of an imposed 15-year or greater sentence.

At one point we looked at 471 career criminals convicted and sentenced as a result of ATF investigations. Collectively, the 471 had a total of 3,088 felony convictions. A summary of their felony convictions were: 46 for murder, 232 for armed robbery, 942 for burglary, 410 for narcotics violations, and 210 for firearms violations. From the data we can construct a profile of the average career criminal.

One out of three is convicted of murder, attempted murder, aggravated battery, rape or a crime against a child.

Eight out of 10 have felony narcotics convictions.

Eight out of 10 prisoners are convicted of a firearms violation or assault with a deadly weapon.

Sources of Weapons

ATF special agents then interviewed 100 convicted armed career criminals. Members of the study group who responded to the question on how they acquired firearms identified four major sources of firearms. These sources are street sales, robberies, or from criminal associates, retail firearms dealers and from personal acquaintances.

Targeting violent criminals in possession of firearms is a very important part of our firearms enforcement program. ATF inspectors work with the special agents to uncover purchasing patterns and weapons commonly used as crime guns to aid in the apprehension of criminals who purchase firearms for use in crime.

"A mandatory 5-year penalty for possession of a firearm . . . will help to take the most dangerous criminals off the street."

Using intelligence from law enforcement, inspectors examine dealer transaction records to identify likely violators such as convicted felons, "straw man" purchasers, gang members and illegal traffickers.

A mandatory 5-year penalty for possession of a firearm by a person who has been convicted of a violent felony or serious drug offense will help to take the most dangerous criminals off the street.

In addition, increased penalties for supplying false information to firearms dealers will have an effect on "straw man" purchasers because they will face tougher penalties for aiding criminals in procuring firearms. Also increasing the time period which defines "multiple sales" from 5 to 30 days will make it more difficult for "straw" purchasers to go undetected.

We are constantly opening investigations dealing with firearms trafficking.

The demand for drugs fuels the demand for firearms and vice versa. Two examples show the extent of the problem. New York City alone seizes some 17,000 illegal weapons each year with 96 percent coming from outside the State.

Two Virginia Beach, VA, men were recently arrested by ATF and charged with conspiracy to falsify information to a Virginia firearms dealer in a scheme to sell six TEC-9 pistols in New York City at four times their retail value.

ATF is going after the tools of the trade used by the career criminal and our firearms seizure statistics reflect this increase. In fiscal year 1984, we seized 9,400 firearms; by fiscal year 1990, that number had increased to over 12,400 firearms.

Recently, the U.S. Ninth Circuit Court of Appeals issued a ruling that a Federal felon whose civil rights had been restored by a State after completion of a prison sentence could possess a firearm.

A uniform standard as to whether a person is disabled under the Federal firearms statutes, at least when the conviction is for certain violent crimes, [is necessary]. Without a uniform definition of a felony conviction, records checks are rendered useless. Although fully convicted of a felony, underlying State expungement or restoration of rights procedures may mean individuals can legally buy all the guns they want without the specific investigation to restore that ability that is provided for in the relief from disability procedures in the Gun Control Act.

Currently I'd like to comment on limiting the size of gun clips and magazines to 15 rounds. The core of this proposal is that regardless of how a firearm functions, firepower is a product in part of how many bullets can be fired without reloading. Reducing the firepower of all firearms restores a balance between the police and the violators.

Tools Needed to Catch Criminals

Our streets have become killing zones where our youth are learning that the gun and the bomb are the enforcer. The President's comprehensive crime proposal gives law enforcement further means to take back our streets one at a time.

These firearms proposals are fully consistent with the important work which has been done from the original armed drug trafficking and career criminal statutes through gun-free school zones legislation.

Whatever other approaches are added to dealing with armed violence, we must have the enforcement tools to go after the serious criminal, the criminal who is already armed and is not about to surrender voluntarily.

Banning Handguns Would Reduce Violence

by Coalition to Stop Gun Violence

About the author: *The Coalition to Stop Gun Violence (CSGV) is a coalition of religious, professional, and educational organizations that supports the elimination of all handguns from the United States. The following viewpoint, from a CSGV pamphlet, presents a series of questions and responses concerning handguns in America.*

Q. What is the severity of the handgun problem in the United States?

A. In 1980, some 11,522 individuals were murdered with handguns—half of all homicides that year. And over 300,000 robberies, rapes, and assaults were committed with handguns. In 1979 nearly 12,000 people were killed in accidents and suicides involving handguns. With 60 people killed and over 700 more wounded each day, it is no surprise that handguns have been labeled a "public health problem" in the *Journal of the American Medical Association.*

Q. How does the number of Americans killed with handguns in the U.S. from 1963 to 1973 compare with the number of Americans killed in Vietnam during that period?

A. From 1963 to 1973, 46,121 Americans were killed in the Vietnam War. Over the same period, 84,644 Americans were murdered by firearms within the United States. Of this total, about 80 percent were killed with handguns, although handguns account for only 20 percent of the nation's firearms.

Children and Guns

Q. To what extent are young people victimized by handguns?

A. Calling for "nothing short of a total ban" on the sale of handguns, the Surgeon General's Select Panel for the Promotion of Child Health traced the recent "epidemic of deaths and injuries among children and the youth" to one source—the handgun. Among adolescents and young adults, murder accounts for nearly one out of every eight deaths, and handguns are responsible for half of all murders in the U.S. And not surprisingly, a substantial number of the 5600 young people who took their own lives in 1977 used handguns. In fact,

Excerpted from *20 Questions and Answers*, a 1981 brochure of the National Coalition to Ban Handguns, now known as the Coalition to Stop Gun Violence, Washington, D.C. Reprinted with permission.

firearms were used four times as often as poisoning, the second most common method. Finally, loaded handguns killed hundreds of young people—ranging from infants to adolescents—by sheer accident.

Q. Is there any connection between the availability of handguns and the rate of violent death?

A. Definitely. The handgun murder rate in the United States per 100,000 population is 100 times as high as the rate in England and Wales, where access to handguns is sharply restricted. It is 200 times as high as the rate in Japan, where it is almost impossible for a private citizen to secure a handgun.

> *"Many groups concerned about handgun violence advocate a comprehensive national law to ban the manufacture, sale, and private possession of handguns."*

In the United States, the highest rate of handgun ownership is in the South, where the overall murder rate is by far the highest. Of every 100,000 inhabitants in the South, 13 are murdered each year. But in the Northeast and North Central states, where handguns are less common, the annual murder rate is only 8 per 100,000. From these statistics, the U.S. General Accounting Office concluded, "The ease with which firearms are obtained is a contributing factor in firearms crime."

Moreover, where there are more handguns, there are more accidents and more suicides. In the ten states with the strongest handgun control laws, the handgun accident rate is 0.2 per 100,000, and the handgun suicide rate is 2.4 per 100,000. In the ten states with the weakest laws, the handgun accident rate is 0.6 per 100,000, and the handgun suicide rate is 5.9 per 100,000.

Social psychologists now believe that the mere sight of a handgun may be enough to stimulate aggressive or violent behavior. Dr. Leonard Berkowitz, the first to observe this phenomenon, has labeled it the "weapons effect." Since people "sometimes react mindlessly and impulsively to the presence of guns," he argues, "the more control the law exercises over the availability of guns, the better." . . .

A Drop in Crime

Q. Do handgun control laws now on the books work?

A. Yes. Within three years of the passage of the Washington, D.C., law banning the sale of handguns, the murder rate in the District dropped 25 percent. In Boston, after two years under Massachusetts' Bartley-Fox law, homicides declined 39 percent. And in South Carolina, after handgun laws there were tightened in 1975, the murder rate fell 28 percent. Naturally, in each case the reduction in the handgun murder rate was even more dramatic.

Unfortunately, a scattered few state laws cannot completely solve the problem of handgun violence. Even in states with strict controls, it is very difficult to regulate the influx of out-of-state handguns. In 1973, for example, 96 percent of the handguns used in New York City crimes had originally been purchased out of state.

To eliminate the present hodgepodge of inconsistent and incomplete state laws, many groups concerned about handgun violence advocate a comprehensive national law to ban the manufacture, sale, and private possession of handguns.

Q. Wouldn't registration and licensing help to eliminate handgun murders?

A. Both registration and licensing are useful but limited responses to the problem of handgun violence. Registration would make it easier to trace handguns used in crimes. Requiring a license to purchase a handgun would screen out those persons who have previously committed a felony offense. Either of these proposals is a good first step, but only a partial response. Handguns would still be widely available, and people would still be killed—in accidents, in suicides, and in crimes of passion. As long as Americans still keep handguns under the mattress, in the closet, and in the glove compartment, none of us is safe.

Saturday Night Specials

Q. Wouldn't outlawing the sale of "Saturday Night Specials" solve the problem?

A. Banning "Saturday Night Specials" would be a useful first step toward an ultimate solution, but by itself it is no real cure for the disease of handgun violence. While definitions of "Saturday Night Special" vary, one 1979 study showed that only 27 percent of the handguns used in urban crimes are committed with Saturday Night Specials. Undoubtedly, prohibiting the sale of these hand-held weapons would start the necessary process of draining American society of its handguns. But if a ban on Saturday Night Specials would save some lives, a ban on all handguns would save more.

Q. Won't handing out heavy jail sentences for all handgun-related crimes stop handgun violence?

A. Mandatory prison sentences might deter some handgun crimes, but requiring stiffer penalties would (at best) solve only part of the problem. Nearly 12,000 people are killed annually in accidents and suicides involving handguns. Moreover, less than 25 percent of all handgun murders take place during the commission of felonious acts. Most murders are "crimes of passion" committed during arguments between people who know each other—not during bank robberies or liquor store holdups. A law requiring minimum prison terms would only prevent deaths in those cases where the of-

> *"As long as Americans still keep handguns under the mattress, in the closet, and in the glove compartment, none of us is safe."*

fender had the time and the presence of mind to consider the consequences of his act. It is absurd to assume that this threat would have stopped Mark Chapman from killing John Lennon, or John Hinckley from shooting President Reagan. Like licensing and registration, mandatory sentencing is only a partial solution to the handgun violence problem. Until the private possession of handguns is banned, any serious reduction in the handgun body count is unlikely.

Self-Defense and Handguns

Q. Doesn't a handgun provide necessary protection for the household?

A. The handgun is rarely, if ever, an effective instrument for protecting the home against intruders. It does not deter burglars, who, seeking to avoid confrontation, almost always enter unoccupied homes. Nor does it often thwart robbers, who usually act too swiftly for the victim to react. In those few cases where firearms might be useful, long guns—particularly shotguns—offer much stronger stopping power than handguns.

Q. Even if handguns are not the best protection, why shouldn't Americans have the chance to guard their homes and businesses as they wish?

A. Most handgun owners buy their weapons for protection. They don't realize that every time one of them buys a new handgun, the rest of us have greater reason for fear.

A handgun kept at home for "protection" is more likely to kill a friend, a neighbor, or a child than a criminal. For every intruder killed by a handgun, six homeowners or their children are killed by accident.

Even a secure, well-kept handgun is a menace to the community. Each year, at least 150,000 handguns are reported stolen from the homes and businesses of law-abiding citizens. By some estimates, four times as many thefts are never reported. It is therefore no surprise that more than half of all criminally used handguns are stolen in residential burglaries. By definition, these weapons have fallen into the hands of burglars, robbers, and thieves.

> *"For every intruder killed by a handgun, six homeowners or their children are killed by accident."*

It is also no coincidence that 70 percent of all stolen firearms are handguns. Though there are four times as many long guns as handguns in this country, thieves consciously steal easily concealable handguns.

The dangers of handgun proliferation were never more vividly illustrated than in November 1979, when three 15-year olds broke into the Washington offices of the National Rifle Association and stole several handguns from an employee's desk. Several days later, those same handguns were used in the murder of a cancer researcher from the National Institutes of Health.

Such examples of negligence are common, and as a result the courts have begun to conclude that owners are accountable for their handguns, even if they are stolen. Like bartenders who by law may not serve a drunken customer, owners must ensure that their handguns are not at risk of being stolen, lest they harm the innocent.

Q. Isn't banning handguns simply a "foot-in-the-door" mechanism for making all guns illegal?

A. No. Groups that support a ban of handguns recognize that the primary function of a handgun is to kill a human being. In contrast, rifles and shotguns serve a sporting purpose. Moreover, because the handgun can be easily concealed, it is the most efficient and, therefore, the most common instrument of criminal violence. It is the concealable handgun that threatens and intimidates the citizens of this country—not the rifle and not the shotgun.

Rifles and shotguns make up nearly 80 percent of the firearms in this country, but they account for less than 10 percent of all firearms misuse. Handguns, only 20 percent of the firearms, account for 90 percent of all firearms misuse, criminal or accidental.

Q. Is it true that "when guns are outlawed, only outlaws will have guns"?

A. No. A ban on the private possession of handguns does not mean that no one may own a firearm. When handguns are outlawed, the American people will still possess rifles and shotguns. The police and other law enforcement officials will still have access to any firearms they need, including handguns. But when handguns are outlawed, the source of supply for criminals—legal sales and stolen weapons—will shrink, making it much more difficult for criminals to secure them.

> *"The unchecked proliferation of handguns taxes America's resources in numerous, often unseen ways."*

Q. If handguns were banned, wouldn't people simply turn to other weapons?

A. It is not true that a handgun can always be replaced by another weapon: only handguns can kill with such deadly certainty and such chilling efficiency. According to an FBI analysis, firearm-inflicted wounds are seven times as likely to result in death to the victim as injuries caused by all other weapons combined. And among firearms, the handgun is by far the criminal's first choice. Unlike a rifle or a shotgun it is easily concealed and requires infrequent reloading.

The Social Cost

Q. What is the present cost to the nation of handgun deaths and injuries?

A. No one can quantify the pain, suffering, and grief inflicted by the deadly handgun, but some experts have attempted to measure its economic impact. In 1978, according to an analysis in the *St. Louis University Law Journal*, the nation spent $500 million on hospital care alone for victims of handgun wounds. Since then, the yearly cost has spiraled steadily toward $1 billion, and it can be expected to go still higher.

Health care expenses—both in and out of hospitals—represent only a tiny fraction of the total cost to society. The unchecked proliferation of handguns taxes America's resources in numerous, often unseen ways. Americans are forced to spend extra dollars on higher insurance rates, unemployment compensation, increased use of the prisons, the courts, and the police, funeral expenses, and welfare payments. The true price America pays for its indifference to handgun misuse is staggering—perhaps $10 billion a year—(this from an industry that does less than $200 million a year in retail sales). The shooting of the President provides an excellent example of the financial burden handguns impose on American society. John Hinckley slipped into a Dallas pawn shop and bought a pair of .22 caliber revolvers for $45 each. The cost of just the hospital care for President Reagan and Hinckley's three other victims, every penny borne by the American taxpayer, now totals over $250,000.

Q. What do law enforcement officials have to say about the need for stronger handgun control laws?

A. Many of the leading figures in the law enforcement community have spoken out for tougher handgun legislation. The late J. Edgar Hoover, longtime director of the FBI, once said: "I think strong laws should be passed restricting the sale of guns, but when you try, you run head-on into collision with the National Rifle Association." More recently, Charles P. Monroe, who heads the FBI's criminal investigative division, stated: "I believe that handguns should be for only law enforcement personnel and the military, period. A handgun is designed to kill people." And New York City Police Commissioner Robert J. McGuire is most direct. "Gun control," he observes, "now is the overriding public imperative of this hour.". . . The Attorney General's Task Force on Violent Crime . . . reached the same inevitable conclusion: a serious crackdown on crime is impossible without a serious crackdown on handguns. . . .

Q. Is a national law restricting the sale and ownership of handguns politically feasible for Congress?

A. Yes. For years, a large majority of the American people have favored stricter controls on handguns. A Gallup poll showed that seven out of ten Americans want tougher handgun laws, and most of them support an outright ban on the possession of handguns, except by the police and other authorized persons. More than *nine* out of ten Americans favor a 21-day waiting period in order to give authorities time to check whether a prospective owner has a criminal record or a history of mental illness.

Social Change Is Needed to Reduce Violence

by Gary Amo

About the author: *Gary Amo, a free-lance writer and political consultant, is a former Peace Corps volunteer, Job Corps counselor, and English teacher.*

In other, more tranquil times, religion and politics were the topics of passionate debate, subjects to be avoided in civilized discourse. Today, nothing excites the emotions more than the subject of gun control. Even such highly emotional issues as abortion and capital punishment cannot drive otherwise rational individuals to the levels of vehemence inspired by gun control.

Guns—particularly handguns—are seen by many as the root cause of crime and violence in society. Others look on firearms as nothing more than tools which must be handled carefully and safely and can be used in a variety of shooting and hunting sports, as well as in the legitimate defense of home and family in a crime-ridden society. The debate transcends profession, political affiliation, class, age, gender, place of residence, and virtually every other demographic characteristic. But once passion replaces reason, the name calling begins.

Stereotypes Cloud the Issue

On one side, the National Rifle Association is viewed as an evil empire and its nearly three million members are widely viewed as coarse, beer-bellied rednecks—and worse. Proponents of gun control do not come off any better. They are often characterized as communist-loving, limousine liberals, secure behind their locked gates, protected by elaborate security systems, and with their collective heads buried in the sand. Politicians, albeit carefully, seize on the issue of gun control as a way to make their political reputations. Newspapers can be counted on to fill their editorial pages with righteous opinions concerning some aspect—or all aspects—of the private ownership of firearms, fanning the emotions on both sides of the issue.

And so the debate continues. . . .

There is the very real possibility that the National Rifle Association and its members are right, that gun control is not the true problem, but only a cosmetic

Excerpted from Gary Amo, "Gun Control: Myth and Reality," *Los Angeles Lawyer,* June 1989. Reprinted with permission.

panacea to mask the deeper ills of society, the festering sores that breed crime and violence. In the heated furor of the debate over gun control, too much is ignored. Politicians feel the pressure from their constituents to do something about crime. A gun control measure gives the appearance of addressing the problem of crime and the politician can tell the voters in the district, "I've done something."

Citizens and Criminals

But a certain amount of logic is lacking. No one has yet satisfactorily answered the question of how disarming the law-abiding citizen will take guns out of the hands of criminals who ignore society's laws.

Some 20,000 laws across the nation already regulate firearms. It is already against the law for convicted felons to possess firearms. It is already illegal to possess a fully automatic firearm. California, for example, has a 15-day waiting period between the purchase of a handgun and when the buyer may take possession. There is a national registration system where firearms sales are recorded on forms required by the federal government. New York City and Washington, D.C. have some of the most stringent firearms

> *"No one has yet satisfactorily answered the question of how disarming the law-abiding citizen will take guns out of the hands of criminals."*

regulations in the nation and yet no one looks on those cities as models of utopian paradises, free of crime and violence.

The National Rifle Association, like Cassandra, trumpets these facts, but anti-gun groups, politicians, individuals and the media refuse to listen, dismissing these points as NRA propaganda.

But the NRA has read some studies that should be required reading for everyone, on both sides of this issue of gun control, crime and violence.

James D. Wright and Peter H. Rossi have spent much of the last decade or so examining the issue of guns, crime and violence. The results of their studies—sponsored by the National Institute of Justice—are major contributions to an understanding of the entire problem. Wright and Rossi write:

> The progressive's indictment of American firearms policy is well known and is one that both the senior authors of this study once shared. This indictment concludes the following particulars: (1) Guns are involved in an astonishing number of crimes in this country. (2) In other countries with stricter firearms laws and fewer guns in private hands, gun crime is rare. (3) Most of the firearms involved in crime are cheap Saturday Night Specials, for which no legitimate use or need exists. (4) Many families acquire such a gun because they feel the need to protect themselves; eventually, they end up shooting one another. (5) If there were fewer guns around, there would obviously be less crime. (6) Most of the public also believes this and has favored stricter gun control laws for as long as anyone has asked the question. (7) Only the gun lobby prevents us from embarking on the road to a safer and more civilized society.

The more deeply we have explored the empirical implications of this indictment, the less plausible it has become.

Professor Wright, in particular, admitted to an anti-gun bias in his academic
work and assumptions before becoming deeply involved in the studies that were
to be published as *Under the Gun: Weapons, Crime, and Violence in America*
and *Armed and Considered Dangerous: A Survey of Felons and Their Firearms.*

> *"The control of guns is
> not equivalent to the
> control of violence."*

Professor Wright, now at Tulane
University, and Professor Rossi were
both at the Social and Demographic
Research Institute of the University
of Massachusetts, Amherst, when
the studies were conducted. They
can hardly be considered mouthpieces for the NRA. In fact, the studies have
been criticized by both sides of the debate. But the conclusions of the two studies are inescapable: firearms are not the true issue.

Evidence Refutes Simplistic Solutions

The policy implications of these research studies are far-reaching and anath-
ema to the simplistic solution of gun control as a solution to much greater problems in society. The authors write:

> First, the control of guns is not equivalent to the control of violence. Violent
> acts would undoubtedly continue even if a complete ban on possession of
> firearms were put into place and were effective . . . people will continue to rob,
> assault, and otherwise prey upon each other whether they have firearms or not.

And:

> One of the NRA's favorite aphorisms is that "if guns are outlawed, only out-
> laws will have guns." There is more truth to this point than the sophisticated
> liberal is usually willing to admit. It follows by definition that laws are obeyed
> only by the law-abiding! If we were to outlaw, say, the ownership of hand-
> guns, millions of law-abiding handgun owners would no doubt turn theirs in—
> most of them people who would never even contemplate, much less commit, a
> criminally violent act. But would we expect a person who owns a handgun for
> illicit reasons to turn his in? Anything illicit that this person might be contem-
> plating is *already* against the law. Can we expect him to abide by a gun law
> when he routinely ignores our other laws anyway? It is assuredly not in the in-
> terest of progressive causes that we be foolish about such things.

But such evidence, and it is backed by scholarly evidence, means little when
more gun control laws are introduced. . . .

What about the criminal misuse of firearms?

Again, Wright and Rossi addressed this issue in another complex and exhaus-
tive study published as *Armed and Considered Dangerous*. In that study, they
surveyed nearly 2,000 felons in state prisons around the country. One of their
findings was that:

The criminals in our sample preferred to own, and actually owned, relatively large, well-made weapons. . . . The more a felon used his guns in crime, the higher the quality of the equipment he possessed. Among the truly predatory criminals in the sample, the small, cheap handgun was not the weapon of choice.

In describing the policy implications of this Wright/Rossi study, James K. Stewart, director of the National Institute for Justice, wrote, "The findings suggest that, for career criminals at least, vigorous enforcement and tougher penalties for those who commit crimes with firearms may be more effective than regulation. Our emphasis ought to be on 'use a gun, go to jail.'"

> *"The root causes of that violence in society is not to be found in firearms, nor will the stricter control of firearms provide the answer that we need as a society."*

Writing in *The Public Interest*, Wright summarized much of the research efforts, along with the "indictment" usually presented by anti-gun advocates. Wright discusses the "crime of passion" so often cited by those who would ban firearms:

The "crime of passion" most often discussed is that of family members killing one another. One pertinent study, conducted in Kansas City, looked into every family homicide that occurred in a single year. In 85 percent of the cases examined, the police had previously (within the prior five years) been called to the family residence to break up a domestic quarrel; in half the cases, the police had been there five or more times. It would therefore be misleading to see these homicides as isolated and unfortunate outbursts occurring among normally placid and loving individuals. They are, rather, the culminating episodes of an extended history of violence and abuse among the parties.

Both *Under the Gun* and *Armed and Considered Dangerous* debunk many of the myths perpetuated by Handgun Control, Inc. and the National Coalition to Ban Handguns, which are given widespread credence by the media. Yet simple logic dictates that they are exactly that—myths. While conducting his research, Wright underwent a transformation.

In the course of my research, however, I have come to question nearly every element of the conventional wisdom about guns, crime, and violence. Indeed, I am now of the opinion that a compelling case for "stricter gun control" *cannot be made*, at least not on empirical grounds. I have nothing but respect for the various pro-gun control advocates with whom I have come into contact over the past years. They are, for the most part, sensitive, humane, and intelligent people, and their ultimate aim, to reduce death and violence in our society, is one that every civilized person must share. I have, however, come to be convinced that they are barking up the wrong tree.

The National Rifle Association and its members, like all other civilized Americans, want to see death and violence in society reduced. But the root causes of that violence in society is not to be found in firearms, nor will the stricter control of firearms provide the answer that we need as a society.

Assault rifles recently have taken the place of handguns as the "cause" of violence and crime in American society. The media, legislators, police chiefs and gun control advocates point to the tragedy in Stockton, California where children were gunned down in a school yard by an individual with an assault rifle, and to gang killings and drug wars to form their rationale

> *"The American dream must be attainable for the people, as well as the privileged."*

for banning assault rifles. But once again, the problem of violence in society is attacked from the wrong direction.

A ban on assault rifles will not stop violence, any more than virtual bans on handguns in New York City and Washington, D.C. stopped violence in those cities.

California's Assault Rifle Ban

In Stockton, Patrick Edward Purdy lived out some terrible nightmare. Everyone laments the tragedy. But Purdy had six arrests on his record, with charges ranging from weapons violations to drug charges to attempted robbery. He received two misdemeanor convictions. The sentences were 12 months probation with five days in jail and two years probation with 30 days in jail.

In the aftermath, bills were introduced in the California legislature, bills which will eventually ban the sale and possession of assault rifles in one fashion or another.

The author of the senate version, David A. Roberti, has been quoted in the *Los Angeles Times*, saying, the senators "now recognized that we have a common obligation to get assault weapons out of the hands of the general public."

How will taking assault rifles away from the general public stop crime and violence in society?

Patrick Edward Purdy was not one of the general public, not with his disturbed mental state and arrest record.

Drug dealers and gang members are not the general public.

In California, if the ban on assault rifles allows law-abiding citizens to register and keep the rifles they already own, these citizens will comply with the law, simply because they *are* law-abiding citizens. They may not like the ban. They may grumble and complain about being treated as criminals, but they will comply with the law. Their rifles will not be used in the commission of a crime.

How many psychopaths will comply with such a law? How many drug dealers and gang leaders will comply with such a law?

Tougher criminal penalties and stricter enforcement of our laws will help reduce crime and crime-related violence. But even such measures provide only a part of the answer.

Much has been made of civil rights, equal opportunity, affirmative action, but too little has been actually accomplished. Too many people in America are homeless, go hungry, lack the basic skills that would be provided by a truly equal education, have little prospect of ever breaking the vicious chain of events that keeps them impoverished intellectually and economically. Is it of little surprise that so much interpersonal hatred exists in our society? Is it a shock to find that we are raising generations of angry children? This nation was founded and exists on great ideals, the greatest ever realized, even partially. But our society must fulfill those ideals. The American dream must be attainable for the people, as well as the privileged.

Reducing Gun Violence on TV Would Reduce Violence

by Marjolijn Bijlefeld

About the author: *Marjolijn Bijlefeld is a free-lance writer and gun control activist.*

It could be any prime time cop and robber shoot out. The bad guys couldn't hit a larger-than-life target if it were standing in front of them, and the good guys, in even the most precarious situations, manage to hit the bullseye. It always works that way for the heroes, right?

Wrong, that's fiction. Facts are much more sobering and don't reflect the "justice" we've grown accustomed to seeing on television and in movies.

The fact is that 22,000 people die each year because of handguns. Annually, 12,000 people commit suicide with handguns and another 1,000 die from unintentional fatal injuries. Every year, there are about 9,000 handgun homicides in this country. In addition, there are more than 200,000 injuries due to handguns annually.

The fact is that it is not simply a cut and dried good guy versus bad guy battle. In 1985, of the 9,000 homicides reported in this country, only 167 were cases of justifiable homicide. For that small number of people, the handgun was perhaps the only way out of a life-threatening situation. For thousands more, it was the weapon that ended their lives.

The fact is that 60 percent of the people murdered are killed by someone they know. Friends shoot friends. Neighbors shoot neighbors. Wives shoot husbands or ex-husbands.

Bloody Slaughter of Innocents

However, much of what we are exposed to in the media does not reflect the bloody slaughter of so many innocent lives. Can we simply blame violent television shows for a blatant disregard for reality, or does the problem lie deeper—

Marjolijn Bijlefeld, "The Hero and the Handgun," *Engage/Social Action* (now *Christian Social Action*), May 1987. Reprinted with permission.

with this country's dangerous fascination with guns?

The media plays an interesting role in the issue of handgun violence. While some shows flagrantly misrepresent and idealize the heroism of handgun-toters, others make a genuine effort to discuss the issue. Not to be overlooked for its enormous contribution to the education of the American public is the news media. Daily, television and newspaper reports inform us of another handgun tragedy that occurred. The constant reinforcement of hearing about senseless deaths that are often avoidable and always disturbing helps shape the opinion that handguns cause more harm than good.

> *"Much of what we are exposed to in the media does not reflect the bloody slaughter of so many innocent lives."*

Indeed, the majority of the people in this country do share that concern. According to a Gallup poll released in May, 1986, an overwhelming 60 percent of those questioned wanted more stringent laws on handgun sales. Another interesting question in this poll asked if people favored a community ban on handguns. Of the respondents, 47 percent said they favored such a ban, an increase of 7 percent over the previous year.

Those numbers are encouraging, not only to people in the handgun control movement, but to federal and state representatives willing to make handgun control an issue. Not many years ago, the powerful gun lobbies could threaten political extinction to anyone voting against their interests. However, the continual appearance of polls that reflect a general trend among Americans favoring stricter handgun policies must serve as an indicator to these politicians that, not only is it safe to speak out on handgun control, it can even be politically sound.

Myths About Guns

However, as positive as these steps are, the road toward a sane handgun policy is a frustrating one. Encouraged in part by ideas presented in the media, many persons believe that a handgun is the weapon with which we can save ourselves from all plagues on society—anything from varmints to criminals to a Russian invasion. For example, letters came into the office of the National Coalition to Ban Handguns after ABC broadcast "Amerika," the controversial series about a Russian takeover. One reads: "I've watched 'America' on TV for almost a week, and now, as a result, I'm going to join the National Rifle Association and all it stands for. I thought that you should be the first to know. I'm an AMERICAN. I don't want to become an AMERIKAN."

This letter presents the tragicomic attitudes so prevalent among some people. Many people honestly believe that when push comes to shove, they'll beat the odds and protect themselves in heroic manners. In all of 1985, only 167 times was someone able to shoot justifiably and kill the bad guy. Incidentally, only about half of those killed were strangers to the person. The others were relatives, acquaintances and friends. Never mind those statistics; people feel *they* can handle themselves under great and life-threatening pressure. After all, Dirty Harry, the Equalizer, and Rambo, do it all the time.

Death as a TV Plot

From the time children are little, they see death as a plot for television and movies. They sit on the edge of their seats while the suspense on the screen builds—the bad guy is stalking our hero through a vacated building. The hero is holding onto his arm where he was just grazed by a bullet from the villain's gun. That will undoubtedly be the best shot the villain gets in before he meets his well-deserved end. And all of a sudden, when things look as if they couldn't get any worse for the brave soul, the bad guy gets befuddled, a box falls on his head and our hero gets a clear path to shoot and kill. He then staggers back outside in the dazzling bright sunlight—the victor. We breathe easier, knowing next week he'll have no scars and he'll be ready to confront any new contemptible and vile character that comes his way.

These scenes are repeated over and over until the line between reality and fiction becomes blurred beyond distinction. Most of us don't live our lives from one perilous adventure to the next. We don't have need to be constantly on the lookout for the next two-bit creep who's waiting to get revenge for something that happened to him last television season. We all go to sleep at night thinking about how clever the hero was and how utterly much more clever we would be in the same situation. We see replays of the dramatic scene with ourselves as the star.

> *"The television media . . . has some obligation to reflect the truth."*

However, in the morning we read in the newspaper that none of that really happened. Instead, the headlines rudely awaken us to the tragedies that took or injured human lives—real lives, not fictitious ones.

• In Oakland, California, an 81-year-old blind man discovered the person he shot was not a burglar, but his 80-year-old wife.

• A prep school student, after being caught drinking on school grounds in Arizona, went on a shooting rampage on campus, wounding an administrator and a teacher before being shot to death by police.

• In Lewiston, Montana, another teenager, intending to kill his teacher because he was failing, was charged with shooting the substitute teacher instead.

• In Bridgeport, Connecticut, a 45-year-old man was shot to death while fleeing a crowd of people who believed he hit a young bicyclist.

• In Fort Worth, Texas, a 20-year-old woman was charged with shooting her boyfriend in the head in an apparent dispute over a Christmas present.

This is not the stuff prime time television is made of. This does not translate into a half hour of good, clean entertainment. It reflects instead intense suffering for families and friends of these victims whose lives were senselessly ended or permanently altered in the blink of an eye.

Such stories are far more than could be edited into a half hour of television time. Every day, 62 people die because of a handgun. One of those is under 14 years old. Even more frightening is the statistic that in 1985, 165 children under the age of 15 were murdered with a handgun. These are not just unintentional fatal injuries which could have been prevented by removal, or at the least, safe storage, of a handgun; these were cases of murder, the intentional shooting of children.

An Obligation to the Truth

Certainly, there is a very real problem with handgun violence in this country. The media can feed our frenzy and fascination with its repetitive empty plots of good guys emerging triumphant over bad guys. But we cannot simply blame the media. "Sheol and Abaddon are never satisfied, and never satisfied are the eyes of man" (Proverbs 27:20, RSV). Naturally, intensity sells the show. The temporary diversion into fantasy is not necessarily bad. But the television media, focused on here because of its preponderance of weekly series filled with violence, also has some obligation to reflect the truth.

Indeed there are several shows that have questioned the validity of handgun ownership and made it an issue in the show. An episode of "L.A. Law" focused on the district attorney's decision not to buy a handgun for herself, even though she had been shot in the arm by a young man seeking revenge for a friend she had prosecuted. She made a forceful speech stating if she did buy a handgun, it would only prove that she had no faith in the criminal justice system. During some faltering moments in her conviction on the issue, she went in to a gun store to look at guns. The dealer, trying his best to sell her a handgun, seemed only to disgust her when he asked her if she didn't agree that it was a sexy weapon. She put the handgun on the counter and walked away.

> *"Violence on television can plant the seeds of violence and retribution in the lives of those who watch and enjoy such programs."*

In an episode of a daytime soap opera "All My Children," one scene was about a child who found a loaded handgun. It discharged, not hurting anyone, but the child's mother expressed her fury at her husband for bringing such an obviously dangerous weapon into the house.

On a "Cagney and Lacey" episode, the show tracked a collector's pistol through its theft and subsequent shooting of one of the show's stars.

An amusing exchange arose when Sgt. Cagney informed the gun owner of New York City's strict handgun laws. He asked her, "Doesn't the right to keep and bear arms mean anything to you?" She asked in reply if he was planning on raising a militia.

Indeed, the show did reflect a serious concern. As did the gun-owning character on the show, many people feel that they've got their handguns well-protected, making them impossible to use as dangerous instruments. But generally, most handguns that are used in crimes are taken in burglaries. Handguns are one of the most popular items to steal from homes. Their concealability makes them easy to walk out with and frequently they're readily available, being "hidden" in the drawer or cupboard. Finally, handguns are easy to resell on a criminal market. It's much more convenient and profitable for a criminal to walk out with a handgun than a color television set.

> *"The distinction between what is right and wrong is difficult enough without having television glorify those who use their handguns to complete heroic deeds."*

The Seeds of Violence

In conclusion, the existence of handgun violence on television and in real life is obvious. The question that remains to be asked is if there is a connection between the two. In two of the gospels, Matthew and Luke, the relation between what one sees and how one lives is clear. "Your eye is the lamp of your body; when your eye is sound, your whole body is full of light; but when it is not sound, your body is full of darkness. Therefore be careful lest the light in you be darkness" (Luke 11:34-35). Nearly the same passage is found in Matthew 6:22-23.

On television, violence begets violence and retribution. An extension of that is that violence on television can plant the seeds of violence and retribution in the lives of those who watch and enjoy such programs. Violent actions and thoughts are not part of God's will for Christians. "The Lord tests the righteous and the wicked, and his soul hates him who loves violence" (Psalm 11:5).

The idea of accepting into the heart things that are seen through the eye was a topic of discussion in the movie, "Witness," about a young Amish boy who witnesses a brutal murder. The child's family hides a wounded police officer who was trying to protect the boy. After the boy finds the officer's loaded revolver, his grandfather sits down to talk with him. On the kitchen table lay the revolver and several bullets.

"This gun of the hand is for the taking of human life. We believe it is wrong to take life. That is only for God. . . . Would you kill another man?"

"I would only kill a bad man."

"Only the bad man, I see. And you know this bad man by sight? You're able to look into their hearts and see this badness?"

"I can see what they do; I have seen it."

"And having seen, you become one of them. Don't you understand? What you take into your hands, you take into your heart. Wherefore come out from among them and be ye separate, saith the Lord. And touch not the unclean thing."

The distinction between what is right and wrong is difficult enough without having television glorify those who use their handguns to complete heroic deeds of vigilanteism. The stark truth is that those deeds are not translated into the "real" world. Instead, this nation suffers dramatic losses of death and injury, hurt and suffering. Every year, nearly 200,000 people are injured and 22,000 people die—some old, some young, some virtuous and some with problems, but all human beings, worthy of living to the fullest the lives for which they were created.

Practicing Gun Safety Can Reduce Gun-Related Accidents

by National Rifle Association of America

About the author: *The National Rifle Association (NRA) is the largest organization of gun owners in the United States. It works to fight gun control laws and to promote the safe use of guns.*

Guns are neither safe nor unsafe by themselves. When people practice responsible ownership and use, firearms are safe. The number of accidental firearm fatalities has dropped 52 percent between 1967 and 1988, according to National Safety Council surveys. This decline is a direct result of the increase and effectiveness of gun safety programs.

NRA and Public Safety

The National Rifle Association has promoted firearm education and marksmanship training for more than 100 years. NRA's concern for public safety led to support of the earliest hunter education courses and continues today through many gun safety and training programs. But all of us share the responsibility for learning what firearm safety involves. With guns found in about half of all American homes today, gun owners as well as non-gun owners should know gun safety.

[Gun owners] should understand and be able to apply:
• The basic elements of gun safety—attitude, knowledge and skill;
• The fundamental rules of safe gun handling;
• How to identify and unload different types of firearms;
• The different types and uses of ammunition;
• How to clean and care for guns;
• Factors for evaluating gun storage options.

Understanding these points will enable [gun owners] to enjoy the many benefits of gun ownership and participation in shooting activities.

Nearly 70 million Americans own firearms and enjoy their safe and positive uses. Guns provide us with the means to participate in a variety of recreational, competitive and educational pursuits. Nearly 18 million people in this country hunt. Millions more enjoy competition and recreational shooting, gun collecting, and historical reenactment. Guns are tools for personal protection, and they are the elements upon which popular collegiate and Olympic sports are centered. People from all walks of life own guns and participate in shooting sports. Many people become involved in shooting at a young age and stay active throughout their lives. Guns offer American society a vast opportunity for shared experiences—as long as we share the responsibility to learn and diligently apply safe gun handling practices.

> *"Guns are neither safe nor unsafe by themselves. When people practice responsible ownership and use, firearms are safe."*

None of us would allow someone to be injured if it could be prevented. The fact of the matter is, accidental gun injuries can be prevented by accepting responsibility and taking the necessary actions. We are responsible for gun safety!

Home accidents involving guns generally result from one of two causes: ignorance or carelessness. The three basic elements of gun safety—positive attitude, knowledge and skill—eliminate both causes. Understanding the meaning of these elements is the first step toward accepting responsibility for gun safety.

A positive attitude is the *most* important element in gun safety; it is simply a matter of accepting the responsibility to act safely. It is a mental awareness that safety is always first and foremost when dealing with guns.

Knowledge means knowing and understanding the gun safety rules and how to apply them to any situation. It is knowing how guns and ammunition operate and how to handle them correctly. Knowledge is also being aware of what you do not know and when or where to go for help.

Skill in handling firearms safely means actually applying the gun safety rules. Skill is perfected through practice.

Fundamental Gun Safety Rules

There are three fundamental rules of gun safety. These rules apply when handling any gun under any circumstances:

1. Always Keep the Gun Pointed in a Safe Direction.
2. Always Keep Your Finger Off The Trigger Until You Are Ready to Shoot.
3. Always Keep the Gun Unloaded Until Ready to Use. . . .

The phrase "ready to use" needs some explanation. A gun kept in the home for protection is essentially always in use and may be kept loaded if special care is taken. The gun must be stored in a secure place, inaccessible to unauthorized users (children or adults) and in accordance with local laws. As a general rule, guns used for any purpose other than personal protection should never be loaded in the home. Guns used for hunting and competition, for example, are not ready for use until the hunter reaches the field or the target shooter steps to the firing line.

Parents who own guns have a special responsibility to practice safe gun handling. Be positive role models and talk openly about safety practices. The worst danger comes when a child considers guns a taboo or mystery that should be investigated when alone. The parent must, through example as well as instruction, set guidelines for children to follow.

Deciding when a child is old enough to receive training for any potentially dangerous situation can be difficult. The first time a child shows an interest in guns, regardless of age, is a signal that some type of safety training is necessary. The child may simply ask a question or act out "gun play." He or she has probably already seen examples of unsafe gun handling on television, in the movies, or in toy gun battles with his or her friends. The point here is that a child's gun safety training should begin as soon as he or she shows an interest in guns.

> *"Home accidents involving guns generally result from one of two causes: ignorance or carelessness."*

The type of safety training that should be taught depends on the maturity of the child. A parent's earliest guidelines may allow the child to touch a gun, but only with permission and only if a parent is present. An older child may be allowed to hold a gun, under adult supervision, while keeping the muzzle pointed in a safe direction. Should the child come across a gun without a parent present, he or she should be taught to:

- STOP—DON'T TOUCH
- LEAVE THE AREA
- TELL AN ADULT

Parents also need to make sure that a child understands the difference between pretend and real life. They need to explain that shootings seen on television are "pretend"; they do not reflect real life. Never assume a child knows the difference.

Accidents Are Preventable

Virtually any accident involving a gun can be prevented if a person accepts and practices the responsibility of learning safe gun handling rules and understanding how guns operate. However, the operation of different guns varies, and it is essential to read the owner's manual and understand it before attempting to unload a particular gun. Should you have any questions about how a firearm operates, do not experiment! Consult a knowledgeable individual for assistance. . . .

The proper storage of firearms is the responsibility of all gun owners. Education and the careful consideration of all factors that relate to your individual needs are the key to this responsibility. If you apply the safety formula and the basic safety rules to each situation, a firearm in the home is as safe as any other equipment you may own.

Gun ownership has been and will continue to be part of American society. Each year millions of Americans, young and old alike, share the unique experiences that the various shooting sports and activities offer.

The choice of being a shooter or not belongs to the individual. The responsibility for safety, however, must be shared by us all. This responsibility begins with education and matures through the development of proper attitudes, knowledge and skills. . . .

ALTHOUGH EDUCATION CAN PROVIDE THE ESSENTIALS, APPLYING THIS KNOWLEDGE AND ACCEPTING THE RESPONSIBILITY TOWARD SAFETY ALWAYS REMAINS WITH YOU.

Making Gun Manufacturers Liable for Gun Crimes Would Reduce Violence

by Garen Wintemute et al.

About the author: *Garen Wintemute is an associate professor of community health at the School of Medicine, University of California, Davis, a physician at the UC Davis Medical Center, and an expert on firearm injuries and policies. This viewpoint was excerpted from* A Nation at War with Itself: Firearm Violence in the United States, *a report prepared by Wintemute and five colleagues for the Henry J. Kaiser Family Foundation.*

There are an estimated 160-200 million firearms in the United States. Roughly 50% of all households report ownership of one or more firearms, and 25-30% own one or more handguns.

Firearms rank as this country's eighth leading cause of death. Over the next decade, we may well see firearms replace motor vehicles as the leading cause of traumatic death in the United States—as they already have done in Texas. Since 1933, when complete death registration was established, there have been more than 1,200,000 firearm-related deaths in the United States. There are now some 32,000 such deaths each year, including more than 18,000 suicides and 12,000 homicides; less than 5% of fatal shootings are unintentional.

Firearm mortality dominates intentional violence statistics in the United States. Sixty percent of our nation's homicides and suicides are committed with firearms; even higher percentages pertain among young people. Recent increases in homicide and suicide rates, particularly among young people, result almost entirely from firearm violence.

Nonfatal Shootings

For every person who dies by firearm violence, an estimated 7.5 nonfatal shootings occur. In 1985 there were an estimated 235,000 nonfatal shootings in the United States, of which 65,000 required hospitalization.

Excerpted from Garen Wintemute et al., *A Nation at War with Itself: Firearm Violence in the United States*, a report prepared for the Henry J. Kaiser Family Foundation, January 9, 1992. Reprinted with permission.

The associated economic impact is enormous. The lifetime cost of firearm deaths and injuries sustained in 1985 was estimated to be $863 million for medical care alone and $14.4 billion in total. Some 85% of the medical costs of firearm injuries are borne by public funds; major urban trauma centers may spend $200,000 to $300,000 in a single weekend, often without compensation, to care for these injuries.

Criminal justice statistics paint a similarly dramatic picture. According to the National Crime Survey (NCS), conducted by the U.S. Department of Justice, more than five million violent crimes (homicide, aggravated and simple assault, rape, robbery) occurred in this country in 1988. The rate of most of these crimes has increased since the mid-1980s.

"More than five million violent crimes (homicide, aggravated and simple assault, rape, robbery) occurred in this country in 1988."

Firearms play a major role; an earlier NCS study estimated that, even with homicide excluded, there were more than 800,000 major instances of firearm violence in the United States each year.

Aggregate statistics do not convey the special impact of crime involving firearms. Offenders who use guns are more likely to complete their crimes than are those who use other weapons, even if the gun is never fired. This is particularly so in the case of rape. When a crime also produces an injury, the consequences are most serious when a firearm is used.

The Impact of Handguns

Handguns are far more likely than either rifles or shotguns to be used in crimes or cause an injury. More than three-fourths of firearm homicides involve handguns. Each year, on average, 639,000 Americans "face an offender armed with a handgun," according to the National Crime Survey. These crimes include an average 12,100 rapes, 210,000 robberies and 407,000 assaults. Similarly, several special studies suggest that handguns are used in 70-75% of firearm suicides.

These statements gain added meaning from the fact that handguns still make up only 25% of firearms in the United States, and less than half of recent production. All handguns, not just cheap, low caliber, Saturday Night Specials, are at risk for criminal use. Criminals seek the same characteristics in handguns as others do: concealability and power. Not surprisingly, therefore, they often gain their weapons from non-criminal owners; as many as 70% of handguns used by one nationwide sample of gun felons had been stolen.

The risk of firearm violence is greatest among some minority groups and among those who are disadvantaged or vulnerable by virtue of socioeconomic status or age. Firearms are now the single leading cause of death in the United States for black males ages 15-34 and black females ages 15-29. The handgun crime victimization rate is three times higher for blacks than whites, and 1.7 times higher for Hispanics than for non-Hispanics.

Minority youth are most affected. By 1988, black male teenagers were 2.8 times more likely to die by firearm violence than from all natural causes combined. From 1984 through 1988, the homicide rate for black males ages 15-19 increased two-fold; the entire increase resulted from firearm homicide. The firearm suicide rate for this group also doubled from 1984 to 1988, while non-firearm suicide increased 16%. Forty-eight percent of *all* deaths among black male teenagers, and nearly 20% of *all* deaths among black female teenagers, now result from firearm use.

Low socioeconomic status is a far more potent risk factor for violence than is generally recognized. For example, homicide rates rise dramatically—by a factor of four or more—among both whites and blacks as socioeconomic status declines. With few exceptions, this variation is greater than that between whites and blacks at the same socioeconomic level. Homicide rates among poor whites may thus be substantially higher than those for more affluent blacks. Our present understanding of violence as fundamentally a race-related phenomenon is at least in part the result of our data-collecting practices. Information on race is routinely collected on police reports and death certificates, and socioeconomic data are not.

> *"Homicide rates rise dramatically—by a factor of four or more—among both whites and blacks as socioeconomic status declines."*

In recent decades, women have been particularly affected by increases in firearm violence. Firearm mortality rates for women are far higher than ever before. The annual rate of victimization in handgun crimes for black women is about 25% higher than that for white men, and is nearly three times higher than the rate for white women. Since the early 1970s, firearms have been the leading method for committing suicide among women.

The elderly are at relatively low risk for firearm crime. However, a 50-year decline in the suicide rate among those over age 65 ended in 1982; a 20% increase since that time is largely attributable to firearm deaths.

Firearms and the Quality of American Life

Some of the most telling information on the impact of firearms in the United States can be derived from surveys and anecdotal accounts. For many years, graduating high school seniors have cited crime and violence as the leading problem facing the nation. They well may be speaking from direct experience. Florida and California schools both reported 40-50% increases in firearm incidents in recent years. An 18-year-old District of Columbia high school student, testifying before the House Select Committee on Children, Youth, and Families, stated that eight of her friends and relatives had been shot to death.

In March, 1991, the *New York Times* reported that architects now design schools with an eye to violence prevention. New York City children recognize that if they play with guns at all, they should use translucent toys so they are not mistakenly shot. Elementary school children (and in one case a pre-schooler) have brought loaded firearms from home to class for show and tell. Permanent crisis teams have been established in major cities to provide counseling to children who witness violence at school or at home. In many urban neighborhoods, children become experts in combat survival—as they must do. Families drill their children in such techniques.

Witnesses to violence suffer psychological effects which last for decades. According to UCSF [University of California, San Francisco] child psychatrist Dr. Lenore Terr, children who witness serious violence view the future as "a landscape filled with crags, pits and monsters." Adults are not immune. Parents of murdered children sometimes experience severe anxiety when they consider having other children.

> **"We have repeatedly chosen not to regulate the product itself, but rather to regulate the behavior of its users."**

The mother of a teenager whose gunshot wound left him in a persistent vegetative state told an interviewer, "It's like having a baby—but worse. Sometimes I hope that he dies before I do, and you know why? Because there's not going to be anybody else to care for him the way that I care."

Efforts to Reduce Firearm Violence

It is widely noted that the United States has over 20,000 gun laws, yet retains unacceptably high levels of firearm violence. This is not the paradox it seems to be, but is a direct and predictable result of the direction our regulatory efforts to reduce firearm violence have taken. Particularly at the federal level, we have repeatedly chosen not to regulate the product itself, but rather to regulate the behavior of its users.

No agency with a mission to protect the public's health has any regulatory authority over firearms. Federal firearms law is generally administered by the Bureau of Alcohol, Tobacco and Firearms (BATF), a branch of the Treasury Department. BATF has at times been aggressive in identifying the holders and makers of illegal firearms and in curtailing illegal commerce in guns, activities which grew out of this country's fear of domestic terrorism in the 1960s and 1970s. With this exception, BATF does not believe it has a mission to safeguard the public from the hazards associated with the widespread availability of firearms. . . .

In 1990, the District of Columbia became the first jurisdiction to enact a product liability reform law to reduce firearm violence. The District Council adopted a statute which would have held the manufacturers of assault weapons liable for the injuries caused by these weapons (the statute as originally drafted applied to all handguns). The statute was repealed in 1991 by the Council when Congressional opposition jeopardized a $100 million in operations funding for the District, then reinstituted by referendum. As of early 1992, action by Congress to disapprove the referendum was anticipated. Nonetheless, cost shifting through allocation of liability represents a very promising approach for the future. . . .

Firearms themselves are virtually unregulated. Machine guns, and criminal use weapons such as short-barrelled shotguns, cannot be manufactured for sale to the public. With these few exceptions, there are no mandatory standards addressing the design, quality, type or number of firearms manufactured in the United States for civilian use. . . .

BATF is a law enforcement agency; it licenses dealers and, in collaboration with the Department of Justice, oversees statutes and regulations addressing commerce in firearms. (The Internal Revenue Service collects federal excise taxes on firearms from manufacturers.) BATF also administers the standards which apply to imported firearms. These standards, established pursuant to the Gun Control Act of 1968, set minimum criteria for quality of construction, concealability and purpose. Domestically produced firearms are legislatively exempted from these standards. Thus, when BATF detects an instance of poor quality or design in a domestic firearm, it has no authority to act.

> *"Without doubt, product liability litigation has played an important role in restricting the firearms industry and in shaping firearms policy."*

For example, the General Accounting Office concluded that 30% of all unintentional shootings could be prevented if firearms were universally equipped with trigger arrestors (to prevent inadvertent pulling of the trigger) and loading indicators. Neither of these devices is required at present, and in the case of handguns, both are usually absent. Under current law, no agency is empowered to require these design improvements.

Litigation and Firearm Violence

Without doubt, product liability litigation has played an important role in restricting the firearms industry and in shaping firearms policy. Most successful cases have addressed specific defects in design or manufacture. Cases have also been brought, particularly against handgun makers, on the premise that the products involved are inherently and unreasonably dangerous even if no specific design defect exists. It has been argued that manufacturers should therefore be held liable for all injuries caused by these guns. Only one such case has been successful, but it had a major effect. In *Kelley v. R.G. Industries*, the Maryland Court of Appeals held that such liability did exist for the manufacturers and distributors of Saturday Night Specials. This decision, coupled with earlier defective product verdicts against R.G. Industries, put the company out of business. It was at the time the largest U.S. assembler of Saturday Night Specials from foreign parts. Moreover, the *Kelley* decision led directly to the establishment in Maryland of a Handgun Review Board, which has prohibited the manufacture and sale of such handguns in Maryland. . . .

Conclusions and Recommendations

During the 1960s and early 1970s, soaring firearm death rates and assassinations of our nation's leaders produced a level of public concern not seen before—or since. Four separate high-level federal commissions, including those on the causes and prevention of violence and on the reform of the federal penal code, recommended that the production and sale of handguns be completely banned or severely restricted, as part of a wide array of measures to reduce firearm violence. With few exceptions the recommendations which addressed firearms were never implemented. The legislative focus in particular has come to rest almost entirely on the regulation of gun users' behavior, and ignores the inherently lethal nature of firearms themselves. In effect, we have chosen to allow a hazardous product to become widely available, and have then attempted to regulate the further distribution and use of that product.

No campaign to eliminate the hazard associated with a consumer product can succeed without addressing the product itself, and the industry which produces and markets that product. The past decades' declines in motor vehicle fatality rates and in per capita cigarette consumption establish this point firmly. Public interest researchers and advocates focussed deliberately on the crashworthiness of motor vehicles and the production and marketing of tobacco. Previously protected industries were forced to enter the public

> *"Particular attention must be given to the firearm industry, and firearms themselves as unreasonably hazardous products."*

debate over injuries caused by their products. The product-based approach has provided innovative channels for action; HHS [Health and Human Services] Secretary Louis Sullivan's call to boycott sports events which are sponsored by tobacco companies is a highly visible recent example.

There is a real possibility that, over the next decade, such product-based activities will produce unprecedented success in efforts to prevent firearm violence. Research published since 1987 has painted, for the first time, an accurate picture of the size of the problem. Other studies just now being released begin to address a fundamental point: the risk-to-benefit ratio, at the individual level, of firearm ownership. Still others have evaluated public policies in this area with new accuracy and sophistication.

Such new knowledge, coupled with a series of successful legislative efforts (which themselves grew from and were supported by empirical data) has in-duced a growing number of policy makers and interest groups to become active on a subject which earlier had seemed risky and unproductive. Researchers and other experts are increasingly involved in policy development, and in the defense of new policies from challenges in court and in public debate. . . .

Particular attention must be given to the firearm industry, and firearms themselves as unreasonably hazardous products. The campaigns to reduce the adverse health effects of motor vehicles and tobacco will provide useful models for this effort. A variety of channels for intervention will be required. These include legislation and regulation, but extend to litigation, direct citizen action, and continued research. . . .

We have repeatedly advocated the use of structured litigation to achieve public policy reform. Support is needed for an assessment of such programs in other areas, and the design of a similar program designed to hold manufacturers and retailers accountable for injuries caused by the products they sell. Among the expected benefits of such a program are a reduction in the easy availability of firearms generally, and the elimination of targeted classes of firearms from circulation.

Chapter 5

Are Other Nations' Gun Control Measures Effective?

CURRENT CONTROVERSIES

Gun Control in Other Nations: An Overview

by Charlotte A. Carter-Yamauchi

About the author: *Charlotte A. Carter-Yamauchi is a researcher for Hawaii's Legislative Reference Bureau in Honolulu and the author of* A Clash of Arms: The Great American Gun Debate, *from which this viewpoint is excerpted.*

Most technologically advanced nations have far stricter gun control laws than the United States and less violent crime. In some of these countries, the laws regulating individual firearm ownership amount to a virtual ban. Accordingly, many gun control advocates attempt to demonstrate the effectiveness of restricting private gun ownership by comparing the gun control laws and crime rates in the United States with those of other industrialized countries.

The statistics are shocking indeed. Handgun Control Inc. reports that in 1985, handguns were used to murder:

- 46 people in Japan,
- 8 people in Great Britain,
  31 people in Switzerland,
- 5 people in Canada,
  18 people in Israel,
- 5 people in Australia, and
  8,092 people in the United States.

Similarly, a 1988 United States Department of Justice comparison of crime rates revealed the United States's violent crime rate is at least several times higher than other countries'. For example, murder, rape, and robbery occurred four to nine times more frequently in the United States than in European countries. Easy access to handguns was cited as a major reason for the higher crime rate in the United States.

Crime Rates in Seattle and Vancouver

A 1988 article in the *New England Journal of Medicine* would appear to support this conclusion. In the article, a group of physicians reported statistics they had gathered comparing crime rates and handgun registrations in Seattle and

Part II of Charlotte A. Carter-Yamauchi, *A Clash of Arms: The Great American Gun Debate*, State of Hawaii Legislative Reference Bureau, 1991.

Vancouver, which have similar geography and socio-economic conditions but significantly different firearm laws. Seattle's firearm restrictions are fairly loose; whereas in Vancouver, carrying concealed weapons is forbidden, buying a handgun requires a restricted weapons permit, and buying a long gun requires a firearm-acquisition certificate.

The doctors calculated the homicide rates per 100,000 residents and found that the rates for non-firearm homicides were nearly identical between the two cities, but that handguns were 4.8 times more likely to be used in homicides in Seattle than in Vancouver. Similar findings are reported for aggravated assaults: Vancouver had slightly more non-firearm aggravated assaults than Seattle, but Seattle had 87.9 aggravated assaults involving the use of firearms per 100,000 residents compared to Vancouver's 11.4. The doctors suggested that the lower homicide rate in Vancouver was attributable to restricted access to handguns.

> *"The doctors suggested that the lower homicide rate in Vancouver was attributable to restricted access to handguns."*

Factors Affecting Crime Rates

As is frequently pointed out, however, comparisons of United States crime rates with those of other countries fail to take into consideration the vast historical, social, legal, and cultural factors that contribute to the differences in crime rates. For example, in an article examining Japanese gun laws and crime rates, [David B. Kopel] asserts that:

[G]un control has little, if anything, to do with Japan's low crime rates. Japan's lack of crime is more the result of the very extensive powers of the Japanese police and the distinctive relation of the Japanese citizenry to authority. . . .

Partly because the Japanese are so unified and homogenous, they accept and internalize social controls. It is this attitude of obedience and impulse control that matters most in the low Japanese crime rate. Guns or not, the Japanese are simply the world's most law-abiding people.

Besides the police and the military in Japan, only hunters are allowed to possess guns, and that possession is strictly limited. Hunters must store their rifles or shotguns in a locker when not hunting. Civilians are forbidden to possess handguns, and even the possession of a starter's pistol is allowed only under certain detailed conditions.

After discussing the history of Japanese civilian firearm ownership and the disarmament of Japan following World War II, the commentator concludes that:

The contrast between the individualist American and the communal Japanese ethos is manifested in everything from behavior at sporting events to industrial labor organization. As a result, pressure to conform, and internalized willingness to do so are much stronger in Japan than in America. This spirit of conformity provides the best explanation for Japan's low crime rate. It also explains why the Japanese people accept gun control.

A comparison of firearms and crime between the Netherlands and the United States resulted in a similar conclusion. The authors of the study found that:

(1) Americans possess 300 guns per 1,000 people versus 9 guns per 1,000 people in the Netherlands;

(2) Laws restricting gun ownership are much more stringent in the Netherlands than in the United States;

> *"Americans possess 300 guns per 1,000 people versus 9 guns per 1,000 people in the Netherlands."*

(3) Police in the Netherlands are very concerned with enforcing firearm laws, seizing about 34 guns per 100,000 people annually compared to an estimated 2 guns seized by the federal government per 100,000 people in the United States, plus another 1 or 2 guns per 100,000 people in each state; and

(4) Crime rates are higher and guns are used more often in crimes in the United States than in the Netherlands—in 67 percent versus 37 percent of the murders and in 45 percent versus 18 percent of the robberies.

Cultural Values: A Comparison

The authors, [G. Jan Colign, David Lester, and A. Slothouwer,] note that, because their comparison is correlational, it does not permit any cause and effect conclusion to be drawn. Nevertheless, they suggest that the data support the argument that death and serious injury are less likely to occur if criminals are prevented from using guns. However, they also acknowledge that cultural values significantly affect these conclusions:

> In the Netherlands, none of the violent robberies we studied resulted in the death of the victim, and the criminal use of firearms brings no greater risk of death (or serious injury) to the victim than the use of another weapon. In the USA, the picture is very different; firearm injuries result in death three to four times more often than blade-weapon injuries. It would appear that the attitudes and motives of criminals are different in the two cultures. Robbers in the Netherlands, though they may carry guns, are not motivated to kill (or seriously injure) their victims, whereas robbers in the USA may be so motivated. . . .

> These cultural attitudes may be the crucial factor in national differences in the possession and use of firearms. Americans possess guns in large quantities and clearly desire to do so. American criminals carry guns and are prepared to use them in the commission of their crime. Those in the Netherlands do not need to own guns; and even when they do carry guns, are less likely to use them to produce serious injury.

Crime rate comparisons with England, where firearms are strictly regulated, also are criticized. Critics point out that both the rates of firearm ownership and of violent crime were extremely low in England for decades before strict gun control laws were passed and also that these laws have not prevented a sharp increase in gun crime in England in the past decade.

A recent examination of the effect of 1977 Canadian legislation strictly regulating the acquisition of firearms on violent crimes, suicides, and accidental deaths found that the stock of firearms in general and handguns in particular has actually grown since the law's implementation. After reviewing the trends in Canada over the past ten years for various types of violent crime, suicide, and accidental death relative to the United States, the author concludes that the 1977 legislation has had few perceptible effects.

Pro-gun advocates frequently point to Switzerland, where high-powered guns are readily available, to support their contention that guns do not cause an increase in crime rates. Switzerland has a murder rate which is a fraction of that of the United States and which is less than that of Canada's or England's, where guns are strictly controlled, or Japan's where guns are virtually prohibited.

For centuries, Switzerland has maintained a policy of armed neutrality with a well-armed citizenry. Today, military service is universal for all Swiss males. After an initial training period, conscripts are required to keep their guns, ammunition, and equipment in their homes until the end of their term of service. Enlisted men are issued M57 automatic assault rifles and officers are given pistols. Each man is given a bolt rifle after being discharged from the service.

In addition, the army sells a variety of machine guns, submachine guns, anti-tank weapons, anti-aircraft guns, howitzers, and cannons to purchasers

> *"Robbers in the Netherlands, though they may carry guns, are not motivated to kill (or seriously injure) their victims, whereas robbers in the USA may be so motivated."*

who have an easily obtained cantonal (roughly equivalent to a state) license. These weapons are required to be registered. Other firearms also are easily obtained. The purchase of long guns requires no special permit or procedure. Handguns are sold to those with a purchase certificate, which can be obtained from a cantonal authority by any applicant over eighteen who is not a criminal or mentally infirm.

Social Control and Gun Control

After reviewing Switzerland's stable, integrated community structures and the many factors that contribute to the inter-generational harmony that exists in Switzerland to inhibit age separation, alienation, and growth of a separate youth culture, [David B. Kopel and Stephen D'Andrilli] conclude that:

> Guns in themselves are not a cause of crime; if they were, everyone in Switzerland would long ago have been shot in a domestic quarrel.

> Cultural conditions, not gun laws, are the most important factors in a nation's

crime rate. Young adults in Washington D.C. are subject to strict gun control, but no social control, and they commit a staggering amount of armed crime. Young adults in Zurich are subject to minimal gun control, but strict social control, and they commit almost no crime.

One of the foremost researchers in the area of gun control [James D. Wright] sums up the inconclusive nature of these international comparisons as follows:

> It does not take advance training in research methods to see that in the absence of more detailed analyses, such comparisons are vacuous. Any two nations will differ along many dimensions—history, culture, social structure, and legal precedent, to name a few—and any of these differences (no less than the difference in gun laws or in the number of guns available) might well account for the difference in violent crime rates. Without some examination of these potentially relevant factors, attributing the crime difference to the gun-law or gun-availability difference begs the question.

Phrased differently, in the absence of controlling for the historical, legal, social, and cultural differences in these international comparisons, any inference that crime rate differences are attributable to differences in firearm availability is gratuitous.

Canada's Low Gun Homicide Rate Proves the Effectiveness of Gun Control

by Catherine F. Sproule and Deborah J. Kennett

About the authors: *Catherine F. Sproule and Deborah J. Kennett are professors of psychology at Trent University in Peterborough, Ontario, Canada.*

Several studies have not yielded clear or unequivocal evidence for the effectiveness of gun control in the United States. On the other hand, Sproule and Kennett demonstrated a significant decrease in shooting homicide rates in Canada after the introduction of stringent gun control legislation in 1976. We propose that the discrepant findings regarding the benefits of gun control between Canada and the USA are likely the result of differences in the rigour and pervasiveness of gun control.

Canada's Stricter Gun Control

In comparison to Canada, gun control in the United States, particularly pertaining to handguns, is remarkably lax. There are an estimated 70 million handguns in the USA, but in Canada, handguns are restricted weapons. Permits for ownership of handguns in Canada may be obtained only by a) police and others, such as security personnel, who demonstrate a need for handguns in their work, b) members of bonafide gun clubs, c) bonafide gun collectors, and d) persons who demonstrate a need for handguns for protection. As far as we can ascertain, permits for handgun ownership have actually been granted only under the first three criteria. Further, infractions of the gun control provisions are indictable offences under the Criminal Code of Canada. In contrast, gun control provisions and criminal law in the United States are not federal but reside in each state or jurisdiction. In the USA, then, avoidance of local gun control regulations may be accomplished simply by crossing jurisdictional boundaries. Thus, not only are provisions for gun control much looser in most, if not all, of the American jurisdictions than in Canada, but also these less stringent regulations cannot be as well enforced as in Canada with its stricter federal gun control legislation.

The purpose of the present study is to examine the incidence of killings with guns in the two countries. Given the demonstrated effectiveness of Canadian gun control, it is expected that the rate of killing by guns will be lower in Canada than in the USA. Further, since the most rigorous regulations on firearms in Canada are for restricted weapons, i.e., handguns, the difference between the two countries' killing rates is predicted to be greater for handgun killings than for those committed by other firearms.

> *"In comparison to Canada, gun control in the United States, particularly pertaining to handguns, is remarkably lax."*

Canadian data for the rate at which victims of homicide were killed by handguns, by firearms other than handguns, or by methods not involving firearms, for the years 1977 to 1983 inclusive, were derived from Statistics Canada's annual publication on homicide. American data for the same years for victims dying by the same methods were derived from the 107th Edition of the Statistical Abstracts of the United States 1987.

It is important to note that the American data are murder rates whereas the Canada data are for the more inclusive category of homicide (i.e., first and second degree murder, manslaughter and infanticide). Comparison of this more inclusive category of homicide to that of the more restricted category of murder should mitigate finding support for the hypotheses.

Equally important to observe is that standardized rates adjusted for age could not be calculated because the age of the victim was unknown. Although changes in age structure have been demonstrated to affect crude rates, a comparison of killing rates by different methods between two nations with similar demographics is unlikely to be affected by the use of crude rates.

Canadian and U.S. Homicide Rates

Table 1: Canadian and U.S. average crude killing rates per 100,000 and (standard deviations)—1977 to 1983.

	Handguns	Firearms Other than Handguns	Nonshooting Methods
Canada	0.276	0.666	1.790
	(.0443)	(.1190)	(.0935)
USA	4.047	1.321	3.309
	(.4108)	(.1716)	(.2070)

244

The crude killing rates per 100,000, averaged over the years 1977 to 1983, are shown in Table 1 for killings by handguns, firearms other than handguns, and nonshooting methods for both Canada and the United States.

A 2 x 3 analysis of variance was performed on killing rates per 100,000 for the independent variables nation (USA vs Canada) and method of killing (handguns, firearms other than handguns, and nonshooting methods) over the years 1977-1983. Both main effects were significant. For all methods, the average American murder rate was significantly higher than the average Canadian homicide rate. As well, Scheffe's post hoc multiple comparison test for the significant main effect of method of killing revealed that the mean killing rate for the two nations combined was significantly greater for nonshooting methods (2.55) than for handguns (2.16) and for firearms other than handguns (0.99). In addition, the mean rate of killing by handguns (2.16) was significantly greater than the mean rate of killing by firearms other than handguns (0.99).

"The average USA murder rate for handguns . . . was found to be significantly greater than the average Canadian homicide rate for all methods of killing."

The significant main effect of method of killing, however, becomes less important in light of the significant interaction between nation X method of killing. Employing Scheffe's post hoc multiple comparison test, all simple mean comparisons were significant except that no significant difference was found between the average Canadian homicide rate for handguns (0.28) and the average Canadian homicide rate for firearms other than handguns (0.67).

In addition, our prediction that the difference between the two countries' average killing rates over the years 1977 to 1983 would be greater for handgun killings than for those committed by other firearms was supported. The mean difference in rates between the two countries for the years 1977-1983 for killings by handguns and for killings by firearms excluding handguns were observed to be 3.77 and 0.66, respectively.

U.S. and Canadian Murder Rates

Equally important are the following significant comparisons. First, the average USA murder rate for handguns (4.05) was found to be significantly greater than the average Canadian homicide rate for all methods of killing (2.73). Second, even though the average American nonshooting rate of 3.31 is significantly higher than the average Canadian nonshooting rate of 1.79, significantly more Canadians were killed by nonshooting methods (1.79) than by shooting methods (0.94). Third, the American shooting rate of 5.37 was observed to be significantly higher than the Canadian shooting rate of 0.94.

In strong support of our hypotheses and in a clear demonstration of the benefits of Canadian gun control, we found that Canadians kill less with firearms than Americans and that the difference between the two countries is larger for handgun killings (which are restricted weapons in Canada) than for those committed by other firearms. As well, American murder rates are higher for handgun killings than for killings by other firearms and for killings by nonshooting methods. Indeed, American murder rates for handguns are higher than the total Canadian homicide rate. The present findings combined with our earlier demonstration of a decrease in the Canadian shooting homicide rate after the introduction of gun control in Canada emphatically show that Canadian gun control, especially the provisions pertaining to handguns, does have the beneficial effect of saving lives.

In addition, these findings undermine the apparent claim of gun control opponents in their slogan 'people kill, guns don't,' which appears to mean that gun control does not affect the likelihood of killing but rather only the means by which death is accomplished. Also, the present findings allay a concern we raised regarding a finding in our comparison of methods of killing in Canada before and after gun control. Our results reported in a previous study indicated that there was a marginal tendency for nonshooting homicides to increase subsequent to gun control implementation, suggesting that gun control may encourage murderers to use other methods than firearms to kill. The findings we present here, however, do not support the claim that gun control operates simply to induce killers to find alternate means to kill. More specifically, in Canada, the definition of handguns as restricted weapons is not associated with higher rates of killing with other more accessible firearms:

> *"Canada's favourable situation regarding murder relative to the United States is to a large measure the result of Canadian gun control."*

the Canadian homicide rates for killing with handguns and with other firearms did not differ significantly. As well, the Canadian rate for other firearms was lower than the American rate for firearms other than handguns. Similarly, evidence against the claim that gun control facilitates the use of other methods was found for nonshooting killings. Although Canadians kill more with nonshooting than shooting methods, the Canadian nonshooting rate is significantly lower than the American nonshooting rate. Finally, in our earlier study we demonstrated that Canadian killers using firearms killed more victims than Canadian killers using nonshooting methods: a killer with a gun is more likely to have multiple victims than a killer without a gun. The high American murder rate for shooting methods may be attributable, in part, to the multiple victims of a killer with a gun.

Guns and Crime: Comparing Seattle and Vancouver

Additional support for the effectiveness of Canadian gun control comes from John Henry Sloan and his colleagues' comparison of crime, assault and homicide rates in Seattle, Washington, and Vancouver, British Columbia, from 1980 through 1986. Although crime rates were similar in the two cities, assaults involving firearms were seven times higher in Seattle than in Vancouver and differences in homicide rates in the two cities were virtually all accounted for by the 4.8-fold greater risk of being murdered with a handgun in Seattle than in Vancouver.

Because Canadian gun control is clearly beneficial, we are concerned about recent reports of a proliferation in gun clubs and gun club memberships whose apparent aim is to obtain handgun permits and also of an increase in the number of handguns confiscated by Canadian customs at the border. Because Canada's favourable situation regarding murder relative to the United States is to a large measure the result of Canadian gun control, Canadians must be vigilant against any erosion of our gun control provisions. Further, because gun ownership (at least in Detroit) is inversely related to individuals' confidence in collective institutions to protect their security of person and property, maintenance of Canadians' confidence in the police and justice system to protect our collective security is an important means by which to deter gun acquisition. Above all, the important role played by gun control in Canadians' collective security must be stressed and more widely recognized.

Israel Has a Successful Gun Control Policy

by Abraham N. Tennenbaum

About the author: *Abraham N. Tennenbaum, a former police lieutenant in Israel, holds a law degree from Hebrew University in Jerusalem. Tennenbaum is a teaching assistant and doctoral candidate at the Institute of Criminal Justice and Criminology at the University of Maryland in College Park.*

There is no clear right to carry a gun in Israel. Nothing similar to the Second Amendment even exists. In theory, the policy is very strict. No one may own or carry a gun without showing a reason to do so. A special permit by the Interior Ministry is then required. The permit has to have the approval of the police, and includes information about the owner and the gun type. It is easy to get a permit for a handgun to a law-abiding citizen (with no criminal record).

There is no distinction between carrying a gun and possessing it. If you have a permit to own a handgun, or other weapon, you are allowed to carry it on your body (concealed or not concealed). The police even recommend you carry it, because then the gun is protected from thieves or children. The result is that in any big crowd of citizens, there are some people with their personal handguns on them (usually, concealed).

The police and the court take seriously the felony of possessing a firearm without a permit, which almost always means that the gun is stolen. People with previous criminal records who are caught with firearms are generally sentenced to a year or two in prison.

Reasons for Owning Guns

According to Israeli law, an owner of a gun is responsible for it. If the gun is lost or stolen, he has to inform the police within 24 hours about the loss of the firearm. The owner will then be prosecuted on the misdemeanor offense of "negligence in keeping a firearm."

Perhaps the main serious difference between the Israeli and American practice is the reasons citizens possess guns. In Israel, the main function of guns of all kinds is the military function and self-defense against terrorism. People have

Abraham N. Tennenbaum, "Israeli Gun Laws and Their Impact," a paper presented at the 1991 meeting of the American Society of Criminology. Reprinted with permission.

guns for other reasons too, such as hunting or target shooting, but the main function of a gun is for self-defense.

While, as noted above, Israeli law limits possessing guns through a system of permits, there are other reasons guns are readily available. Most of the guns in Israel are not owned by the people who use them. They belong to the army, the police, or to other authorities, but not to private citizens.

Some examples will explain the huge distribution of firearms:

1. There is mandatory service in the army (three years for males, two years for females). In addition, most of the males are recalled into the army for approximately 30 to 45 days each year. Most of them get firearms of some kind, which they take home with them each leave period. In part, because this is the best way to take care of the weapon. The result is that in any major crowd (bus stations, trains, main streets), there are armed soldiers on the way to or from home.

2. Each school trip to the countryside requires companions with firearms (usually, some of the students' parents and teachers). In order to obtain firearms, one of the teachers has to go to the local police station and be assigned some firearms, which he will return after the trip.

3. The Israeli police operates a body called "Civil Guards" which handles all the police volunteers. One of its functions is to operate voluntary patrols during the night in some neighborhoods. The patrols are equipped with firearms, which are issued at the beginning of and are returned at the end of the patrol. Many of the volunteers are high school students (ages 16-18). After a short period of training, they carry firearms like any other volunteer.

Israel's High Gun Density

In simple words, the "gun density" in Israel is very high, despite the laws. This density is caused, of course, by the situation in the region, and it is not likely to be changed soon.

Israel is a very small and isolated country. For practical reasons, these facts can be very helpful. For example, there is only one big file (The Criminal Records Chart), which includes the criminal records of all Israeli citizens, including cases where there was a decision not to prosecute. Another example is the way the police handle cases of kidnapping (very few criminal kidnappings have occurred

> *"In Israel, the main function of guns of all kinds is the military function and self-defense against terrorism."*

in Israel in the last forty years). Volunteer teams go out to search the forests and caves, while the media call on people to be aware of the situation and try to locate the missing person.

It is not surprising, therefore, that the philosophy of gun control in Israel is that we can distribute many weapons to authorized people. And therefore guns are, by comparison to the U.S., very available.

Are guns available to criminals? Criminals can get guns in Israel, but it is not easy. Usually, handguns are stolen from private citizens while rifles, grenades, and explosives are stolen from the army. Basically, the "free market" with the rules of supply and demand governs the prices. An important feature of the gun is its history. A gun that was used in the past in a murder or robbery is a "dirty" gun which can cause troubles for the buyer, because ballistic tests can accuse the buyer of old crimes.

> *"Gun control laws and tough punishment cannot prevent criminals from obtaining firearms, but the laws can perhaps make it harder for criminals to get them."*

Another result of the situation is the greater use of explosives and automatic weapons in murders. Their availability to criminals (by stealing them from the army) seems to contribute to people's ability to use them.

To summarize: It is not as easy to get a firearm in Israel as in the U.S.A. but it is possible. However, the phenomenon of drug dealers or other criminals going with a firearm in their pocket is totally unknown in Israel.

The homicide rate in Israel has always been very low (40-60 cases of murders a year, in a population of four and a half million people). It is clear that the murder rate in Israel is much lower than it is in the United States. This is despite the greater availability of guns to law-abiding civilians.

It is unclear how much we can learn from a small homogenous society like Israel for the situation in other societies, but perhaps two broad statements can be suggested:

First, it seems that gun control laws and tough punishment cannot prevent criminals from obtaining firearms, but the laws can perhaps make it harder for criminals to get them.

Second, the relationship between density of firearms to the murder rate may not be generalizable. We can perhaps suggest that it is culturally correlated. What is important is the distribution of, and the underlying reasons for, this density.

The problem with the Israeli case is that we do not have any control group. The gun control laws and the density of guns are a long-term situation in Israel. It has never been seriously changed, and it is unlikely to change in the near future. Perhaps, with a lower density of guns or with easier gun control laws, the situation could be different. Who knows?

Israel's Gun Control System Works

The most fascinating point in the Israeli system is the combination of seemingly contradictory components. On one hand, the gun market is strictly regulated. On the other hand, guns are available and used by almost every law-abiding citizen at one time or another.

The result of this strange combination seems to work together. The question is if this combination can be implemented in other societies. Perhaps a combination of local unique conditions is what makes the Israeli system successful. Perhaps not. Perhaps the results will be the same anyway.

Future research is needed to better understand these interesting phenomena.

Japanese Gun Control Laws Are Oppressive

by David B. Kopel

About the author: *David B. Kopel, an attorney in Denver, Colorado, advocates the rights of gun owners. Kopel is the author of* The Samurai, the Mountie, and the Cowboy: Should America Adopt the Gun Controls of Other Democracies?

For gun controllers, Japan is a dream come true. The law is simple: "No-one shall possess a fire-arm or fire-arms or a sword or swords."

Japan's crime rate is very low, and its gun crime rate virtually nil. Anti-gun lobbies tout Japan as the kind of nation that America could be, if only we would ban guns. Handgun Control, Inc., quotes a Japanese newspaper reporter who writes: "It strikes me as clear that there is a distinct correlation between gun control laws and the rate of violent crime. The fewer the guns, the less the violence."

Japan's Strict Gun Control

But while Japan may be a gun-banner's dream, it's a civil libertarian's nightmare. Japan's low crime rate has almost nothing to do with gun control and everything to do with people control. Americans, used to their own traditions of freedom, would not accept Japan's system of people controls and gun controls.

Other than the police and the military, no one in Japan may purchase a handgun or a rifle. Hunters and target shooters may possess shotguns and airguns, under strictly circumscribed conditions. The police even check gun licensees' ammunition inventory, to make sure that there are no unaccounted shells or pellets.

A prospective gun-owner must take an official safety course; and then pass a test which covers maintenance and inspection of the gun, methods of loading and unloading, shooting from various positions, and target practice for stationary and moving objects. The license is valid for three years. When not in actual use, all guns must be locked away.

So comprehensive are the gun laws that even possession of a starter's pistol is only allowed under carefully-detailed conditions.

Excerpted from David B. Kopel, "Japanese Gun Laws and Crime," *American Rifleman*, December 1988. Reprinted with permission.

As to standards for the granting of gun licenses, the gun law offers no standards, just the vague statement that licenses must be denied "any person (taking into consideration also relatives living with him) who there is reasonable cause to suspect may be dangerous to other persons' lives or properties or to the public peace." Membership in the wrong political group will disqualify an applicant.

There are about half a million licensed shotguns, although their numbers have declined by about 20% in this decade. While new rifle purchases have been banned since 1971, Japanese who owned rifles before the ban have been allowed to keep them, providing of course that they keep their gun permit valid. About 27,000 licensed rifle owners remain.

A Low Crime Rate

The Japanese gun crime rate is very small. Handguns were used in 209 crimes in 1985. About two-thirds of all gun crimes are committed by *Boryokudan*, organized crime groups.

Across the board, the Japanese crime rate is dramatically lower than the U.S. rate. Tokyo, the world's safest major city, suffers muggings at the rate of 40 per year per one million inhabitants. New York City's rate is 11,000.

According to government statistics, Japan had 1.2 homicides per 100,000 citizens each year, and America had 8.4 in 1988. Actually, the gap between U.S. and Japanese homicide rates is not quite as large as the official statistics indicate. The F.B.I. overcounts American murders, by listing what [Florida professor] Gary Kleck estimates to be the 1,500-2,500 legal, defensive fatal shootings of criminals as illegal homicide.

> *"For handgun murders, the U.S. rate is 200 times higher [than Japan's]."*

Whatever the exact numbers, it is clear that Japan's actual homicide rate is far less than the U.S. rate. As for handgun murders, the U.S. rate is 200 times higher.

Robbery in Japan is about as rare as murder. Japan's annual robbery rate is 1.4 per 100,000 inhabitants; America's is 220.9. Do these statistics prove that America needs to import Japanese gun laws? Before saying "yes," let's take a look at the broader picture of Japanese crime control.

The Japanese criminal justice system bears more heavily on a suspect than any other system in an industrial democratic nation. One American found this out when he was arrested in Okinawa for possessing marijuana: he was interrogated for days without an attorney, and signed a confession written in Japanese that he could not read. He met his lawyer for the first time at his trial, which took 30 minutes.

Unlike in the United States, where the *Miranda* rule limits coercive police interrogation techniques, Japanese police and prosecutors may detain a suspect indefinitely until he confesses. (Technically, detentions are only allowed for three days, followed by 10-day extensions approved by a judge, but defense attorneys rarely oppose the extension request for fear of offending the prosecutor.) Bail is denied if it would interfere with police interrogation.

Even after interrogation is completed, pretrial detention may continue on a variety of pretexts, such as preventing the defendant from destroying evidence. Criminal defense lawyers are the only people allowed to visit a detained suspect, and those meetings are strictly limited.

Partly as a result of these coercive practices, and partly as a result of the Japanese sense of shame, the confession rate is 95%.

For those few defendants who dare to go to trial, there is no jury. Since judges almost always defer to the prosecutors' judgement, the trial conviction rate for violent crime is 99.5%.

The police routinely ask "suspicious" characters to show what is in their purse or sack. In effect, the police can search almost anyone, almost anytime, because courts only rarely exclude evidence seized by the police—even if the police acted illegally.

The most important element of police power, though, is not authority to search, but authority in the community. Like school teachers, Japanese policemen rate high in public esteem, especially in the countryside. Community leaders and role models, the police are trained in calligraphy and Haiku composition.

Fifteen thousand *koban* "police boxes" are located throughout the cities. Citizens go to the 24-hour-a-day boxes not only for street directions, but to complain about day-to-day problems, such as noisy neighbors, or to ask advice on how to raise children. Some of the policemen and their families live in the boxes. Police box officers clear 74.6% of all criminal cases cleared. Police box officers also spend time teaching neighborhood youth judo or calligraphy. The offi-

> *"The police also check on all gun licensees, to make sure no gun has been stolen or misused, that the gun is securely stored, and that the licensees are . . . stable."*

cers even hand-write their own newspapers, with information about crime and accidents, "stories about good deeds by children, and opinions of residents."

Lack of a Supportive Relationship

The police box system contrasts sharply with the practice in America. Here, most departments adopt a policy of "stranger policing." To prevent corruption, police are frequently rotated from one neighborhood to another. But as federal judge Charles Silberman writes, "the cure is worse than the disease, for officers develop no sense of identification with their beats, hence no emotional stake in improving the quality of life there."

Thus, the U.S. citizenry often does not develop a supportive relationship with the police. One poll showed that 60% of police officers believe "it is difficult to persuade people to give patrolmen the information they need."

The Japanese police do not spend all their time in the *koban* boxes. As the Japanese government puts it: "Home visit is one of the most important duties of officers assigned to police boxes." Making annual visits to each home in their beat, officers keep track of who lives where, and which family member to contact in case of emergency. The police also check on all gun licensees, to make sure no gun has been stolen or misused, that the gun is securely stored, and that the licensees are emotionally stable. Gun prohibitionists might rejoice at a society where the police keep such a sharp eye on citizens' guns. But the price is that the police keep an eye on everything.

Policemen are apt to tell people reading sexually oriented magazines to read something more worthwhile. Japan's major official year-end police report includes statistics like "Background and Motives for Girls' Sexual Misconduct." In 1985, the police determined that 37.4% of the offending girls had been seduced, and the rest had had sex "voluntarily." For the volunteers, 19.6% acted "out of curiosity," while for 18.1%, the motive was "liked particular boy." The year-end police report also includes sections on labor demands and on anti-nuclear or anti-military demonstrations.

A Comparison of Criminal Justice

Broad powers, professionalism, and community support combine to help Tokyo police solve 96.5% of murders, and 82.5% of robberies. In America, the police clear 74% of murders, but only a quarter of all robberies. Seventy percent of all Japanese crimes end in a conviction; only 19.8% of American crimes even end in an arrest. A mere 9% of reported American violent crimes end in incarceration. Compared to the Japanese criminal, the American criminal faces only a small risk of punishment. Is it any wonder that American criminals commit so many more crimes?

"In 1985, the Japanese police seized a record high 1,369 illegal guns. A big-city police force in the U.S. might confiscate that many all by itself."

Additionally, Japan's tight, conformist social culture does an excellent job of keeping citizens out of crime in the first place. As the head of Tokyo's Police Department explains, "A man who commits a crime will bring dishonor to his family and his village, so he will think twice about disgracing them."

Having lived together for several thousand years with very little immigration, the Japanese have developed the world's most homogenous and unified society. America's ethnic diversity causes tensions and crime, as the first or second generations of immigrants sometimes face the challenge of a new society, difficult economic circumstances, and sometimes substantial discrimination.

But even if immigration does cause some crime, our policies certainly seem more humane than the ethnic policies of Japan. When Japan, under severe American pressure, admitted 100 Vietnamese boat people, a leading publication called them "the sword of an alien culture pointed at Japan."

Many Korean families have lived in Japan for longer than Michael Dukakis' family has lived in America. Although born in Japan, the Koreans have "impure" blood, which makes them forever ineligible for Japanese citizenship.

Responsible Citizens Commit Few Crimes

Partly because the Japanese are so unified and homogenous, they accept and internalize social controls. It is this attitude of obedience and impulse control that matters most in the low Japanese crime rate. Guns or not, the Japanese are simply the world's most law-abiding people.

Japanese-Americans, who of course have access to firearms, have an even lower violent crime rate than do Japanese in Japan. Likewise, prisoners in jails in Japan and in America have no guns, but American prisoners perpetrate many homicides each year, and Japanese prisoners none.

Dr. Paul Blackman of the National Rifle Association's Institute for Legislative Action points out that if gun control were really the major cause of the low Japanese crime rate, it would be impossible to explain why Japan's non-gun crime rate is so much lower than America's non-gun crime rate. America's *non-gun* robbery rate, for example, is over 60 times Japan's. In Japan, a person can leave a bag of groceries on the sidewalk outside a store, and come back a half hour later to find it still there.

Notably, while Japan's homicide rate is low, it's about the same as the rate in England and Wales—a shooter's paradise compared to Japan. And the rate is the same as in Switzerland, where the government supplies assault rifles to all adult males, and which are required by law to be stored at home.

Japan's experience also suggests that gun control may have little effect on a nation's suicide rate. While the Japanese gun suicide rate is one-fiftieth of America's, the overall suicide rate is twice as high as America's.

Japan suffers from many double or multiple suicides, called *shinju*. Every day in Japan a child is killed by his or her suicidal parent, in *oyako-shinju*. Japan's tight family structure, which keeps the crime rate low, is not an unalloyed blessing.

> *"One important reason the Japanese voluntarily accept disarmament is that their government does the same."*

America's leading pro-gun-control scholar, Prof. Franklin Zimring, observes, "Cultural factors appear to affect the suicide rates far more than the availability and use of firearms. Thus suicide rates would not seem to be readily affected by making firearms less available."

Zimring's observation fits with the evidence in America. All ethnic groups have equal access to firearms, but Jews are less likely to use guns as their suicide method, while blacks and Southerners are more likely to use guns. Although American blacks are more likely to use guns in suicide, the black suicide rate is below the American average.

A Gun-Free Society

There is only one level at which Japanese gun controls are unquestionably successful. Almost the entire population has no personal familiarity with guns. Most of the Japanese tourists who shoot at the Hawaii Gun Club on Oahu have never even seen a gun before.

Drying up the availability of guns might be much more difficult in America than in Japan. Japan never had a significant stock of non-military guns, so gun control was simple to mandate. But in America, there are already about 200 million guns. In 1985, the Japanese police seized a record high 1,369 illegal guns. A big-city police force in the U.S. might confiscate that many all by itself.

An island nation, Japan has an easier time sealing its borders against illegal gun imports. Yet even if gun manufacture in America vanished, and all present guns were confiscated, illegal imports and production could quickly rebuild the American gun supply. Tulane University's James D. Wright warns that handgun prohibition might provide the same kind of boost to organized crime that alcohol prohibition did, opening up a new lucrative market for the sale of illegal goods.

> *"Japan's gun laws are part of an authoritarian philosophy of government."*

While many Americans are quite attached to their guns, and would refuse to obey many types of gun control, almost all Japanese obey the gun law, and feel no loss; in Japan, never seeing a gun is hardly a deprivation, for Japan developed only the most minimal cultural attachment to firearms.

When Portuguese trading ships arrived in the middle of the 16th century, Japan's many feudal leaders investigated guns for use in the ongoing civil wars. Long before the "Southern Barbarians" (Western traders) ever arrived, Japan had far outpaced Europe in metallurgy. Within a few decades, the various Japanese armies had more, better-built guns than most European armies.

A military dictator named Hidéyoshi was particularly expert in firearms tactics, and Hidéyoshi finally conquered Japan and ended the civil wars. In 1588 Hidéyoshi decreed the "Sword Hunt," and banned possession of swords by the lower classes. The pretext was that all the swords would be melted down to supply nails and bolts for a hall containing a huge statue of the Buddha. Instead, Hidéyoshi had the swords melted into a statue of himself.

After Hidéyoshi, the Tokugawa Shogunate took power, and ruled Japan until the late 19th century. The Shogunate used guns extensively in its invasion of Korea. But after the invasion was repelled, Japan turned inward, rejecting all forms of Westernization. Western contact was limited to a single Dutch trading mission, which was required to stay on a small island in Nagasaki harbor.

The Tokugawa began the gradual process of eradicating all Western influence from Japan, including the use of firearms. There was no need for a "gun hunt," since firearms had been used mainly by the feudal armies, not the people. Under the Tokugawa, peasants were assigned to a five-man group, headed by landholders who were responsible for the group's behavior. The groups arranged marriages, resolved disputes, kept members from traveling or moving without permission, maintained religious orthodoxy, and enforced the rules against peasants carrying firearms or swords.

The Shogunate's gun control eventually disarmed not only the peasantry, but also the Samurai warriors. Gunsmiths were restricted in the number of apprentices they could adopt, and eventually sales to anyone besides the government became illegal. The Samurai did not mind, though. While American pioneers considered their guns a symbolic badge of honor, the Samurai revered swords as the true symbol of knighthood. For combat, Samurai disdained guns because they allowed fighting from a distance, rather than face to face, and required the combatant to assume an undignified crouching position. Further, there was little practical use for long guns, since there was not a great deal of big game to hunt.

> *"Without a culture of civilian firearms ownership, the Japanese never saw strict gun control as anything out of the ordinary."*

Thus, in the 1850s, when Commodore Perry re-opened Japan, Japanese were still using matchlock guns similar to the type the Portuguese had introduced over 300 years ago. Led by American manufacturers, the rest of the world had long ago replaced matchlocks with flintlocks, and then with percussion caps.

Without a culture of civilian firearms ownership, the Japanese never saw strict gun control as anything out of the ordinary. And because the crime rate is so extraordinarily low, the Japanese, unlike many Americans, perceive no need to own a gun for individual self-defense.

Government's Disarmament Policy

One important reason the Japanese voluntarily accept disarmament is that their government does the same. After the disaster of World War II, war was perceived as an unmitigated horror, and the army was drastically curtailed.

The police carry guns, but rarely shoot them, instead using their black belts in judo or police sticks. In an average year, the entire Tokyo police force only fires six shots. Even if guns vanished from America, it is difficult to imagine a big-city American police force firing only six times in an entire year.

In a top-down society such as Japan, when the government disarms itself, it creates a powerful moral climate for citizens to do the same. Needless to say, a disarmed military and police are not likely in the United States, and neither is voluntary compliance with gun control.

In many American cities where it is nearly impossible to legally carry a gun for self-defense, many people do so anyway. Many more own illegal weapons at home for self-defense. Thus, many American gun prohibitionists insist that strict gun controls be accompanied by mandatory jail terms. The gun banners recognize that without mandatory sentences, judges and juries would rarely send their fellow citizens to jail for an illegal self-defense gun. Without the certainty of jail, strict controls are often ignored. But in Japan, the citizens voluntarily comply with the gun law; accordingly, there is no mandatory minimum penalty for unlicensed firearm possession.

Should America Import Japan's Gun Laws?

In the 1910 debate preceding New York's Sullivan Law (the first major American gun control law affecting citizens recognized as entitled to full civil rights) one writer recommended that New York copy Japan, "where intending purchasers of revolvers must first obtain police permits, and sales must be reported to the police." In 1987, a letter to the editor of *The New Republic* announced that Japan has so little crime because "citizens forsake their right to own guns in return for safety," and that America must do the same.

Yet it is not so easy for one country simply to imitate the laws of another culture. Postwar Japan was ordered to follow American criminal procedure and anti-trust rules, but soon stopped. The rules did not work in a culture used to unlimited police power, and enamored of paternalistic conglomerates. . . .

Just as Japan functions without a right to bear arms, the nation gets by without many other rights as well. Not only the laws regarding protection of criminal suspects, but freedom of speech, of intimate conduct, and of religion are far narrower than in the U.S. Japan even has an official religion, Shinto. The Japanese military consecrated a deceased military hero as a Shinto god, although the man was a Christian, and his widow objected vehemently.

Pressure to conform, and internalized willingness to do so are much stronger in Japan than in America. The spirit of conformity provides the best explanation for Japan's low crime rate. It also explains why the Japanese people accept gun control.

Theoretically, America could adopt a gun ban like Japan's. But that ban would be completely alien to our society, which for over 300 years has had the world's freest gun culture. Japan's gun laws are part of an authoritarian philosophy of government that is fundamentally at odds with America's traditions of liberty. Such laws do not make sense for our country.

Australian Gun Control Measures Are Ineffective

by Ned Kelly

About the author: Ned Kelly, a notorious Australian outlaw (1854-1880), is a pseudonym used by the American author of this article, which originally appeared in American Rifleman *magazine. The author, an electronics engineer, occasionally travels to Australia.*

As Handgun Control, Inc., (HCI) said in its literature, "In 1985, handguns killed . . . five in Australia and 8,092 in the United States. God bless America." HCI would have us believe that the difference between the two figures is attributable only to tough restrictions on handgun ownership in Australia.

It's not surprising that HCI would mention Australia in its propaganda; from the gun prohibitionist perspective, Australia is a model country. To legally possess a handgun, the owner must be licensed, the gun must be registered, the owner must be a member of a recognized gun club, and the gun may be transported only between home, range and the gunsmith's shop. Police estimate compliance with the handgun registration laws at about 85%.

Long Guns Are Less Regulated

What gun control advocates *will not* mention is that these same restrictions do not uniformly apply to rifles and shotguns, and long guns are plentiful. The number of firearms in private hands in Australia has increased from 2.7 to 3.5 million in 10 years. That's one firearm for every four Australians in 1990.

In spite of the proliferation of firearms, the Australian homicide rate has remained roughly constant since the turn of the century. Firearms homicides have also been dropping as a percentage of the homicides since 1955. They presently account for 40% of all murders committed in Australia.

HCI would say that this is definitive proof that mere restrictions on handgun ownership would cut America's homicide rate. The number of murders committed with firearms could be reduced without affecting private ownership of long guns. But gun owners might look at these same statistics and reply that cultural factors would probably keep Australia's homicide rate low even if handgun laws were liberalized.

So who's correct?

That's pretty obvious if one takes more than a superficial look at the statistics. The annual homicide rate for Australia for the period 1972-1987 was about two per 100,000 people or about 100 per year. For the same period in the U.S., the annual homicide rate was roughly eight per 100,000. Approximately 60% of these American homicides were firearms related.

In the unlikely event that an effective gun ban was enacted in the U.S., our homicide rate would still be 60% higher than Australia's. The rate at which Americans died of knife wounds in 1987 was 1.6 per 100,000, which is comparable to the 1987 Australian murder rate for all causes combined. Cultural differences, not gun laws, account for the difference in the homicide rates.

A Variety of Gun Laws

Handgun ownership aside, generalizations concerning firearms ownership and gun laws in Australia will be in error. Australia is a federation of six sovereign states and one territory. The states have considerably more autonomy than states in America, and, like in the U.S., gun laws vary considerably from location to location.

Tasmania and Queensland have the most liberal conditions of firearms ownership. Owners do not need a gun license, and rifles and shotguns are not registered. Tasmania permits private ownership of machine guns, provided the owner is a licensed collector or machine gun dealer. (The term "dealer" is a bit anachronistic since dealers can't sell to private citizens, and the police don't buy from dealers. Dealers legally can only buy and sell among themselves and collectors.)

Western Australia, the Australian frontier, sits at the other end of the gun law spectrum. Licensing of shooters and registration of long arms have been in effect in this state since 1935, longer than in any other Australian state or territory. To purchase a rifle or a shotgun for target shooting, the prospective Western Australian gun owner must show membership in a gun club. To purchase the same firearm for hunting, the prospective hunter must provide the police with written permission from two landowners to hunt on their properties. An application for the purchase must then be filed with the police, and the police can deny the application without any explanation.

"The situation in Western Australia is similar to having a state the size and flavor of Texas with gun laws like Massachusetts."

Most of the constraints faced by Western Australian gun owners aren't the law, by the way—they are merely police policy.

The situation in Western Australia is similar to having a state the size and flavor of Texas with gun laws like Massachusetts. Western Australia and Victoria

261

have both banned high-powered rifles; and, possession of semi-automatics is prohibited unless a person can demonstrate a need to own one.

What shouldn't surprise American gun owners, however, is the absence of any correlation between restrictive gun laws, homicide rates and gun crime. The violent crime rate in a liberal-law state, Tasmania, population 500,000, even appears to be decreasing. In 1987 there were *no* firearms homicides on the island; and, in 1988, there were *no* armed robberies.

> *"The push for gun control received extra impetus as a result of two massacres in 1988 that occurred within a week of each other in Melbourne."*

In 1987, the latest year for which statistics are available, the homicide rates for Queensland, Western Australia, Victoria and New South Wales were six, five, six and seven per million inhabitants, respectively. The percentages of total homicides committed with firearms in these states were 26%, 29%, 36% and 32%, respectively. Victoria and Western Australia may be the national leaders in harsh gun controls, but their firearms homicide rates are not significantly better than the one for Queensland, which has no controls at all.

Although the Australian homicide rate is remaining stable, the same cannot be said for crime in general. The robbery rate has doubled since 1972; the rape rate has tripled; serious assault is up by 350%. Even if the frequencies of these crimes are still far below rates for the U.S., most Australians find the trend alarming.

Many Crimes Do Not Involve Guns

The fact that 98% of the rapes, 95% of the personal robberies, 98% of the serious assaults and 54% of the commercial robberies are committed *without* firearms, however, seems to have escaped both the state and federal governments. Their irrational but predictable response to increased crime and violence has been progressively harsher gun laws.

These laws, obviously, will have no effect on the vast majority of criminal activity, which occurs in the absence of firearms. Of all the categories of serious crime, only commercial robbery might be seriously affected by tougher gun laws, but statistical and historical evidence suggest that even this will not be the case.

In Queensland in 1981, police reported 110 serious incidents involving weapons. In 53% of these cases, the weapon in question was a firearm; slightly over half were handguns. Handguns have been completely restricted in Australia for more than 50 years. Whether the Australian public will wait 50 more years to see if restrictions on long arms have any similar effect on crime remains to be seen.

The present restrictions on handgun ownership were enacted at the state level in the 1920s. In this era, the colonial governments of Australia and New Zealand tended to rubber stamp laws that were passed in England. Gun control legislation was no exception to this rule.

When the red scare of the 1920s broke out in Europe, handguns were portrayed as an ideal weapon for Bolshevik revolutionaries because they were cheap and concealable. England banned them. By 1930, as Australia plunged into the Great Depression, all of the Australian states and mainland territories had followed suit.

Australia suffered greatly in the global economic crash. The turmoil that produced the Nazis in Germany and the Brownshirts in England also produced the New Guard in Australia. This right wing irregular army was formed to resist the policies of [the] Labor Party government in New South Wales. Members of the New Guard started using .303 cal. Enfield rifles in paramilitary exercises and parades that justifiably alarmed the then unpopular Labor Party of New South Wales. In 1931, the state government petitioned the federal government for national legislation to prohibit importation of rifles of a military type that fired ammunition larger than .22 cal.

> *"Recommendations to state governments were: a ban on all semi-automatic firearms . . . and licensing of all shooters."*

At the conclusion of World War II, a considerable number of firearms started finding their way back to Australia from the Pacific and Middle Eastern theaters. (One Australian told this American author that, "for every nine coffins with bodies, there was one coffin filled with guns.")

The state governments still feared that these rifles might play a role in civil insurrection. In Australia, as well as the U.S., many assumed that the end of the war would mark a return to the depression and its accompanying social unrest.

A campaign was begun to ban ownership of all firearms that used military cartridges. In spite of the efforts of the newly formed Sporting Shooters' Ass'n of Australia (SSAA), New South Wales passed such legislation in 1947. This law remained in force until 1978. Its most enduring legacy was a number of interesting conversions of military rifles to civilian calibers such as the 7.7x54R.

The effect these laws had on Australia's crime rate is unknown. They were passed primarily to protect the government from real or imaginery threats from people, not to protect the people from themselves. Within the past decade, however, gun laws have been proposed as a means of reducing violent crime and, if possible, preventing firearms from getting into the hands of psychopathic killers.

Melbourne's Gun Massacres

The push for gun control received extra impetus as a result of two massacres in 1988 that occurred within a week of each other in Melbourne, Victoria. In the first of these shootings, a gunman armed with a semi-automatic version of the M14 gunned down five people on Hoddle Street.

Julian Knight, the first of the gunmen, was captured alive. A check of police records showed that he was out on bail, after being expelled from Duntroon Military Academy for the attempted murder of a sergeant. Knight had also been arrested a few days before the Hoddle Street shootings for carrying a loaded rifle on the street, but he had not been charged or detained under the provisions of the Firearms Act. Failure to enforce existing gun laws contributed directly to loss of life; Knight's gun license had not been revoked by the police at the time of the shootings.

> *"Shooters who have re-registered their guns in good faith are seeing their licenses revoked by the registrar of firearms."*

The second catastrophe also involved a gun owner who had been licensed by the police. In this case, the license had been granted only a few days before Frank Vitkovik opened fire on the public at Queen Street. He shot 13 people, killing eight of them, before throwing himself off the 12th floor of the Australia Post Building. A subsequent investigation showed that Vitkovik, who was a university student, had a history of psychiatric counselling.

The firearm used by Vitkovik was a .30 cal. M1 carbine. This particular type of gun had been banned in Victoria as a "machine gun" from the 1950s to 1972. Vitkovik had sawed the rifle off—a violation of existing gun laws—and had destroyed the gun's gas cylinder and its self-loading capability. It had to be operated as a single-shot.

Political Turmoil Surrounding Gun Control

Both of these mass murders received considerable attention from politicians and the press throughout Australia. They also set the stage for a year of political turmoil that revolved around the issue of gun control.

Barrie Unsworth, then premier of New South Wales, asked Australia's prime minister, Bob Hawke, for a Special Premiers' Conference that would draw up a national gun-control strategy. The meeting was scheduled for Dec. 23, 1988, a mere three months before an election in Unsworth's home state. The premiers (equivalent to American governors) of Australia's states were asked to personally attend the gun summit in the national capital, Canberra, or send a senior cabinet minister in their place.

The haphazard and hasty nature of the conference was obvious from the beginning. John Bannon, premier of South Australia, confessed that he learned of the meeting through news reports, not by invitation. He sent word that he wouldn't attend as he was scheduled to attend a "tall ships" ceremony that day.

Among the people who did show up were Barrie Unsworth; Bob Hawke; John Cain, the premier of Victoria; Mike Ahern, the premier of Queensland; and John Bennet, the attorney general for Tasmania.

In the words of Premier Ahern, "The summit was held in high emotion and was not conducive to sensible debate." Queensland wanted more time to study the situation and was skeptical of additional gun controls. Tasmania was out-and-out opposed to them.

Unsworth charged that Tasmania and Queensland were being uncooperative in a time of national emergency. "I suppose that it will take a massacre of the proportion we have seen in Queen Street and Hoddle Street to bring Tasmania and Queensland around."

Bennet shot back, "If you look at Tasmania's record, compared with New South Wales and Victoria, I think Barrie Unsworth is the last person who should be telling us how to suck eggs." Bennet subsequently walked out of the meeting.

Calls to Ban Firearms

While the summit was still in conference, a government spokesman started announcing to the press what firearms were going to be nationally banned and what new restrictions were going to be placed on gun owners.

Recommendations to state governments were: a ban on all semi-automatic firearms, restrictions on the availability of manuals that showed how to make weapons, and licensing of all shooters. At the same time, the federal government announced its intention to prohibit the importation of all semi-automatics. Also announced was the formation of a national committee to study violence and its prevention.

When a consensus did not emerge from the summit, each of the governments was left to go its separate way. Bannon made up for his absence at the conference by announcing bans on semi-automatics, restricted ammunition sales and new rigorous licensing procedures for gun owners in South Australia.

> *"Will gun owners be able to get a 'fair go' when firearms issues are next considered? Only if they insist on one."*

In New South Wales, Unsworth pressed on in his campaign to confiscate more than one million firearms from private citizens.

And, in Victoria, John Cain's Labor Party government announced that it would ban the private ownership of all firearms except those owned by farmers, security services and gun club members. The ban would take guns away from 90% of the states' gun owners. A three-month moratorium on issuing shooters' licenses was announced.

The leader of Victoria's opposition Liberal Party, Jeff Kennet, said that his party would support the government proposal, and he faulted Cain for not implementing it sooner. This left Victoria's gun owners with no voice in the state parliament aside from a few members representing the minority National Party.

Ted Drane, then president of the SSAA, decided to stiffen the backbone of the

Liberals and make it difficult for them to abandon the firearms community. A newspaper advertising campaign on behalf of gun owners was started; bus trips were organized to transport protestors to gun rallies and 10,000 posters were printed up calling for a gun owners march on the state Parliament House on January 30.

The march, expected to draw five to 20,000 people, succeeded beyond everyone's expectations—83,000 people showed up, making it the largest political demonstration in Australia since the Vietnam War. The media, especially ABC, the Australian government's TV, attempted to reduce this figure, day by day, in follow-up news stories.

> *"A call-in telephone poll . . . showed 77,575 calls in favor of firearms ownership and only 26,199 calls endorsing the government ban."*

Newspapers started filling up with angry letters to the editors. Membership in the Victorian chapter of the SSAA quintupled in two weeks. And a call-in telephone poll conducted by Channel 10 News showed 77,575 calls in favor of firearms ownership and only 26,199 calls endorsing the government ban. It was the largest response to any poll conducted by the station.

The Liberal Party realized that it needed to switch sides in the gun debate or lose its constituency to the pro-gun National Party. Kennet appeared to do an about face.

A Gun Ban Measure Fails

After Victoria's gun ban was approved in the Lower House, it stalled in the opposition-controlled Upper House. Premier Cain then went to the state governor—in this case a Labor Party appointee—and asked for emergency enforcement of the ban and moratorium in spite of the fact that parliament had not passed it. Permission was granted, but Cain's government was in danger of violating the state constitution by governing outside of parliament. Petitions sent to the governor, demanding an end to Cain's actions, were ignored.

Kennet again changed sides in the fight and came to Cain's rescue, explaining that he didn't want the premier to be embarrassed by the legislative impasse. The Liberal Party announced that it would not block introduction of the bill into the Upper House.

The Victorian government finally announced that it would let gun owners keep their semi-automatic rifles, provided they were re-registered as prohibited weapons. The SSAA ran newspaper ads charging that this policy would degenerate into immediate confiscation. Cain was outraged by the ads and called the SSAA "liars." There was much truth in the SSAA's claim. Shooters who have re-registered their guns in good faith are seeing their licenses revoked by the registrar of firearms. And, guns like the .223 Ruger Mini-14 are being confiscated as "assault rifles." Compensation is being paid, but thousands of semi-automatics in public hands are simply vanishing.

Although the ban on semi-automatic rifles was passed in Victoria, the remainder of the items suggested at the national gun summit were not enacted throughout Australia. The defeat of Barrie Unsworth, in an election he personally called "a referendum on gun control," sent shock waves through Australia's political community. Another election, this time in Victoria on Oct. 1, 1988, succeeded in returning Cain to office; but, he lost additional seats in Victoria's Upper House to the pro-gun National Party.

As part of his drive to restrict gun ownership in Victoria, Cain had appointed fellow Labor Party member and gun control advocate Steve Crabb to the office of police minister. Crabb's job was to supervise enforcement of both existing and future gun laws. While both Cain and Unsworth were hysterically telling the press that gun bans were necessary to avert repeats of Queen Street and Hoddle Street, Crabb was quietly conceding that no gun ban could guarantee public safety.

The real target of the legislation, it seems, was a reduction of Victoria's homicide rate. Queen Street and Hoddle Street were being exploited to pass laws that would not affect the type of killer that terrified the public most.

While the Victorian government was admitting that new gun laws were incapable of keeping firearms out of the hands of psychopaths, it should also have conceded that the laws would have no effect on organized, drug-related crime. This cruel reality was demonstrated to the police of New South Wales in January 1989.

On January 10, Federal Inspector Colin Winchester (the U.S. equivalent of Deputy Chief of the FBI) was shot twice with a .22 cal. rifle as he was stepping out of his vehicle at his residence. The wounds were fatal, and the killer made a clean getaway.

Gun Control: No Effect on Crime

The state government of New South Wales, at an estimated cost of $250,000, called in 68,000 .22 rimfire rifles in an attempt to match the ballistics of the murder weapon against the ballistics of a registered rifle. The effort was fruitless. Months later, a rusty, unregistered .22 was found abandoned in some bushes; ballistics positively identified it. The case is still open, and police have few leads.

> *"Gun licensing, gun registration and gun prohibition have had no success in reducing crime in either Australia or the U.S."*

Gun licensing, gun registration and gun prohibition have had no success in reducing crime in either Australia or the U.S. But the myth lives on. Much of the debate on gun ownership in Australia subsided temporarily while the National Committee on Violence, that was created as a part of the gun summit held in Canberra, performed its study.

The committee's report, *Violence, Directions for Australia*, finally was delivered early in 1990.

The results of the study were predictable. One of the members of the committee was Judith Dixon, a Labor Party parliamentarian who had been thrown out of office by shooters in the Victoria election. And the chairman of the committee, Prof. Duncan Chapel, had stated on his appointment that he was going after guns.

In spite of the statistical data that was presented in the study (some of which was used in the writing of this article), the committee rendered its predetermined opinion, "There is no doubt that a significant disarmament of the Australian public would save lives and prevent injury."

Government Recommendations

Among the recommendations made by the committee were: national restrictions on ownership of firearms; prohibition of all automatic weapons; a national computerized firearms registration; an end to mail order gun sales; mandatory storage of handguns at pistol ranges; registration of all private gun sales; mandatory measures for safekeeping of all weapons in an inoperable condition in secure storage; and, last, something called a Positive Generic Import Statement to restrict importation of firearms into Australia.

In April 1990, Sen. Michael Tate, Australia's minister for justice, prepared to submit the Import Statement to the national Police Ministers' Conference. He was told by the police ministers that the proposed law had been discussed with gun owner organizations, but further investigation revealed that the police departments of the various states had only consulted each other. Shooters, in fact, had never been contacted.

The statement was dropped from the agenda, and Sen. Tate and his staff travelled Australia to talk with the nation's shooters. Perhaps the effort was sincere. Will gun owners be able to get a "fair go" when firearms issues are next considered? Only if they insist on one. Are firearms rights about to become part of Australia's past history? Who knows? If Australia's shooters will pull together before confiscation is upon them, that day may never arrive. Until then, gun control will remain one of the most contentious topics in Australian politics.

Jamaican Gun Control Laws Have Not Reduced Gun Violence

by William Calathes

About the author: *William Calathes is a criminal justice professor at Jersey City State College in Jersey City, New Jersey. His paper, from which this viewpoint is excerpted, was awarded first place in the International Paper Competition in 1990.*

Jamaica, located in the southwest Caribbean, is a one-island state of 4,244 square miles with a population of approximately 2.3 million. Controlled by the British from 1655 following a short Spanish occupation, Jamaica was the first British West Indian territory to gain political independence. . . .

The social structure of Jamaica consists of three hierarchal organized classes: upper, middle and lower classes. The upper class is comprised of junior partners of finance, exhibits a colonial mentality and is socially and politically reactionary. In the mind of the upper class, poverty and lack of culture have the same connotations of disgrace and shame as Negro blood in southern United States.

Jamaica's Class Differences

The middle class is small in number and avoids ideological identification with the lower classes. From the birth of modern Jamaican politics, usually dated from the labor movement of 1938, the middle class supported the JLP [Jamaican Labour Party], and was fearful of the PNP [People's National Party] because of its early socialist orientation. However, once the PNP purged the left wing element of its party, some of the middle class began to support it.

The upper and middle classes are separated from the lower classes by sharp breaks on the socioeconomic scale. The cultural difference between the upper and middle class is relatively slight however. [Author Michael Garfield Smith states:] "Materialism provides the formative principle or reference point in the value system of the upper section, while social status dominates the value sys-

Excerpted from William Calathes, "Gun Control in a Developing Nation: The Gun Court Act of Jamaica," *International Journal of Comparative and Applied Criminal Justice* 14 (1): 322-36. Reprinted with permission.

tem of the intermediate section, and values of immediate physical gratification are central among the third section, spiritual as well as secular values reflecting these principles."

Political Violence

This plural model has historical relevance. It may be argued that much of the behavior of the lower classes in Kingston was consistent with "the culture of poverty." Much of the post-colonial behavior of the Jamaican lower classes can be explained in terms of socioeconomic problems and needs. Social mobility was difficult. Race and color carried important implications, but they were less critical than economic stratification.

Following the end of the Second World War, political power became associated with the middle class. During the PNP administration lasting from 1956 to the eve of independence, the link between the upper and middle classes was forged. This link persisted through the first decade of independence.

Of great significance in any discussion of class, politics and Jamaican criminality is the lumpenproletariat. During the late 1960's these were the many people who were armed by the political parties in the battle between the PNP and JLP for Western Kingston. [In *Violence and Politics in Jamaica*, Terry Lacey writes:] "After this short introduction to politics within the system, some of these gangs reverted to ordinary criminal activities, others turned to more revolutionary politics and some used their newly-acquired guns to terrorize the rest of society, particularly, the national bourgeoisie."

> *"Individuals given firearms for political purposes soon realized that other criminal purposes could be pursued as well."*

The lumpenproleteriat utilized by both PNP and JLP politicians to fight their political battles was volatile and became very much out of control by the early 1970's. By the early 1970's their energies, once more or less controlled by the politicians, were increasingly directed against the entire economic, social, and political system. Individuals given firearms for political purposes soon realized that other criminal purposes could be pursued as well. . . .

The PNP, led by Michael Manley, controlled the Parliament from 1972 to 1980. The Manley years were characterized by attempted social and economic reforms, problems and inefficiencies of administration, much opposition from the business community, the JLP, and the United States, and an increasing wave of firearm crime and criminality. Within this societal context the Gun Court Act, a mandatory piece of firearm legislation, was passed in 1974 and survived in its most repressive forms through 1982.

The Gun Court Act established a special court to deal with the offense of the illegal possession of firearms and other offenses involving firearms where the offender's possession was illegal and provided for a mandatory and indeterminate sentence for illegal possession and use of firearms. In order to fully understand the reasons behind the passage of the Gun Court Act, it is necessary to examine the background to its passage as well as its provisions.

By 1973 an increasing number of Jamaicans were adversely affected by the increase in crimes of violence in which firearms, unlicensed or illegally obtained were used. Jamaica had become "a small Vietnam." Citizens not only feared going out in the evenings, they also feared staying at home. There were accounts of family members keeping vigil in their homes in many sections of Kingston for fear that sleep would mean immediate death.

Persons were shot and killed by day and by night in the course of robbing, rape and other offenses, or for no apparent reason. Witnesses for the Crown at trials of persons accused for such crimes were often intimidated. Victims of the crimes themselves were not infrequently killed or shot at, most probably with a view to their elimination as eyewitnesses who could testify against the perpetrators of these crimes. Even Counsel for the Crown in one case was not immune from the use of a firearm. Intimidation and attack did not come only from the offender. It also came from associates of the offender especially where the offender was a gang member. The serious nature of the situation was judicially noticed in the first set of appeals from the Gun Court.

> *"Many . . . believed that . . . more concern should be directed at removing the liberties of the hardened criminal."*

Murders occurred at an increasing frequency and were reported by the media. But it was not until the media horrified the nation with reports of the occurrence of three murders in particular that tremendous pressure was felt by the government to take immediate action. The first of these was the shooting in March 1974 of Leo Henry, a prominent businessman. The business sector in Jamaica, in particular, was outraged. One newspaper headline simply read, "Get the Guns." Then on March 16, Robert Stennet, an attorney, was shot in his home. Another attorney, Paul Ritz-Ritson, the Chairman of National Sports, was also murdered by gunmen in Montego Bay shortly thereafter.

Theories on Increased Gun Crime

A variety of "modernization" explanations as to the causes of increased firearm crime during the early 1970's were postulated: 1) social, economic and cultural change; 2) rising material expectations; 3) unemployment; 4) population growth; and, 5) miscellaneous factors such as the world oil crisis, capital flight in the wake of nationalization efforts, emigration of talented and skilled Jamaicans, and abuses and violence which party leaders were not always capable of preventing.

However, interviews conducted with a cross-section of the Jamaicans indicated a general public consensus that dramatically differed from modernization explanations. The most prominent theories advanced to explain the increase in firearm crime were: 1) crimes were political in nature; and, 2) the society's respect for prosperous citizens and societal institutions had deteriorated. These are interesting findings because they are somewhat inconsistent with newspaper accounts at the time (e.g., letters to the editor). *The Daily Gleaner* published public opinions which were supportive of the government taking a forceful approach to the rising crime problem. For example, many wrote that they believed that the liberties of law-abiding citizens were being eroded and that more concern should be directed at removing the liberties of the hardened criminal. Others expressed the belief that bail should be withheld in certain cases and that the death penalty should be extended to some crimes of violence. Many who advocated the death penalty justified their positions by stating that this punishment should be extended not so much to deter crime, but to rid society of these offenders. While these suggested remedies seem harsh, review of newspaper comments were indicative of support for taking a forceful approach to the problem. . . .

> *"Violent criminals in Jamaica did not have to choose an alternative weapon to achieve their goals. Firearms were readily available."*

The basic provisions of the Gun Court Act remained virtually unchanged from 1974 to 1982. During its legislative life approximately 1,200 individuals were convicted under its authority. The constitutionality of the Gun Court Act and the debate as to the social, political and economic problems of Jamaica, are of course, vital matters. But no less vital is the most elementary question of all: namely, did the Gun Court Act fulfill its stated purpose of deterring firearm-related crimes?

Crime Control

One of the primary aspects of the prolonged controversy over firearm control is whether such legislation is inherently capable of reducing the number of firearm-related crimes. In the United States, much of the past research on suppression of crime has focused on the impact of gun control measures. In the majority of these studies, the strictness of gun control laws in many areas (e.g., states) has been correlated with crime rates in those areas. The results of these studies have been mixed, with a tendency to find that gun control reduces crime.

The opponents of increased control, tacitly admitting that empirical evidence is one of the means of measuring the effects of firearm regulation, contend that expert opinion and compelling evidence seem to indicate that the amount or kind of crime in a community is not substantially affected by the relative ease with which a person can obtain a gun or by the relative severity and mandatory nature of firearm offense sentences. [In *Studies in Criminal Homicide*, Marvin E. Wolfgang says:] "Few homicides due to shootings could be avoided merely if a firearm were not immediately present . . . the offender would select some other weapon to achieve the same destructive goal." During the 1970's and early 1980's violent criminals in Jamaica did not have to choose an alternative weapon to achieve their goals. Firearms were readily available. This fact appears to be equally true prior to and following passage of the Gun Court Act.

Failure of the Gun Court Act

To appreciate the problems and difficulties of firearm crime during this period in Jamaica, it is useful to offer an overall picture of the trends of firearm crimes. The sources of the data used were the officially recorded statistical data and publications of the Jamaican government and a detailed analysis of newspaper reports. Crime rates were calculated from official reports of crime known to the police and national census reports and the annual abstracts of statistics. National crime statistics are collected and recorded by the national police agency—the Criminal Investigations Department (CID) and published in the *Economic and Social Survey* by the National Planning Institute. Statistics are collected from the 169 police stations around the country and are recorded in the agency's Criminal Statistics Register. . . .

Despite the limitations of the data and analysis, a general empirical assessment of the Gun Court Act can be made. The data indicates that following an initial decline, there were overall increases for all categories of firearm-related crimes throughout most of the study period. Although it is beyond the scope of this paper to analyze possible intervening variables, it is readily apparent that the Gun Court Act did not succeed in lowering the rate of firearm-related crime. Initially, as was illustrated by two earlier, but limited studies of the Gun Court Act, there were overall declines in the firearm crime rates following the first

> *"In the absence of a 'reasonable excuse,' the law-abiding citizen was treated as being in illegal possession of a firearm . . . [and] was liable to arrest without bail."*

year of implementation. These results, however, proved to be short-lived. The fear generated by severe punishments for firearm crimes and its concomitant increase in police efforts to apprehend firearm criminals did not succeed.

Many Jamaicans believed that the perpetrator of firearm crime committed the theft or rape, then shot the victim. This was an element in much of the violence which characterized Jamaica during this time period. If this was indeed the case, then firearm violence, complex in its own right, becomes more difficult to comprehend. Moreover, statistically, during this period, living conditions within the urban areas of Jamaica generally improved. Unemployment rates dropped; shanty towns were severely reduced; and education programs improved. Despite the presence of the Gun Court why then did firearm crime continue to increase? . . .

It is difficult to determine how much of the increase in firearm crime was attributable to such factors as: 1) the loss of respect for human life and the resulting acceptance of criminality as a necessary evil of the day; 2) the failure of successive governments (the JLP won the general election of 1980) to strengthen the efficiency and morale of police and improve their relationship with the public; 3) the failure of successive governments to take necessary steps to ensure accommodation and an enlarged judiciary and to provide suitable essential conditions for the efficient discharge of their functions; and, 4) the social and economic conditions which existed and the failure to focus attention on finding meaningful solutions to these conditions.

> *"The attempt to control firearm criminals through passage of mandatory firearm legislation failed."*

However, the majority of individuals interviewed who were not directly affiliated with either political party offered a completely different picture of firearm crime during the time of the Gun Court Act. Explanations offered included: 1) use of strong-arm men, gunmen and gangsters in the political arena; 2) widespread victimization in the allocation of jobs and contracts by successive governments and by local authorities; and, 3) interference by politicians with the police in the execution of their duties.

Legislators passed the Gun Court Act to help curb the rate of firearm crimes. Statistics indicate that illegal firearms were still in the hands of many criminals during the years the Act was implemented. The attempt to control firearm criminals through passage of mandatory firearm legislation failed, and political motivations seem to have been important reasons for this failure. Since the Act was an empirical failure, then two critical questions must follow: 1) What function did the Gun Court Act have; and, 2) What was the nature of firearm crime during this period?

The Act in Operation

The Gun Court Act was legally and politically oppressive. An example of its legal oppressiveness was its rules of evidence, which ran heavily against the accused. In the absence of a "reasonable excuse," the law-abiding citizen was treated as being in illegal possession of a firearm. He or she was required to offer an explanation satisfactory to the Resident Magistrate, and in the meanwhile was liable to arrest without bail pending trial. Other oppressive legal provisions and procedures included the mandatory sentence and guilt by association.

The Act was also difficult to properly enforce and administer. Accidental circumstances often gave rise to a charge. Allegations of illegal possession of firearms could also easily be concocted and substantiated. For example, someone with a grudge may have left, or procured some person to have left, a bullet in the room of a person against whom he or she bore a grudge and then informed the police. The police, doing their duty, would search and find the offending article, and thereafter that innocent citizen was headed straight for detention without any additional evidence. A firearm need not be recovered. These tactics could have been used by politicians who wanted to eliminate their opponents either before, or at election time. The Act also led to much discretionary enforcement and hence much corruption.

The Act's political oppressiveness was first evidenced by the fact that many street officers and police supervisors did not perform their duties in a completely impartial manner; thus giving rise to public complaints and a diminishing level of public support and respect. Internal investigations by the police were rarely conducted and, with few exceptions, results were not conveyed to the public. The police failed to convince the public that complaints were being thoroughly investigated and errant police officers punished.

While the upper and middle classes initially supported the Act, the sentiments of the lower classes became mixed immediately following passage. This observation may be close to obvious, for following passage, shootings and increased police activity occurred in the poorer neighborhoods. Under the Act, members of the lower classes could easily be accused and they knew of no one who could exonerate them. They also could not afford private defense counsel. The lower classes' opinion of the Act, which was somewhat mixed initially, changed to complete opposition by the end of 1974 because by that time, the Gun Court prison started to become filled with their own.

> *"During elections one side declares war on the other. If they thought that you were with the other side, they would kill you."*

Living by the Gun

Rivalry between the two political parties continued following passage. One young factory worker interviewed stated, "Political parties gave guns to people in certain neighborhoods, strongholds of the opposition party to stir trouble; in order to create unhappiness and perhaps gain a political foothold." Another person stated: "During elections one side declares war on the other. If they thought that you were with the other side, they would kill you; not so much in the rich areas, but in the poor areas. You see we can't afford to pay off the police for protection."

Some of those interviewed stated that they turned to political firearm violence because they perceived no better way to survive in an economically disadvantaged country. They began to "live by the gun." One self-proclaimed political gunman stated that turning firearm violence was one way of receiving "free money:"

> Well, it was called free money because most of the time you would do nothing and you would still collect it. I used to work for one of the parties. Sure I knew that what I was doing was illegal and I knew that there was a chance that I would be caught and sent to Gun Court for the rest of my life. But I needed money and I was told that I needed to do what they were telling me to do so that the government would change and things would get better.

The targets of the Gun Court Act were those individuals who participated on the middle and lower echelons of the political game and common apolitical street criminals. Top-notch gunmen were not apprehended. Their connections with the politicians of both parties protected them. Gunmen worked for both the PNP and the JLP. For all intents and purposes, therefore, the Act may have been aimed at the population which contributed the least to the high level of firearm crime.

Following passage, the law enforcement community was pressured by high-level politicians to make full usage of the Act by increasing surveillance and arrest activities of lower-level political and street criminals. At given points the government also believed it necessary to involve the Armed Forces in the control of crime. The instances of Armed Forces intervention were marked by increases in the number of law enforcement officers killed while on duty and by information leading to the belief that a rapidly increased number of organized gunmen groups were terrorizing the country. Instances of clashes between the Armed Forces and the police were also recorded.

"The Jamaican bi-partisan system created fierce loyalties which . . . had zealous supporters in either party resorting to strong-arm methods."

Gun Violence Increases

The passage of the Gun Court Act led to more violent law enforcement-citizen encounters. Many citizens interviewed saw an historical reason for the existence of armed groups in the country. They knew that the Jamaican bi-partisan system created fierce loyalties which at given times in history had zealous supporters in either party resorting to strong-arm methods. All political leaders interviewed condemned the existence of even the remnants of groups using strong-armed methods, but acknowledged their continued existence by blaming the other political side. Nevertheless, it was generally believed among those interviewed that such groups continued to exist and operate.

The situation became so serious that accounts of police brutality and false arrests were becoming quite commonplace almost immediately following the Act's implementation. In fact, Justice E.G. Green, the first Presiding Magistrate of the Gun Court, on the occasion of his first acquittal of a gun crime, said that he would regret to see the day when policemen would plant a bullet on a person. These possibilities began to occur with increasing frequency.

By the end of the first year of the Gun Court Act's implementation, the public seemed to accept street killings as a way of life. The 1972 election and its resulting violence also created a by-product which is interesting to once again note. A number of individuals were known to be associated with gunmen, or were gunmen, and were highly respected in certain communities. For example, in downtown Kingston there were individuals who were able to secure respect from the youth of the community, and, may not have been convicted of a crime for one reason or another, but were known supporters of gunmen or were gunmen themselves.

It appears that these "political criminals" were freely perpetrating firearm violence following passage of the Gun Court Act. Most of the gun criminals of this sort had some political factors associated with their lives. These people were given firearms and money by both political parties. The public was aware that there were gun criminals who had political connections which protected them. For example, following an arrest it was not unlikely for a politician to frequently go to a police station and successfully demand the release of certain people. Certain people would be released because police officers may have feared the politician or police officers themselves may have been politicized.

"Ranking" gunmen tended to have short life-spans and were often killed brutally. These types of criminals were above the Gun Court. For some political reason they were never brought before the Court and consequently were permitted to continually perpetrate violence. Moreover, once in possession of firearms, many of these gunmen utilized them to perpetrate non-political criminal offenses. "The police and the Gun Court were useless when it came to 'ranking' gunmen.". . .

The Gun Court Act Endures

Following the election of the JLP in 1980, the Gun Court Act remained in effect with its most oppressive features for two years. By early 1982 many individuals interviewed stated the failure of either government to remove, or at least substantially amend the Act, was a challenge against all class interests. For example, a small local merchant stated, "When the previous government was in power, the legislation was necessary as an emergency measure. But that was 1974. The Act has proved to be a mistake and yet the new government did nothing at all to change it. We have to start wondering why this Act has been in effect so long."

Bibliography

Books

Jervis Anderson	*Guns in American Life.* New York: Random House, 1984.
James J. Boulet Jr.	*Firearms Folly in Maryland: Official Corruption Overcomes the Constitution.* Springfield, VA: Gun Owners Foundation, 1989.
Charlotte A. Carter-Yamauchi	*A Clash of Arms: The Great American Gun Debate.* Honolulu: Legislative Reference Bureau, 1991.
Verna Casey	*Gun Control: A Selected Bibliography.* Monticello, IL: Vance Bibliographies, 1988.
Robert S. Clark	*Deadly Force: The Lure of Violence.* Springfield, IL: Charles C Thomas, 1988.
Alan M. Gottlieb	*Gun Rights Fact Book.* Bellevue, WA: Merril Press, 1988.
Ted Robert Gurr, ed.	*Violence in America: The History of Crime.* Newbury Park, CA: Sage, 1989.
Stephen P. Halbrook	*That Every Man Be Armed.* Oakland, CA: Independent Institute, 1990.
Gary Kleck	*Point Blank: Guns and Violence in America.* New York: Aldine de Gruyter, 1991.
Dave Kopel	*The Samurai, the Mountie, and the Cowboy: Should America Adopt the Gun Controls of Other Democracies?* Buffalo: Prometheus Books, 1992.
Elaine Landau	*Armed America: The Status of Gun Control.* Englewood Cliffs, NJ: Julian Messner, 1991.
Robert Emmet Long, ed.	*Gun Control.* New York: H.W. Wilson, 1989.
Robert L. Nay, ed.	*Firearms Regulations in Various Foreign Countries.* Washington: Law Library of Congress, 1990.
Lee Nisbet, ed.	*The Gun Control Debate: You Decide.* Buffalo: Prometheus Books, 1990.
Deborah Prothrow-Stith	*Deadly Consequences.* New York: HarperCollins, 1991.
Paxton Quigley	*Armed and Female.* New York: Dutton, 1989.
Gerald D. Robin	*Violent Crime and Gun Control.* Cincinnati: Anderson, 1991.
Janelle Rohr, ed.	*Violence in America: Opposing Viewpoints.* San Diego: Greenhaven Press, 1990.
William R. Tonso, ed.	*The Gun Culture and Its Enemies.* Bellevue, WA: Merril Press, 1989.
William W. Treanor and Marjolijn Bijlefeld	*Kids and Guns: A Child Safety Scandal.* 2d ed. Washington: American Youth Work Center and the Educational Fund to End Handgun Violence, 1989.
U.S. Bureau of Justice Statistics	*Handgun Crime Victims.* Washington: U.S. Government Printing Office, 1990.
James D. Wright and Peter H. Rossi	*Armed and Considered Dangerous: A Survey of Felons and Their Firearms.* New York: Aldine de Gruyter, 1986.
James D. Wright, Peter H. Rossi, and Kathleen Daly	*Under the Gun: Weapons, Crime, and Violence in America.* New York: Aldine, 1983.

Periodicals

Daniel Abrams	"Gun Smoke," *The Nation*, July 29-August 5, 1991.
Jerry Adler	"Armed and Considered Dangerous: Citizens Weigh the Risks of Shooting Back," *Newsweek*, September 24, 1990.

Gun Control

Daniel K. Akaka and Steve Symms	"Should Congress Pass the Brady Bill?" *The American Legion*, August 1991.
American Rifleman	"Sheriff Makes the Point: Instant Background Checks Work," May 1991.
Michael Beard	"If Guns Could Make Us Safe . . .," *Christian Social Action*, July/August 1991. Available from the General Board of Church and Society of the United Methodist Church, 100 Maryland Ave. NE, Washington, DC 20002.
James S. Brady	"Congress Didn't Want to See . . .," *The New York Times*, April 3, 1990.
William F. Buckley Jr.	"Guns and Children," *National Review*, October 21, 1991.
John Canham-Clyne	"Gun-Control Bills Shoot Blanks at U.S. Violence," *In These Times*, May 22-28, 1991.
Sharon Carrico-Martin	"How I Bought a Gun in Forty Minutes," *Time*, October 28, 1991.
Tristram Coffin	"Crime in the Cities," *The Washington Spectator*, June 1, 1991. Available from the Public Concern Foundation, PO Box 20065, New York, NY 10011.
Congressional Digest	"The Brady Handgun Violence Prevention Act," entire issue on the Brady Bill, June/July 1991.
Clayton E. Cramer	"State Constitutions and the Second Amendment," *American Rifleman*, February 1992.
Robert F. Drinan	"America Needs Gun Control if It Is to Call Itself a 'Civilized Society,'" *National Catholic Reporter*, May 24, 1991. Available from 115 E. Armour Blvd., Kansas City, MO 64111.
Alan Farnham	"Inside the U.S. Gun Business," *Fortune*, June 3, 1991.
Don Feder	"Gun Control Doesn't Work," *New Dimensions*, April 1991.
Glamour	"Handguns: Should Buyers Be Subject to a Seven-Day Waiting Period? 73 Percent Say Yes," June 1991.
Jeanne A. Harris	"Armed and Female," *New Dimensions*, August 1990.
Linda M. Hasselstrom	"A Peaceful Woman Explains Why She Carries a Gun," *Utne Reader*, May/June 1991.
Sue Huck	"Gun Control: A Hardy Perennial of the Liberal Agenda," *Conservative Review*, April 1991. Available from the Council for Social and Economic Studies, 6861 Elm St., McLean, VA 22101.
Don B. Kates and Patricia T. Harris	"How to Make Their Day," *National Review*, October 21, 1991.
Gary Kleck	"The Value of Civilian Arms Possession as a Deterrent to Crime . . .," *American Journal of Criminal Law*, vol. 18, no. 3, 1991. Available from University of Texas School of Law, 727 E. 26th St., Austin, TX 78705.
Robert W. Lee	"The Campaign to Disarm America," *The New American*, June 4, 1991.
Robert W. Lee	"Police Protection or Self-Defense," *The New American*, April 20, 1992.
Mark D. McLean	"Gun Control and Sheep for the Slaughter," *The Wall Street Journal*, January 6, 1992.
Tom Morganthau	"It's Not Just New York . . .," *Newsweek*, March 9, 1992.
Lance Morrow	"Childhood's End," *Time*, March 9, 1992.
The New Republic	"Tom Foley, Gun Nut," January 28, 1991.
Ron Rosenbaum	"The Brady Offensive," *Vanity Fair*, January 1991.
Jay Edward Simkin	"Control Criminals, Not Guns," *The Wall Street Journal*, March 25, 1991.
Kathleen Sylvester	"A Little Bit of Gun Control," *Governing*, July 1991. Available from Congressional Quarterly Inc., 2300 N St. NW, Suite 760, Washington, DC 20037.
Jackson Toby	"To Get Rid of Guns in Schools, Get Rid of Some Students," *The Wall Street Journal*, March 3, 1992.
Joseph B. Treaster	"Teenage Gunslinging Is on Rise, in Search of Protection and Profit," *The New York Times*, February 19, 1992.
Franklin E. Zimring	"Firearms, Violence, and Public Policy," *Scientific American*, November 1991.

Organizations to Contact

The editors have compiled the following list of organizations that are concerned with the issues debated in this book. All of them have publications or information available for interested readers. For best results, allow as much time as possible for the organizations to respond. The descriptions are derived from materials provided by the organizations. This list was compiled upon the date of publication. Names, phone numbers and addresses of organizations are subject to change.

American Bar Association (ABA)
Section of Criminal Justice
1800 M St. NW
Washington, DC 20035-5886
(202) 331-2260

Founded in 1921, the ABA's Section of Criminal Justice is comprised of attorneys, law students, judges, law professors, and law enforcement personnel interested in the quick, fair, and effective administration of justice. The ABA supports a ban on assault weapons and a waiting period for gun purchases. It believes gun control measures are both constitutional and effective. Among the ABA's many publications are the quarterly magazine *Criminal Justice* and various reference guides, books, course materials, and legal analyses.

American Civil Liberties Union (ACLU)
132 W. 43rd St.
New York, NY 10036
(212) 944-9800

The ACLU champions the rights set forth in the Declaration of Independence and the U.S. Constitution. It opposes the suppression of individual rights. The ACLU interprets the Second Amendment as a guarantee for states to form militias, not as a guarantee of the individual right to own and bear firearms. Consequently, the organization believes gun control is constitutional and that because guns are dangerous, gun control is necessary. The ACLU publishes *Civil Liberties* quarterly and *Civil Liberties Alert* monthly in addition to policy statements and reports.

Center to Prevent Handgun Violence
1225 Eye St. NW, Suite 1100
Washington, DC 20005
(202) 289-7319

The center is a national, nonprofit organization that aims to educate the public concerning the dangers of handguns and ways to reduce this danger. Through school programs, the center attempts to teach children about the hazards of handguns. The center produces written and audiovisual materials that are available to the public.

Citizens Committee for the Right to Keep and Bear Arms
12500 NE Tenth Pl.
Bellevue, WA 98005
(206) 454-4911

The committee believes that the U.S. Constitution's Second Amendment guarantees and protects the right of individual Americans to own guns. It works to educate the public concerning this right and to lobby legislatures to prevent the passage of gun control laws. The committee has more than 600,000 members. It provides pamphlets and other materials to the public upon request.

Educational Fund to End Handgun Violence
PO Box 72
110 Maryland Ave. NE
Washington, DC 20002
(202) 544-7227

The fund is a nonprofit educational charity dedicated to ending gun violence, especially violence against children. It provides information to researchers, journalists, attorneys, legislators, and the general public concerning handgun violence, firearms marketing and production, and firearm design. The fund sponsors educational programs and publishes materials such as *Assault Weapons and Accessories in America*, a study of assault weapons, and *Kids and Guns*, a study on gun-related suicides, homicides, and accidents involving youth.

Gun Owners of America
8001 Forbes Pl., Suite 102
Springfield, VA 22151
(703) 321-8585

Gun Owners of America opposes gun control measures as unconstitutional and ineffective. The group lobbies legislatures to prevent gun control measures from becoming law. It provides information to the public in the form of pamphlets and brochures on gun ownership and gun control.

Handgun Control, Inc.
1225 Eye St. NW, Suite 1100
Washington, DC 20005
(202) 898-0792

Handgun Control, Inc. is a nonprofit organization that lobbies Congress to pass federal gun control legislation. It sponsors speakers and programs to inform the public about the dangers of America's inadequate gun control laws. It provides speeches, articles, and reports concerning gun control to the public.

National Crime Prevention Council (NCPC)
Information Services
1700 K St. NW, Second Fl.
Washington, DC 20006
(202) 466-6272

The NCPC is a branch of the U.S. Department of Justice. It works to teach Americans how to reduce crime and addresses the causes of crime in its programs and educational materials. It provides readers with information on gun control and gun violence. The NCPC has a comprehensive computer database of crime-related information and a resource center that includes more than one thousand books.

National Rifle Association of America (NRA)
1600 Rhode Island Ave. NW
Washington, DC 20036
(202) 828-6000

The NRA, with nearly three million members, is America's largest organization of gun owners. It is the primary lobbying group for those who oppose gun control laws. The NRA believes that such laws violate the U.S. Constitution and do nothing to reduce crime. The association does support a national, computerized system that would check the backgrounds of individuals attempting to purchase guns. In addition to its monthly magazine *American Rifleman*, the NRA publishes numerous books, bibliographies, reports, and pamphlets on gun ownership, gun safety, and gun control.

National Shooting Sports Foundation (NSSF)
555 Danbury Rd.
Wilton, CT 06897
(203) 762-1320

The NSSF is an organization of hunters and others who use guns for recreation. It provides members and the general public with information on the history, safety, and use of guns for sport. NSSF publications include pamphlets such as *NSSF Handgun Guide, When Your Youngster Wants a Gun*, and *The Ethical Hunter*.

Second Amendment Foundation
12500 NE Tenth Pl.
Bellevue, WA 98005
(206) 454-7012

The foundation is dedicated to informing Americans about their constitutional right, as stated in the Second Amendment, to keep and bear firearms. It believes that gun control laws violate this right. The foundation publishes the quarterly newsletter *The Second Amendment Reporter* in addition to monographs such as *Waiting Periods: Myth Exposed, Semi-Automatic Rifles,* and *The Police View of Gun Control.*

United States Revolver Association (USRA)
96 W. Union St.
Ashland, MA 01721

The USRA, founded in 1900, opposes gun control. Its members believe that owning guns in general, and revolvers in particular, is necessary for Americans to be able to defend themselves against criminals and against foreign invasion. The association supports increased sentences for criminals who use guns. It provides information to the public concerning revolvers and legislation that would threaten gun ownership.

Violence Policy Center
1834 18th St. NW
Washington, DC 20009
(202) 265-1920

The center is an educational foundation that conducts research on firearms violence. It works to educate the public concerning the dangers of guns and supports gun control measures. The center's publications include the books *NRA: Money, Firepower, and Fear* and *Assault Weapons and Accessories in America* in addition to an information packet and other materials that are available to the public.

Index

The Myth of the Happy Child

Books by Carole Klein

THE MYTH OF THE HAPPY CHILD

THE SINGLE-PARENT EXPERIENCE

Carole Klein

The Myth
of the
Happy Child

Harper & Row, Publishers
New York, Evanston, San Francisco,
London

FIRST EDITION

Designed by Dorothy Schmiderer

Library of Congress Cataloging in Publication Data

Klein, Carole.
  The myth of the happy child.
  1. Child study. 2. Emotions. I. Title.
BF723.E6K56 1975   155.4'18   74–1825
  ISBN 0–06–012422–9

---

75 76 77 78 79 10 9 8 7 6 5 4 3 2 1

For Emily and William Klein,
children I love—people I respect

Contents

Acknowledgments

Before this book officially begins, I want to thank some of the people who helped make it possible. First of course are the boys and girls whose experiences and perceptions so vividly increased my understanding of what it means to be a child. I spoke and listened to great numbers of children in the course of this writing. Many of them you will meet inside these pages. Others, who are less visible, nonetheless provided me with invaluable background material. I wish also to thank the parents of these children, for allowing me to share in their sons' and daughters' lives. A special word of thanks to Ms. Bette Distler, Poet in Residence for the "Project Moppet" program of the Woodbridge Township Public School system in New Jersey. Her students regularly contributed writings to my collection of creative expressions by children about the feelings of childhood.

A word of thanks now to people who figured in a somewhat different way in the development of this book. To Mrs. Barbara Lindeman, a friend and enlightened critic, who never failed to give sharp insights about the material I was exploring. Her questions served to clarify my own thinking, which in turn strengthened my writing.

To my husband, Ted Klein, who provided consistent encouragement and belief that the book would achieve the goals I had set for it.

And finally, to my editor, Mrs. Frances Lindley, whose wise suggestions and range of thinking helped me reach those goals.

CAROLE KLEIN

New York
March 1975

Introduction

Susan, eleven, lies on the hot beach in front of her family's summer home sucking orange soda from a bottle as if the bottle's mouth were covered by a nipple. Her free hand strokes the sand in steady rhythm just as she used to stroke the blanket in her crib. Another child suddenly looms over her and she quickly drops the bottle from her mouth, soda trickling now in orange paths down her cheek. The child makes a jeering comment and tears well up in Susan's eyes as she jumps to her feet. Then, lips still puffy from sucking, she spits in her "friend's" face and runs wildly into the welcome cover of the sea.

Eight-year-old Jimmy dreams that his father pushes him into the washing machine and covers him up with soapy water. Over and over and over he spins around the metal prison, looking out at his father each time his head makes the circle past the window in the front of the machine. His father only smiles at him, seeming not to notice Jimmy's horrible discomfort. The boy wakes up screaming. Still half asleep, he pounds his pillow as if it, not his dream, held him captive. Even after his parents calm him, he refuses to go to sleep unless the door and all the windows to his room are left open.

Bruce comes home from school. The front door is unlocked but his mother isn't there. He runs from empty room to empty room, not able to contain his panic. "Mommy, Mommy, please come out, Mommy!" he screams, throwing open closets, looking under furniture as if he were playing some bizarre version of hide-and-seek. His mother drives up a few minutes later and is horrified at his behavior. She tells him nine-year-old boys don't act this way, and he should be "ashamed" of himself. . . .

He is.

He hangs his head, unable to look at her, but unable also to stop his sobbing. She tells him to go upstairs to his room and "calm down." Meekly he obeys her instructions, and when she follows along just a little bit later, he is asleep—fully dressed, sprawled out on his bed as if hurled there by the force of his emotion. His cheeks are crimson and damply hot with the perspiration of fear.

Bruce and Jimmy and Susan are ordinary children. They have not been introduced to serve as dramatic contrast to what most other children are really like.

("Thank God my Jennifer's not like them!") But of course Jennifer is.

As you follow me through these pages you will meet many children who are very much like your own. Healthy, normal boys and girls who, within that normality, are often extremely happy but often, too, will be quite desolate. A child's world, no matter how much we might like it, cannot be plotted on the map of our illusions: a map that says the landscape of childhood is enchanted, delighted, filled with innocent pleasures and joy. In the vast country of psychic pain, we do not line up in size places. Indeed, evidence now exists that when we have hardly any size at all, we are already learning the conflict attached to being human.

An obstetrician named A. W. Lilly has ascribed a "personality" attribute to a fetus. He believes that the uterus, as softly padded cocoon, doesn't totally protect its developing charge from sensory input. Much of the world outside the mother's womb actually does affect this minuscule pre-person. He will be startled by a sudden noise, hear his mother's heartbeat, is sensitive to her physical restlessness. Experiments show that he responds actively to a needle's touch or the feel of a cold solution. X-rays prove that fetal limbs flail wildly during labor, and that if the baby's head is compressed just a tiny bit during a contraction, its protests are intense and violent. And so the child, it appears, enters his new world already poised for pain, having known its stings as part of the price of being born. And it continues.

The notion of a child's life as idyllic and uncontaminated by significant distress erodes still further in the face of some of these statistics: It has been estimated that on a national level, 10 percent of all children have emotional problems significant enough to warrant professional help. One study of eight hundred elementary school children in a New York suburb, for example, concluded that well over half could have benefited from some form of outside assistance. And these figures fit with disarming neatness into another report by that relentless chronicler of our lives *The New York Times,* which reveals that increasing numbers of children are in fact seeking this assistance. There seems, we are told, little question that the "kiddie on the couch" is more and more a part of the therapeutic scene. Actually, this image is misleading, since few children work out their problems in the traditional horizontal pose. But it's an image that serves to illustrate the report's dramatically contemporary finding. In the years between 1966 and 1971 alone, there was a 63 percent increase in the number of children being treated at a mental health facility. And this startling expansion doesn't include the vast numbers of boys and girls who received some kind of private care.

The rationale behind these statistics varies, with most people feeling that it's the parents' greater sophistication about psychological help that brings the family looking for help. In other words, children are not necessarily more disturbed because they flock in greater numbers than ever before to the therapist's office.

At the same time, the child today, with all his enriched opportunities for experience, has more opportunity for experiencing stress. When asked why this was so, Dr. Robert Traisman, an Illinois psychologist, answered tersely, "Why? Pick up a newspaper!" The doctor then fleshed out his reply, touching in the process all the bases of life's emotional assaults—family tensions, academic pressures, uncertain values and, finally, the fact that we are increasingly a more isolated and "less personal society."

Yet if this book is written to acknowledge that raising a child, especially today, is a worrisome business, it is also written to assert that the stresses a child feels, and yes, many of the effects of stress, lie within the range of what can realistically be called "normal" emotional bruises. So whether outside help is sought or not, there's a larger truth the myth of childhood happiness eclipses: it is incredibly difficult to become a person.

Even with parents' most dedicated efforts to fill their child's life with pleasure, the child will experience many moments of real emotional pain. Anger and fear and loneliness and guilt are only some of the feelings that leap unbidden into children's developing lives. For indeed, they are feelings inevitably connected to growing up.

This inevitability is too often overlooked in the bombardment of material aimed at contemporary parents. The disturbing impression lingers that our slightest blunder will forever maim our child's emotional health. The sight of children "unhappy" fills us, then, not just with loving concern, but with guilt. We remember the too harsh scolding, the preoccupation when we should have been listening, the misreading of signals that totally botched up our ability to meet a need. Surely it was some such behavior that changed the emotional climate. Surely these worries and fears are an index of *our* inadequacy.

It is time to recognize that we often assume unnatural responsibility for feelings natural to the process of growth and development. Certainly we adults are flawed and fallible, as people and as parents, but the reason yesterday's giddily joyous son or daughter now huddles miserably in a chair does not necessarily relate to a particular parental transgression.

Instead these boys and girls are exhibiting behaviors built into their formation as separate people. And however much we ache in empathy for our children's painful feelings, we must acknowledge their right to experience them. Knowing it is not "our fault" will help us do this. We will not have to feel defensive as they make their struggles of self. Understanding the limitations of our ability to change the course of growing up, we can stand by lovingly, ready to offer whatever help we *can* give as they meet the inescapable challenges of childhood.

It is not, I should add now, the purpose of this book to

argue that there is no such thing as emotional illness, or to convince parents that no child will ever find his problems overwhelming. But clearly we live in an age when words like "normal" and "abnormal" must be opened up to a broader range and be judged in a newly relativistic light. Normal for what circumstances? By which person's criteria? As Thomas Szaz says of his profession's own confusion, "Ask six different psychiatrists what 'normal' means and you'll get six totally different answers!"

So nowhere are there agreed-upon definitions. Such uniform thinking belongs to our past, to far more stable times than those we know today. Yet there seems little point in regretting this loss of semantic security. For "stability" as a goal often clothes us in strait jackets, narrowing the life space so much that only our steady breaths provide any excitement. Bruno Bettelheim, that veteran of child-raising, refers to this dulled image of the "good" life when he says: "high on my list of priorities for childrearing in the future is to correct the current fallacy that it's desirable to rear children who are insulated from the frustrations and difficulties of life . . . we must teach them from childhood on that the success of living is in the ability to meet the difficulties; to struggle through."

I remembered this when I read the report of psychologist Morris Hymowitz about yet another study. This time it involved nearly two thousand boys, followed over a twelve-year period, revealing at study's end only fifty who showed no visible signs of any psychopathology. Dr. Hymowitz's addendum to the report supports Dr. Bettelheim's belief that yes, perhaps struggling through is more important than fitting in. For even as I wonder, awe-struck, what kind of soil this tiny elite group of fifty was nurtured in—even as I nervously speculate if I could ever develop a similar green thumb with my own children—I am told that the uniquely stable handful of trouble-free children were also "lacking in imagination and creativity, and were highly limited in their interests and activities." The calmness I am inclined to covet seemed also to spell passivity and dully repetitive behavior.

Incredible! The impossible dream, attained, brings only yawns. Nonetheless, despite such challenges to our innocence, even with enormous holes rent in the illusion that any time of life, as we know life today, can be paradise, we still hope *our* children will have childhoods of innocent contentment.

It is such a hope that often tempts us to renovate reality. So mothers will pick up their children from school (perhaps after their own regular analysts' appointments) and smile benignly at each other as they watch the play and listen to the shrieks and laughter. That a boy leans against the wall only watching, that a girl hunches her shoulders in mortified awareness of developing breasts, that a child still smarts from the sharp sarcasm of a teacher, that invitations to a birthday party leave uninvited children feeling marked as lepers—this the mothers too often do not (will not?) see.

There is a particular dynamic to this myopia—what no less an authority on man's lopsided eyesight than Sigmund Freud referred to as "childhood amnesia." As the phrase quite simply and powerfully suggests, it is difficult to understand a child's world because it is impossible to recall what our own world, in childhood, was truly like. For when we look back at our own early pasts, we don't so much remember as reconstruct. I who remember am not the person I am remembering. I am an adult woman, with scars and fears, with needs and interests and goals far different from those I had when I was four or six or even fourteen. Yes, of course, I can remember events out of the past—chronological signposts that thread through the years, tying together significant times in my life—but I cannot feel the climate of the country that I traveled.

So I can say to my child, "I remember how it felt not to be invited to a birthday party," but the fact is I do *not* remember. Yes, I can recall rejection similar to what she experiences now, but I cannot in empathy touch her aching soreness, for it is, after all, only the event I recall and not its emotional essence.

Even the most vivid childhood memories are only fragments, half-truths that don't tell the whole story of who I once was. I can tell you that I remember being critically ill when I was four years old. And I even catch sight of my father, dressed in a leather jacket and a woolen cap because the windows all had to be open despite the frigid weather to aid my breathing. But I cannot tell you through the retrospective blur how it felt to lie in bed trying to breathe, or how it felt to me to have him there beside me. I don't know what expressions ranged across his face: love, or anger, or fear—or how those nonverbal communications were heard by me. My own adult truth submerges the truth of that child in bed, and she remains, in ways that matter, a stranger.

Psychiatrist Ernest Schachtel, an authority on memory, says that "even the most profound and prolonged psychoanalysis does not lead to a recovery of childhood memory; at best it unearths some incidents and feelings that had been forgotten."

Emphasis here is on the word "some," as the doctor's use of it is particularly significant in this age of analytic encounter. For no matter how earnestly we try, no matter how often or expensively we pour out our pasts to a "significant other," the past remains shrouded by the accumulated experiences and repressions of our developing selves.

Repression is, as indicated, the powerfully resistant factor in childhood amnesia. In countless ways we're taught to deny those aspects of ourselves that don't fit in with family and cultural values. We are tamed, inhibited, trained to be part of society's machinery. By the time we're adults, we've learned the mechanics of the machine too well. We don't carry with us, from those earlier selves, responses that go against the people we've become. The intense emotional experiencing of a child's world is out of place in this no-nonsense, achievement-oriented, grown-up world we now call home. And so when we look at children, they are quaintly foreign—visitors from another country, even though their country was once our own.

Schachtel explains neatly: "Childhood amnesia covers those aspects and experiences of the former personality which are incompatible with the culture."

It of course has always been true that adults and children have faced each other across the divide of time as long as they have coexisted. But as with so many other aspects of living, it's the same, only more so, today. If adults historically haven't been able to identify with what a child really feels, they could at least identify with his patterns of growth and development. After all, a child moved pretty well through the same tunnel to adulthood as had his parents, placing his feet in paths well marked by those who had come this way before. At the end of the tunnel, light shone on a world equally pretested and familiar. He would be a grownup, like his parents.

But he is very, very different from his parents, this child

today. Margaret Mead, a lady who has watched several generations from several worlds come through the tunnel, compares contemporary parents and children to what happens when a tribe in New Guinea is suddenly "exposed to airplanes and transistor radios," or when "children of cannibals go away to medical school."

The analogy is graphically apt, if jarring to urbane self-concepts. Despite martinis and master's degrees, we are in many ways primitives when compared to our children. The frame of reference for us to share is uncomfortably limited.

A child grows up and into a world assaulted with a technology that is massive, and with massive implications for how he *views* the world. From television to the bomb to space travel, he's the product of an age that raises questions his parents never dreamed of, and defies answers they may have built a life by. There is often a widening discrepancy, as the child grows, between his parents' "truth" and that of the world outside. His parents say one thing, his experience another—creating a kind of confusion children have never quite felt before. How to make sense of it . . . ? Where are the guidelines?

Dr. Mead comments, "No one, teachers, physicians, parents, knows anything about dealing with the child who [is] someone they will never be, and about whom we can make no prediction," adding to that, lest we not get her message, ". . . we have no idea at all what the world is going to be like 40 years from now."

So, to a startlingly new degree, a child today is at the center of his own "becoming." It has always been difficult, painful, profoundly wrenching to make life coherent, but now it is particularly hard.

Knowing this, my response deepens to a girl named Greta,

who is a child you'll meet often as this book unfolds. Greta is six, youngest child in a family with three boys. She has long brown hair and a dimple that sits higher on her cheek than any dimple I've ever seen, just at the top of her cheekbone, so that when she smiles it seems to point the way to her eyes, their deep brown color so appropriate to their sloping almond shape.

Today there are tears in Greta's eyes. She'd had a troubled night, bad dreams that reflected a plaguing discomfort about the challenges of first grade.

"I wish," she said finally, tears spilling over now, "I wish I knew . . . *everything!* If I knew everything, I could"—she takes a deep breath, and scales the heights of her despair, and comes up with the ultimate conquering of experience's peak —"I could sleep with the lights out!"

It seems to me—and hence the reason for this book—that the only way to help Greta sleep with the lights out is to turn them on in the many rooms of her childhood. Understanding the experiences the rooms contain will help us understand Greta. And in seeing her, and all our children, as the people they really are, we can help them escape the tyranny of imposed perceptions of what they're "supposed" to be.

I am what I am
Don't make me be what I'm not
Because . . .
It won't be me.
                    —BETH (age 10)

To me it seems that youth is, like
spring, an over-praised season . . .
more remarkable, as a general rule,
for biting east winds, than genial
breezes.
                    —SAMUEL BUTLER

1 / The Myth
and Its Effects

A child breaks a toy and cries as if his heart also lay in scattered pieces. We soothe him briefly and then, when the crying continues, push him (however gently, it *is* a push) aside . . . ready ourselves to move on to more important tasks.

We snap at a child who hangs around the kitchen after school, refusing to go out to play because "nobody likes me."

"You have lots of friends," we assure him briskly, and send him on his way. Later, when he comes home clearly wounded by rejection, we accuse him of deliberately not having a good time. Our anger rises with surprising swiftness and we treat his sadness as though it were a flimsy, inappropriate costume—not the real clinging cloth of his experience.

Nancy is ten. She is small-boned and fragile-looking. Her thick hair, which she wears in one long dark braid, appears too heavy for her rather tiny face. The hair seems to belong to someone older and stronger. When you first look at her, your vision seems almost to divide—first the face and then the hair, the contrast too sharp to have fused yet into one image. Interestingly, this is almost a metaphor for Nancy's

1

personality. She is, her mother sighs in frustration, like two people. The oldest of three children, she sometimes seems the youngest. Her moods are volatile, buffeting her equilibrium and that of everyone else around. In the middle of a crying, kicking tantrum, she may run out to the garden and pull up all the flowers, jumping up and down on them until they're thickly perfumed dust.

Or she will literally tremble with fear over some "tiny" event. A simple quiz in school, a new baby-sitter due for an evening. Her body shakes and her voice catches in her throat when she tries to tell her mother what it is that has suddenly created her spreading panic.

And then, at other times, she's as wise as though she had lived for many years beyond her actual ten. When I talk to her during such periods, I can completely forget, in the intellectual meeting, that this is according to any calendar a child. She has the rare ability to strike directly to the bone of a situation—sizing it up and wrapping it up with no string of pretense left hanging. For example, when we were talking about some mother in the neighborhood who considers herself a playmate of her children, Nancy was unimpressed. Yes, she agreed, the woman did sometimes go sleigh-riding and roller-skating with her daughter, and did make the most elaborate birthday parties of any of her friends, but, said Nancy, "that's just doing, not being. Anyway, if I were her kid, I'd always have a stomach ache. It's like she starves you when she doesn't feel like feeding you, and then she stuffs you full of things when she wants to show off her cooking."

Last summer, thinking it might help strike a balance between the babyishness and grown-up sensitivity, Nancy's parents sent her to camp. Predictably, letters covered the range of her personality—sometimes lyrically enthused, often perceptive, occasionally poetically unhappy.

A note dashed off quickly before a play rehearsal, filled with proud excitement about her starring role, would be followed by: "Counselors aren't much different than teachers. They treat you like you're a lump of clay. . . . They like little statue people, not real kids." Or: "I was very, very homesick yesterday. It made me feel like an old lady sitting on a broken bench with her mouth closed."

On visiting day at camp, Nancy's parents barely drove up to the gate before she hurled herself out from behind it and threw herself into their arms. It was clear from her sun-flushed face that she had been watching for them for hours.

The force of her greeting was overwhelming. As Nancy's mother untangled herself from the embrace, she said with a little laugh, "You couldn't have missed us all that much!" And before Nancy could insist she had, her father showed her the treats they had brought, snacks and games and comic books, pulling them out of the bag as though they were objects of seduction. There was an edge of tension, almost palpable, to the scene, as the parents looked around, self-consciously gauging the relative drama of other family reunions.

If the children in this book are all "normal" children, the parents are all "normal" parents—men and women who don't go out of their way to ignore their sons' and daughters' pain. Neither are they all uniquely insensitive people who, because they have never felt what their children feel, can't begin to understand what it means to be hurt, or frightened, or lonely.

No, it is precisely because we ourselves often know these emotions all too well that we avert our eyes from the truth of childhood. As suggested, it is the harsh reality of adult life that deepens the need to believe in myth. Relentlessly disappointed, we want our children to be hopeful. Disillusioned with love, we hope our children never question love's benevolence. Cheated by the false rewards of acquisition, we delight in our child's eager sense of promise.

Similarly, since it sometimes seems that the more we learn, the more we see life's absurdities, we find a child's "naïve" approach to experience enchanting. . . .

"When I'm with a bad baby-sitter, I don't come out of my room all night," says six-year-old, ever articulate Robert—flaming red hair, perfect nose, huge blue eyes sketching myth's child (anxiety about abandonment, plaguing bad dreams, ever present fear of failure—in spite of dramatically high IQ—making him very much reality's child). "Why don't you come out?" I ask him, and he tells me, "Because this way, I can say she's not there."

Judy, a chubby five-year-old—new to kindergarten, hating the walk to school every day because she's the smallest child on the block and is sure the "big third-graders" are laughing at her (many times she's right)—understands exactly what Robert is saying. She confesses a "secret"—that lots of times she walks all the way to school with her eyes closed. I had noticed, and like Judy's mother been puzzled by, the unusual number of bruises on her legs. Now it was explained. Eyes screwed tight, she kept bumping into telephone poles and garbage cans while she walked. But it was a fate she preferred to a visual collision with what she perceived as towering menaces to her newly emerging independent self.

In our envy of the child's apparent belief that he can erase what he'd rather not see, we recognize neither the confusion that requires an eraser nor the shadow that always remains, stubbornly resisting the rub. Judy's fear doesn't disappear because she won't focus on its source. It is only temporarily dimmed. Yes, Judy and Robert through their make-believe can detoxify reality to some degree. Indeed, with the limited powers of childhood, pretending is often the only way *to* deal with unpleasant situations. But ironically the situations may be perceived as far more unpleasant than they actually are. And it is this truth that should keep us from being wistfully amused by the naïveté behind barricaded door and eyes squeezed closed.

Obviously neither the baby-sitter nor the third-graders are real physical threats. But for a variety of reasons (many of which are discussed in the chapter on fears) they are perceived as threats. In the same way, the interplay of all experience is given a subjective as well as an objective reading by the child trying to make sense of the characters and plots in his expanding life. What *seems* to be happening is frequently as real as what actually *is* happening. Down through the ages, adults have said in horrified wonder to parents become less awesome, "But I always thought you disapproved of me," or "thought I was dumb," or "preferred" a brother or sister.

Yet so real were some of those pains when they happened that they probably shaped our lives, influenced the decisions we made, the directions we took. Therefore, when Greta says to me one morning, her voice bleak, "Daddy took my brothers to his office," I hear in her voice and read in her face total and utter rejection. And even though I know her father adores her, I am sure her unhappiness is, in this moment, real.

When we talk, there's an outpouring of evidence about why she was deliberately left behind. Her brothers are smarter, Daddy can play ball with them, she spills her milk all the time—a litany of grievances against herself. She shuffles her sandal on and off her foot, not looking at me, refusing in head-down mumbling to accept my suggestion that she talk to her father and tell him how much she would like to visit his office too. Maybe, I say rather desperately, knowing it is true, he just doesn't realize how much it means to her.

Eyes still fixed on her jiggling shoe, she answers me, her voice so low that I have to strain to hear it:

"I did say something, and he said I wouldn't have anything to do there all day. He said someday he'll take me when he has time for us to go out to a movie or something. . . . It's okay," she says then, and I'm chilled by her way of closing down conversation. "It's okay. . . . I didn't want to go anyway."

I am chilled because I see in Greta's response what R. D. Laing has called the "politics of experience." By this he means that in a family there is a "power struggle" over whose perception of an experience will be called real. Parents needing the order of a quiet evening, for example, decide a child is sleepy, so he'll go off to bed in spite of the fact that his body feels not the least little bit fatigued. The myth of happy childhood perpetuates this pattern of separating a child from his real experiencing. For it helps adults guiltlessly accept their own arguments.

Greta's father, believing that he has a happy little girl, who certainly is always sure of being loved, can keep his day less complicated by not having to amuse her. He tells himself, and can believe it, that she wouldn't have a good time in his office. Needing her father's love (which she is not at *all* sure of), Greta tries to believe it too. The myth prevails as she kisses him good-by without further complaint. But in the process, she has taken one more step toward self-estrangement; has sacrificed one more piece of her autonomy on the altar of approval.

Aggrandizing the myth and the child's inherent helplessness "excuses" adult self-righteousness. It allows us to justify, as Greta's father did, the restrictions and repressing dictums we inevitably lay down on children. After all, the helpless need protection. They must be told whom to trust, and taught how to behave so that the world accepts, not rejects, them. And we do want the world to accept them.

For we are, however unhappy in the job, licensed franchisers of that world. Generations of parents have gathered their children around society's counter and enticed them to buy, even as they themselves did, what Nancy referred to as "little statue people"—replicas of what the culture thinks they should be. "Adjust," we nervously say, "fit in, conform. . . . Here—accept these imperatives. No, no—repress those impulses."

The urgency stems from increasing uncertainty about where we ourselves fit in. Therefore, not just in my child's successful adherence to rules, but in his smiling face as he follows them, lies, I think, my own redemption. A happy child is evidence I'm doing my work well. Anxiety about my role and function is soothed. What have I accomplished in life? Well, look right here—I have a happy child!

Understandably, then, when the child broods, and attacks, or is frightened, he frightens me. For divergence from the myth of happiness also carries implications of a parent's failure. If my child is *not* happy, as the myth says he should be, then something I did or didn't do has caused his "atypical" pain.

Is it any wonder, then, that many parents, like Judy's, try

to shut their eyes to behavior that might if really confronted cause *them* pain?

In the study mentioned earlier, where it was concluded that a large proportion of the eight hundred children being observed could have benefited from professional help, it was also concluded that the reason they rarely got the help was because parents resisted the idea it was needed. Largely inappropriate feelings of responsibility for what was "going wrong" made mothers and fathers bury their heads in the sand while they insisted everything was all right.

Inevitably this no-news-is-good-news, what-I-can't-see-won't-hurt-me approach to the real experiencing of childhood often leaves children in lonely possession of their discomfort. As we saw with Greta, very early in life, long before they learn to read, they begin learning the scripts of what they perceive as being "acceptable" expressions of self. When Nancy's parents came to camp, they whirled through the day in circles of distraction from her unhappiness. They took her to the most coveted local restaurant for lunch, participated with genuine glee in all her camp activities, were wildly enthusiastic about even her smallest triumph. But as surely as if they had bound and gagged her, they made it impossible for her to communicate what she was really feeling. With their love for her undisputed, their obsession with producing a happy child turned the spigot to "off" for any expression of emotional pain.

Study after study proves that children sense what feelings are unacceptable to their parents and carefully edit them out of their meetings. Little boys, for example, whose fathers cling to the machismo image do not, no matter how loving they are with their fathers, talk about being afraid to play ball. And Nancy's plaintive comment, as her parents drove away, that "Mommy doesn't like me to be sad" paints a smile on her face while she waves good-by, even though tears flow silently inside. Dr. Irving Markowitz, who heads a major family service agency in the New York area, says that in a sense, children in these situations are being asked to be their "parents' therapist." The child creates an almost analytic encounter, assessing his parents' needs and calming their self-doubt by steering their relationship in the need's direction. But, says Dr. Markowitz, children when they do this are "faking" childhood. And it is never comfortable to breathe behind a mask, no matter how cheerfully smiling it may be.

Obsession with happiness slaps masks not only on children but on ourselves as well. Our eagerness to keep them "happy" paints confusingly cheerful faces over tearful experience. When Jimmy's grandmother died, he was "protected" from seeing any real expression of grief. As if she were in the middle of sex, his mother guiltily arranged her emotions whenever he entered the room.

"He never saw me cry once," she says proudly, adding in sighing explanation of her self-denial, "After all, he has time enough to know how much it hurts to lose a person you love." But I wonder—and it's not an idle question—will he really be able to deal with loss, or with love, when that time comes? Dr. Markowitz reflects the views of many of his colleagues who, like himself, make archaeological digs into patients' long-calcified feelings, when he explains that we serve as models for our children's emotional life. So that in "denying that the death of someone we love is such a terrible loss, we are implying that no relationship should ever be taken too deeply."

In such an antiseptic emotional climate, the air grows thin, the depth of experience runs shallow. Surely this is not a very meaningful heritage for any child. Yet guilt because the myth isn't working causes the most loving parents to deny children perhaps their most meaningful inheritance—the right to total possession of the fullest spectrum of their feelings.

2 / The Argument Against the Myth

If this book questions the mythology of childhood, it clings to believing in its miracles. The imagination is stunned at the idea that this writhing newborn infant sleeps under a blanket made from the history of the world. Yet generations of ancestors have passed on their genetic story, now to be told by him.

Skeptical though we are of old moralities that made sex and procreation a holy sacrament, the joining of sperm and egg seems, even in its admitted randomness, miraculous. Why that particular night's union and not another?

So it's still awesome to think that this tiny ball of instincts and movements was only nine months ago a single cell. What we may not know in our initial confrontation is that nine months from now, we'll be even more awe-struck when those infant movements will have already been incorporated into countless numbers of complex skills—each one making the child more aware of himself as a developing person.

He will, for example, no longer lie inertly in his crib, but instead will frequently grasp at things outside it, exploring with the excitement of first discovery their newness and special meaning. Some objects will particularly please the senses, like soft toys and bottles filled with warm milk. And he can perceive differences and make associations between animate and inanimate objects. The puppy that dances on the animal mobile above his crib swings back into position after he pokes it with his fists; the family dog runs yelping from the room at a similar prod through crib bars. So, too, the child begins to attach different emotional meanings to his perceptions. Only a live puppy is capable of licking his face in affection, and only the living animal's heartbeat under his hand can be so comforting.

A child is the center of his world, but the world expands continuously as he grows. When he pulls himself to his feet in his playpen, his life has radically changed. He now stands like other human beings, alongside them and opposite them, and can begin to get a wider sense of himself as a person who shares the experience of life and being human.

All this is the process of becoming a person—the story of how an infant gradually grows into full membership in society. And the process is, by its very definition, part one of the three-part argument against the myth of the always happy child. For it tells us that childhood is *developmental.* And because this means "becoming," rather than "being," the sands continuously shift underfoot, with no steady spot to nurture the contentment known through security. Yes, as a child whirls in the dizzying dance of developmental change, there may certainly be peaks of incredible joy, but they cannot be counted on to last. The calendar's turn into another growth period plummets him crazily to the tilting ground. Ground that is cold now where yesterday it was warm, hard and rough now where it was recently lush and rich.

The growth of a person involves far more than learning to

speak and walk and grasp widening sets of techniques. As he moves through the stages of physical development, the child experiences that development, experiences his world in ways unique to him.

Unfortunately, his uniqueness is frequently not recognized, which is one of the pieces of evidence in development's case against contentment. For although there are patterns of growth—babbling before speech, crawling before walking—the trip is not the same for all travelers through childhood. No matter how many charts are drawn about developmental curves and average behavior, a particular child cannot totally be captured by statistics. So the idea that all young passengers should be at a particular developmental place at a designated time leaves too many children breathlessly trying to catch up, more convinced with each frustrated effort that they'll always be lagging behind. They strain at the uniform of childhood, longing for some right to variation in its design. Rarely is it given. Like some mass-produced quartermaster's stock, identical clothing is issued to meet the turbulent weather of childhood's real climate.

For this reason, impressively bright Robert comes home from first grade in hot-faced humiliation, painfully sharing his "stupidness" over not being able to master the small muscle control six-year-olds are "supposed" to have, the better to tie shoelaces without teacher's help.

It's important to remember that the objective turmoil of development is always influenced by the subjective emotional perception of experience. Events and interactions and exchanges filter past a screen through which the child "feels" what is happening, even as he takes part in the happening itself. Therefore, if enough six-year-olds in the classroom *can* tie their shoes, and if the teacher cares enough about the accomplishment, Robert's trailing shoelaces can indeed form the word "stupid" for all, but most of all for himself in self-contempt, to see.

What a child sees in his personal mirror is very much influenced by what Harry Stack Sullivan called the "reflected appraisals" of other people. So Robert looks in the mirror and sees his physical self. But how he and children in general evaluate that self relates in large part to how significant people in their lives have judged their reflection. Too often it's the other person's perception that shapes their own—the other person's truth that comes perilously close to being the truth.

While parents are the most significant people in most children's lives, other people also have a great deal to do with how they see themselves—other people like, for instance, teachers.

In research on the forming of self-concepts, school weighs heavily on the scale of both positive and negative developing perceptions. One study of children from elementary school through college age had a quarter of the respondents referring to school as a factor in what they liked or didn't like about themselves. And it should be quickly added that the bulk of these responses showed school a much more fertile ground for nurturing self-contempt than self-esteem. Its towering certainties about what children are supposed to be make children feel even more inadequate and helpless about what in their chaotic development they really are. It's no wonder that fantasy about school often reflects a sense of powerlessness and the eager wish for magical gifts of strength. . . .

"If I were magic," recites Judy, "I would turn every school into a big, big pile of ants. But they'd still be ants so they'd be tiny and so I would be much more bigger and I would jump up and down and jump up and down until they were squashed in a dirty lumpy pile." She finishes breathlessly. Then, as I'm about to speak, she turns and adds a finishing fillip: "And then I'd take off my shoes and scrunch the school dirt in my toes and wash it off in the shower so it all ran down the drain." This last image sends her into peals of giggles, a raucous level of gaiety I have heard only when formerly religious friends tell some ultimately blasphemous joke.

So powerful a force can school be in a child's response to his own development that it can even take precedence over the family's more sympathetic atmosphere. Robert's mother laughs and kisses him when he confesses his morning's failure. "Who cares about such a silly thing?" she asks gaily. "I promise you: by the time you go to college you'll know how to tie your shoes." Robert tries a smile to match her own, but what his mother doesn't know is that in his weakened self-regard, as surely as Robert knows his name he knows that the boy named Robert will never be smart enough to go to college.

No; just because there's evidence to support adult measurements of a situation—this is a "big deal," that's only a "little thing"—it still doesn't mean very much to the child caught in the hurricane center of his feelings, who continues to wrestle with the subjective aspects of his experience. Picture eight-year-old Jimmy, for example, who finds his wiry but undersized body shameful. His friends are all bigger, often stronger, able to reach higher in basketball games and jump broader hurdles in gym class. Jimmy's parents understand his distress, although they don't share it because they know, and tell him, that everyone in their family is just a "slow grower." And indeed Jimmy's father grazes six feet, and his older brother gained nearly a foot when he hit adolescence. So see, Jimmy, they say consolingly, you'll "catch up" with your friends later on.

But catching up isn't the same as being equal now. And Jimmy, in childhood, is rooted in now, although many negative perceptions he forms about himself will affect his self-view for years to come. In the same way that studies show fat children "feel" obese long after they've become really thin, physical characteristics that a child is unhappy with, like shortness, can distort the self-image even when his head is clearly lintel instead of only table high.

Even when a child doesn't feel distressingly "different," he will feel that the mirror of developing self is at times the mirror of an unfunny fun house. Periodically it distorts the image he expects and wants to see. For the real point is that the image isn't fixed. No child can say "This is who I am" and have a reasonable sense of confidence that when he looks again he will recognize whom he sees. Inevitably, in the spinning physical and emotional and intellectual changes of development, the person in the mirror will sometimes be a stranger. It will be a person whose responses you can't count on, or in any way predict.

In all stages of growth, including those labeled particularly peaceful, like the years before real adolescence, lifting the label always shows some very untranquil developmental activity. Many of the ten- and eleven-year-olds, and certainly the twelve- and thirteen-year-olds I dealt with proved to me that their conflicts, however well concealed, had by no means ceased to exist. Much of their trouble had to do with the total newness of their experiencing. The steps they were taking away from childhood and into adolescence were so tentative, so experimental. There was no history to support a feeling or response, let alone a bravely taken action.

For some children the mirror's unsteady reflection can bring particular pain. Again, so much of the unhappy response relates to a discrepancy between what they would like to be physically and what they actually see they are. Children like Susan, eleven, whose bulky body is a body she agonizes over endlessly, can work herself up to frenzies of despair over both her inner and outer image. The still shapeless contours (will they ever be otherwise? she wonders) of her flesh are only matched in the self-hating pain they provoke by the unwelcome shapes of feeling inside her head, currents of chaos that sweep her along till she sometimes loses control.

One morning recently she spent forty-five minutes changing and rechanging her clothes for school. The blouse worn outside makes her look "pregnant"; the blouse tucked in declares her lack of a waistline; the body shirt pulls at her stomach and accentuates the deficiencies of her totally nonaccented chest; the sweater stops just at her hips, outlining their width. Each outfit makes her face more flushed, her eyes more damp. Each outfit gets thrown in furious rejection onto the bed, wrinkling the pile of clothes already bitterly discarded.

Finally she leaves for school, knowing as she bolts from her mother's annoyance because she hasn't eaten breakfast that her mother will soon be furious at the sight of her bedroom, and that the anger will be waiting for her at three o'clock. She knows, too, that hunger will, as her mother predicts, take over the morning and knows what her mother doesn't know: that its pangs will relentlessly call her attention to the body she hates now with such total passion.

Later that morning, Susan comes to our writing class. She seems lethargic and doesn't participate in any discussion. But when the class is over, she hands me this poem.

THE MEANING OF BEING ME

Who Am I? Who Am I?
Growing up isn't easy, no matter what you think.
No. No. It's hard. It's hard.
It's standing on the brink
of a mountain that
    you're afraid of.
    Sometimes I ask you who I am, but you don't tell me.
    Sometimes I ask myself who I am. . . .
Still a kid?
Soon a grown-up person. (Will it be better then?
Can you tell me that . . . can I believe it?)
I hear a certain song and I get
    tears in my eyes. . . .
I see a person and I get so angry—and he never even
    said a word. . . .
It's hard, growing up . . . it's so hard. Why must it
    be so hard. . . .
The littlest rough spot and there I go—crying,
angry . . . up to my room to break down—to kick—to have
    bad dreams—
I hurt you, and you, and you, sometimes—but I hurt me
    more times.
I don't want to hurt you, and I don't want to hurt me—
But it hurts so much not to know
    how to answer,
Who am I?

Susan would not show this poem to her mother at the time
she wrote it although her mother would certainly have empa-
thized with its turmoil. Instead she burrowed deeper into her
misery, made worse now by isolation. Worry about what she
is "supposed" to feel frequently keeps Susan from the com-

fort of sharing her feelings. It is a worry that relates to the second argument against the myth—the overwhelming *dependency* that is the counterpoint rhythm of childhood. From the time he lies in his bed hungry, needing someone else to bring food to make hunger disappear, dependency for his emotional and physical survival encircles a child. As he grows, his awareness of his continuing inadequacy imposes false fronts on instinctual responses and feelings. For he must, he feels, please the people whose care he needs, even those whom he would perhaps like to defy but is not yet strong enough to.

Take Nancy, for instance, who generally puts her "best" face forward in school, and is approvingly labeled by all her teachers as extremely "cooperative." On her last report card the teacher wrote, as if she were bestowing a gift, "Nancy is a delight. She never fails to do what is asked or expected of her." But in one of our writing groups, we play a metaphor game, and this same blandly yes-saying child writes, in a resentment undimmed by its neat lettering and perfect spelling: "I am a new house with no locks on my doors—everyone walks into my rooms without knocking."

Actually Nancy has created an analogy that describes with chilling accuracy what children's lives are often like. The invasion of privacy inflicted on a child is great and, often, the act of adults who have the most sincere respect for other people's rights. We do shove the Nancys and the Roberts and all the other growing selves called children into unlocked rooms, where paradoxically they're kept prisoner by our constant surveillance. They have no way to keep us from barging in at random whim, usually to teach another variation of socialization's favorite game—learning "right" from "wrong." We tell them what to do, how to act, what to think, and even how to look. The battle over hair and dress imposes grown-up taste on a child's developing one—and his need for our approval encourages him to "understand" that ours is the only "right" one.

That there's so little resistance to this dominating intrusion relates to fear of what lies outside childhood's unrespected perimeters. To one standing on the world's sidelines, the action in the center can seem pretty grim. It's a world that seems essentially an unfriendly place, with evil perhaps lurking, as in Hansel and Gretel, behind every falsely welcoming door.

Ask a child why there are rules and laws, and he'll tell you somberly, as four-year-old, darkly handsome George told me, "so that people don't go around killing and robbing each other."

What kind of people? I ask. "Everybody," he answers, obviously surprised at the silliness of my question. Don't tell *him* about internal control. Much realer chains keep all our villainy in line. Even when they're considerably older than George, this life view persists. Without rules, children imply, man's basic meanness would blossom. Left to people's own judgment, justice rarely would reign. This wild-garden view of life, a far cry from the mythic, gently flowering idea of how a child thinks, increases children's worries about their helplessness.

So it is their sense of inadequacy, not hostile malevolence, that provokes a discussion like the one between Greta and her mother when they were caught in a sudden snowstorm. During the frighteningly slippery automobile trip home, Greta asked worriedly about the possibility of their having an accident. Her mother started to say something reassuring about the lack of real danger, but Greta waved away the answer. She clearly wanted to get to the heart of the issue. What if, she asked, they have an accident and her mother is killed. Who will take Greta home? The questions continued —grotesque background for the harrowing ride.

Will Daddy be able to really take care of her—make her lunch and braid her hair? Does he know where her piano teacher lives, and will he be too strict about homework?

With heroic composure, her mother answered all the questions, drawing the lines of security tighter back around the child, so that finally she was satisfied. Humming a favorite song, Greta sat back in the seat, while her mother told herself silently that self-fulfilling prophecies don't really come from six-year-olds.

The excessively intense relationships within the nuclear family contribute to the problems children today have with dependency. Margaret Mead has written that with only two people to give security, a child always lives with the anxiety that one will disappear, leaving him with a meager half loaf only. This is quickly obvious when you work with children in writing about their worries and feelings. Family "fights" are mentioned over and over as threats to emotional well-being. . . .

"Arguments always scare me," writes eight-year-old Cathy. "I'd even rather my mother got mad at *me* than at my father."

"I get so scared when my father doesn't come home from work on time," Robert tells me, "but it's worse when Mommy yells at him when he does come home."

And ten-year-old Andy, whose outside self—all athletic skills and muscular build and jutting chin—belies the poet who lives inside, says that if he were invisible, "I would seal my mother's mouth with honey so that when she talked to my father all her words would sound sweet because they had to push out through the honey before he heard them!"

Many psychiatrists I talked with believed that the nuclear family's dependency forces a child into unfortunately narrowed experiments with self-fulfillment, for his fear of losing these exclusive sources of security makes him behave only in ways that are sure to win parental approval. And the sad fact is we do engage in a kind of trade-off with our children's dependency. It's the rare parent who doesn't exploit a child's need for approval and love in order to shape his behavior. The kiss or the spank become symbols of love or rejection, and when one is needed so badly, and the other is feared so terribly, they far outweigh their superficial significance.

"I don't understand what he's making such a fuss about," Dougie's mother says in embarrassed exasperation. With three-year-old curiosity (and competition for the attention I was receiving), Dougie had emptied all the drawers in the living room. The sight of playing cards, coasters, rubber-bands, tissues, toothpicks and cocktail napkins piled into messy collage had moved my friend to grab her son and lay a not very heavy hand to his bottom. Fortunately, they live in a private house, for surely in an apartment the screams would have alerted neighbors to a child's being battered on the other side of the wall. And indeed, in a way, Dougie was feeling battered by his mother's anger. His own walls of security were suddenly crumbling, admitting strong gusts of wind he well knew he couldn't resist on his own. Later, when his mother hugged and kissed him and wiped away the burning tears, the walls were solid again, protecting him from experiences he couldn't at this point in his development handle by himself.

Critics of our style of socialization call such giving and

taking of affection "anxiety conditioning," meaning exactly what the phrase implies. Children often learn to be "good" because there's so much anxiety involved in being "bad." A conditioned response gets attached to a forbidden action and not only precludes taking the action but makes the idea behind it, in effect, unthinkable. To allow the thought or feeling or impulse is to go against the guidelines for keeping love. Better stay within them while you try to make sense of your developing life.

And it is often so hard to make sense of it all. . . . A long time ago, the philosopher Descartes crawled into a stove to puzzle the mystery of man. At the end of the day, when he climbed out, he said, "I think, therefore I am." Children in a way reverse this tale. Their inability really to understand and clarify their thoughts makes it hard for them to grab hold of the meaning of their lives. Delicately blond Cathy writes, in our metaphor game, "I am a cloud. . . . I drift around in the sky and never really know where I am." And Jimmy, who first uses his despised shortness as the core of his self-concept, saying, "I'm a forty-five record. . . . My music always shuts off before anyone listens," later dictates, "It's really hard to describe me. I think that maybe if I tried I could, but what could I really say? I'm happy that you want to hear my feelings, but I wish you could come inside my head and sort them out first." And then he adds, as if I, this omnipotent grownup, could really see inside his head and he'd better protect himself, ". . . but I don't want you to tell out loud what you find." Jimmy's belief that I can see and tell him who he is indicates the *cognitive confusion* that is the final third of the argument against the myth of the happy child. For intellectual development is also still in process and this means that children will frequently gain the approval they need so badly by behaving in ways whose logic totally escapes them.

"I want it!" Dougie wails when his mother takes back a truck he's pulled from another child's hand. He is told it doesn't matter that he wants it—it "belongs" to someone else. He is told in simply stated words but a highly serious tone of voice about property rights and asking for permission. And all the while his eyes are fixed on the shiny red wonder of the truck, and his hand fairly tingles with the remembered tactile joy of it, ready as it was to be pushed in careening pleasure across the room. He reminds me of an alcoholic being given a temperance lecture in a liquor store; and I feel his bewilderment at having to sacrifice immediate gratification for concepts that can have no real meaning at this stage in his intellectual development.

The point is that, at three, a truck in hand is much more meaningful than any strength of character attainable through resisting temptation. Just as it's "better" to eat with your face right over your plate when the food smells so good that way. Just as when I whisper to George to lower his voice while he criticizes his sitter, he is clearly puzzled. Why should he deny what he's genuinely feeling in the name of some abstract principle of social behavior? Indeed, when I ask children to list questions they have about "rules," they pour out as from buckets of bewilderment so vast there isn't any seeable bottom. Why be nice to people you don't like? . . . Why take baths when you don't mind being dirty? . . . Why clean up your toys if you don't mind the clutter? . . . Why not interrupt people when you have something to say? . . . Why not cry when you're hurt, or kick when you're angry, or be nasty to the teacher or sitter if she's nasty to you? . . .

Long into childhood this confusion exists. Until obedience gives way to understanding, a child feels the distress of being outside his experiencing, the puzzled observer of his own behavior. The linkage between possessing your life and possessing your ideas is very real, and the emotional pain until that linkage is forged is also, and awfully, real.

So real that if he's sufficiently perplexed a child may box himself into an even tinier corner of experience than childhood normally allows. Studies on the "rigid" child show that uncertainty about what he is "supposed" to do, and lack of understanding about why it should or shouldn't be done, encourage many children to play it safe in particular restricting ways. They will push experience into broad categories of "right" and "wrong" and stand stiffly between them, unable to make the slightest adjustment. I met many children who became really upset at a deviation from routine, and who clearly needed the security of repeated familiar behavior. Desperate to "know," they clung to certainties and insisted on constants. I remember one day when Cathy and I were having cocoa in the school classroom how she refused to stir the cup with her finger when I added much-needed sugar. No matter how I assured her it was okay, and that it was my "fault" for forgetting the spoon, she would not and, I saw by her tension, actually could not dip her finger into the beckoning liquid. Mommy didn't like her to stir things with her hands, she told me again and again. But this is "different," I countered each time, not being aware enough in my own frustration that for Cathy there could be no "different." You don't get your fingers dirty, period. It doesn't matter that it's now a cup of cocoa instead of a once dirty diaper, or that there are extenuating circumstances for violating a family rule of manners. To make such a distinction would suggest an individual evaluation of experience that Cathy is too uncertain to make right now.

Dr. Arthur Jersild says that toward the end of childhood a child can "disengage himself from the unpremeditated flow of feeling and thought and examine the flow, question his ideas, inquire into his motives and scrutinize the fabric of his life."

But in childhood itself most children can act only in consonance with conditioned responses and sometimes, like Cathy, must keep these responses well oiled by rigid repetition. Studies on children who are far more rigid than any children in this book illustrate the ultimate effects of spending too long a time obeying without understanding. One fascinating if frightening bit of research was aimed at seeing how children can accept variations in a scheme. A group of eleven-year-olds was asked to classify a collection of objects —items that covered a very broad field, toys to kitchenware to tools. The results showed that children who were considered "rigid" could not classify the items in any other way but their obvious functional relationships. In other words, while the nonrigid child could see the connection between the redness of a toy and the redness of a wrench, the rigid children could not. Toys were in one pile, tools in another, pots in another—and there was no other way of sorting they could think of.

Similarly, when given a series of cartoon pictures which showed a child breaking a rule that was written across the top, they could not qualify the rule's moral judgment. For instance, one picture showed an old woman sprawled on the street, the contents of her shopping bag littered around her. The child in the picture is offering her help, although the written rule says "Don't talk to strangers."

As with Cathy, the rigid children absolutely could not relate to the idea of extenuating circumstances. The old woman must stay right where she was despite her obvious distress. Their own need to avoid the distress of wondering whether they were doing the "right" thing forced them into the kind of unequivocal thinking that left no room for independent reasoning.

But the cognitive bind of childhood doesn't stop with rigid postures and inflexible judgments. For the lack of "knowing" that is part of being a child is in fact a double bind. If children are often unhappy over having to behave in ways they don't understand, they're also frequently anxious because their limited intellectual powers distort what they're trying so hard *to* understand. Half-truth upon rumor upon childish folk tale are strung together into a bit of totally "logical" wisdom that can be terrifying in its subjective truth.

"If you dig too far you'll fall into China; if you swallow a pit a tree will grow in your stomach; when you start kindergarten you're already expected to know how to read. Babies come from seeds and storks and plants; and when you die a witch comes to take you away in the middle of the night; and if a light goes out inside a tunnel when you're driving, it means there's a crack in the wall and all the cars will fill with water and everyone will drown." These are just a few of the awesome absolutes of childhood, often shared in spine-chilling "can you top this one" horror with other small truth-seekers, but rarely communicated to the grownups who might separate fact from fantasy fear.

For the same reasons that children smilingly obey rules that they resent, don't understand, or are unhappy with, they keep much of their misinformation to themselves. They are afraid of criticism, of disapproval, of ridicule, and what's more, they're not being taught to believe that anyone is really interested. As Dr. Jersild says, "a policy of encouraging children to evade rather than face their personal concerns is deeply imbedded in our culture . . ." so that "a wide gulf often exists between a child's most pressing preoccupations" and what he thinks those around him really want to know.

This communication blockage has some really unfortunate implications, not the least of which is that a child frequently hauls around the bulky burden of false and often nightmarish conclusions. Recently Robert served as grisly, but graphic, illustration of what I mean. He had been an observer of the rapid deterioration from cancer of their next-door neighbor and closest family friend. After an almost total wasting away, the man died, just before his thirty-fifth birthday. During the same period, perhaps out of a new consciousness of the calendar, Robert's father put himself on a diet. With the usual tedious self-involvement of the dieter, how much weight he was losing dominated nearly every family conversation.

Robert's father's birthday was in the spring, and as winter melted along with his excess poundage, it became obvious that his son was acting somewhat strangely. Always sensitive, now he was moved to tears by the slightest criticism. Never happy about being separated from his mother, now he had an infinite number of new excuses for not going out to play, and a thousand and one body ailments to justify staying home from school. Added to this was a suddenly voracious appetite. He would gulp down his food at the dinner table and request second helpings while his parents had barely begun eating. And when they stopped eating he would reach over with his fork and grab anything left on their plates.

"Even vegetables, for Christ's sake," his mother says now, remembering (still rather grimly).

Finally it became apparent that there was a message in Robert's behavior. Though he wasn't saying anything with words, he was clearly communicating quite serious distress. Sufficiently upset herself, his mother consulted their pediatrician, who referred them to a child psychologist. It took only two visits to discover that Robert was living with the fear that his father was going to die in April, on his thirty-fifth birthday. With the inescapable "logic" of his own six years, Robert could not escape from what his parents' friend's death, his father's loss of weight and his father's approaching birthday all added up to. The eating binges reflected his anxiety over the terrible emptiness of this dreadful totaling. Acting out the fear it was so hard to express, he tried to fill up the imminent void of his security by a gulping symbolic expression of his feelings.

As soon as he could admit his feelings, could, with the help of the doctor and his parents, put them into words, escape was newly possible. By being brought out into the open, his concerns could be dealt with.

Yet much of childhood continues to be lived in the dark. As Dr. Jersild and others suggest, we do not educate our children either to reveal or to study themselves. At the same time, as this chapter suggests, for a long, long time, even with encouragement, the results of that study for a child will be extremely limited. As a child, he must spend a good part of his time divorced from real understanding. And to live without understanding means he must always walk the precipice. He never really knows where the next pitfall is, whether the turn up ahead is dangerous. Because he doesn't know, he must depend on others for guidance. And his inability to make the trip alone deepens his sense of inadequacy.

What's more, as he walks, grasping tight the other person's hand, bodily and emotional changes buffet him, make him weave from side to side—sometimes giddily, but sometimes in trembling, throbbing pain.

Childhood, then, is process and, as process, a trip through time and personal space that we can only begin to understand from the places we ourselves have arrived at. . . .

We are watching television one afternoon, and a child star is infuriating the handful of children who share my den. He's so "phony," "unreal," "snotty." "He thinks he's so tough" . . . "acts like he's so big." Nancy turns to me in disgust and says, "How can anyone think he's like a real kid?"

Casually I ask, "What is a real kid?" knowing the discrepancy has something to do with the young actor's air of arrogant confidence. We're not trying very hard for clues to childhood today, and so words only dust the room, without anything really getting settled. But then, after a commercial for a favorite candy, Andy says, amused at the thought, "Being a real kid is like being a candy bar. You keep melting in your hands!"

What feelings they hold in their hands, these real, not mythic or media's children, with all their stains and changing shapes, are the stories we will continue telling now. . . .

3 / Fear

"Every day I'm afraid of dying"

"As soon as I found out that my two guinea pigs, Perry and Juanita, were dead I was terribly scared. That morning I had fed and played with both of them. I just ran up to my room and cried. When I was done I told my parents to please get rid of them. I was very very sad as I cleaned out their cage and threw out the food. Now, in drama, when we're asked to think of something scary, that's what I think of. How the next morning when I went downstairs and when I passed the place where their cage was I got very upset and I got an empty feeling . . ."

A while ago, Greta was hospitalized with some minor but necessary surgery. It was not a hospital that allowed parents to stay overnight, and Greta's mother was assured such emotionally protective procedures weren't actually necessary for the "average" child's well-being. The magic word had been said. Who wants a child who's "different"? So she bowed to the hospital rules and left her six-year-old daughter each night to return home to her other children.

The first signs of trouble appeared one morning several

days after the operation when a nurse stopped Mrs. Walters as she came off the elevator. It seemed, Greta's mother was told (with disapproval clearly piercing professional blandness), that Greta was taking toys from the other children in her four-patient hospital room. During the night she would climb out of bed and raid the night tables of her roommates. In the morning, her own table would be piled high with their books and games and candy boxes. Understandably, Greta's roommates were outraged, and "obviously," the nurse said tersely, the hospital could not tolerate such disruptive behavior.

Mumbling that this was very unlike Greta, and feeling as if she'd been struck by some terribly foreign force, Mrs. Walters hurried to her daughter, who was lying with her face to the wall. Hardly the picture of an aggressive predator, she seemed even tinier than usual. Her body looked shrunken, as though some powerful pain were crushing it. Yet Mrs. Walters knew that Greta was free by now of any real physical discomfort.

Conversation between mother and daughter was sparse, with Greta claiming in halting whispers that she was "too tired" to talk. So Mrs. Walters could only sit tensely by her side, silently wondering what was happening. She could understand that Greta might be depressed over being in the hospital, but why to this extent? And what were the roots of her bizarre behavior? By the time the surgeon came around for his daily visit, Mrs. Walters was quite frantic. She gestured with urgent pantomiming that she wanted to speak with him, but the doctor didn't respond to her invitation. Instead he pulled a chair up close to Greta, from whom no invitation at all had come. As with her mother, she maintained a stony silence, answering the doctor's questions with barely audible brevity. The doctor, however, stayed on, taking the little girl's hand in his and stroking it gently while he talked.

"Greta," he said, "I hear you've been piling up a lot of stuff every night on the table here."

The body under its white hospital blanket stiffened, seemed to withdraw even farther from accusatory sight.

But there was no accusation. Only a sharing of information. A kind of "telling" aimed at releasing Greta from her confused and frightened isolation.

"You know, I had a patient here last week," the doctor said. "She was just about your age. She was very worried that while she stayed in the hospital her brothers and sister would take all her toys and books and records. . . ."

He paused, to let the words be heard fully, and then continued. "I told her that lots of times children in hospitals worry about such things. They're even afraid that when they go home or back to school, people will have forgotten them altogether. I told her that this was just a kind of hospital worry, and that people would never forget who she was. . . . And you know what?" he asked then. "She called me yesterday and said her family gave her a big welcome-home party, and that instead of her toys being gone, she had even more than before, because she got so many presents!"

The doctor let his words penetrate the murky veil of Greta's fear, keeping his hand over hers, so she could grasp it. She turned now, the tears flowing freely and visibly down her face. Sadness still covered her like another blanket, but she was no longer hiding under it, and her eyes already seemed less haunted. For, as had happened with Robert's anxiety about his father's dying, the doctor had put into words what Greta, at six, was not able to articulate even to herself. In these early years of her childhood, there were no clearly printed labels to be pasted on her terrors. Ideas like separation anxiety and fear of displacement and lack of control over life are adult vocabulary. But the emotions they describe can flood a child's being, as they flooded Greta every night.

Since to a certain degree the word creates the thought, helping Greta concretize her thoughts by giving her the language to express them began to evaporate her tension. Till now, all she could do was what Robert had done with his compulsive eating—act out her feelings through her behavior. The displacement she felt from her family was, in the absence of words to express it, translated nonverbally into stealing. She was quite simply doing to other people what she was so terribly afraid was being done to her. While her roommates slept she invaded their lives, taking their favorite possessions when they couldn't protect them. And each stealthy grab at a book or toy paralleled what she unconsciously believed was taking place back home behind her defenseless back.

Blessedly, the alert physician was able to interpret the language of Greta's behavior and respond to its anguished cues. In talking about it, Greta was also given the relief of a significant discovery—her apprehension wasn't unique. Other kids in her position felt the same way too. This is no small source of comfort, for children too often see their fears as a contemptible symptom of weakness, to be hidden, above all, from other people's sight. Dr. Arthur Jersild says that in our culture's preoccupation with courage, "a child may be driven to the point where one of his fears is the fear of showing fear." Therefore, he continues, "when a frightened child feels free to express his fright, and is struck by the fact that others also are afraid, at least a small dent has been made in the vicious chain of fear and blame through which [he] becomes alienated from others and from himself."

In any case, whether it's because they fear the shame or ridicule or punishment which admitting their worries might bring, or because their anxiety is too free-floating to give it a name, children are frequently locked with their anxiety into starkly empty rooms, with only nightmarish specters as company. Innumerable studies document the myth-shattering truth that children have a great many more fears than their parents ever realize. In one study, for example, of six hundred children between the ages of six and twelve, each child was questioned about twenty-four different fears and asked to tell which were the most upsetting. In arriving at the list, the study's author, Dr. Eve Lazar, carefully eliminated concerns that were already known to trouble most children, as well as some that, according to other studies, generally bothered very few.

The table now contained a broad spectrum of heart-thumping possibilities, from realistic worries like being late for school, to semirealistic ones like being an adopted child, to what would seem completely imaginary anxieties like being attacked by lions, tigers and snakes. It was obvious from the results that being afraid, even "unrealistically," is a normal part of a real child's childhood. In evidence, some findings: 80 percent of the children worried about someone in the family getting ill or having an accident. Almost 75 percent were scared of being attacked by lions, tigers or snakes. Nearly 73 percent were worried about their house burning down, while the same percentage were very frightened at the idea of strange people following them. And 70 percent were terribly afraid of being kidnapped. (With the recent escalation of kidnapping as a way of instant wealth or political statement, there's reason to believe this statistic would go considerably higher were the question asked again.)

There's no neatly packaged theory to explain why children are so afraid. A variety of explanations contain fear's quaking rationale, but all support our basic premise. It is, for instance, likely that children get caught in anxiety's web because they can't escape awareness of their dependency, a dependency that relentlessly reminds them of their vulnerability and, what's more, tells them that it will not only take someone older and stronger to protect them from harm, it will take someone wiser to *define* the harm. Which is friend, which is enemy? Which path is clear, which is dangerous? Yes, there must also be some understanding of the expanding world's mysteries before a child can learn not to fear them. . . .

Dougie runs screaming into his parents' bed during a thunderstorm while Greta can, if not terribly happily, remain in her own. The few additional years of living she has had have brought enough flashes of lightning through her room so that she knows they really aren't going to strike her. Safe confrontations with experience expand a child's still limited ability to understand the experience, and thus make it less ominous.

But where uncertainty exists, the fear exists. Simplistically, when I began writing with children in this emotion-packed area, I imagined poems about loud noises and stormy turbulence. Instead their stories and poems ran to the other extreme. The silent menace of the unknown, the subtle terror of a deceptive quiet. A clear relationship, then, between the icy mystery of the hidden danger and the blood-chilling throb of fear.

"Fear is nothing," recites Bruce, beginning a collaborative poem:

No foot shuffling
No talking
Like a very dark night when the shutters swing outside
With a creak you feel more than you can hear. . . .

Picking up on his image, Beth, a serious ten-year-old with large hazel eyes and hair the color of butterscotch, writes:

Fear is like a cold night,
When the darkness begins to creep in
And the cup of hot cocoa in your hands is suddenly
Too cool to warm you. . . .

And Susan continues:

Fear is taking a big step in the snow
    but making no footprints. . . .
Fear is winter when you wake in the night
    and the house is very quiet and you have no covers on. . . .

Later, Robert dictates a poem to an older child who sits at the typewriter. Never having heard the morning's contributions, still this is what he says:

Being afraid is like being in a very quiet room.
There's no noise
at all . . .
Like the no-noise of
a too-soft ball
rolling down a dark and empty hall.

The sense of physical and intellectual inadequacy that comes from being so small in a world that looms so large makes a child hostage to a host of fears—that all in some way relate to his overriding worry of becoming separated from the protective clasp of his parents.

The intensity of Greta's fear of abandonment involved the special reality stress of enforced separation. She had exchanged the warmth of her home for a coldly impersonal, often pain-producing place, where physical weakness and isolation made her particularly defenseless.

But a child's meals need not be prepared in institutional kitchens for him to dine on the indigestible food of separation anxiety. . . .

Jason, four years old, very blond, small for his age, with a vocabulary that would ring true for someone many times his age and size, plays house with a friend. It is a game-playing that, like much make-believe, helps express fear's conflicts.

Jason pretends not to hear the other boy's knock on the door. Finally, however, in a high, ostensibly female voice, he answers, "Go away. You don't live here anymore!"

Eric, his friend, now pretend son, excitedly argues that he does so live here, and he *must* be let in. But Jason is adamant. In sweeping pantomime, he holds the door wide and peers out angrily. Eric's cheeks are flushed, his stance defiant. But he's no match for Jason, who glowers a few minutes longer and then slams the door shut, saying in a voice so loud that it threatens to crack, "Get out of here. I don't recognize you. . . . I can't remember who you are."

Eric's face crumples in terror, matched only by the panic Jason himself knows. As director of this drama, he's led them both into the most revolutionary theater. He has experimented with unimaginable danger, depicted life's most grotesque experience—being deserted by your mother.

Even when the desertion isn't conceived of as deliberate, the out-of-sight, out-of-mind idea keeps children apprehensive. They want to grow up but are afraid to leave the protected circle of home. Afraid that if they step out of the circle the sands of time will cover up their footprints.

So, "If I don't see her, will I ever see her again?" is the persistently haunting question of childhood.

It's a question that sends Dougie screeching down the park path looking for his mother, when he has glanced up from his play and seen she is no longer sitting on the bench where he'd left her. His sobs bring her racing from the water fountain where she's gone for a drink, and her distress is obvious when she hears the source of his hysteria. Sympathy for his fright is touched with concern that he is so "irrationally" afraid.

"How can he get so excited about my being gone for just a minute!" she asks.

But when I ask Robert and a group of his friends to think of the scariest thing that ever happened to them and Robert answers, "One time when I was in the department store with my father and we went down the escalator and I looked up and saw I was standing next to the wrong man"—when I ask my question, and he gives his answer, there is mirrored in his friends' faces full understanding of the descent into hell that brief escalator ride had to have been. And I am able to understand newly that to a child, a minute or two is more than enough time to know the fear of abandonment. Any situation in which a child feels unprotected, in which he can't trust himself to manage the challenge, will be a time so filled with fear that no clock or calendar can accurately measure it.

For one thing, the concept of time, like other concepts, is

in development. Dougie's stomach lunges in immediate panic at a moment's lapse in the continuity of his mother's presence, where Robert might continue playing a bit before becoming really alarmed. But even at Robert's age, understanding of time is limited and unsophisticated. There's little more grasp of its clicking-away complexities than of the difference between morning and afternoon, or day and night. And even these distinctions are made primarily in relation to life's activities. Nine o'clock is when you go to school . . . twelve o'clock is when you have lunch . . . half past six is when Daddy comes home.

But what does "today" really mean and why is tomorrow today when it comes, and how come if I'm smaller my birthday comes before Mommy's . . . ? These are questions whose answers are far beyond a growing child's real grasp (even if a parent could come up with answers she herself was satisfied with). Unfortunately, careless if unwitting adult abuses contribute to this confusion and thus to time-related fears. When we call home from an appointment to tell the sitter we'll be late, and assure the small voice who first answers the phone that we'll see him in "just a few minutes," arrival nearly an hour later fertilizes the field of misunderstanding. Distorted perceptions thicken, making waiting alone in the house "just for a minute, for heaven's sake!" while we run next door for a bottle of milk, seem a sentence of solitary confinement that can stretch to terrifyingly endless lengths.

All through childhood, the absence of security-giving voices through the open doors of other rooms allows fear to move in and take possession of the premises. . . .

"I hate it when Mommy drives the sitter home, and stops off at the store," Beth says. Even the memory seems to distress her. "I always hear these terrible noises, like someone's breaking in."

With her mother in the next room, Beth can tune out the creaking pipes and slapping shutters. But when she is alone, and unprotected, they become newly sinister. The fear of strange noises is great in children of all ages. Indeed, to some extent it can become greater as a child grows older. For the baby in his crib has no concept of burglars. If a noise upsets him, it's only because the sudden sound is startling. It's a different story for Beth, who reads and hears stories about rape and murders and robberies, and so knows that despite its emotional security, her house is not physically immune to invasion.

Understanding this, I am prepared for the story she herself writes, again using pretense to face a real fear. It's a fantasy about a girl whose mother "sometimes put a big block of ice in her stomach so no one could ever touch her without freezing to death." This way, Beth wrote, "when the girl had to be by herself, she was cold, but she wasn't scared. Because she knew robbers couldn't hurt her."

After a few adventures from which the heroine emerged icily intact, the story ended in an obviously anxious author's version of the happy ending. "When the girl's mother came home, she gave her daughter a special drink that made the ice all melt, so the girl could be warm and comfortable again."

When the girl's mother came home . . . Once more the ballad of dependency. A ballad whose recurring refrain should remind us that an aspect of vulnerability is to make the people who protect you heroic in size and importance. And this means that it will never be easy to replace the sustenance of their presence.

Considering the fact that just about half of all mothers today work, and one out of three leaves behind a child under six, we're facing a very realistic dilemma. Society's stubborn clinging to the mythic image of home-centered mother, with nothing more on her mind than what to cook for dinner for her mythically happy children, leaves those children without any well-conceived structure of surrogate care. Too often instead they're subject to hit-and-miss arrangements, under the hands of uninterested, inadequately trained, unresponsive people, people whose presence often fans rather than quiets anxiety. . . .

"I don't like the lady who stays with us when Mommy and Daddy go on vacation," Andy says tensely.

Why doesn't he like her?

"Because," he answers after thinking hard for a minute, "because she smiles too much."

Before we smile in return, amused at the childish illogic, step over to Andy's side of the experience. And remember that the hidden danger is particularly terrible to the child trying so very hard to understand life. Andy can't see behind the obvious pretensions of the lady living with him for two weeks. So for Andy, this gushing lady's false face of friendship is very, very frightening, because it is so clearly false, hiding who knows what awful visage underneath?

At ten, Andy can't, as I can, see the benign quality of the woman's posing. He can't, as I can, distinguish between malevolence and remoteness. He only knows that hidden messages are peeking around her smile's upturned corners, so that he does not feel at all the way a smile is supposed to make him feel. And the impreciseness of it all contributes to his fear, for it reminds him yet again that he can't read the book of his experience by himself.

I ask George, then, about his live-in baby-sitter. Tension tightens the marvelously expressive face when he says he doesn't like her. As with Andy, I seek some hard data, more clues to a child's subjective view of human interaction. But again, as with Andy, the grievances are vague. His rejection and distaste are based on this only: "I don't like the way she talks," followed in quick anger by: "and I don't like the way she looks." It is a sweeping summary that goes no further, and I have heard it before and will hear it again from other four- and five-year-olds, who, like George, are too young to reach even Andy's level of specific criticism. There is no real cognitive grasp yet of false smiles and effusive insincerity. But George has clearly sensed the contradictions in the young woman's behavior, and I know he shares with Andy an anxiety-inducing perception. These people in their lives are too uncertain to bring security. Does she really like him or only say she does? If she gets angry, will she go away? If something hurts him, will she *really* help him? These are the inevitable puzzles of childhood, as children try to figure out relationships. These are the half-formed, fear-forming questions in the struggle to feel safe, to know friend from enemy. These are struggles that at four, in moments of particular confusion, become an anxious assessment of the troublesome person. "I don't like the way she talks, and I don't like the way she looks."

It's interesting to note that how a child himself "talks" is often a barometer of his fear. Indeed, considering the limitations of childhood speech, it may be a better gauge of his feelings than anything he actually says. For example, the quality of George's voice went through obvious changes when he shut the door on his baby-sitter, casually off somewhere else in the apartment, and took me back into the center of his room. I was to be happy captive audience to an elaborate commentary on his collection of hats worn at birthday parties and an intriguing bottle of "magic rocks" and the wonders of his much beloved Slinky toy. There were vitality and vibrancy to his voice now, with his tone changing to match what he was saying and doing: high-pitched glee when wearing a certain headdress, earnest resonance when giving "scientific" explanation.

But listening to the language of the voice behind the spoken word sometimes brings other sounds. Some that ring shrill and tense, or dull and flat. It is a kind of communication that often indicates the emotions inside the small speaker are simply too much for him to handle. They may swirl so fiercely in his chest that he can only shout harshly. They may feel as if they're choking him, so his throat closes up and his speech becomes muffled and difficult. Or his feelings may be so totally deadened by fear that his voice comes out in dull monotone, droning on sluggishly and tonelessly.

When Jason, for instance, talks about his nursery school teacher, his voice is suddenly thick, as if something is burning his throat. Which, of course, it is. The hot lava of his fear of a new place and a new person constricts his chest and tongue. As he tells me these stories . . .

"My teacher follows me home." He meets my eyes, daring me, it seems, to contradict him. When I don't, the impassive response seems to spur creativity. Grimly he continues:

"She wants to hit me . . . she waits downstairs in the lobby so she can punch me. . . . Sometimes she pushes me off the slide in the park. . . . She's going to open the lion's cage when we go to the zoo with my class."

The line between fantasy and reality is a wavering one for children Jason's age. And a very wavering one for the frightened child. So when the elevator doors slide open in the lobby of Jason's building and he looks to see what shadows lurk in the darkened corners, or when the gaily painted nursery school doors swing closed behind him, locking him into four hours of contact with a person he distrusts, his sense of menace is shudderingly real.

The line we speak of is, by the way, not only wavering but circular. For research shows a child who is afraid will read maliciousness and even deliberate cruelty into the behavior of adults who are really quite harmless. So if this woman's personality has heightened Jason's sense of insecurity, his insecurity will distort how he interprets what she says and does.

Indeed, it is this off-center perception that creates Jason's final fantasy about her maliciousness—that she plans to release a lion from his cage, the better to attack her four-year-old victim. Irrational as the fear may seem, studies like the one mentioned earlier prove that logic is not the material from which objectivizations of fear are formed. Not just Jason but great numbers of children worry about being pursued and eaten up alive by wildly roaring animals. From the clammy clay of anxiety are sculpted the moving statues who chase helpless children down manicured park paths or peaceful suburban streets. And the fact is that just as adults influence time-related fears, we have also made our contributions to these childish attempts to give terror a shape.

For in truth many "fantasy" fears are related to the way grownups have conceptualized danger. Greta, for example, is frequently very "worried" about her parents when they go out for an evening.

"It's really absurd," her mother says with a laugh that isn't totally amused. "I actually find myself keeping a curfew for her. Who'd have thought I'd give up my mother's control over my social life for a five-year-old's? There I am, partying, dancing, having a terrific time, and I suddenly feel I have to go home, because she might wake up and be 'worried' that we're still not there. God knows what she's worried about!"

Greta, not just God, knows quite well what she's worried about, although she's too embarrassed to confess it. Instead she masks her concern behind a generalized discomfort that frustrates baby-sitters and continues to puzzle her socially frustrated parents. But after all, since Greta has learned to walk and talk, she's been warned about the dangers in the street. The cars that can run over you, the people that you mustn't talk to, the corners turned that can make you hopelessly lost. How can she not feel worried when her parents are out there, unguarded, in great unnamed spaces, to return, in childish time confusion . . . when?

Similarly, any child who has visited a zoo, and seen lions and tigers and snakes loping and slithering in cages, is able, even with his limited perceptual powers, to figure out they're in cages because they're a threat to his safety. It's perfectly reasonable then to focus feelings of helplessness onto their overpowering threat; a set of fears that in their dramatic proportions crystallize the many things he doesn't feel ready to cope with.

Involved also in fears of this kind is growing awareness of the body's frailty; an awareness that ghoulishly feeds into confusion about bodily functions as well as the healing process. The lion's symbolically gnashing teeth can rip holes in this stuff called skin, and break apart this hard stuff called bones, and the whole business can hurt terribly, and maybe make you some kind of freak for the rest of your life.

Anxiety about mutilation and disfigurement is acute in childhood, appearing of course most distinctly at times of particular stress. Before surgery Greta had enormous anxiety about the prospect of anesthesia, an emotional response well documented in any study of hospitalized children. Asleep, who knows what that knife-wielding surgeon may cut off or take out by mistake, or perhaps by punitive intent? Even simple tonsillectomies will focus light on this haunting projection of doom. When Robert, for example, went to have his tonsils out, he objected wildly at having to put on a hospital gown.

"Why do I have to take my pants off if I'm just going to have my tonsils out!" he demanded shrilly. And in his clutching grip on his jeans is the story of crippling terror. When he wakes up, maybe some part of him much more important than his tonsils will be permanently gone.

Judy went into a panic when her stitches from a minor head injury had to be removed. She clung to her mother, burying her head in her bosom with each snip of the surgical scissors, so that she had to be literally pulled back by the pediatrician each time. But to see the full range of her anxiety we would have to know how Judy pictures her body—that, like many children her age, she envisions it as a kind of container; inside, a bunch of organs bunched together, like cookies inside a cookie box. The stitches that held her together were like the cookie box sealed. The stitches opened were like the box open, its contents now able to spill out, to be (surge of panic) emptied completely. And how quintessentially horrible the knowledge of what happens to cookie boxes when they *are* completely empty . . .

For now, Judy could only cling in terror to her mother, trying not to see those little white fragments piling up on the floor, which were to her mother clearly cotton threads but to Judy maybe not, maybe instead parts of her—parts of her that she was particularly anxious about in this time when new challenges presented themselves, like learning to read. In the worry over meeting those challenges, why not wonder whether the threads weren't really pieces of her brain, and so why not wail at the final snips, and the final flutter to the ground, *"Mommy!* Can I still learn how to *read?"*

Judy's awful measure of anxiety grows out of another aspect of childhood fear. An oppressive sense of retribution. The feeling that, as Jason once said, "it's very bad to be mad" makes many children apprehensive about feelings that are actually, in their childhood, inevitable. For the short-circuiting of pleasure that we call socialization cannot help but be frustrating and anger-producing.

No, you can't have candy, stay up late, mess your pants, hit your brother, come with me to the party, be fresh to Grandma. . . . The list is never-ending, the response always unhappy, even if bitterness is kept deeply buried. Many authorities therefore believe a child's fears often symbolize the nagging worry that sooner or later (and he'll never know when) he's going to be punished for rebellious and angry thoughts.

Such fears are often particularly intense when there's a family crisis like the death of someone close. Studies of bereaved children prove conclusively that they frequently feel they are responsible for the tragedy. For instance, Bruce's much loved but senile grandfather spent the last few months of his life in Bruce's house. His sometimes abusive ranting and senseless demands were very upsetting, and many times Bruce muttered under his breath that he wished the old man had never come to live with them, and he wished he would go back to his own house, and yes, on a number of occasions he wished he would "hurry up and die."

How awful that memory when, a few weeks later, Grandfather unexpectedly did die. Almost immediately, Bruce became tremendously fearful. He read danger into experiences he had happily mastered many months before. Going on bike rides with friends or playing with neighborhood animals were suddenly fraught with danger. Like a criminal on the run, Bruce lived in breathless terror. Perceptive probing by his parents helped him deal with reality and rid himself of the fantasized guilt which, as we shall see elsewhere, can create so much pain.

To some extent Bruce's dismay relates to the earlier-mentioned research into childhood fears that showed children are, in addition, extremely afraid of dying and death. Even children much older than those involved in the research prove, in other studies, to be a lot less sure of immortality than they may appear to be. Those cool, somewhat contemptuous adolescents, it turns out, worry a great deal about life coming to an abrupt and too early end. Perhaps at the wheel of the family car they may arrogantly demand to be allowed to use.

Almost 40 percent of teen-age girls, for example, according to one study, are extremely anxious when they're driving, while 47 percent of teen-agers in general, despite long-suffering protestations to parents not to be so "up tight—Billy's a terrific driver!" are rigidly nervous passengers when Billy does the driving.

Yet few parents are aware of this crack in the adolescent's self-confident façade, just as few parents in Dr. Lazar's study knew how much the fear of death darkened their younger child's horizon. One of the more interesting aspects of Dr. Lazar's research was her attempt to discover how aware mothers were of what their children were really afraid of. In every category there were great discrepancies, with mothers invariably ascribing far fewer fears to their children than they really had. The widest discrepancy, however, involved the fear of dying. Only 10 percent of the mothers thought their child ever worried about death, while more than 80 percent of the children in wild-eyed yes-saying immediately admitted to the fear. . . .

Like Jason, Robert and a friend play make-believe.

"Bang, bang, you're dead!" Robert shouts, and his friend cooperatively falls to the floor. Robert looks down at him, cheeks flushed, and then suddenly pulls him to his feet. "I don't want you to be dead that long. Get up . . . get up!"

They go into the kitchen to have a snack, but even as cookies and milk cover up the last few minutes' tension, Robert retains the mind-boggling knowledge that something happens to people that makes them stop being people and, unlike this game, it is not reversible.

That night when Robert goes to sleep he has a nightmare, where a "death man" comes to take him away. And the next morning he asks his mother all kinds of questions about how long members of his family live and whether it hurts to die, and do you talk when you die, and where do you go when you die, until his mother nervously succeeds in changing the subject, if not, however, the direction of Robert's thoughts.

There was no conscious desire in Robert's mother to isolate her son with his fear. It was simply that she, like the mothers in the study, turned away from children's death-related terrors out of frustration, because they didn't know how to answer questions about death in terms comprehensible to a child. Furthermore, we live in a time when there's little cultural glorification of death, and most of us are uncertain about religious beliefs that once gave the end of life meaning. So the questions our children ask remind us of our own brooding inquiries and we would rather not be reminded, thank you.

Also contributing to children's fears, as well as to parents' discomfort in handling them, is the fact that the world we're all part of is an increasingly fearful place to be in. Anger and despair bubble underneath the surface of all our encounters.

Beth and her mother witness a mugging. . . . Robert's father is verbally abused by a stranger in a restaurant parking lot who feels his "space" has been taken. . . . Andy sees a young man having a "bad trip" on the subway. . . .

And how do we explain that in addition to our list of holidays commemorating famous people's birthdays, we now remember the days of their assassinations? And what about the murders, and bombings, and kidnappings, and hijackings that bound into our living rooms with electronic intimacy?

There is clearly a sense of danger in the contemporary air. Yet our awareness of violence makes it even more important to tune in to the fears which that violence engenders in our children. It is not really a parent's job to provide evidence why they shouldn't be afraid. What is needed instead is our acceptance of their right to *be* afraid, lest we help to force a child's fears underground, entrapping him in the loneliness of the mythic childhood, where it can become more and more difficult to feel "safe."

4 / Loneliness

"Feeling lonely is how the street looks
just before it gets dark"

Nancy writes this description of her lonely feelings after her family has gone out for a Sunday walk, leaving her at home to nurse a cold. Her grandmother, here on a visit, is resting in the next room, so Nancy isn't afraid of being alone in the house. Yet she is suddenly overcome with anxiety and a deep feeling of sadness as she sits curled up on the window seat in her bedroom. Outside on the street she sees her father playfully pulling at her sister, and her mother laughing and hugging her brother. The glass that separates Nancy from the happy cluster seems to condemn her to isolation, as the sun shining on the intimate scene outside rapidly fades and darkly colors her vision.

Jeremy is twelve. He is awkwardly tall and much too thin, seeming to be all bony legs and arms. His days are marked by clumsy accidents that frustrate him sometimes to the point of (secret) tears. He is leaning against a tree in the school playground while his class team finishes a game of ball. A little while ago he'd heard the coach insist that he be given a chance to play, and heard, too, the team's grudging acquiescence. When Jeremy, nervous, fumbling, made a mess of his pitching, disgusted shouts followed him from the field. Now, off alone, he feels his eyes smart, and he keeps looking down at his hands as if they still held the baseball, as if he were figuring out just the right curve it would take to strike out an opposing player. With such a victory, he might be accepted by the team and, more importantly, by himself.

Tommy still has nightmares over his bunkmate's drowning at camp last summer. It was Tommy who noticed the boy's absence, and who tried to track down the wet bathing suit that would say Steven had indeed returned from swimming and was just off by himself somewhere, the way he tended to be.

Tommy at fourteen is an immensely capable person. He is stocky and of only average height but extremely well coordinated. The supremely methodical member of a family of disorganized artists, he has always enjoyed the structure of camp life and frequently found Steven's inability to deal with it quite maddening. Steven was, among other noncamp things, a "loner," the child who so often seems apart from the places he is physically part of. Whether Steven's isolation was self-imposed or only meek capitulation to other people's rejection Tommy now, terribly now, will never know. For Steven's bathing suit was not found that afternoon. He was still wearing it when his body was dredged up from the lake several hours later.

The emotional state of the campers that night didn't reflect their earlier attitude toward the dead boy. Tears and shrieks and sobs rolled over and through the gaily cluttered cabins, in one of which, despite the late hour, one bed was glaringly well made. Tommy alone remained stoic, seemed untouched by grief. His mother, who came to visit when she heard the news, was troubled by his apparent lack of feeling. It seemed so strange, because the counselor told her that Tommy was the only person who had ever made Steven any real overtures of friendship. However, it soon became apparent to Tommy's perceptive parents that his remoteness was in fact connected with the tragedy, even if they couldn't figure out exactly how. All that summer and on through fall he retained the thoughtful, quick-to-anger manner that spoke of some desolate inner turmoil.

Tommy and I were friends. We visited often and talked about many things. But he never discussed the drowning until one day just before Christmas when he told me about getting a letter from a girl at camp, who was starting a scholarship in Steven's name. Everyone thought it a fine idea, she said, but it was clear Tommy didn't think so at all. His cheeks were flushed with resentment, and he threw the letter on the ground after reading it to me.

"She's such a phony," he spat out bitterly. "She never would even say hello to him. None of them ever knew he was alive. . . ." And then he showed me a poem he had written, which he was enclosing with his parents' generous contribution to the fund—a chilling addendum to a warm human gesture.

> Steven Hines, not known to all
> Became well known when he went
> and died and
> Left all the girls crying
> Popular now in death
> a damn shame in life
> that I was his only friend
> up there
> The one who didn't cry just
> for the heck of it.

While Tommy believes he did try more than his camp-
mates to touch the depths of Steven's loneliness, he is
haunted by guilt that he didn't try enough. That evening,
over a dinner I shared with his family, it all poured out. The
retrospective evidence of how he had so often, too often,
turned away from Steven's outstretched hand. The walks he
didn't take with him, the games he declined to play with him,
the conversations he cut short so quickly. A relentlessly
negative bill of particulars that was climaxed by Tommy's
harsh whisper to his father—the choked suggestion that
maybe there was some terrible connection between Steven's
loneliness in life and the fact that his life was now over.

Tommy's parents quieted his disproportionate feeling of
responsibility for the other boy's death, but the thought that
Steven may have taken his own life is not simply the melo-
dramatic musing of an adolescent. The ugly fact is that suicide is the second major killer of children Tommy's and
Steven's age. Only accidents rate higher, and who is to say
how many of those accidents are not themselves premedi-
tated decisions? Is the drowning really from a stomach
cramp? Is the car crash really the result of inexperienced
driving? Is the overdose of drugs only the arrogant refusal of
youth to consider consequences?

There is hardly a way to know. But what *is* known, brutally and inescapably, is that more young people than ever
before are trying to kill themselves, and equally escalating
numbers are being irrevocably "successful." The wish to end
life before much of it has begun now affects about eighty
thousand young people every year, with data accumulated on
children attempting suicide when they are only ten years old.
About ten thousand children from ten through adolescence
make melancholy intent a final reality, a figure twice what it
was fifteen years ago. Proof once more that contemporary

stress makes it harder to be a child. On examination, it turns out to be the stress of loneliness that is chiefly responsible for these suicides. The difficulty in communicating, the feeling of separateness, the dreadful sense that your presence is neither needed nor noticed make some children want to cease living at all. Fewer than 30 percent of these boys and girls who kill themselves even leave a farewell note behind. No one to talk to in life, why bother trying one more time, in death?

I am in no way suggesting that every child who feels lonely is or will be suicidal. The despair of the young people responsible for these burgeoning statistics doesn't fall within that range of "normal" feelings we are considering. Their pains are greater than those known by the children who live inside these pages. But once again, behavior seen in its extreme can often make clearer the continuum between "normal" and "abnormal." There's a recognizable truth under the exaggerated act, and it is this truth, the truth of loneliness in childhood, that we pause to look at.

Actually, the experience of loneliness is remarkably elusive. There are so many nuances and degrees, so much variation in its expression, that no one, psychiatrist or poet, really believes he can totally define its slithery shape. Nonetheless, young poets in particular will often try. . . .

Beth writes:

> Loneliness is like an asthma attack
> I feel sick
>   and sick
> it's hard to breathe
> my lungs hurt and hurt
> Happiness goes

> in and out
> in and out. . . .

All the children agreed when Beth read this that there is often real physical pain attached to loneliness. Headaches, stomach aches, muscle cramps and certainly chest constriction can be body signs of a child's battle with its multifaceted terror. And it *is* multifaceted, this exquisitely painful feeling, which is why it is so particularly hard to define. And why, also, it so encircles childhood—making some experience of its isolating presence inevitable.

There is, to begin with, the loneliness that grows out of a growing child's need for love. Children are, we know, born with the need for warmth and tender contact. Quite apart from their dependence on others for physical survival, their sense of worthwhileness and emotional security comes from other people giving and showing love. Experiments prove conclusively that the hand that feeds must also hold and stroke if an infant is to escape emotional and maybe even physical crippling. A study was carried out at Johns Hopkins University among children who were extremely undersized. Their problem was thought to be hormonal, until investigation showed they were all deeply lonely—that they were boys and girls who came from families where tenderness was conspicuously absent. The hospital staff was instructed to show expressions of love along with the standard medical care. Cuddling and caressing and intimate conversation became part of the therapeutic scene. The results were rapid and, as the report reads, "remarkable." There was dramatically noticeable growth in these bodies that had apparently been stunted by emotional isolation.

The loneliness of childhood, as it relates to being taken

care of with or without tenderness, is mirrored in the stories of these biologically "atypical" children. But the most physically normal "normal" child will also experience loneliness when he temporarily loses the security he knows through love. Invariably in descriptions of loneliness, children will refer to feeling cut off from intimate contact. . . .

Greta dictates, "Being lonely is eating lunch with your family in a restaurant, and no one talks to you."

An older girl writes wistfully, "When I feel lonely, I remember when I was a baby and looking for my mother through the bars of my crib. All of a sudden, it's like here I am again, in an empty room, still only looking."

And an adolescent's imagery also captures the bleak sense of estrangement so often felt by the lonely child:

> I try to shake hands
> with my father
> across a fence.
> But,
> his side is higher
> than mine.

The intense longing for interpersonal intimacy and love that's part of childhood is heightened by the restricted possibilities of the nuclear family. The lonely feeling of "separateness" feeds into and is fed by fear of separation. Because this is so, another loneliness-related problem takes shape. That utterly desolate idea that we deserve our despair (an idea most adults grapple with for a lifetime) begins in these early days. As a child tries to understand his pain when he loses sight of love's face, he can only blame himself for failing to keep it nearby. Jason, for example, has no capacity yet to appreciate his mother's artistic talent or understand her need to express it. All he knows is that five days a week the door slams shut behind her and for long stretches of time he is, in spirit, alone. It's quickly obvious, when I talk to him, that at the age of four, two and two put together frequently total self-blame. Something about *him* makes her prefer her studio to being home. If he were better, nicer, she would want to keep him company. The mornings in school with his "mean" teacher, the trips to the park, where so many other kids come with their mothers (not like him with a grumpy nursemaid), are his fault. It's his fault he's lonesome. He is essentially unlovable.

If this seems an extravagant reading of Jason's perceptions, I assure you it's not. While such reasoning does not always dominate his thinking, at various vulnerable moments it will do exactly that. Just as it will for other children Jason's age who are in similar situations. As "magical" center of all experience, with little understanding of the many influences on an event, young children often have only themselves to blame when the magic and resulting event are black.

It's out of this kind of thinking, in fact, that another kind of loneliness comes. The terribly alienated feeling that they must keep parts of themselves guiltily hidden from other people and, to some extent, even from themselves.

Andy writes this poem one morning, his face flushed with anger. The capital letters and their implications are his own.

> My brother bothers me. . . .
> My mother gets mad at me when I hit him
> I never hit him
> I never tell on him either
> I never tell anyone what he does to bother me

I MIND NOT TELLING
I love my brother.

Andy has been taught it's "wrong" to be seriously angry with his brother and to express that anger physically or verbally. The conflict over what he feels and what he's "supposed" to feel is obvious in his quick assurance that he loves his brother after that instinctive upper-casing of his resentment. But as Andy denies his spontaneous feelings, his isolation deepens. For he gets further and further away from his instinctual self. And a conviction grows, whispers bleakly in his ear, that if people knew what he was really like, they would not, could not, should not love him.

This shame-tinted, isolating secrecy extends to confessing even loneliness itself. There's something not nice about being lonely, including the kind of loneliness that's profound and profoundly justified. Greta, for example, knew in the hospital the loneliness that speaks life's basic truth: Each person stands, in certain moments, alone. For Greta during those two weeks there were many such moments. The fundamental separateness of existence hovered around her as yet limited comprehension; she went, alone, through the terrifying technology of tests; received, helplessly, the smothering mask of anesthesia and was wheeled down corridors on narrow canvas stretchers without the power to stop the process. All children, even if they never set foot in a hospital, will at certain times (away at camp, entering a classroom full of strange faces) catch a glimpse of this solitary side of the human condition. Unable, afraid, to share this vision, they feel their confusion and loneliness deepen.

Rollo May called loneliness the "yawning void," and over and over again children spontaneously use the concept of emptiness in their descriptions of what it feels like to be lonely, once again proving they are much more aware of the complexities of emotions than adults think they are. It's the rare child who doesn't know very early in life that being lonely is a lot more complicated than being physically alone. Witness a potpourri of definitions not found in any dictionary. . . .

"I'm inside a deep dark pit. . . ." "It's a huge opening that sucks me inside. . . ." "The walls are as high as the sky and there's no way to climb out. I have to inch my way up the walls, but I keep slipping. . . ." "There's an invisible tunnel that only I can see. It stretches forever, ahead of me forever. There's no opening in sight. . . ." "There's an empty curving hole in the ground that I sit in all by myself. . . ."

So bottomlessly terrible is this emptiness sometimes that children aren't beyond sharing its space with the most dreadful kinds of creatures. It's as if the ghosts and witches and monsters that haunt sleep and even the waking world are still preferable to being lonely. As Dr. Jersild says sadly, it may "be better to have a corpse for company than to have no companionship at all."

The need for companionship is great in childhood and how the need is filled is very much a part of the story of loneliness. There is a lovely children's book that speaks to this yearning —*Charlotte's Web,* by E. B. White. In it, a pig named Wilbur searches the barnyard desperately for a friend. After he has been rejected over and over again, Charlotte the spider makes the commitment. But there's a lot about Charlotte that troubles Wilbur, and he finally says to himself, "I've got a new friend, all right. But what a gamble friendship is!"

There is (again quite contradictory to the mythical child surrounded by smiling chums) a sharp consciousness in children about the "gamble" aspect of friendship. And a great many will often skip the game rather than chance losing. They'll settle for superficial contacts based mostly on shared activities, but they hold back from the kind of intimacy that really could counteract loneliness. For while a friend is described with wistful regularity as being someone you can "trust," who will "help you" and "be on your side," the real truth is that few boys and girls I talked to felt such a relationship existed in their own lives.

Trying to grow up is hard and it's a competitive struggle that pits one child against another. Each person wrestles with his own need for popularity and acceptance, making it almost impossible really to be open to anyone else. Jules Henry, the anthropologist, writes about children and friends: "The fact that everyone can be chosen or rejected . . . makes for enormous uncertainty in interpersonal relations; it makes for great sensitivity to looks, stares, smiles, and criticism, and originates the endless inner questioning, 'Am I liked?' "

Dr. Henry's observation proves faultlessly on target as I see the results of a story game that has friendship as its theme. The children are to make up stories or poems about a set of pictures. George, when I show him a picture of two boys his age laughing, says, "They're telling a secret. . . . I feel sad. . . . They like each other." And Robert dictates this poem about a picture of a gray bird:

> This is a lonely bird that
> I have heard
> is the loneliest bird in the world.
> It sits all day in
> a rotten way . . .
> that lonely bird with
> no friends.

And Cathy writes this about two girls who have just won a trophy:

> They feel fine
> They feel like a person
> They feel like someone
> They feel like friends.

If friends make you a person, no friends can make you a lonely, invisible nonperson.

"I had a dream," Nancy writes . . .

> No, more a nightmare
> I was in school, and they all didn't know me
> I felt so alone when no one knew me
> I looked in my mirror and I was ugly
> I looked in my mirror and I saw nothing
> I'm ugly, I'm nothing when I'm alone.

The feeling of validation that comes from acceptance by other children, and the deepened loneliness when it does *not* come are greatest for the older child. As adolescence approaches, the child begins to detach himself from the family. To an increasing extent, he must come to terms with himself as an independent person rather than as his parents' child. While this process is inevitable and necessary, it can also be very lonely. . . .

"There were many nights," Tommy's mother remembers unhappily, "when he'd cry out in his sleep from a nightmare about Steven's drowning. I'd wake him up and would just ache to hold him and rock him in my arms. But of course he'd be furious if I did anything like that. So I'd just give him some water, and leave him alone."

Thus the child who is emerging from childhood must look harder than he's perhaps done till now for what Balzac once called a "companion for his fate." This is a period, after all, of particular turbulence, when new yearnings and doubts engulf the body and the mind. To know someone, and preferably many someones, also struggling with the turmoil can be extremely comforting. Even if the intimacy level is really low, with competitiveness dominating the scene, having "friends" still makes the landscape less threatening. The mere fact that he belongs to a group makes the child less lonely, for he is, if nothing else, part *of* a group.

So there is comfort, however small, in numbers. Several lonely young people, struggling with growing up, can lessen the individual experience of loneliness. But what of the boy or girl who stands outside the crowded circle? They, too, have to make identity experiments, separate from and become independent of their mothers and fathers. What if, when they let go of their parents' hands, there's no companion's hand to grasp instead—how do they withstand the buffeting of developmental storms?

And the question goes beyond just losing the comfort of sharing experience. There's a concept in children's friendships called "mutual mirroring," according to which a child of any age can, in effect, see himself through his friend's eyes. He can identify with his friend's behavior and adjust his own to conform to what he wants his friend to perceive. The child who has no friends—what can he do? How does he learn to be part of the world if he never enters into its social give-and-take? His mirroring is not mutual but solitary. The image he sees is always his own, unchanged by anyone else's perspective.

What a desolate idea . . .

But maybe . . . not.

For there is another side to loneliness. A side that recognizes the power of each unique image and is not afraid of the single reflection. Children left alone by contemporaries and often by adults as well are in many ways particularly free to discover themselves. And so they frequently do, in highly creative, exciting ways. It was no coincidence that many of the most sensitive, curious and intellectually aware children I talked with had always spent and still do spend a great deal of time alone. Nor was it a surprise to check this finding against the early lives of people who have made significant contributions to the world, and discover that they, too, in childhood had to do without acceptance by their crowding-together peers. For example, Albert Einstein, when reflecting on his life, said his work grew out of very personal and instinctive drives.

"For the most part," he said, "I do the thing which my own nature drives me to do. . . . It's shameful to earn so much respect and love for it."

"Of course," he added, "arrows of hate have been shot at me too, but they never hit me, because they somehow belong to another world, with which I have no connection whatsoever. I live," he concluded "in that solitude which is painful in youth, but delicious in the years of maturity."

It can be delicious, too, in its way, even *during* youth, the pleasures of self-discovery outweighing the pains of isolation. When I see Robert walking home from school alone, while the other kids group into twos and threes, my heart aches for him. His face is down, and I can't see its expression, and I wonder what he thinks as he walks past pairs and hears shared laughter. But then he bursts through the door and tells his mother he has to call the planetarium "right away," because he has a question his teacher couldn't answer. I hear his discussion with the scientist on the other end of the phone, and the conversation has a legitimacy that seems almost bizarre when Robert hangs up and wets his talked-dry throat with eager gulps of chocolate milk from a dearly loved Yogi Bear drinking cup.

And George, who as an apartment dweller cannot open a front door to a street full of other children but must wait for mother or sitter to take him to the park, has a curiosity about my tape recorder that dominates our interview. How does it work . . . why does it distort his voice . . . can he try it for himself? And he does try it, and in only moments masters it, and there is a delight in his mastery that promises an appreciation of his own uniqueness.

But obviously, of course, even the most well-adjusted child who is most creatively alone will sometimes wish he were not alone. It's at times like these that he may use his creativity for an ultimate invention: giving life to an imaginary companion. Studies show that bright children are particularly likely to invent a fictitious playmate, using its presence to meet very particular needs. For Robert this need is an acceptance of his scientific interest, which so many flesh-and-blood contemporaries find "weird." But to Bo-Bo, Robert's fantasy friend, a "superfish" goldfish, who wears U.S. Keds and Levi's and rides back and forth on a horse, to him Robert's "lectures" on newly learned information are never tedious. No matter how long they last, Bo-Bo's gills never close with drowsy boredom. Greta, on the other hand, uses her imaginary friend, Ming (an orphaned Chinese princess), as a collaborator. Feeling frequently overwhelmed by her brothers' presence, Greta knows Ming is faithfully committed only to her. When the boys dominate conversation, Ming and Greta whisper to each other, often planning intricate plots of aggression that make Greta feel newly powerful.

Greta's relationship with Ming demonstrates that you don't have to be an only child to be in ways a lonely child. Indeed, much of Greta's lonesome sense of separateness relates directly to the fact that there are several children in her family. For there is in childhood an enormous concern with what's "fair," and in the subjective, tentative logic of these years, that evaluation can get quite distorted. So it is that Greta becomes terribly upset when her brothers get bigger slices of cake or more heaping dishes of ice cream than she does. The loneliness of rejection cuts into that smaller piece of cake she's been served, even though realistically it's all she can comfortably eat. Yes, she hears the argument that the boys are bigger and so have larger appetites, but what she feels is a lonely hunger for as much cake (read as much acceptance) as they get. Dr. Jersild explains that children are frequently more preoccupied with the idea of "proportion" than they are with "amount." Therefore, the proportion of loneliness can be quite great for a child who, with other siblings jostling for position, feels she's not getting her fair share of her parents' love.

On the other hand, loneliness has its own particular shape for the child who doesn't share childhood with brothers or sisters. He may indeed use aloneness well, but there are times when it hangs heavy. The lonely feeling that Jeremy described as like "when you're the only person left and you don't know where to run" can be accentuated when there isn't anyone to run alongside. Many only children I talked to clearly preferred the idea, if only at certain select times, of having another child in the family. Andy summed it up for many children when he said he thought "two kids were just right." Why? "Well," he answered seriously, "because one is lonely, and three's a crowd, but two—that's company."

One of the times that company is needed, most children agree, is at meals. Eating alone is an experience that children clearly dislike and that accentuates feelings of loneliness.

This unhappy truth again shows how problems are caused by clinging to a mythic image. Many women's groups are quite properly agitating for provision to be made by school systems so that the child whose mother works can lunch comfortably at school. All across the country there are local ordinances based on some idea of family that makes this impossible. The assumption that children should eat lunch at home makes no provision for children whose mothers cannot be home at lunchtime. And it leaves a child like Beth, through the disapproving dispensation of the principal, sitting on a cold gymnasium bench eating out of a paper bag, along with a scanty number of other lunchtime pariahs.

Living as she does in a quite traditional community, where large families and home-based mothers prevail, Beth, as the only child of a working mother is set apart (as the city child might not be, her life style being more modern than mythic, and her schools recognizing her needs). But for Beth, the solitary lunching intensifies the loneliness of being "different." For this reason, while she frequently enjoys the special pleasures of being an only child, when she sits on the concrete bench at noontime she would welcome being crowded by a brother or sister.

Unfortunately, if eating alone can accentuate loneliness, eating itself can become loneliness's antidote. In the months after her parents' divorce, Susan began putting on weight at an alarming rate, and traces of gargantuan feasts still jar her mother when she comes home from work. When I talk to Susan one day, she is eating potato chips, and hospitably offers me some. After I take some in my hand, she eats her own directly from the family-size bag. A look of tension comes over her face and she reaches for the chips with increasingly staccato movements. The eating is clearly joyless and clearly compulsive, and I know in terrible certainty that she will not be able to check the jerky bag-to-mouth motions until there is nothing left in the greasy cellophane sack but crumbs. Hunger, at least physical hunger, has long ceased to be a factor in the food she currently consumes.

To my surprise she admits this, initiates a conversation about her eating.

"I don't remember the last time I was really hungry," she says in a mixture of defiance and apology. "I know I should go out and play more, but I'm always so tired. So I just come home and watch TV and eat."

She pauses, and then, licking the salt from her fingers, she says, "Anyway, it's nice, when I'm in school, to think about what I can eat when I come home. It makes me feel better about coming home when no one's there."

How many jams and candies and spongy breads and sickly sweet drinks are sold to feed the gnawing emptiness of children hungry for human contact?

As I write about loneliness and its impoverishments, I, a non-animal lover, am newly responsive to puppies and kittens and all the other furry, single-mindedly devoted creatures who fill the lonely spaces of a child's life. Far better than Susan's sucking salt from her fingers, or gulping sandwiches and sundaes, would be a puppy's tongue ecstatically licking her face. . . .

"My favorite possession," Jimmy writes for an assignment, "is not really a possession. It's my dog, Mr. Mouse-face. My parents named him that because they think he's runty. But to me he's beautiful. He's always waiting for me when I come home. He kisses me and slobbers all over me and it's sticky and yukky but everytime he does it, I feel great."

And Beth saved for a big tin of her dog's favorite "cookie," and wrapped it in Valentine paper when the animal came home from the vet's after surgery. Inside the box was this elaborately illustrated poem:

> Since you've been gone, I've had
> nothing to do
> but look at
>   the rain and think
> about you and sing a lonely song.
> I cried in my prayer and I
> hoped God would hear.
> Now you're back!!!!
> I look in your
>   corner
> and you're there to see.
> Oh! your old love-face—it
> makes
> a brand-new me!

A brand-new me is often perceived by children as being an unlonely me. An apologetic self-consciousness is fostered by adult denial that loneliness can affect one very early in life. Yet even Harry Truman, certainly a more pragmatic than philosophic man, was able to recognize the truth of this experience. He's reported to have always gone out of his way to speak to children because he accepted and understood that "it's a very lonely thing to be a child."

Allowing a child to acknowledge this sometimes painful truth can help him hang on to his inner self, a self he will, because he accepts it, feel freer about revealing to someone else. And in that act of unafraid intimacy will be, of course, loneliness's primary antidote.

5 / Guilt

"I do a lot of bad things"

Freud called guilt "the most important problem in the evolution of culture." At the same time he saw guilt as the means by which a culture survives. With a sense of guilt, people can relate to each other productively. Without it, they would be like the psychopath, who sees all other people only in relation to his own predominant needs—needs that recognize no moral measurement of "right" and "wrong."

We already know that feeling guilty is one of the ways a child becomes a dues-paying member of society. When he does something he's not "supposed" to do, he feels the hot surge of self-blame. Inner critic drowns out inner friend, shrieking accusations, warning of terrible retribution for disobeying a parental "shalt not." Similarly, just anticipating guilt inhibits all kinds of behavior that the instinctual self cries out for. . . .

Greta sits over a dish of ice cream and chocolate sauce that she's eagerly watched me prepare. The moisture in the dish is matched by her salivating—but suddenly there's an enormous problem. She's asked me the time and I've told her it's four-thirty—an hour, it turns out, that's past her mother's permissible snacktime.

Greta's conflict is painful to watch. I have the feeling that suddenly her hand is really not able to pick up the spoon and put it into that creamy luscious mound and bring it, heaping, into her hungrily waiting mouth. In front of my eyes she is becoming leaden, stiff, a robotlike example of the "good" child—good here defined as accepting her mother's value that it's "bad" to eat sweets before dinner.

I feel terrible to have unwittingly created this dilemma. And it's literally a dilemma, for neither solution to Greta's problem will in fact *be* a solution. (Definition of dilemma: "any situation necessitating a choice between unpleasant alternatives"!) If she resists the treat, she'll be more than physically starved. Her repression of self's appetite will cause grave tension; a tension, some would argue, that in itself contains much guilt. For in her righteous stoicism, she will have ignored spontaneous needs, and so, according to this view, will experience the guilt of self-estrangement.

On the other hand, if she surrenders to temptation, her flesh will crawl with apprehension. Guilt has been called "moral anxiety," and I find it a particularly accurate description as I watch Greta anxiously wrestle with the decision to eat or not eat the already melting ice cream. It's a decision I'm helpless to influence. I had, in my own guilt, reached for the dish, brightly assuring her I didn't mind wasting its contents. But her eyes filled with tears of deprivation and I quickly pushed it back in front of her. She stared at it a few moments longer, then grabbed the spoon and began to eat.

She had scaled the mountain, jumped from the highest diving board. The plunge into experience was dramatic. The fear of descent was obvious in the racing movements of her eating. No escaping criminal could hurry so to destroy the evidence and thus evade detection.

At Greta's age, being guilty is primarily involved with

being caught. Her anxiety now, for the most part, centers on whether or not her parents "find out" she has broken their rule. Lawrence Kohlberg, in his studies on moral development, sees this response as part of a process of moral reasoning, a process he divides into three levels: pre-conventional, conventional and post-conventional. Within these levels are six ascending stages in a hierarchy of moral valuing. Each step is a bit more sophisticated than the one before, moving toward a kind of ethical system that bears little resemblance to the simplistic morality of the young child.

To Greta, at the pre-conventional level, "right" is what she can get away with. "Wrong" is getting caught. Consequence is her morality, not principle. Many of the problems children have in early life relate to grownups' difficulty in accepting this piece of pragmatic truth. The six-year-old who cheats on a simple test is coldly condemned by his teacher and suffers scary disapproval from his parents. He, not just what he did, seems to be labeled as "bad." This is a self-perception that causes great pain. And it promises far more unpleasant implications for the future than any to be drawn from his passing off someone else's knowledge as his own. Yet while the child called bad may accept the judgment and carry it with him through the years, actions like cheating at this time of life are in reality no barometer of character or any indicator of future moral development.

Continuing with Kohlberg's widely accepted theory, the next level of moral reasoning is the conventional stage, where, as the name implies, a child assumes the conventions of the family. Now he is prim preacher of their doctrine, not only conforming to the rules himself but "justifying" and "supporting" them to other people. Listen to younger and older children playing and you get a vivid picture of this parrotlike process at work. Senior members of the group dress up in grown-up values in a fancifully imitative game of moral "house."

Jason is playing with a bunch of children in a neighbor's apartment. Uneasy about the relatively unfamiliar territory, but unable to withstand his body need a minute longer, he asks where the bathroom is. Inside, he starts to take down his pants, when he hears the ominous thud of the door closing behind him. Immediately his face reddens with fear and he clumsily hobbles to the door and opens it. Lisa, his friend's ten-year-old sister, primly tells Jason, "We don't leave the door open when we go to the bathroom."

"Yes we do!" Jason yells. He pushes the girl's hand away before it can repeat its assault against his security. His pants are open and falling around his knees. The other children have come near to see the source of the noise. Their giggles reinforce Jason's physical and emotional distress. His penis is now pulsating, his pants slipping from his awkward clutch. He is mortified by his nakedness, and the naked evidence of his fear; and miserably confused by the squirming feeling of guilt brought on by his attempt to satisfy a need for human contact.

Social training has conditioned the older children to recoil at someone's leaving the door open when he uses the toilet. A set of negative emotional responses has created a modifying effect on their behavior. *They* would *never* do anything like *that!* And despite his fear, their disapproval affects Jason, who quickly cleans himself and flushes the toilet, and runs down the hall to his own apartment, something he was not supposed to do. He'd been instructed to wait for his sitter to claim him, but the empty hall and the sitter's scolding were preferable to the other children's guilt-producing disdain. While Jason's mother has already begun to teach the unwelcome lesson of closed doors for private acts, the children's jeering disapproval rapidly reinforces this commandment. You can be sure that Jason will have considerable conflict over leaving bathroom doors open in the future. What's more, if he should inadvertently enter a bathroom that someone else is using, his face will burn with Peeping Tom guilt.

He has learned aversion's lessons well.

Children may move through the stages of moral development at different rates of speed, and at certain times of their lives may be half in one and half in the other. Kohlberg also believes, and observations seem to support him, that people can stop completely at some point in the process. Much work in delinquency, for example, tries to expand and continue the development of moral reasoning so that the "criminal" can really understand why what he's done is called a crime.

Such understanding is best gained in what's referred to as the post-conventional stage. Generally this doesn't occur until young adulthood, although certain of its beginnings can be seen in adolescence. In post-conventional moral reasoning, autonomous valuing takes over. Reason examines shalts and shalt nots, and analyzes absolutes. A distinction now is made between stubbornly upholding cultural mores and developing a set of moral principles, principles that are relativistic rather than based on rigid obedience to any set of rules.

This stage of thinking makes guilt much more complex. We're guilty because of acts against our principles and our fellow man, not simply because of a particular misdeed. So Tommy could feel a lingering sense of guilt over not touching his friend Steven's loneliness while the boy was alive, even though he was in no way involved in his eventual death.

If in this way we can trace the development of morality to see where it takes us, we can also turn backward to see how the guilt attached to this development begins in early childhood. How it flowers in those first days when a child realizes he's a separate person from his parents. In countless ways he starts to understand that his needs often run counter to his parents' wishes. And in that realization is the first planting of the fertile seeds of guilt. For he is bound to do (and to want to do) things his parents won't approve of.

In the process of dealing with this beginning dilemma, he develops what we have come to call a conscience. In psychoanalytic terms it's the superego. To Walt Disney's Pinocchio it was Jiminy Cricket. To a child it's personified in a variety of ways. . . .

"A conscience is something that remembers everything you don't want it to," says Greta in immediate and resigned answer to my question.

"A conscience is an eye in the back of my head under all my hair that sees inside and out," Cathy adds.

Robert thinks for a while, then jumps up and runs to the mirror. He twists his face into a host of shapes, then holds one that's all downward curves and furrowed brows.

"This is what a conscience is," he says excitedly. "A big worried face! It worries about everything I do. It worries about what I say. It's a face that never smiles."

"My conscience," dictates Andy, "sits in a dark room thinking about all my troubles. He's always very, very tired." Andy's voice reflects the same fatigue. His energy seems sapped by the relentless "thinking" of this darkly brooding thing inside him.

The conscience, then, sits in judgment, just as the parent does. Indeed, its authority is often much more heavy-handed than a parent's would really be. Without the intellectual capacity to distinguish between her "sins," a child can torment herself over even the tiniest transgression. . . .

"I broke the plate!" Judy howls the minute her mother enters the door. Her face is taut with worry. All afternoon she'd tried to figure out how to hide the incriminating pieces of glass that shone inside the kitchen wastebasket, so glaringly corroborating her guilt.

Earlier, in bed for a nap that of course wouldn't come, Judy had an idea. She'd dressed and run into the kitchen and climbed on top of the wastebasket, her bottom dipping inside it, her legs awkwardly hanging over the side. It was very uncomfortable, but no matter. When she sat this way you couldn't see the fragments.

For over an hour she sat there, with no TV set to look at, with no one to talk to. Just sitting there. Ready to go on sitting there for how long?

After a while, however, the sitter woke from her own nap, and when she came into the kitchen she burst into laughter at the sight of Judy on top of and half inside the wastebasket. Judy's fair skin went quickly red, her eyes turned to the wall. Shame, the frequent companion of guilt, was along for the ride.

Even when the sitter tried to make things better, pretended not to find her behavior as "silly" as she'd already called it, even when she said Judy's mother wouldn't be upset over a "cheap dessert plate," guilt in all its pain remained. As we have said, a child doesn't distinguish between ideas like expensive and cheap. (Judy still believes five pennies is a much better present than just one quarter.) So what matters to her is not that the plate was made of glass instead of crystal. What matters only is that she, Judy, broke it. That she, Judy, is "bad." And only Judy's mother's repeated assurance that she isn't angry, that she still loves her, that she knows she's really "sorry" can quiet the nagging, frightening voice of self-blame.

At Judy's age, she finds it perfectly conceivable that her misdeeds might result in horrible consequences. She can, this child who has never been spanked, anticipate torturous punishment or that her parents will totally reject her, maybe even throw her out of their lives completely. This bizarrely exaggerated vision of retribution rests with what we know is children's sense of inadequacy, the unhappy feeling that they don't handle things well on their own. . . .

Andy tells this story one morning:

"A boy gave me two chameleons to keep for him when he went to camp, and one died right away, and I didn't want to tell him. And then we went to see my Grandma, and I forgot to leave food, and the other one starved. I felt really bad because the boy was angry at me, but I felt worse for the chameleons because they didn't have a chance."

Beth stands up stiffly and requests a turn as soon as Andy finishes speaking. He starts when she jumps to her feet, as if he expects her to hit him. But she's on a guilt trip of her own. In brittle voice, she tells how she washed her best sweater, her newest sweater, and shrunk it beyond any possible use.

Andy looks up, to share a hurtful moment:

"Did your mother spank you?"

Beth tells him grimly that her mother never spanks her, but that she'd told Beth "lots and lots and lots of times it was a *stupid* thing to do." Her voice comes down hard on the word "stupid." It resounds in the room like a slap, and I realize again that there are ways and ways to inflict guilt bruises on a child inadvertently. And if I needed proof, Beth

gives it to me later, when she writes, and reads aloud, this
poem:

> It's TERRIBLE!
> It's terrible.
> I can't read
> I can't write
> It's terrible
> I never learned
> I'm not bright.
> Can't you see—it's like
> I'm blind
> I can't do anything right
> I'm poor
> No one needs my poor dumb blindness
> Oh, it's terrible!

What's terrible really is that the most perfectly obedient,
well-behaved children with parents who truly delight in them
still can't entirely escape guilt's grasp. For there are certain
guilt feelings that stem simply from desires, whether or not
they turn into deeds. We need only focus on a child's battle
with his sexual feelings to see this process. By the time he
reaches Jason's age, for example, he's already very aware
that certain parts of his body are, in relation to others, a lot
more interesting. But even with such permissive parents as
Jason happens to have, no child will escape being affected by
our cultural taboos against sexual curiosity. That terrific
feeling that comes when Robert strokes his penis, or when
Judy fingers her vagina, stops when the baby-sitter gives a
funny look or the teacher sharply instructs one to sit up
straight. In its place they are suddenly self-conscious, uneasy

in the sense that somehow, no matter how good it feels, they're doing something "wrong." Faced with the perception that such feelings aren't nice, the pleasure the feelings bring is diluted by guilt. Similarly, Tommy's fantasy over what a female classmate looks like without her clothes on makes him gulp as guiltily as when she turns to him as if he'd been caught in the act of disrobing her. And even when sex isn't part of the conflict, the wish to break a rule makes the wisher a frightened sinner. So it is that the desire to cheat on an important test makes Nancy, now old enough to understand the stigma of cheating, flush with guilt when the teacher calls her name, even though her eyes have never left her own desk.

Since it *is* so inevitable for children to feel guilty, it behooves us to examine the many ways guilt may manifest itself in a child's life. For it does, chameleonlike, take on many, sometimes ingeniously disguised, forms. Nightmares, for example, along with a nightmarish number of daytime fears, are often the creations of a punishing conscience. But guilt can harass the body as well as the mind, and so it is often the churning of guilt that produces the painful stomach ache. It is, understandably, hard to digest even the most coveted food when a guilty conscience sits through the meal. And it's equally hard to breathe easily when worry about being "caught" constricts your throat. So the rasping attack of asthma, more often than realized, may have been triggered by guilt.

Oppressive feelings of guilt can even affect a child's posture, his stooping shoulders graphically illustrating a self-punishing weight too hard to bear. In the same way, sudden speech problems may result from losing the battle with guilt. Psychiatrist Sanford Rado explains that, without understanding why, the stammerer "gets scared." There is the nervous feeling that self-expression may bring discovery for secret sins, that what this disobedient, unworthy person says may be (deservedly) held against him. So, says Dr. Rado, "Guilty fear promptly stops his speech, as if to say 'watch your step.' "

However it manifests itself, secret feelings of resentment toward no-saying parents are at the heart of much early guilt. (And as we have already seen, every parent at some point must be a no-sayer.) The range of what's permitted may be greater in some families than in others, but it's a space that has some eventual limits. At some point the gate slams shut, and then anger blossoms. The hostility a child feels mixes badly with his love for and need of his parents. What seem totally imcompatible feelings head toward each other and crash in the harsh dissonance of guilt.

As I've indicated, children are frequently harsh judges of their own crimes. Beth's poem certainly showed that her self-contempt was greater than her mother's annoyance could ever be. I was therefore very conscious when she read her poem aloud that there was at least some element of wanting to punish herself in this declaration of her "stupidity" to her classmates. The self-punitive aspects of guilt are, sadly, nearly always present, affecting, as a result, nearly every aspect of the developing life.

Problems with school, for instance, can frequently be traced to a need to do penance for some infraction or rebellious feeling. When Susan's parents were divorcing, her schoolwork suffered markedly. Her mother assumed her powers of concentration were affected by the tensions at home. She was only partially right, for there was a more subtle slope to this academic decline. In counseling, it was quickly evident that Susan was tormented by the extent of her anger about her parents breaking up. She was also caught in that terrible paradox of childhood perception—helpless to stop disaster, responsible for disaster. So she was guilty, miserably, impotently guilty, thanks to the feeling that it was somehow her fault the family was crumbling. The solution? Punish herself. The sentence? Fail in school. Helping Susan understand that her hostility wasn't unique and that she had a right to feel it and, too, that she had no part in her parents' interpersonal problems broke the cycle of failure. But failure of some kind, in relationships, in school, is a recognized, if demonically destructive way of trying to soothe the wrath of one's conscience through self-punishment.

Guilt can also put brakes on normal feelings of competition and aggressiveness. When I watch Jeremy play ball with seventh-grade classmates, I find myself wondering whether he is not, in effect, "throwing the game." I feel some unconscious bagman has bought him off and that he's making no real effort to win. I am told when I discuss this with psychiatrists that a great many children do indeed slow down inside competition's circle when, out of self-punishment, they can't allow themselves the joy of victory. Reprehensible sinners, they must silently refuse such undeserved rewards as winning games or the approval of their peers.

But at least Jeremy does play, however slowed his pace. Robert at this point in his life won't engage in any competitive sport. The burden of guilt would be too great for him if the team he was part of should lose. Children never have trouble finding evidence in the case against themselves. Robert, at a bumpy stage of development, intuitively stays away from situations that might provide him with additional justification for self-blame. This pulling back from experience out of a fear of being responsible for failure is a bit of footwork most children will engage in at various points in their lives. They generally need help in understanding that they don't have to live up to particular expectations in order to be worthwhile. But in as competitive a society as ours, this isn't an easy perception. Hence the nagging feeling that they've "disappointed" their parents by not getting the lead in the play, or made their friends angry because their poor playing "ruined" the game. Better then, perhaps, not to try out at all for a part or a place on the team.

It should come as no surprise by now that there's an interestingly new wrinkle on the face of contemporary guilt. A great many parents are amazed at the idea that their child should be troubled by guilt. As they react to the idea that their children are fearful, parents recoil from the thought that their child feels guilty.

"Why, I bend over backward *not* to make him feel that way," Bruce's father says unhappily, echoing in his frustration the voices of many other men and women, people who didn't want to "lay that goddamn guilt trip I hated so much on my own kid!" The more I talked to parents, the more I realized that in this time of sophisticatedly antiseptic environments, of polio vaccines and fluoride treatments, we earnestly, if naïvely, try to inoculate a child's spirit against the contaminating germ of guilt. Not to govern through guilt is such an important parental goal, it's a very harsh irony to discover that in spite of it their children frequently do feel guilty. But an even greater irony is that the goal may itself be unnatural, actually creating more problems than it eliminates.

When I visited Dougie's mother one afternoon, for example, he interrupted our conversation with the relentless regularity of a metronome. Each intrusion was a little louder and a little longer than the one she had just smilingly dealt with. There was an air of desperation to Dougie's interruptions, which only seemed to lift when his mother finally put an end to them. Her gentle but firm command that he play by himself until we were done talking calmed rather than aggravated his querulous mood. As if—could it be?—he was looking for some limits to be set, for that line to be drawn soon between permissible and *verboten* behavior.

Yes, it *can* be. For professional opinion confirms what Dougie's mother instinctively knew; that the other side of freedom is often chaos. When all restrictions lift, leaving unlimited space, impulses and feelings can't be rooted or placed in perspective. So while excessive pronouncements of "right" and "wrong" may make children feel excessively guilty, no standards at all can increase rather than diminish discomfort. What *is* right? What *is* wrong? Not knowing makes every action a possible mistake, and makes the limitless space too wide open to feel safe in.

And when they *do* commit a "wrong," children clearly prefer to be punished clearly. Many parents, in the name of liberal parenting, hold back on what seems too authoritarian a response to transgression. Yet there was absolutely no question that the vast percentage of children I talked to preferred direct methods of punishment to the kind of subliminal disapproval their parents indulged in.

"My mother gets this funny look on her face," Susan says. "She looks like a prune, all scrunched up . . ." and she tightens her own face into rigid wrinkles to demonstrate the dry shape of her mother's rejection.

"My father doesn't talk when he's mad at me," says Bruce. "He just says yes and no and makes believe he doesn't hear me when I ask him something. Sometimes it lasts for days.

I can never tell"—he sighs wearily—"how long it's going to take to be over."

Robert has been listening to this discussion of moodily amorphous discipline, and now he interrupts.

"Boy, when my mother gets mad, she yells her head off!" His voice is amused and almost gay, and yes, I see the envy on the faces of our group.

It's interesting to note that punishment itself, not just openly stated disapproval, is also frequently welcomed as a way of wrapping up guilt so it can be disposed of. Jules Henry writes that it may be startling for people in a "permissive culture" to realize that not to be given the emotional pain of punishment can actually "be felt as a deprivation." Yet, says Dr. Henry, "many children would far prefer punishment, for their guilt unpunished becomes emotionally far more painful."

Of course, the punishment must be appropriate and above all fair. No discussion of childhood guilt can leave out the dominant idea of fairness. If guilt thrives on secret resentment, resentment is enormously stirred by a child's eagle-eyed analysis of how just his parents' impositions are. From a remarkably early age, the difference inherent in "do as I say, not as I do" is a difference perceived, and often deeply angering. In one study of children's concepts of authority and rules, it was found they made a clear distinction between rules and fair rules. Invariably the measurement of "fair" was made by how standard it was across all kinds of lines, that it wasn't more restrictive for children than it was for adults.

Children learn morality. As in the case of speaking and walking, they begin to do what they have observed other people doing. But we don't sneakily walk on all fours after we model an upright position for our children. Nor are speech patterns, except maybe for some discreet censoring, very different in or outside a child's earshot. On the other hand, there are often very different definitions of right and wrong for the big and little participants in life's morality play, a difference children are deeply aware of. So while fear and dependence may make them obey a commandment, they are not thereby convinced that justice is being done. Similarly, not even genuine love for their parents will make children blind to the way justice is sometimes bent to fit an adult's temporary requirements. . . .

A few days after Beth had ruined her sweater she came to our class visibly troubled.

She told us that her mother had taken the controversial garment back to the store she'd bought it from, claiming it had shrunk on the very first hand-washing. In fact, it had withstood several washings, and only when Beth plunged it into very hot water in the washing machine was the damage done.

"My mother says they should have warned her it was delicate," Beth says, her voice carrying a tone almost of pleading, as if she wanted someone to reassure her that what her mother said and, more importantly, what she did was right and did not merit the criticism Beth was guiltily feeling.

It was a reassurance not to come from this group. They'd walked this way too frequently themselves. As happened with us at other times, Beth's stories opened up the floodgate of their experience of preaching versus practicing.

"My mother talks on the phone for hours, but I can only stay on for three minutes. . . ."

"My father walks our dog when my neighbor's away so it can go on their lawn. . . ."

"My mother tells her office she's sick when she goes to a party the night before. . . ."

"My mother promises things she says later she didn't mean," Greta announces loudly. "Like letting me cook dinner sometimes, or use the sewing machine. She says she doesn't remember saying I could, but I *know* she said them!"

Her voice rises on the shrill note of guilty rebellion. The class is properly horrified. Breaking a promise, to a child, is an almost immeasurable sin. And indeed, Greta's mother would agree with their perception. Except that the generational difference in assessment of experience makes Mrs. Walters comfortable about her lapse of memory, for she knows she would never break an "important" promise. But —need I even say it?—who is measuring "important"?

Not Greta, that seems certain; whose resentful conflict is unmistakable. Because of childhood's difficulty in freely expressing feelings, she turns her angry feelings inward to fester, and build up, and become distorted. Unable to direct her hurt and anger appropriately, she begins to feel guilty about being hurt and angry.

Perhaps because guilt seems one of the *most* bottled up of children's feelings, they frequently select it from lists of feelings to write about. Because they do, I am able once more to leave the final statement of another childhood experience to those who experience it firsthand. . . .

"Guilt," writes Nancy,

> is like a terrible mess
> A messy rag
> A mess of dirt
> An overflowing garbage can
> that has only my garbage.

And Cathy draws a picture of a big luminous ball and labels it GUILT, and says, "Guilt has a color. It's clear. It makes me feel still and sleepy and think a lot. It makes my house a house no one lives in even when everyone is there."

Robert, too, draws a picture. Of a boy and his shadow. And in perhaps the ultimate statement of guilt and conscience, he dictates:

> This is my shadow.
> He always sees what I do.
> Sometimes my shadow walks behind me
> Sometimes my shadow walks in front of me
> Sometimes when I'm bad my shadow
> punches me
> —because he hates me.

Fortunately, most of the time Robert can believe his shadow finds him fit to live with. But much of the time, nonetheless, the shadowy forms of guilt will hover over his and every child's continuing struggle with impulse and restraint.

6/Anger

*"Anger turns you into a blackboard
that everybody scratches on"*

Dougie is playing in the park sandbox. A little girl at the other end makes her way toward him. She stares down at Dougie, who does his best to ignore her. (He knows too well what's brought her here.) She's got her eye on his pail and shovel—toys that benevolently, but in far too limited numbers, are supplied by park fathers. The drama unfolds. Girl reaches down and grabs. Dougie jumps up and swings. Competed-for shovel now convenient weapon, the better to express Dougie's hostility toward this intruder. Her screams are piercing as a trickle of blood appears on her forehead. But they seem only to whet the avenger's appetite for violence. He comes at her with the pail, dumping its sand mixed with water over her head. Globs of gritty muck cake her face, sting her eyes as she frantically rubs them, make blood-tinged trails of mud down her cheeks.

The screaming victim's mother is horrified, but the triumphant villain's mother is no less so. For if we are inclined to cover up the reality of a child's emotional life, we pull the covers particularly tight over the feeling of anger. Yes, we might, however reluctantly, abandon the myth of childhood's contentment in order to soothe a boy or girl who's afraid, or reach out to one who is lonely. But there's something so . . . unattractive about the child who's angry, who, like Dougie, blatantly shows his animosity toward another person, or, like Nancy, will whirl ferociously in the blazing center of a temper tantrum. Nancy's furious kicks at the family garden when she's frustrated over some restraint frighten her mother because they seem such an extreme statement of rage. We are a culture that is afraid of the darker side of man's nature. We prefer not to recognize its presence, in others and in ourselves. And certainly we don't want to see it or hear its strident sounds in our children. The fear of what an angry child implies about us as parents, or suggests about how he really, not mythically, sees his world, makes us wash his mouth of the bubbling expressions of bitterness before they're articulated in any direct or indirect way. Dr. Arthur Jersild comments wryly that, indeed, we seem to raise our children in an atmosphere that makes anger immoral, as if, he says, "the eleventh and greatest commandment were, 'Thou shalt not show anger' . . . nor even feel it!"

Yet if we often seem to make little sense in our approach to children, our rejection of the anger they feel is particularly lacking in logic. For the fact is that unpleasant as its scowling face may be, anger is a necessary human characteristic. It is one of the most important ways children can define themselves as people. In anger a child begins to answer life's basic question, "Who am I?" by relating the query to self-assertion. The demands he makes, the rights he defends, his resistance to people who frustrate or hurt him are shaped by the sharp edge of anger. Like a child who is afraid, an angry child is finding a way to cope with an oppressive situation. Dougie, as well as his sandbox adversary, could, after all, have dealt with confrontation by fearfully running to their mothers instead of belligerently heading toward each other. By this measure, then, their defiantly polarized positions were positions of strength which expanded instead of restricted their developing experience.

Dougie and his companion will of course gradually learn to be more civilized in handling their discontents, but their capacity for anger will be an important factor in the people they become. Indeed, one of their greatest "becoming" challenges, as it is with all children, will be how to handle their anger in ways that are strengthening rather than destructive. Learning what aggressive behavior is appropriate and what is not, learning how to mute impulsive rushes of rage, learning what evidences of anger will be tolerated by the grownups in charge and which will be punished are all issues that take up a great deal of a child's time as he tries to figure out what his life is about.

Like many other experiences of childhood, anger to a large degree begins at the very beginning, with a physical response from the infant in his crib. The hungry baby screams to be fed. His clenched fists, his perspiring face and his piercing yell can easily be called anger. But his feelings are unfocused. No enemy has been sighted yet. By the time this baby reaches George's age of four, it will be a tensely different story. A particular person will cause frustration, and so the wish to strike out now takes on a direction.

For example, when I went to see George one afternoon he quickly designed a pattern for our visit. We would simulate host and guest, companionably watch the afternoon fade while we sipped tea together. His baby-sitter had offered to bring me tea, and George told her he would like a cup too. (At four, the kitchen stove is off limits, so he can't on his own implement his design.) While we wait, he takes little bites from the huge gingerbread cookie I've brought as evidence of friendship. To my own need-to-be-accepted pleasure, he breaks off a piece of the cookie and gives it to me, suggests I "save" it to eat with the tea, just as he's going to save the rest of his. Anticipatory delight has given him the ability to delay gratification, but still he impatiently checks the door of his room to see if the young woman is coming. Finally she does appear in the hallway, and George happily stands back to let her enter with the tray that carries only one cup, meant, unmistakably, for me.

There is a rush of expression across George's face as she lightly brushes over "forgetting" his request. Frustration and resentment vie for dominance as they head in her direction. The feelings combine and, in their joining, define the inevitability of anger in a still helpless child's life.

Dependency makes children unhappily accept not only such restraints to pleasure, but also other people's perceptions of their behavior. The labels grownups attach to children infuriate them, since they feel so incapable of tossing them off. Anger smolders silently as boys and girls are given a sweeping summation of their flaws.

"She thinks she's the big boss of words!" George says when the sitter leaves the room after telling him not to be "a baby." While Andy, on another day fresh from being publicly labeled "a slob" by his teacher, grumbles bitterly, "My teacher's a pencil and she writes all over me."

A related and widely held theory about anger in children sees the emotion as growing out of hurt feelings. The loss of face and status darkens childhood with impotent rage and frequently results in grotesque fantasies of "getting even."

Jason and Eric talk about an older child who's been making fun of them on the nursery school bus.

JASON: "I'm going to cut off all his hair and glue it on his nose so he can't breathe."

ERIC: "I'm going to make him drink four bottles of milk without stopping so he throws up all over the floor."

JASON: "Then let's tie him up on the roof of the bus with no clothes on . . . and then . . ."

Now Jason whoops with delight as he gets back not only at the bully but at the restrictive limits of acceptable language. ". . . and then all the birds will make poo-poo on him, and we'll cover him around and around with toilet paper, and he'll be all sticky and dirty smelly!"

Minutes later Jason and Eric are singing a TV commercial jingle. Their rage has passed like a sudden storm. In these preschool years particularly, passion runs fast and high. Had Jason and Eric been strong enough during their flash of anger, they would gladly have killed the taunting classmate, without wasting one thought on the act's morality. On the other hand, the boy himself could soon become a welcome friend should he decide for some reason to be more congenial. Hatred and friendship are equally unstable in childhood, slipping into ever changing shapes while the calendar flips its pages. But clearly, as time moves along its continuum, anger toward someone or at some interference will make young minds and bodies smolder in raging discomfort. This truth of childhood is immediately obvious in the infinite number of references children make to anger's physical aspects. . . .

"When I'm angry," Cathy writes, "I feel like a rotten apple with worms crawling all around me, eating pieces of my insides." And Tommy expresses the rather bleak thinking of adolescence when he creates this terse image: "My body is brittle when I get angry. Like a brick that's used to hole up a fireplace. When you pick the brick up it burns your fingers and then it breaks into pieces."

On the other hand, Robert, at six, is sweepingly dramatic in his descriptions. He colors a piece of drawing paper with huge Magic Marker letters that say "BLIP-BLOP-BOOM!!!!!!" Then, writing skills exhausted, he explains, "Being angry is like being punched in the stomach with a monster's fist." And Lisa, obviously influenced by the day's muggy weather, says, "Feeling angry is like having to drink a big cup of pollution."

As suggested, anger can tear at the mind as well as the body in its jagged ripping of contentment, an experience often perceived as completely enervating. . . .

"To me," Beth writes, "anger is feeling like you're nothing at all. It's when you don't care about anything or anyone."

Jeremy shares this alienating vision, writing:

> Anger makes nighttime come,
> > even though it's day,
> You feel trapped,
> > even though you're
> > > free.
> You're absent,
> > even though you're
> > > there.

One of the reasons anger marks children "absent" is that they rarely feel free to reveal its blistering presence. Although the most important antidote to the toxicity of anger is action, a direct and immediate and appropriately directed expression of the feeling before it festers, children are not generally permitted such release.

In the powerlessness of childhood, they cannot alter the

experiences that fan their anger. Instead, in their helplessness, anger will only grow.

Hear then this tale of impotent rage. . . .

> Last month on vacation we went to see a movie in New York. The movie started at 12:30 and we all woke up about 10:00. My brother and me begged our parents to go early so we'd be sure to get in and get good seats. We were all ready to go at 10:30 but my folks kept telling us to do things . . . that we couldn't go until we did them. I got a real bad stomach ache from being so angry at them . . . (we didn't miss it, but it wasn't a good day anyway because I was so nervous and mad before we got there).

Largely because they don't always feel free to reveal anger to adults, children often exhibit a startling Jekyl-and-Hyde demeanor in their daily life. It quickly becomes clear when you spend any length of time observing children that they are often very different people from those they usually let grown-ups see.

Teachers have been known to reel in horror at seeing films of "prize" students theoretically left to their own devices. The quiet, placidly studious pupil who never speaks without raising her hand is suddenly raucously silly and abusively rude to her classmates. Countless schoolrooms, islands of cooperative order when authority is there, become frenzied competitive jungles when the teacher isn't sitting in judgment. Each child stands poised to ostracize, exclude, separate into ins and outs, lightning quick to locate the sore spot in another personality and relentlessly press on it in "better you than me" glee.

One reason schools provide particularly fertile ground for

both feeding and trying to hide hostility is that, for the most part, they make a child ashamed and frightened of his anger. The judgment appears to be handed down that it's not only bad to act angry but, as Dr. Jersild suggests, it's almost as bad to feel angry. Numerous studies show that children fuse and confuse wrathful feeling with aggressive action and see "having a temper" as a very serious defect, to be hidden and disguised as much as possible. Like a pimply face or obese body, it is something to be ashamed of.

Similarly, many children make apologetic analogies between possessing a temper and what it must be like to be "possessed" by evil spirits. Susan, for instance, describes her temper like this:

> It wants this . . . it wants that. . . .
> There is nothing
> that it doesn't want. . . .
> When I try to go away
>   it always makes me
>   stay
>   and hear
> all those awful things it whispers
>   deep inside my ear.

When a child himself can whisper that he does in fact feel angry, there is not only relief, but often a cessation of unproductive yet uncontrollable expressions of his hostility. Harry Stack Sullivan once said that it's a great deal easier to "swallow anger than to digest it," and the fact is that anger swallowed only stores up inside, until finally, often at a trivial provocation, it erupts. One study had as its goal reducing "inappropriate aggressive behavior" in third-grade classrooms. With a study group of 106 children, attempts were made to have them understand the source and accept the legitimacy of their angry feelings. The hoped-for goal was that by "digesting" their hostility in this way they would be able to modify its expression. And indeed, when they did achieve self-awareness in regard to their anger, they were able to apply behavioral brakes to disruptive expressions of it.

This study notwithstanding, schools continue to cultivate a child's indignation by reducing his sense of individuality, as well as his sense of personal freedom. The school as "jail," the feeling of being "locked up" or like "an animal in a cage," appears again and again in children's descriptions of the place they are obliged to go to every weekday (days whose emotional tone Andy described as "giving the Monday morning blahs all the way till Friday").

Andy smiled when he made that comment, but he did not smile when he recited this poem, written after his teacher had "unfairly" included him in a punishment resulting from another student's disruptive behavior:

> I am stuck inside my teacher's desk
> She keeps me inside it
> I keep saying
> LET ME OUT
>   LET ME OUT
>   I keep kicking
>   at the drawer
> One day I'll get it open
> and then
> All she'll have inside it
>   will be

A picture—
that never even looked like me.

Like Andy, many children are often enraged at the loss of emotional and physical integrity that takes place inside school doors. That they must, for example, be given "permission" to go to the water fountain when they're thirsty, or first convince a teacher they're not "faking" before they can seek the nurse's help for a stomach ache, fills the heart to bursting with bitterness. And the ultimate outrage is having to ask permission to go to the bathroom. That someone else has control over their own bodily needs intensifies the futile anger of dependency. Because the level of fury is so great, teachers as permission givers can become the objects of the most passionate hostility unless they have moved into new perceptions of their role and of children's rights. Absolutely nothing spurs a child to faster and fiercer creativity than asking him to fill in sentences that begin, "My teacher . . ."

Jimmy, for instance, begins a go-around one morning by saying, "My teacher is a dangerous weapon because her mouth always punches me. . . ." Robert picks up on this image, seeing, as many children do, the teacher's "mouth" as a major weapon in the school's bruising emotional assaults.

"My teacher," he says, "is a train. Her mouth gives off hot steam that makes you choke if she comes too close. . . ." But it's Cathy who is moved to newly expressive heights by this assignment. She stands stiffly in the middle of our circle. Her voice quivers with feeling as she spontaneously creates this poem:

Teachers are made of sour dough
a broken toe
dirty clothes
and
a broken nose . . .
out of mud and grime (especially *mine*).
Teachers have a spider on top
of their ugly hair mop.
A teacher's job
is to say no, and
go
to the office . . .
and you're BAD—because you forgot your spelling
book.
I'd like to catch one on a fishing
hook,
and slit her down the middle
after I washed off all her hate.
Then I'd stick her on a griddle, preheated to
a thousand and
eight.
I'd bake her till she got crisp, then put her on
a broken plate.
And I'd bring her to the office so
the principal would eat her
and get a stomach
ache.

The children listened with wide-eyed fascination to this troubadour of violence, and when she was done there was a standing ovation. The excitement of her anger was heady stuff. And it opened up a discussion of a child's-eye view of the restraints to pleasure which authority places along the path of growing up. It is a perspective that clearly relates its level of resentment to how fair the restraints seem to be. Cathy's teacher's blind disregard of her rights, her arbitrary impositions on Cathy's life, her lack of sensitivity to her needs make this eight-year-old girl murderously furious. The bitterness that children feel at having so little choice, so few options, of having to be so totally dominated by someone else's orders is tremendously deepened when they perceive no justice in those orders that *are* laid down.

Even family commands often seem tyrannical to children, and bitterness lingers as the image of themselves as submissive serfs is reinforced. It is an image that binds their writing together when their anger is shared in a collaborative poem. It is to be called simply "Orders" and Jimmy begins it by saying:

"*Jimmy!* Don't talk with your mouth full!"

His mouth has barely closed on the line before the next child speaks—then quickly the next, and the next, while the poem turns into this:

> DO . . .
> say hello to my friends . . .
> go to bed . . .
> eat your meat. . . .
> COME HERE . . .
> and take out these garbage cans . . .
> and take your punishment like a man. . . .
> STAY THERE!
>   when I tell you to. . . .
> DIDN'T YOU HEAR ME
>   when I called you?
> CUT YOUR HAIR! You look like a girl. . . .
> You're a girl

WEAR A DRESS!
You look like a SLOB!
You smell like a PIG!
Sweep out this MESS!
You do what I *tell* you to. . . .
Who do you think you're *talking* to?
CLEAN . . .
the basement . . .
your face . . .
your shoes. . . .
WASH . . .
your hair . . .
your feet . . .
your hands. . . .
GET ME! my briefcase. . . .
BRING ME! my sewing. . . .
Clear the table. . . .
Set the table. . . .
Don't you know what side the forks go on? . . .
DO IT AGAIN!
DO IT RIGHT!
STOP!!
GO!!!
NOT YET!!!!
NO!!!!!

I listen and my head bobs to their ever-racing rhythm of resentment and constraint. I stop the carrousel, too exhausted to let it continue. (There's fuel enough to keep it running for hours!)

Actually, the anger children feel about arbitrary rules is intensified by the suspicion that giving or depriving them of pleasure is sometimes based more on adult need or mood than on what's best for them. In their lack of self-esteem, many children I talked with sullenly wondered, for example, whether their parents' bundling them off to camp every summer had more to do with grown-up summer fun than with their own. . . .

"My mother gets so excited," Nancy says acidly. "She goes on a diet and buys new clothes, and I hear her making all these dates with friends because she'll have 'more free time with the kids away. . . .' " Nancy's voice trails off angrily as she mimics her mother's cheery response to the summer separation, which Nancy herself has, at best, very mixed feelings about. Yet in spite of the irate suspicion that her mother really wants to "get rid of her," Nancy's anger is relatively benign. For she knows her mother loves her and for the most part has her best interests at heart. So, as Dr. Irving Markowitz explains, the family's "history of altruism" affects how angry a child becomes when altruism temporarily falters. It is only in those relationships where children consistently meet whimsical and arbitrary thwarting of their rights and self-respect that the dissonant sounds of rage may reach fever pitch.

To the degree that a child does feel uncertain about his life's relationships, he will know another, darker side of anger, that tormenting, esteem-eroding feeling we call jealousy. Childhood's need for parental love, for acceptance by other children, for respect and understanding by teachers and caretakers makes any competition for these responses extremely threatening. Many children, encouraged by nuclear-family exclusivity, clearly seem to feel that the acceptance of someone else automatically means their own rejection. . . .

"I hate it when my baby sister sits on my mommy's lap. I wish I could pinch her nose so she can't breathe and then she'd turn blue and then Mommy would think she was dead and would put her in the cemetery where Grandma is." So ends Eric's unabashed tale of hostility and wish for revenge toward the newborn infant who has infiltrated the family after Eric's four years of total rule.

But it isn't only life-changing new brothers and sisters who nourish rancor. Often it's older children, like Greta's brothers, who in their overpowering presence seem to create such unfair competition for her parents' attention. And many children of divorce are also grimly threatened by a parent's new romantic interest, even if every effort is made to have the child feel that his own place in love's circle remains firm. Sometimes a similar uneasy rivalry extends to other family members, as when a grandparent or favorite relative suddenly welcomes a new relationship into his previously child-centered life. Frequently it's an older brother or sister whose wandering affection makes jealousy bloom. Jimmy, for instance, has always had a particularly warm relationship with his eldest brother, the twelve-year difference in their ages making the older boy more parent surrogate than competitor. One Monday morning Jimmy announced that over the weekend his brother had become engaged. Enthusiasm did not color his voice as he described Sunday's celebration. And later that morning, he wrote this small story, so large in its tale of emotional conflict:

> I felt happy and angry when my brother got engaged, and I also felt very sad. I kind of like the girl he got engaged to, but I feel like I'm losing him as a real good brother. I mean he's a real good person, and now he's good with his girlfriend more than he's good with me. I know that he still likes to be with me whenever he can, but I don't know anymore how much that will be. I really want to tell him I care about him,

but it's kind of hard to tell that to your brother or to anyone. I guess she tells him, and maybe that's why he likes her more than me. I don't know what I'll do when he gets married. I think we won't ever be together anymore. I hope he waits a long time to be married. Maybe she'll get tired of waiting and will go away.

Whether jealousy spins the plot of violent retaliation we heard from Eric or the wishful thinking described by Jimmy ("she'll go away" instead of "I'll make her go away"), the fact is neither child can do anything to shift the scenery or change the cast. And this is true of every aspect of a child's anger. For while an adult can deal with his frustration by ridding himself of its source (quit a job, move away, divorce a mate), a child has no such options. He can only run in place, with anger nipping at his heels. A situation that sometimes, sadly, makes him direct his pent-up feelings against the only "safe" target—himself.

Yes, like the crib-bound baby who bangs his own head in frustration, some older children will pummel their own spirits in anger. Susan's jeering comments about her looks— "Aren't I *gorgeous!*" said with a sneer as she prances around in a too tight bathing suit—are clear evidence of anger turned inward. And even more serious symptoms of being the target of one's own anger may be seen in the child who compulsively gets into trouble or is continuously "accident prone."

On the other hand, the child who does wish to strike out rather than turn his hostility inward must often find very indirect ways to do so. Without the power to give full vent to angry feelings, he learns to be quite Machiavellian, showing resentment through deviously ingenious behavioral statements.

When Judy is angry at her parents, for example, she sucks

her thumb, a regressive behavior they find enormously ir-ritating. Each annoyed glance they send in her direction makes the slurps more ostentatiously juicy as triumph gleams in her eyes.

"I say I don't feel like eating my supper when I'm mad at Mommy," Robert says, "even if I'm really, really hungry!" There's great pride in his voice at having found one small way to compensate for his inadequate strength in what may seem life's power struggle. No question: if it distresses his mother for him to go without dinner, a gnawing stomach is a price he'll gladly pay for the sweet taste of revenge.

Similar settling-the-score schemes can be seen behind all kinds of ostensibly innocent behavior. Particularly when deepened helplessness forces a child's anger even further underground, it may pop up again in a variety of deceptively innocuous disguises. So the child who whispers when the teacher is talking, just loudly enough to distract her, may be as hostile as the child who openly defies her. And the little girl who "forgets" to give the sitter an important message from her mother can be gleefully avenging, even though she's so meekly obedient while the sitter is in charge.

Still, while schools and teachers and friends and baby-sitters are all part of the collaborative story of childhood anger, it's inside his home and with his parents that the story becomes most complex. As the first place a child learns frustration, and where his emotional involvement continues to be greatest, anger will naturally be more potentially intense here. How that potential develops, however, relates to several interpersonal elements in the family atmosphere.

Anger is more evident, for example, in homes where parents are so concerned about standards of "good" and "bad" that a child grows guilty about hostile feelings. Anger is also unwittingly encouraged by parents who don't let the emotion die a natural death. An angry child who's behaved inappropriately is sometimes too long reminded of his "sins." The desire to make *sure* he's repentant causes some parents to maintain their disapproval until he feels demeaned and deeply resentful. An unhappily graphic example of this was given by Nancy, when she wrote:

"When my father gets mad because I've yelled at him, he never yells back. He just nags and nags and nags and nags. It's like he's hitting me in the head with an ax so I can't think because every time I try to think my mind bleeds."

But if persistent recriminations breed bleeding anger, inconsistency in standards does so as well. The "All right! *Have* another cookie" kind of exasperated parenting, where rules of behavior are worn down and thrown out for a temporary respite, promises an angry future even if it quiets negative expressions here and now. The child whose temper tantrum is rewarded will have a temper tantrum soon again. The permissible space alluded to earlier must be defined and maintained if a child's anger is to be successfully contained. Indeed, such consistency proves to be a much more significant factor in controlling anger than the strictness of the punishment if the child loses control.

Most important, however, in helping children deal with their hostility is to understand its inevitability. Dr. Jersild says that "children cannot develop normally without becoming angry." This is an idea that should diminish the grown-up desire to sugar-coat the sometimes bitter taste of this part of a child's emotional life. For anger is indeed a life tool, beginning in infancy and continuing through the years. Though encouraged by helplessness and dependency, it is also, as noted, a statement of self, proof that this growing person cares about himself and about his life, and is willing to think deeply and defend developing values. However a child is taught to convert the feeling of anger into socially acceptable expressions, he must be allowed to acknowledge that the feeling exists. This kind of permission gives him custody over himself and promises that no matter how many times he must apologize for certain angry acts, he will not feel the destructive need to apologize for a very deep and significant part of who he is.

7/ Dreams

MY DREAM

All the walls had eyes
and noses like people
and they came after me
and I ran into the kitchen to
look for Mommy, but she wasn't
there, and the refrigerator had
eyes too and it started chasing me and
I ran into my room and jumped into
my bed and the bed started to run
and it just kept hitting the walls
with me in it and my head was hurting and hurting.

Greta's shouts woke her mother. Quickly Mrs. Walters hurried into her daughter's room to find the child sitting up in bed, a terrible look of fear on her still sleep-covered face. Eyes that shone so brightly during the day were now glazed and unfocused, looking backward into the world of darkness, a world children chart in the often blazing, often terrifying colors of their dreams.

Greta had been dreaming, she sobbed to her mother, of coming home from school on the last day of the term to go on a family vacation. She'd hurried down the few streets, "all excited," but then when she came to her block, everything was very quiet, and the car wasn't in the garage, and nobody was home. Greta's voice rose shrilly as she continued the night's story. ". . . And I went into the kitchen, and there wasn't any note for me on the refrigerator like you leave sometimes, and then"—her voice reached a hoarsely high pitch, threatening to crack entirely under the weight of her tension—"then I opened the closet to hang up my coat, and nobody's clothes was there except mine. And I ran outside and then I saw our car all the way down the street moving away, so I got on my bike so I could chase it, but . . . *all the wheels came off!*"

The last line was delivered with a wail of despair that pierced her mother's heart with its obvious revelations of how the child viewed her life and its relationships. Mrs. Walters is a woman with a fairly sophisticated understanding of psychology and a great empathy for her daughter's emotional experiencing, and she could hear the complexities of the legend Greta had constructed in her dream. She realized it was a tale rooted in the six-year-old girl's feeling of inadequacy compared with her older brothers and in the struggle, which seemed to her so hopeless, to win her fair share of their parents' attention.

Hearing her daughter's dream reported, Mrs. Walters had indeed been put in contact with the raw material from which its story was spun. And even if she might not necessarily have been entirely accurate in interpreting the dream's symbols, she'd been completely correct in recognizing that *through* these symbols, Greta was expressing some deep concerns and conflicts. Actually, such recognition is not unique to our sometimes self-consciously psychoanalytic culture. For example, a tribe called the Senoi, who live in the Malay Peninsula, have been the object of much study because of their practice of regularly and openly interpreting family dreams, including the children's. Every morning at breakfast the child, along with all other family members, discusses his dreams, and is directed toward actions meant either to affirm or contravene the dream's message. Senoi people believe that the images inside a dream reflect how a child is viewing and adapting to the outside world. Thus, they feel, if the dream images are negative, and the child keeps them to himself, he may eventually suffer varying degrees of mental illness or at least unproductive amounts of anger or aggression. Encouraging him to express his dreams, they conclude, lessens this possibility. But the Senoi carry their dream validation even further. They teach their children quite specifically to act in ways that will detoxify the negative dreams and reinforce those that are positive.

This means that if a child dreams about an angry shouting fight with a friend, he is told to seek his friend out that day and speak to him lovingly—perhaps even offer him a gift. Conversely, if during the night he dreamed of doing something heroic, he is encouraged to corroborate the dream message by creating something that will truly help the other members of the tribe. Stanley Krippner and William Hughes, psychologists who have studied the Senois and dreams in general, report that this particular group of people claims to have very little violence or pathology among its members. Whether or not this can be proved, clearly, the doctors say, "from an early age the Senoi finds that others accept the feelings and thoughts of his inner life."

This is unfortunately not at all so in our own society. Inherent to this book is the idea that we tend to avoid the rawer formulations of our children's concerns. However, just *because* of this, it becomes particularly important that we listen to the voices of our children as whispered in their dreams. If much in a child's waking experience separates him from his instinctual and emotional self, his dreams can serve as a way of integrating these factors into his total personality. As he falls into sleep, the floodgates open and a host of feelings and fears and impressions tumble forth in all their disorder and half-formed conclusions: feelings and fears and impressions and conjectures that in waking life, for a variety of reasons, he is likely to repress. A maternal frown when he begins to express a concern, for example, can instantly end a discussion not only with his mother but also with himself. Indeed, no matter how warmly welcoming the family actually is, or how receptive to all kinds of emotional confusions, the pressure of life's routines makes extended speculation about feelings and needs almost impossible. The momentum of daily demands catches child and parent alike in its no-nonsense grip, and there is little time for recognition of those tentative wisps of developing thoughts.

In his dreams, though, the child can confront them, and sometimes think them through. Calvin Hall, a pioneer in the study of dreams, called dreaming "thinking that occurs during sleep," and research continues to validate this aspect of the dreaming concept. Yes, a child's dreams are (as Freud postulated they were for all people) a protection against the build-up of buried emotional conflict. They serve as a safety valve to release the pressure accumulating from the never-ending input involved in growing up. But they are also, we now realize, a blueprint *for* growing up; a way for children to "process" all that they see and hear in the course of a day. While he sleeps, the child can roam around through the history inside his memory cupboard and try and make sense of it. He can go over the contradictions, the sanctions and restrictions of his life and, through the imaginary dream experience, get to the heart of a waking problem. Like the travelers on the road to Oz, the young dreamer wanders along a fantasy path to the root of the mystery that lies in his own unconscious.

In his dreams, then, a child experiences himself and his ever changing world. But it is a world that is deeply personal, far more concerned with feelings than with objective events. Dr. Hall reports that even during extravagantly dramatic periods of world history, dreams tend to be much more intimate than global.

So children in the midst of war or chaotic political activities do not dream about the material that makes the newspaper headlines. Their dreams contain instead the stuff of personal diaries—what they think about themselves and how they see the conflicts of their emotional lives.

In this vein, Dr. Irving Markowitz, who works extensively with children and their dreams, sees children's dreams as being particularly "prospective," as opposed to an adult's frequent use of the dream to engage in retrospection. As we grow older, we tend to look backward in our dreams, to review and reminisce and come to terms with our yesterdays. Nostalgia visits us during the night, just as it does with misty-eyed frequency during the day. Children don't dream retrospectively, because there's little material yet for nostalgia. Nor is there enough intellectual development to evaluate past decisions. No, from the very beginning of life, children are oriented toward the future. Childhood is presented as a prelude to being, "being" subtly synonymous with being an adult.

Also, children are, as we have said, painfully aware that the present, like the past, is still not in their hands. And they know they are inevitably growing, developing, moving toward a time when it will be, a possibility that, with their current feelings of inadequacy, blankets soft beds with the harsh cloth of anxiety. For these reasons, although both adults and children use the dream as a "work sheet," children make special use of its planning aspects. The challenges of days yet to come, still shrouded in mystery, are mulled over in their dreams. Sleeping, a child explores possibilities for action when darkness lifts, tests out the responses he might make to experience, along with the possible effects of those responses.

So it was that Judy, before she began kindergarten, had a whole series of dreams that unmistakably related to this larger-than-life event. In sometimes direct expressions of her worry: "I dreamed I got sick in the middle of the class and threw up all over the teacher . . ." at other times in veiled symbolism: "A lady came to the house and asked me a whole bunch of questions so I could win a prize, and when I didn't answer her she threw hot water on my face and said I would have to stay in the house for a whole year before the water could dry . . ." Judy dealt with the idea of leaving home. What if she refused to go . . . what would happen when she did go . . . what would happen if she got sick and needed her mother . . . what would happen to her relationship with her mother . . . what would happen if she couldn't learn as fast as the other children . . . ? These were all part of the night's conjectures.

Because of the particular planning function of their

dreams, children tend to carry their dream speculations to especially catastrophic heights. They will, considerably more than adults, explore in dreams life's most pessimistic promise. They will consider the very worst alternative rather than the most desirable one, with their speculations aimed at coping with the most traumatic trump card life may deal them.

This theory explains why so many of a child's dreams involve death or some other form of abandonment by a parent. Why, for instance, George dreams his mother "forgot him in a taxi," and Jason dreams his mother "fell on a knife and was cut all to pieces," and Robert dreams about being picked up in the mouth of a giant crab when he goes swimming with his father, so that he stays caught in one place while his father unknowingly swims steadily out of sight. These are all dreams that illustrate the depth of dependency that makes the idea of losing a parent's support so terrifying. Yet, through this imagining, strength can be gathered to deal with the awesome but inevitable letting go that is the goal of growing up.

Struggles with dependency are at the root of many of a child's dreams. Dr. Hall, in categorizing types of dreams, labels one large group "freedom versus security," and a child's nighttime conflicts regularly reveal this push-pull process. The safety and protection of dependency, the excitement and challenge of freedom competitively beckon the small dreamer, taking on many guises, but clearly expressing this classic life conflict. "I was going on a trip all by myself, but it started to rain so hard the plane couldn't take off. . . ." "I forgot my lines in the play and Mommy whispered them so loud that everyone heard them and I felt so embarrassed I ran off the stage. . . ." "I dreamt I was sleeping in my old room, in my old crib, and I was wearing my baby pajamas but my legs stuck all the way out because they were so small on me, and I was very cold, and then all of a sudden I got very sad, and when I woke up I still felt sad. . . ."

Not surprisingly, this kind of dream appears with special frequency at transitional times in a child's life. As in Judy's case, when starting a new level of school, or when going away to camp or becoming, with the birth of a new baby, an "older" brother or sister, the anxiety attached to growing up intensifies and reflects itself in symbolic dream arguments for and against maturity. Children faced with particular growing-up challenges will in their dreams struggle to feel competent to face those challenges. How to translate the work sheet's raw material into a working blueprint for what lies ahead?

There is a "rites of passage" aspect to this kind of dream, related to what psychiatrist E. Wellisch calls the struggle to find one's "way." Dr. Wellisch defines "way" as thoughts a child has about his "origins, tasks and aims." Dreams of a "way" often occur, says Dr. Wellisch, when the child senses he has "reached a significant stage in his way of life. He has to undertake a challenging task and, sometimes, to make a decisive choice."

A recent dream of Robert's serves as graphic illustration of this idea. It was a dream he awakened from in tears, but with a quietly resigned character to his sobbing that was very different from his usual dramatic howls of despair. It's a dream he remembers in quite full detail and is clearly, if painfully, willing to communicate. . . .

"I was being buried in a coffin, but I knew I wasn't really dead. A man told me (I *think* he was a nice man, but I'm not sure) that everyone who's seven years old has to be buried before they're allowed to be eight and nine and grow up all the way. He told me it was like going to school. You had to do it before you could be big. And I was scared, but I believed him. I knew that Mommy did it when she was little, and Daddy too. . . ." His face as he talked to me was taut with strain, and he seemed to need to have me understand its source completely.

"I knew I would be unburied after a while," he continued, "but I was still so scared . . . and I watched the other kids . . . my friend David who's in my class, and he was climbing into his coffin, and I was standing behind him on line waiting for mine—you know, like you wait in amusement parks for your car to come along the track and stop for you to climb in. I could see the coffin coming toward me, and the top opened up, and I had this terrible feeling 'cause I knew I *had* to get in. . . . There wasn't anything I could do, because if I didn't get buried, I couldn't be alive again. . . ."

Robert's voice trailed off, and he did not continue. Nor, in fact, had his dream continued. For these are the dreams that we would commonly label nightmares, those often terrifying battles with experience that abruptly end with a sob, a scream, a heart-pounding race to a parent's bed. Freud called the nightmare "a dream that failed." Dr. Markowitz speculates, appropriately to this discussion, that it may be rather a dream that cannot continue. If a child doesn't have enough history, experience and information in his memory cupboard to allow him to formulate an answer to a particular question, whether it be specific, like passing a test, or profound, like Robert's concern about meeting the challenges of maturity, he may simply have to wake up. For he cannot, on his own, finish the dream problem out.

There are other reasons, though, for the night's darker dreams, those that end too quickly or far too disturbingly.

The clash of impulses that are part of a child's learning to be a person creates dream scripts that are rich with conflict. So Dougie throws himself into his mother's arms after a nap. . . .

"I dreamed I was being chased by a tiger, Mommy, and she had *your* face!"

Heroically Dougie's mother comforts him, while she squirms uneasily at this confrontation with her little boy's repressed inevitable resentments.

Since such battles between hostility and love, or impulse and conscience, rage all through childhood, we can better understand not only the plots but the cast of characters who people its dream stories. The police and the convicts, the priests and the sinners, the angels and witches are often representative of a child's image of the different sides of his personality that will act out dramas heavily laced with guilt.

Actually, dreams also *contribute* to guilt, generating uneasy feelings that linger long after a dream has ended. For away from the external controls of waking life, a child will explore ideas in his dreams he would not ever consider acknowledging during the day. Because of this, he may use the bad dream as a way of punishing himself, as if, says Dr. Hall, "the nightmare is the price he pays for doing something wrong." So the punishing conscience shouts its accusations, and fills the dream with vindictive designs of retribution, like electric chairs and fires and furious principals and teachers; while lions and tigers and monsters quickly gain on leaden-footed dreamers.

These vengeful symbols illustrate the secret language of the dream. Symbols, the images of the dream, are the way ideas are expressed during sleep. The concept of symbolism is crucial to any discussion of dreams. But we have in recent years moved away from a strictly Freudian interpretation of these pictures in a dreamer's mind, which gave them rather categorical definitions. Today there is more inclination to see symbols as having individual meaning—in relation to the specific child's life.

Indeed, just because a child's dream symbols *are* so deeply personal, an attempt to respond to them can establish new levels of adult-child communication. Listening to the dream's revelations may give a glimpse of repressed frustrations, may allow parents to see that an ostensibly healed emotional scar is in fact still an open wound. For example, while Cathy was away at camp last summer, her parents had the family cat put to sleep. The animal was sickly and old and a nuisance to everyone but Cathy. Guilt over their legitimate but rather impulsive decision encouraged them to tell Cathy, when she came home from camp, that the vet had recommended the pet be placed in a country home for old cats and dogs. There were vague promises that they would take Cathy to visit her "soon." The story sat uneasily in Cathy's consciousness and, coupled with her longing for the pet's familiar place in her emotional life, she had many moments of really painful sadness. She wanted desperately to believe what she had been told but was unable actually to accept it. Yet fear and guilt and loyalty meshed into a complex conflict that sealed her lips. Till one night Cathy had this dream, from which she woke screaming:

"These people," she gasped, "they sent back a dog they bought because they didn't want him anymore. Then all of a sudden he was in like this big factory . . . and a man put him into a chopper and he came out in a bunch of chops like lamb chops and a lady with a bloody apron said I had to eat it for my dinner . . . and she told me to sit down at the table, and she gave me a knife and a fork, and she put the chops on this big plate in front of me, and it was all filled with blood . . . like soup! . . . and the *dog's face was there . . . it was part of the chop! . . . and the lady said go on . . . go on . . . eat it!*" Cathy shrieked this ending of her dream. It was too horrible to tell about, as it had been too horrible to dream any longer. And Cathy's parents, who had come to comfort their screaming daughter, realized through its grotesqueness that their protective pretense had been futile and that this nightmare cry was a cry for help in dealing with a terribly confusing life experience.

Dr. Markowitz, by the way, does not believe that parents should be hesitant about trying to decipher the symbolic code of their children's dreams.

"You don't have to have all the answers," he says, "to speculate, sometimes with the child, about what a dream might have meant to him."

Indeed, this kind of speculation can, with surprising alacrity, itself provide answers to some haunting problems. With Cathy, this meant that her parents, aware of their role in her distress, did their best to comfort her fears and explain her confusions. Bruce's mother and father made similar use of the dream to confront their child's raw concerns. During the period when Bruce was having problems in school, he had a series of sleep-breaking nightmares. The majority involved attempts to escape hideously ugly monsters or being hopelessly pinioned in their choking grasp. Finally, "although we tried to avoid the thought," Bruce's mother says rather ruefully, "we had to entertain the idea that not only was Bruce obviously really frightened about something, maybe we were in some way contributing to his fears."

With a little help they focused on the idea that there were

some "monstrous" binds in their son's life—monstrous defined as a situation he was helpless to change or control. Monster dreams often reflect exactly this kind of dilemma, although the dilemma itself varies from child to child. With Bruce it was simply the fact that an increased homework schedule was pulling at the rather rigid rules his parents maintained about an early bedtime. To a boy inclined to be rather plodding anyway, the constant tension only made him more so. So Bruce's dreams were a clear statement of the double bind his life had become.

Once aware of his problem, Bruce's parents relaxed some of the family schedules. Dinnertime was delayed a bit so that Bruce could get a good chunk of his work done before it began. In this way he didn't have the feeling of racing the clock from dinnertime on. Bedtime itself was also made more flexible, with his parents' sensible realization that it was far better for Bruce to sleep a little less than have his sleep broken with conflict-produced nightmares.

So Bruce's dreams became a communication tool within the family, a function of dreaming that becomes increasingly significant as dream research continues. One value of such "dream discourse" is that a child can express feelings he would be reluctant to confess in more direct conversation. Somehow the dream has a hypothetical quality that allows him to feel out his parents' attitudes, to try and gauge their degree of receptivity to a feeling or wish, without subjecting himself to the humiliation of the rejection a more open statement of self might bring.

An almost textbook illustration of this occurred between Jimmy and his father. Jimmy had been feeling particularly competitive toward his father, largely because his mother had begun helping her husband in his business and thus was suddenly away from home unusual amounts of time. Both adults were aware of the resentment Jimmy was feeling and also sensed the distress the resentment caused him, as he had always been particularly close to his father. Their sensitivity allowed them to hear the story of anger and guilt behind the dream story Jimmy loudly announced one morning, as he entered their bedroom when they were dressing for work. . . .

"I had this really awful dream," Jimmy said, his eyes focused on his father's image in the wall mirror. "It was about this scientist who invents a terrible monster, a mean, terrible monster. But the scientist was mean, too, and he used to boss the monster around all the time. So then . . ." Jimmy continued, his voice rushing now, words tumbling all over one another, "so then the monster one day sneaked behind the scientist when he wasn't looking and"—now Jimmy's eyes darted quickly away from his father's reflection—"and he punched the scientist on the head and said, 'Take that . . . take that . . . take that . . .' and he punched him until he was dead!"

An air of expectancy hung in the room in the few minutes before Jimmy's father, "acting on a hunch," made this reply:

"You know, Jim, I was dreaming myself last night. I dreamt you were all grown up, and had kids of your own . . . and I started to think how you might have children yourself someday, and how you'll probably try and do a lot of things for your children, but they won't always understand why you do them, or why you have to do other things they don't like at all, and they'll probably be really angry at you lots of times. . . . I remember feeling like that about Grandpa a lot, and I guess you must about me sometimes. . . ."

Father and son's eyes met again in the mirror. Without commenting, Jimmy suddenly turned and left the room, making his father frantically uneasy that he had "gone too far in my do-it-yourself analysis bit." But these fears were quickly allayed, for when he and his wife came down a few minutes later for breakfast, Jimmy was already at the table waiting for them, and waiting to add this addendum to their conversation:

"You know, Dad . . . about my dream . . . I didn't tell it right. The monster wasn't really such a *bad* monster, and he didn't really *kill* the scientist . . . he just kinda beat him up a little. . . ." The boy's voice trailed off and he turned his attention to his cereal, but it seemed very clear that a significant conflict in his life had been at least to some degree eased because he had involved his parents in the private world of his dreams. His father's obliquely empathetic response had allowed Jimmy to work some of his own feelings through. He was able to modify the harsher emotions that had made him feel guiltily murderous toward the man who had "created" him.

Validating the dream life of a child is not just an act of accepting who he is as a total person. It is also strengthening an extremely significant tool for structuring a life of greater enrichment. The kind of thinking that takes place in dreams is the kind that produces the highest level of creative thought. The magnificently bizarre combinations of ideas that take shape in dreams can produce profoundly creative results. Freed from the barriers of language structure and rules of logic, the dreamer can arrange thoughts into new patterns and experiment with the stuff inside his memory cupboard to see what variety of innovative conclusions might emerge. Dreams are flowingly open-ended, while daily life often closes in too quickly and abruptly for creative thinking to take place.

We tend in this culture to be wary of make-believe, and this extends to our feelings about night dreaming as well as day-dreaming. Robert's mother listens to her son's breakfast recitals of the night's adventures and finds herself worrying whether he "dreams too much," as if his explorations into a private world are evidence of faulty adaptation to the public one. In fact, research supports the opposite conclusion. There is a correlation between dreaming during the night and learning skills during the day. The child who can think in images is capable of grasping complex ideas put into words. Say Drs. Krippner and Hughes, "The creative thinker typically accepts and exploits his dreams and the creative elements of his inner experience."

Many children I worked with kept "dream diaries," delighting in sharing their entries with other journal keepers. Listening to them, it was obvious that curiosity soars as the night darkens. Recesses of the mind's darkest corners are suddenly lit, illuminating all kinds of otherwise buried secrets of self. As Nancy writes, to sum up this chapter for me:

> Dreaming is like you're lying on
>   a raft
>   on a blazing hot day.
> Reflections of you shine off the water,
> And you float through them, so that
> all around you
> are pieces of
>   yourself.

8 / Shame

*"Everybody laughed at me when I said
the teacher's name wrong"*

The dictionary has a varied set of definitions for the word "shame." Synonyms range from embarrassment to mortification to humiliation. The experience of shame is described as a loss of pride or self-respect; a sense of being ridiculous, indecent or unworthy. Clearly, there are many nuances to this feeling, and clearly, too, they are part of the unwieldy baggage children carry with them through childhood, banging against legs trying to catch up with experience, and leaving bruises that throb with physical and psychic pain. Even the dispassionate dictionary consistently relates pain to shame, and any work with children quickly validates this connection.

The hurt of shame is inevitable to a self still in formation. For self-esteem will periodically suffer all kinds of blows as certain experiments with freedom end in disaster. . . .

"I tried to cook my own breakfast and I dropped the pan on the floor and I burned a hole in the tile and Mommy woke up and yelled at me and said I could never turn on the stove again," Judy says one morning. Her voice is ragged, her eyes are averted, her self-confidence is obviously submerged under the burning taste of failure.

Erik Erikson, in his theories on identity, links the feeling of shame with the feeling of doubt. The child who is too often shamed by his failed attempts to stand on his own feet can begin to doubt his ability ever to take that stance. Indeed, one of the great dilemmas of growing up is how to emerge from childhood's natural helplessness without still feeling too incapable, too inadequate ever to handle life on your own. Children are so predisposed to thinking themselves incompetent that any condition emphasizing that perception, such as feeling ashamed, will vastly deepen their distress.

No matter how rapidly a child grows physically, secretly shameful feelings of smallness and weakness often pulsate inside, and these feelings must be hidden from sight at all costs. The fear of looking "stupid," of feeling "silly," of being "mocked out," are malevolent threats hovering darkly on the horizon. No wonder, then, that expressions of shame invariably connect the feeling to the idea of exposure. Ashamed, a child wishes to bury his face in the covers, hide in the closet, run away from home. In his dreams, he runs naked along school halls unable to find shelter, looks down when reciting to see pants fallen to the ground, goes to parties with all the wrong clothes on. Asleep or awake, there is the sense of being pinned down under the harsh light of a judging "other," derisive laughter swelling louder and louder around flaming ears.

Not surprisingly, we get this representative image from Robert, his face flushed with emotion, who says:

"It's like your skin is all ripped off your body . . . peeled away in big pieces, and you gotta cry and cry and cry, like Mommy would if she peeled a million onions."

And then Andy, who has reflected a minute on Robert's analogy, adds his own, clearly similar conception:

"Being ashamed is like your head is cut open by a big piece of metal like I saw in that sheet-metal factory we went to with the class . . . and the whole inside of your head is all hanging out."

To be made painfully visible, then, in all their inadequacy, revealing their incompetence and confusion for all to see. If such negative perceptions of self are natural to childhood, and we know they frequently are, shame about that self being seen is aggravated by the way we tend to relate to children. We are often more ready to fix blame than to teach responsibility, and we sometimes exhibit an unlovely predilection for "shaming" as a way of controlling a child's behavior.

Again, nowhere is this distorted interaction more evident than inside our schools, their atmosphere rich with possibilities for learning the pain of mortification, for being taught the guidelines of self-contempt. These are feelings, by the way, not easily checked into school lockers when the day is over. As Alfred Adler writes, many children grow up "in the constant dread of being laughed at," and he goes on to say that ridicule of children "retains its effect upon the soul of the child, and is transferred into the habits and actions of his adulthood."

There is no doubt that if "nothing succeeds like success," nothing reinforces a fear of ridicule more than being made to look ridiculous. Robert's anxiety about his coordination as compared with that of other children can be traced in considerable part to the humiliating mornings in kindergarten when he couldn't tie his shoes, those mornings when his teacher quite frequently, after heaving exaggerated sighs, would call out to some other child in a tone of abject weariness meant to imply (as it unmistakably did) utter disdain for Robert's incompetence, "Will someone please come up and tie Robert's shoes for him so we can go outside for recess? He can't seem to do it for himself yet." And there Robert would stiffly sit—no recourse but to face front—toward tables lined with jeering faces, hearing the barely suppressed giggles, the stage whispers behind loosely cupped hands. There he would sit while some better-coordinated classmate, sometimes a boy, sometimes a girl, would bend over him condescendingly and tie his laces into a bow.

The mortification of those days is beyond even Robert's gift for metaphor, and I would not think of encouraging him to attempt its description. To see his face when he merely begins talking about the experience makes me want to move on quickly to other things, suspecting even as I chatter about a current TV program that he will long retain the memory of those terrible mornings when he first learned the shame of competitive failure.

Jules Henry, talking about our educational system, says that schools teach children how to hate other children as well as themselves. The child who ties Robert's shoes preens in her superiority. Her success is built on Robert's failure, a very common pattern, according to Henry, in the way children are socialized, particularly as they become "educated." As for Robert, the perspiring after-school bouts with his laces did eventually lead him to master a skill. But the rewards of his accomplishment were joyless, because he was motivated not by the desire to succeed at a new challenge but to avoid the ignominy of disgrace. Henry calls this life's "essential nightmare," and goes on to explain that too often, "to be successful in our culture, one must learn to dream of failure," and of course all the humiliation failure brings.

It should be noted here that an aspect of oppression is to reject the person for the very qualities which define him. In other words, the Jew is persecuted for his Jewishness, the Negro for his blackness, the woman for her "womanly" qualities (such as intuitiveness or emotional intensity). Similarly, children are continuously attacked in schools for being "a baby." The contempt attached to the term is fodder for the child's own contempt for himself. Asking a child to do more than he's physically or emotionally able to do and then disparaging him for his helplessness teaches him to be ashamed of who he is, as well as undermining what he feels capable of becoming. He enters school with the limited ego resources natural to his age and then encounters shaming situations which will further inhibit his ego development. Not certain of who he is as a separate person, should he fail to conform to the teacher's perception of who he should be, he becomes ashamed of his own instincts and needs. So, in a hopeless spiral, his shame makes him feel *more* helpless, *more* inferior, less capable of ever meeting the teacher's expectations, less willing to let her catch sight of the vulnerable creature he really is. No matter how carefully books were studied the night before, the fear of making a mistake seals lips tightly shut when answers are asked for.

Not only in its oppressive demands, but also through the constant criticism that's so often a function of the role of teacher, does the school become a particular arena for experiencing shame. In a cartoon strip by Charles Schultz, dealing with the marvelous Peanuts gang, Lucy is saying in disgust that she is going to quit school once and for all, that "yesterday one of the teachers criticized my lunch. She said I had too many doughnuts and not enough carrots. . . . It's time," Lucy then says firmly, "to quit . . . when they even criticize your lunch!"

Unfortunately, Lucy's self-assertiveness is not the norm

for most children. Instead they tend to burrow deeper into feelings of inadequacy, internalizing more and more the teacher's negative judgments. Jason provides this ideal illustration one morning when we are walking in the park: I have my hands in my pockets, and he slips one of his own hands in alongside mine so that our fingers touch. It is a warm and pleasant feeling, but after a minute, Jason makes this comment, obviously reminded of some recent hurt:

"You know," he says bleakly, "my teacher makes me *feel* like a pocket, that's got all the wrong things inside it!"

The pocket was frequently used by children as a symbol of being ashamed—both because it was a place to hide and because it suggested the dark despair of the emotion. Similarly, when we would draw pictures about feelings, shame was invariably colored black, no light softening it, "as if," writes Beth, captioning an all-black canvas, "as if you will see so much dark that your eyes may never see light again."

One of the residual benefits of doing the research for this book was that some light did enter the darkness of shame when children shared the secret of it through their writing and talking. Eyes widened at the realization that they were not alone in experiencing the stings of embarrassment. Harry Stack Sullivan once talked about the "delusion of uniqueness," the feeling that we are different from each other and therefore somehow inferior. So when children bravely volunteered, "I wet my pants the first day of kindergarten . . ." or "Daddy makes me wear baby galoshes in the snow and everybody laughs at me . . ." or "I'm in a special reading class where everyone is stupid . . ." they could begin to feel the strengthening intimacy of being like each other and lessen the alienation of feeling so shamefully "different."

The push toward being like everyone else, to find some

identity in belonging, is, we know, very great in childhood. This is why, once again, school can produce so much material with which a child may begin building an apologetic structure for who he is. The simple dividing up of children into groups that define capability can quickly define the extent of their inferiority. So traditional schools that "track" their pupils or are particularly competitive athletically may be launching children down roads they'll have great difficulty ever leaving. And no matter how many ostensibly compensatory skills a boy or girl may have—being a good athlete instead of a student, or vice versa—if they are too deeply ashamed of their failures they will get little comfort from their success.

Feelings of shame for his inadequacies are fanned by any relationship that doesn't allow a child to take himself seriously as a separate person. The view of the child as an adult's property contributes unhappily to this destructive condition. No matter how the "property" is coddled and loved, the role is demeaning—and it is bitterly resented by the children themselves.

Instant heat, for example, is generated by the word "cute," to express an adult's affectionate feelings for a child. It seems the ultimate put-down, distressingly patronizing. Similarly, ask a group of children what grownups think of them, and the answers are rapid and angry. . . .

"Dumb . . . puppets . . . jerky . . . silly . . . like a toy . . . a plastic doll . . . stupid . . . a pet, just like a dog or cat . . ." Rage rises with each person-denying adjective, until finally, inevitably, the ultimate resentment: "We might as well be invisible."

The concept of invisibility was used over and over again by children talking about the shame of insignificance . . . like

Andy, who, after a classroom scolding, says angrily:

"My teacher sucks me up like a vacuum cleaner till there's nothing left of me to see that she doesn't like." And Susan, after being summarily ordered to wear an outfit she hated for a special family occasion, wrote this self-pitying but graphic poem:

> I talk and no one hears me . . .
> I touch and no one feels me
> Unnoticed
> Unheard . . .
> I'm invisible . . . not a person
> I'm not alive . . .
> So I must be a ghost . . .
> And my life is not a life, just
> A made-up story—
> *A horror movie!*

Invisibility was also used in children's writings to indicate a wish for protection, so that nobody could witness the humiliation of a mistake, in either dress or speech or behavior. At the root of either use of the symbolic image—anger at not being noticed, the desire to hide from critical attack—is the fact that children are inordinately concerned with what other people think of them. Uncertainty about self makes validation by someone else enormously important. As a child grows up, he is constantly tormenting himself about interpersonal relationships: will he be accepted, will he be liked, will he mess things up by doing something wrong? . . .

"I worry all the time!" Cathy wails. "When I'm with a bunch of kids I feel like I'm in a play, on a stage, and they're the audience, and I'm going to make a terrible fool of my-self. . . ." Beth nods her head in understanding and says, "I know. Me . . . I guess it's more like I feel I'm a puppet, and I keep taking me apart. I worry so much whether each piece of me is going to work that I forget how to put myself together. I just lay there in a lumpy pile and can't do any-thing."

Self-consciousness seeps through every day, and sensitivity to any kind of disapproval is intense. Lack of self-confidence makes every action a cause for trembling concern. Judy cries herself into throwing up during Christmas vacation because she is afraid her new haircut is too short and everyone will make fun of it when she goes back to school. (Many did.) And Robert comes into his class one morning shivering from the cold, but when this grade's empathetic teacher asks him where his sweater is, he says he forgot to bring one. Later that morning, the teacher noticed a bulge in Robert's pants that seemed unusual, and when she looked up again, a strip of blue wool was peeking out of his pants leg. Before she could unobtrusively call him to her desk, a classmate's eye followed her own and in a few minutes poor Robert had once again become the object of group derision. Hating the sweater for being too "babyish" (it had a nursery design and was quite short), he had stuffed it into his pants so as not to have to wear it. Memories of shoe-tying days filled him with tension about not seeming as mature as his classmates. Un-fortunately, his solution backfired and trying to save face ended instead with his face again flushed with mortification.

It is terribly painful for a child to step outside the circle of sameness that can quiet his ever present fear of being laughed at. To be "weird" or "queer" is quintessentially awful and fear of the label paralyzes the child with self-consciousness. One study of teen-age boys and girls showed that 52 percent became terribly distressed when even a stranger seemed to be "staring" at them. (And they were quick to give this interpretation to the most casual glance in their direction.) Immediately these children squirm under the imagined scrutiny, check zippers and buttons, straighten hair nervously; often they will leave a subway car or room because of the real torment involved in feeling appraised (knowing as they do, in all their insecure unknowing, that they'll surely be found wanting).

No question, much of the tension involved in being a child is deeply aggravated by shame. Life's relationships are strained, and children alternate between self-demeaning campaigns for approval and defensive withdrawing for fear of disapproval. They limit their experiences because of worry that they won't be able to handle new demands or will be criticized for making the attempt. And worry about being liked keeps pace with self-denigration, for it is the rare child who consistently greets himself with approval.

The concept of "ideal self" is very much present here— that discrepancy between what a child thinks he should be and what external and internal mirrors tell him he is. While the internal mirrorings of self are of course more complex, reflections in actual mirrors can cause their own very intense distress. Once the middle years of childhood are reached, this kind of problem is particularly acute.

As in Susan's case, often the problem is overweight. The tension-releasing comforts of chocolate and ice cream, plus the body's natural changes, pad adolescent forms with hated excess pounds. On the other hand, being skinny brings its own pain, especially when the bosom remains childishly flat while other girls' figures are taking on a sensual new shape.

As for the skin that is most visible, on the face, the blemishes of acne can blister the soul. No ointment will be overlooked that might clear a pore and each new product commercial is received like a promise of salvation. And what of buckteeth, or braces . . . or noses too short or too long . . . or eyes too small or pale, or myopic? The litany of shame is endless.

As we have already indicated, the lack of self-love touches other kinds of reflections. For not just how they look but how they act troubles a surprising number of children. . . .

"I have this real awful laugh," Jeremy says heatedly, as if he is confessing some long hidden perversion. It was Jeremy who had initiated a discussion about what we like least about ourselves. It is a discussion that amazes me in its shame-structured distortions of my objective view of these children. Now Jeremy continues in his ruthless self-analysis: "I sound like a horse. I make these gulping noises and sometimes I have spit in the corner of my mouth."

He closes his eyes in disgust as other children admit, with varying degrees of apology, their own harsh assessments of self in the world. . . .

"I clump around like some dumb cow," Bruce says. "I'm always tripping over things. I wouldn't dance with a girl for a million dollars—I'd probably break both her legs. . . ." "I always ask people for help," Lisa quickly breaks in. "I never make up my own mind about anything! I'm surprised I don't ask what I should make in the bathroom!"

Nobody in the group laughs. This is, each person knows, as serious a conversation as they are likely ever to have.

A good part of this social awkwardness relates to childhood's intellectual limitations. Children are enormously concerned about "knowing what to say." They are so afraid that they'll say something foolish and be ridiculed *for* their limitations. Over and over I was stunned by the discrepancy between children's creativity of expression when they didn't feel they were being judged and the tight-lipped, tight-gripped hold on language when they felt that they were. If this last perception occurs in the presence of adults or older children, it also often plagues them in the presence of their peers. "Shyness" is revealed like a shameful scar when boys and girls talk about themselves. Lisa, for instance, draws a picture of herself lying on an ironing board, and says contemptuously, "This is me talking to a boy. Every time he talks I get stiffer and stiffer, like his words are ironing me flat!" while Bruce says, "I store up all my words like I was a container instead of a person, and I only can talk when I'm so stuffed up they have to burst out."

So the self-conscious child, in the company of anyone but trusted friends, and in any new social situation, approaches conversation with stutterings and stammerings and oppressive silences and nervous giggles, and their humiliating sounds and no-sounds ring in his ear long after the school dance or picnic or party is over.

If many parents don't realize the extent of their children's feelings of shame, they're often equally unaware of how much they themselves may unwittingly contribute to the feelings. It is a collaboration with self-consciousness that often begins at the very beginning of the parent-child relationship—on that day when the proud mother or father supplies the new baby's name for a birth certificate. For an amazing number of children are quite seriously unhappy about their given names. One study had 44 percent of the interviewees distressfully critical of their parents for not being more careful about the names they chose for them.

Thus we find girls like Beth shortening longer names out

of hatred for their "square-o" old-fashionedness, while Greta mumbles her name when asked, sure she'll be teased because it's so "funny" (read "unusual"). Bruce despises his name, which he sees as "faggy," and resents his parents for not having realized its rather elegant overtones would cause their son some embarrassment when he grew older.

And mothers and fathers as people—not just as occasional abusers of parental authority—are the cause of much discomfort to their children (who feel tainted by their relationship to adults who are subject to criticism). Studies of children's attitudes toward their families show that a great percentage are frequently "ashamed" of how their parents act and live. Mothers and fathers who dress "too sexy," who get drunk at parties, who act "gross" by being too sloppy or loud make dependent children ache with conflict. Love for parents mixes with shame for their behavior, and guilt rises, deepening the torment. And if children worry how their parents look to their friends, they worry as well how their parents treat their friends. Even very young children sulk over a playmate being ignored. . . . "Why didn't you smile at Jamey?" Dougie asks his mother angrily when she picks him up at nursery school. "She'll think you don't like her!" Similarly, rudeness, lack of sociability, arguing in front of visiting friends (just like they weren't even there!) make children cringe because of their accountability toward companions whose approval they want so desperately to maintain.

There are many defenses to cover the feeling of shame, not the least of which is a false bravado. Very often the swaggering, most competitive child is really the one who feels least confident about his own worth. Conversely, some children retreat almost permanently from social and competitive contact—hoping perhaps to announce their self-sufficiency but in reality making themselves inaccessible to the people who, they secretly know, would reject them if they met.

Too much shaming as a way of socializing a child can make him determined to get away with as much as possible in secret ways, as well as teaching him to use shaming as a weapon in his own relationships. Jason screams and writhes in the barber chair so the barber can't cut his hair, and Jason's father embarrassedly takes his son home, locks still long. Earlier that morning Jason had been punished, and now, clearly, it was his father's turn. Similarly, adolescents' "freaky" clothes are often, says some psychological theory, a way of shaming parents by vivid public rejection of the parents' values.

There is impotence in shame, whether it is used against others or burns inside the self. And it is an impotence that has at rock bottom a loss of dignity. Children, painfully aware of their powerlessness, are acutely sensitive to any reminder of their weakness. As a child, this growing person must ask for, be given, permission, entreat; daily, in a dozen ways, humble himself. Resentment burns deeply when that unavoidable condition of childhood is in any way exploited.

" 'Please,' " says Jason, "is the worst word I ever heard," and his implication is clear. It is an implication adults would do well to remember when they deal with children whose dependency should not obscure their rights to a sense of dignity about their developing selves.

9/Sexual Feelings

Mothers have eggs inside them and daddys take off all their clothes so they won't get dirty and then they help the mommys cook the eggs so they turn into babies. . . .

JASON

If this book is dedicated to the idea that children should be allowed to tell real, not mythical, stories with their lives, the stories should be free of a censor. They should not be cleansed of the lusty, swirling sensuality that is so much a part of childhood's emotional experiencing. For the truth is that from their very earliest days babies exhibit behavior that can only be called sexual. The sucking on breast or bottle brings gratifications quite apart from the pragmatic food-getting goals of the act. A baby's tongue and mouth and lips are tools for sensual explorations that dominate his attention as he sucks furiously, face reddened with concentration. . . . And when the hunger abates, and the sucking slows down, there is a look of contentment on the perspiring face that tells us other appetites, too, have for a little while been sated.

Yes, how something tastes, how hard it is, how soft it is, how cold or how warm, are filtered through oral membranes and translated into perceptions that may, according to some views, affect the kind of total person the child will become. Even in these days of questioning the absoluteness of certain Freudian theory, there seems to be general agreement that children who have been seriously frustrated in "oral gratification" will know a considerable amount of interpersonal anxiety when they grow older.

Babies are also, in their rich sensory experiencing, acutely sensitive to odors. In this period of animalistic pleasure-seeking, they live much of their lives through their sense of smell. Long before a child recognizes his mother's face, he is familiar with the scent of her body, a scent that may vary with her emotions and so evoke different emotional responses in him.

Psychologist Richard Krebs has written about babies who respond to their breast-feeding mother's sexual arousal in another room. Suddenly, as the woman turns to her husband, the baby wakes from sleep in apparent hunger. The doctor speculates that the sexual arousal of a nursing mother releases the milk from her breasts, and the baby, so sensitive to her smells, is awakened and calls out (competitively?) for her attention.

That there is a sensory and sensual pleasure in the smells of the baby's own body is very evident when he plays in his crib or playpen. He is, for instance, not at all disgusted by the contents of his full diaper—quite the opposite. He likes and is stimulated and pleasured by its warm, moistly pungent odors.

And later, cleaned and powdered, this still primitive new person will show other signs of sexuality. Dougie's mother, for example, remembers being horrified the first time she found her then infant son with an erection. Yet the fact is that babies frequently have erections; one study of nine infants from three to twenty weeks showed that seven of the nine had at least one a day. And each incident was accompanied by observable tension and release of tension, clearly related to an adult's more sophisticated, but no more meaningful, sexual response.

That children's erotic life *is* meaningful is too often overlooked by the adults whose attitudes so influence their lives. Indeed, perhaps in no other area of relating to children is there more denial and condescension than toward their expressions of sexuality. To some extent this complacency allows parents to accept more easily the sexual experience of masturbation. (It's relatively simple to be tolerant of something you don't take seriously.) So when Judy comes shrieking into the kitchen one morning: "Mommy! I found a button inside me just like the elevator button at Grandma's house, and when I push it I go up and down inside!" her mother can smile benignly without an earlier generation's disapproval. (On the other hand, later that morning Judy overhears her mother repeat the story to a friend, and the amusement in her voice makes the little girl's face flush with confused discomfort.)

In reality, a child's body contains nerve endings and organs of touch that make her highly susceptible to tactile stimulation. So no explorer could know more excitement than Judy can, and did, and does from her unexpected clitoral discovery. There are, of course, differences between children's capacities to be sexually aroused, but every child will experience some part of the sensual continuum and know the delicious pleasures of stroking, rubbing and prodding their own genitals. Many children have experienced orgasm even before the age of five, and clearly they did not have to know the name of the feeling to know how good it felt.

Children, however, *do* vary in their sexual development, and that they are pushed by the myth of innocence into one sexual pattern is the source of serious individual conflict. The boy or girl who is sexually "precocious" often suffers severe emotional pain. For our morally ambivalent society is uncomfortable with the child who is "too mature," whose body seems inappropriately developed for her chronological age. . . .

"Put something else on," Cathy's father says before the family goes out for dinner. "That sweater's much too tight on you." Cathy stares at him and flushes in embarrassment. And in her room when she yanks the sweater over her head, the swellings around her nipples disgust her. She is, after all, only eight years old, and if five years from now breasts will be prized, today they are despised symbols of her being "different."

Adults' uncertainty about sexual norms affects all of a child's sexual experiencing, precocious or not. Even with masturbation, which may be intellectually accepted by parents and other adults, residual resistence often appears. An uneasy sense that he'll be "overstimulated" has parents poking into the child's private meetings with himself.

In actual fact, masturbation is generally more soothing than exciting, which is why from infancy on it is usually indulged in at bedtime. The hand between the legs under pajama or nightgown slows down the story of the day's adventures, and helps turn the page into sleep. When boys and girls write about nighttime feelings, invariably they reveal this soft side of sexual pre-sleep activity. . . .

"When I lie in my bed," writes Nancy, "I feel like my body's a candle, that flickers when I touch it . . . and feelings drip from me like wax. I hold on to my body while darkness hovers around and comes closer and closes in on me. I lie very still and touch myself and listen to the quiet, and soon I hear the wind rustling and the trees sound like they're whispering, and the wind blows out the flame and I cover myself with my blanket to stay warm, and I go to sleep."

And Beth writes: "When I lie down in my bed, I feel my body is lying in the middle of a brook. Feelings rush through it, as if over rocks and weeds, smoothing my edges and rough spots . . . shooting around the corners of myself until I feel washed all over, sparkly, silky clean."

Yet despite these poetic testimonials to the comforts of masturbation, Beth and Nancy and many other older children too often feel guilty about it. This despite the fact that as they approach adolescence they are moving into a time of ultimate sexual upheaval, a time when their sex organs will mature and there will be heightened demands to satisfy sexual urges. Actually, in cultures where boys and girls can experience each other early in life, the masturbatory experience is quite rare. In effect, it is our social system of extended childhood that forces the hand to find its own sexual release, and it is yet another irony of a child's life that he is made to feel guilty and weak and ashamed because of this culturally induced activity.

However, since we *are* a society that postpones heterosexual gratification, we quite naturally (if unnaturally!) recoil even more from sex play between children of different sexes. Since some aspect of such play is indulged in by every boy and girl, each "game" helps grind down the myth of the happy child. For the child who "plays doctor," or shows his when she shows hers, soon feels an uneasy element in his temporarily pleasurable tension. The sexual taboos in our ostensibly liberated world run very, very deep, and few children will escape their force. Impulse wrestles with a confused conscience over and over again, as the child tries to understand some very important human differences. . . .

"Look at that!" Jason says, awe-struck, as a classmate accommodatingly spreads her legs after pulling down her pants. He pokes her vagina gently, and gets down to see if he can see up inside it. His curiosity is pure and natural, yet when his teacher walks into the room he flushes guiltily and his friend hurriedly pulls up her pants, bumping her leg in the process. The teacher comforts her, and nothing is said about what she's just witnessed. Nonetheless, both children know, even if they don't know why, that this particular anatomical comparison elicits more grown-up attention than a comparing of noses or hair or height.

The forbidden elements of sex explain its frequent appearance in children's humor. For instance, Judy can't resist a play on words during a kindergarten game of learning colors. The children are instructed to clap their knees and identify the colors of their overalls. Around the room it goes: "blue knees . . . green knees . . . red knees . . ." The closer it comes to Judy, the more I become aware of some inner struggle taking place. She seems to be fighting off an insistent smirk. And the game continues: "yellow knees . . . brown knees . . ." and it comes to Judy, and she looks at her teacher just for a moment, and then at me observing in the back of the room, and she slaps her hands on her hips and shouts, "Hy-nee!" The class is overcome with laughter; ribboned heads are thrown back and chubby fists are thumped on desks in indescribable glee. Surely nothing this outrageously funny has ever been said anywhere else on earth. And surely, too, Judy has learned the power of suggestive language. She shares with her peers a new respect for words like BM and penis and duty and pee-pee and bellybutton. They are part of a young comic's repertoire, guaranteed to bring an anxious laugh from the audience.

And later on in life, the smutty story brings equally loud laughter from clusters of children huddling on the brink of maturity. In classrooms obscene notes are passed, filled with words whose implications are as uncertain as the French or Latin phrases they're supposedly there to learn. For children use humor as a mechanism for dealing with inner turmoils and confusion, which is why their humor is so clearly related to developing interest in the opposite sex. Alternating currents of desire and disgust at the idea of heterosexual sex are both responses from which jokes, nervously "dirty" ones, are made.

But before a child can deal, humorously or otherwise, with the issue of attraction to the opposite sex, he must first resolve the major question of what it means to be the sex he himself is. It's a question whose answer doesn't come ready-made at birth, even though the physical definition is of course there. Early in life, the differences between male and female seem obscure, and a child looks for concrete answers to help explain them. . . .

Dougie comes running into his house from playing outside to announce he's visited a neighbor and seen her new baby.

"How nice," his mother answers companionably. "Is it a boy or a girl?"

Dougie considers the question, suddenly troubled because he's over his head. But then a light flashes across his face. It isn't his fault that he doesn't know the answer. . . . "I couldn't tell," he says brightly. "It didn't have any clothes on!"

To Dougie it is clothing cues, not parts of the body, that tell boy from girl, and his approach to the question illustrates the thinking of the young child. It is too often ignored that children's thinking about the meaning of sex roles is totally different from adults'. "Boy" and "girl" are labels they vaguely know are pasted on their bodies, but when they look in the mirror of themselves, the label's meaning is elusive. So it is that before three years of age, most children will be inconsistent in their answer to the question "Are you a boy or a girl?" and will comfortably play mommy *or* daddy in games of make-believe. Even at four, children will still feel that if you changed your hair style or put on a dress instead of pants, you could become the other sex, and that mysterious future when they will be grownups seems wide open in gender possibilities. . . .

Jason comes running into the kitchen after his father scolds him. He grabs his mother around the knees and buries his head in her lap.

"When I grow up," he says, voice rich with emotion, "I'm going to be a mommy—not a daddy!"

While Jason's vow of course relates to the moment's anger toward his father, it represents, too, the instability in his understanding of sexual difference. So although his mother greets this declaration of love a little uncomfortably, her concern is needless. For the fact is that it will be a while yet till Jason understands that boys remain boys and girls remain girls, and his confusion simply reflects his stage of conceptual development.

By the time children are five, they *do* generally understand the constancy of sexual identity. But the conflicts attached to that perception remain and continue as they grow. For example, despite a relaxed cultural attitude toward homosexuality, many children in the middle years of childhood are terribly worried that they may be homosexual. This anxiety is related to and also complicated by the fact that homosexual feelings, and even experiences, are very common at this stage of development. Indeed, not only are the feelings psychologically natural, but knowing the self-doubt of these years, they are almost inevitable. How can you not admire, envy, covet the beauty of another boy or girl who seems to have escaped your emotional and physical blemishes? But when you do admire, when you do admit to the secret feelings, what torment there is, what terrible secret shame at this irrevocable proof of not being like everyone else, of—oh, ultimate negative label—not being "normal."

Too often the sharp stabs of accusation are public and, however unjustified, may leave many lingering scars. Last year Susan was brutally ostracized by a segment of her school for her obvious crush on a class leader. This other girl was everything Susan herself would want to be—slim, blond, skin smooth, body firm. As she stroked her silk comforter, Susan hungered to touch this girl's overwhelmingly perfect surface. One day, as she was worshipfully standing near her in a momentarily empty classroom, Susan did exactly that. But at the moment her hand made contact with the other girl, a gaggle of students bounded through the door. Susan froze, and her fear was quickly seized on by the crowd and molded into ugly epithets—dyke, lesbian, queer. Crimson, crying, Susan pushed through the group and ran home, screaming to her mother that she would never go back.

Of course, in the powerlessness of her childhood, she did go back, did take the jeers and the abuse, and although her mother talked to her and tried to help her understand that her sense of disgrace was inappropriate, her suffering continued, further eroding her struggle to build a coherent sense of herself. A fragment from Susan's journal from that time proclaims her pain. . . .

> There goes fat girl
> answering a fire
>   inside herself.
> The flames erase the twisted picture
> she . . .
> calls . . .
>   me.

Ironically, while many children like Susan show newly accelerated homosexual concerns, other children encounter the problems involved with an accelerated exposure to heterosexual experience. For if we are a culture in transition, young people have often already arrived at brand-new places on the sexual map. And so boys and girls are often torn between the behavior of their peers and their parents' older set of moral codes. In Tommy's camp last summer, among the campers his age, there were secret underground strategies for an elaborate "bunk fuck." Tommy was ripped with ambivalence. . . . Should he go, shouldn't he go? Ultimately the plans were foiled by an alert camp director. But not before Tommy had written this entry in the journal that he, like Susan and so many other children, keeps religiously:

> The ax of suppression chops at my feelings
> until I'm too weak
>   and afraid

to
scale my parents' barricades.

Studies prove that the pressure to perform heterosexually at earlier and earlier ages is creating, as it did for Tommy, very real problems for great numbers of children. The "sexual revolution" has made unwilling revolutionaries out of far too many boys and girls who in the name of liberation have lost the freedom to say "not yet." Adolescent pregnancies are escalating crazily, while growing numbers of girls as young as ten will turn off an already precocious introduction to the menstrual cycle by becoming pregnant.

And that pregnancy doesn't occur doesn't only imply abstinence. Susan and Nancy and almost every other child I interviewed who had reached the junior high school level casually referred to girls they knew who were "on the pill." Yet these children also revealed, as indeed did their sexually cavalier friends, an uncertainty about sex as troubling as their parents ever knew in their own pre-pill childhoods. Sexual intercourse often serves as a poor substitute for the emotional intimacy really being sought in a relationship, and bodies too often behave in ways unrelated to minds and emotions.

Sex contributes to distress also by the way it can reinforce fears of personal inadequacy. As we've seen, children are constantly measuring themselves against one another and, particularly in this aspect of their self-perceptions, are quick to find themselves wanting. The agony in locker rooms and summer-camp bunks will be intense when the penis which always seemed too small clearly fails the competitive measure, and barely budding breasts seem even flatter next to the swelling bosom of a friend.

The desire to find sexual definition makes almost any part of sexual development a cause for competition. Beth, impatient to begin menstruating, watches her calendar with the concentration of a criminal marking off a sentence—doomed, she feels, to the prison of her childhood while all around her other people are escaping. She pokes herself every night in the bathroom, hoping, hoping to see the toilet tissue tinged pink. Each pristine white strip of paper convinces her she is headed for unwanted medical celebrity—the first girl to go through life never menstruating.

But even as Beth hungers for female validation through menstruation, other girls, like Susan, already padded or tamponed, often seethe with self-consciousness too. Susan's menstrual flows are heavy, and when she stands up in a classroom to recite during those periods, she is flooded with fear. What if a bloodstain has appeared on her skirt? What if the bulge of her padding shows?

Boys, of course, are not immune to concerns about sex-related public exposure. The erection that takes sudden command of tight jeans makes Jeremy double over with emotional pain when the teacher calls on him—pain as real as if he'd been physically struck in that most sensitive part of his body. He feels a terrible shame at being so out of control—a shame that keeps him from engaging his parents in the kind of discussion that might clear up his complicated-by-confusion distress.

Certainly no writing about children and sex can be complete without touching on the distortions their own writings often contain. Whether it's about erections or how babies are made or are born, a child's image of sex is colored by his inability to grasp certain sexual concepts in their entirety, as well as by the emotions those half-comprehended concepts quickly ignite.

Nancy and a boy go skinny-dipping on a dare and their bodies briefly come together underwater, and Nancy, despite an ostensible knowledge of reproduction, spends many sleepless nights convinced she's pregnant. And Jason, who believes babies are hatched from king-size eggs similar to the smaller ones he saw chickens lay on his uncle's farm, freezes with terror when a very pregnant woman takes a seat alongside him on the subway. His mother, standing over him, cannot understand the abrupt change in his mood—doesn't know until much later that Jason was sure the baby would burst out during the bumpy train ride, forcing his own involvement in the—to Jason—not at all blessed event.

And if children are bewildered about themselves as sexual people, they are equally perplexed at the thought that their parents relate that way to each other, or indeed to other men and women. No matter how legally divorced, the mother who comes home from a date flushed with sexual fulfillment can enrage a waiting child. The anger may not be articulated, even to the child himself, but clearly and unhappily it is there. And working with children of even the most properly married parents shows how mind-boggling the idea is of parental life behind closed bedroom doors. To relentless questioning by Jason, for example, about how babies got *in* their mothers' stomachs in the first place, Robert finally, in tremulous voice, answered that mothers and fathers "take off all their clothes and lay on top of themselves."

Robert and Jason stared at each other in sudden silence— Jason trying to make sense of the image, Robert trying to deal with the feelings finally saying *it* out loud had started swirling. Minutes passed and I watched Robert's face, unwilling to intrude in whatever he was working through (even though I sensed his parents would soon be drawn into some clarifying discussion). Finally his face cleared. It was obvious he had settled something in his mind, and now he helpfully passed it on to Jason, who was patiently waiting for his older friend's considered wisdom. "I guess that's why you and me don't have brothers and sisters, because our mommys and daddys didn't like doing that!"

Jason giggles, and Robert grins, and the conversation for the moment is over. What is significant in this discussion is the way in which Robert, out of his reluctance to see his parents in a sexual light, created his own mythology about their sexual behavior. Clearly this is reminiscent of how adults deal with the similar wish to avoid the truth of their children's sexuality. Partially our procedure stems from the way we have repressed our own childhood's sexuality. Partially it is because we continue to aggrandize the myth of innocence. Neither reason is reason enough to continue the pretense that our sons and daughters are not sexual people, for as long as we cling to that deception, children will wander in puzzled circles of feeling, perhaps having to deny aspects of themselves that will permanently impoverish relationships and their lives in general.

10 / Mothers and Fathers

"My friend's mother kisses her all the time"

No discussion about children's feelings can close without bringing into it the two people most involved with a child's emotional life. The relationship between parent and child continues to be an area of ultimate encounter—that place where sensitivities and empathy reach extraordinary heights. It is a relationship that can make adults feel most fully human, and in which the growing child learns to define his own humanity.

A child's basic attitudes about himself and his place in the world are formed within the family. Will he love more than hate? Trust more than suspect? Know more pride than shame? Move out to experience more than he retreats from it? All these questions take shape in childhood, and the answers are primarily determined by the interactions children have with their parents, interactions that involve most of all the crucial idea of love.

The meaning and origins of love are elusive, subject to endless debate by men and women nursing its wounds or savoring its delights. But no matter where the emotion takes us in maturity, its significance in the days of beginnings, in childhood, is overwhelmingly profound. Love places a warm hand on a child's back, guiding him through the often wintry winds of development. Over and over, research proves it is indeed the certainty of love that steadies childhood's step and provides enthusiasm for the rest of life's journey. One study, for example, of 158 "well-adjusted" children (that is, children with no really debilitating problems) concluded that the significant shared quality of these comfortable-in-life young people was that their parents were clearly devoted to them and, more importantly, the children knew they were.

And here, of course, we have love's rub. . . .

For if parents and children inevitably have difficulty hearing each other across the gulf of disparate perceptions, the interpretative gap is widest in respect to the ways adults give and children perceive "evidence" of being loved. It's a problem far more complicated than the difference in the development of cognitive powers. We are talking now about need and the imbalance between a child's appetite for parental love and his parents' ability to satisfy it. Psychologist Alice Rossi points out with a simplicity which belies the problem's dimensions that a child's need for mothering is "absolute," but even in the best of relationships the need of a woman to mother is only "relative." While this truth has always been with us, today it is particularly so, as more and more women try to combine mothering with some interest outside the home.

That closets lined with baby food and diapers are not exciting enough to all mothers to warrant shelving other needs until their children grow up does not of course mean they feel less love for their children. Clearly, many devoted mothers also engage in careers. But the situation does underscore Dr. Rossi's point about the different emotional requirements of mother and child.

It should be pointed out here that "mothering" can often come from fathers. As sex roles become redefined, parenting, too, expands its patterns and emotional responsiveness is less and less limited to biology. But whether it's mother or father (and obviously one would hope it's both) who through affection can bridge the gap of discrepant needs, there are times in childhood when the gap will yawn to an apparently unbridgeable width. In these developmental phases, the child is like a ravenous diner at a banquet, gobbling up every proof of caring—the affectionate touch, the affirming word, the welcoming smile. . . .

"Mommy was so happy to see me when she came home that she started to cry!" Robert says one morning while he shows the class presents his parents brought from their European trip. And the lilting pride in his voice clearly says it was those tears, not these elaborate toys, that are the homecoming's real gift. Robert's entire being is ignited by the glow of love returned. His self-esteem soars through reinforcement of the idea that he is important to the people so very important to him.

Because love's well-being is so total, it's understandable that much children's writing about love involves all their senses—how its presence feels or looks and sounds. Remembering that children are afraid of loud and sudden noise, we can appreciate these descriptions:

"Loving is soft and gentle and quiet," writes Beth. "Clocks make tiny tickings and all the sounds in the house are just hums and everything you touch is like blue velvet."

Jeremy, too, uses a sensory framework, but this time to make a connection between love and self-discovery. "Love makes different kinds of quiet," he writes. "There's a soft silence where you can think anything you want to, and let your mind wander without having to stop it. I like to do that because even though I'm thinking a lot of things, I can rest."

Jeremy's description, through its suggestion that the child secure in love is free to discover himself, illustrates how love unfolds the fabric of self-awareness. Encouraged and appreciated for who he is, he can roam about in his mind to see whom he would like to become. Dr. Irving Markowitz explains that the uncertainty a child feels about his own productions, whether they're goals or feelings or ideas, makes him need immediate response to his efforts at every tentative step. Dougie wanders away from his mother with big-boy bravado when they visit the playground but he returns to her bench in a little while and pats her on the cheek, and receives her hug with a satisfied giggle. His swagger is a little more certain when he leaves her again, for in that affectionate interchange was what has been called "emotional refueling," the self energized by the strength of love.

Similarly, Beth calls her mother at the office to tell her about a test score, while Greta stares hard at her father as she lets go of his hands and pedals off herself on a new two-wheeler. The pride in the children's independent achievements expressed in Beth's mother's voice and on Greta's father's face encourages, as nothing else can, more and more experiments *with* independence, as well as giving the push to develop further intellectual and physical skills.

Studies of children's intellectual development invariably support this conclusion. Once again using the dramatic extreme to illustrate a point's general significance, children who are really love-starved by their natural mothers show enormous acceleration in learning when given continuously tender and stimulating surrogate care. One six-year research project, for example, involved twenty-five "emotionally disadvantaged" infants. Their lethargic dullness caused a scientific projection of a high probability that "they would slip to an IQ of 85 by the age of six." When outside stimulation was provided, by consistently available and affectionate "teachers," the children steadily brightened. Apathy became alertness, passivity stirred and was transformed into resourcefulness. By the age of six every child was reading, and all tested at the "superior" score of 125 to 130.

Obviously the children involved in this book are not similarly deprived and so will not be exposed to the potential tragedy of a stunted intellect. But even with the accepted, economically and emotionally advantaged child, there is a direct relationship between the loving presence and the push to learn. A paper delivered at a recent psychiatric meeting on this subtle interplay concluded that "children who later grow up to be exceptionally competent intellectually probably do not become so because of innate capabilities only." Starting almost in the cradle, the authors of the paper said, "these children have daily experiences in their homes which selectively promote their intellectual development."

The "experiences" referred to didn't mean only how many "educational" toys a child has to play with, or even how much physical time his parents spend as learning-play companions. Presence is indeed important, but presence alone can be more frustrating than nurturing. Judy, for instance, once angrily told her mother, who was restlessly participating in a game of checkers, "You have your back in front of your face!" Thus, at a very early age, children can recognize the difference between dutiful eye contact and real engagement.

Of course, all parents will have moments when they are less than absorbed in their child's chatter or play, but as long as children see the more constant reflection of love such moments will pass without serious emotional incident. It is these steadier images that contain the concept of "reflected appraisals," that process through which a child's idea of how his parents feel about him affects how he feels about himself. Not only do positive appraisals promote self-confidence, they also teach a child about the more profound aspects of a love relationship. When Judy's mother leaves a note on her pillow that night, telling her how much she loves her, and that she's sorry she spoiled her checker game, Judy learns something about generosity and forgiveness. The next morning she tells her mother that "when I have kids I'm gonna say what a sweet mommy you are sometimes." However conditional Judy's praise may sound, in reality she has gone beyond early childhood's totally selfish demands for love to an image of mature caring that she will develop and carry with her to yet another love-needing generation.

Judy's more realistic awareness of love's behavior points up a love-related problem that the mythic image of childhood engenders. Grouping all children together under one happy smile assumes that they have identical love needs. Yet children, as individual people, are actually quite different from one another in their temperaments. They will cover a vast range of emotional ground in both dimension of need and in the intensity of the demands they make on a relationship.

So Robert, who like Judy would like total commitment from his mother, complains bitterly when she goes to two meetings during the same week, even though she has never worked and is extravagantly available to him.

"You're *never* here when I need you!" he wails in deprivation as she leaves him with the sitter, and only awareness of her son's insatiability keeps her from feeling inappropriately guilty.

On the other hand, Beth is, as she has been since birth, enormously self-sufficient. In her baby carriage she would gaze endlessly at the hanging mobile as it swayed in the day's breeze. Now she reads several books a week, writes long passages in her diary, loves to do crossword and picture puzzles. Indeed, so much is the private-pursuit part of who she is that she told the camp director, when discussing summering at his camp, "Yes, all the activities sound very exciting, but I have to have at least one hour a day to be just by myself."

So Beth stands on the other end of need's continuum from Robert. Therefore, although her mother has a full-time job, and even though she does get worried sometimes about being physically alone, her security-giving view of her mother is that she is emotionally available to her.

Clearly, the comfortableness of the fit between parent and child relates at least in part to who the child constitutionally is. But it also relates to who the parents are—as individual people and, perhaps more importantly in terms of their children, who they are as parents. Men and women become mothers and fathers for a variety of reasons. They see the role as satisfying a wide spectrum of needs and behave in the context of that role in many different ways.

Studies that have involved ways of parenting all show that there is indeed broad variation in attitudes and behaviors. Some parents are "indulgent," others "democratic," some "coercive," still others "authoritarian." The correlation between a specific parental approach and a child's development is fragile at best. What's more, it is really academic. For the *real* issue is not which kind of parent is better or worse for a child, but that *for* better or worse, children are raised by the parents they have. Mothers and fathers should not feel guilty about this inevitable situation. Given the fact that we are all human beings, it's unreasonable to believe that another parent's strengths and weaknesses are any more balanced than our own. As long as we recognize our children as separate people, entitled to their own strengths and weaknesses, they will do equally well inside our particular family walls.

Children are of course aware that other families are not mirror images of their own, and are not above making sometimes critical comparisons, often to their own parents' discomfort. When Greta tells her mother about the other mother who "kisses all the time," maternal concern escalates. Should she be more affectionate? Used to older children, who periodically reject physical affection, perhaps she has not been attuned enough to Greta's needs.

Actually, Greta's mother has little reason to feel guilty. True, she is not particularly demonstrative, but she shows her love for Greta in innumerable ways. It is entirely possible that Greta was making only a simple comment, noticing differences that she hadn't been aware of when she was younger. Nonetheless, Mrs. Walters did try to show her affection and approval for Greta more actively after that comparative statement, and she feels, from Greta's behavior, that it was an appropriate response to have made. Certainly there is some validity in weeding out what might be a legitimate message in a child's reports about parental differences. It is not only in their dreams that children sometimes say things to their parents indirectly. However, it should be stressed again that, by and large, we are the people our own childhoods shaped us to be, and as long as we raise our children with good will and love, they will prosper accordingly. . . .

But they will also suffer, and not just because of our flaws or failings. Of course, there are many times when parents *will* be the cause of their children's pain, and we will continue to try and rise as parents above the character problems that make this happen. But no matter how successful our efforts are, our children will know, along with the exquisite joy, bursting hope and delicious excitement of their childhoods, a darker, more violent, bitter side of life.

The reason we have explored this side within these pages is quite simply because there seems no alternative, considering the world we have brought our children into. The flow of experience rushes around us, making it harder and harder to chart a course. The accelerated rate of change that is the dynamic of this time clearly demands that the mythical conception of childhood be challenged. Fantasy's child will not swim well in these unfamiliar currents.

The social pressures and tensions that command the attention of adults do not, no matter how we would wish otherwise, leave children unaffected. It is they, in fact, who are often most caught by the world's confusions. We are a society that too often maintains the idea of the child as property, a perception that allows us to work out adult anxieties and disappointments *through* our children. So as an athlete might groom a son to captain a Little League team, our culture pressures children to achieve in ways it calls important, and also to compensate for inadequacies it may now regret.

For example, postwar concern about losing ground to the Russians (called by psychiatrists "sputnik anxiety") resulted, says one psychological report, in a "breakneck acceleration of scientific curriculum" that was often "harassing" to the children it was imposed on. Similarly, these last transitional years have made children the vehicles of many grown-up struggles with social change. Studies of those troubling issues of "bussing" and school prayer conclusively proved that the needs and feelings of the children, in classrooms or in transit, were rarely important factors in agitation either pro or con.

We must abandon the perception of a child as "possession" if he is to learn how to take responsibility for his own life. And if children have always had to do this as they grew into maturity, it is a particularly important life goal today. For more than at any other time in our history, adults are becoming inadequate models for a child's socialization. As indicated at the start of this book, much of what we were taught to believe in and live by may not prove the most useful equipment for today's child. The old verities are not nearly so helpful as learning to feel comfortable with less rigidly defined behavioral directives. A child today must be flexible, unafraid of unknown challenge; above all, he must move more and more confidently into independence and autonomy. Children today must be choosers, who will not panic at the unlimited number of choices their lives will present them with.

They must, therefore, achieve the consciousness of self that will allow them to pause in order to choose, rather than be forced into behaviors that have little to do with their inner needs. A coherent plan of action comes from knowing who you are, and only a person who is encouraged to be whole can know this. If a child pushes part of his experience underground, he may become separated from parts of himself that are necessary to form the wholeness of the person he is becoming.

The myth of the happy child encourages children to repress and deny too much of their real experiencing. The impact and implication of feelings are left unexplored, even though these feelings make up their self's sense of place in the world. So it cannot be overstated that the myth of happiness imposes far too negative an imperative on reality's child.

There are other reasons, too, for dispelling the myth of the happy child—reasons that also relate to the child's search for a meaningful sense of himself. The wish to have our children always happy may prevent them from meeting some very necessary challenges. According to Dr. Irving Markowitz, and he is only one analytic voice out of many on this subject, it is impossible to find happiness in maturity if unhappiness in childhood isn't dealt with at least to some degree.

A childhood that was truly as blissful and carefree as the myth implies would mean the crucially important labors of development had not been engaged in. It would place the self in a hothouse, not where it should be, in the open air. Yes, the temperature of the hothouse is soothing, but it stifles the growing personality, so that, according to Dr. Markowitz, the "happy child" may turn into an emotionally stunted adult, bewildered and frightened and still dependent as he moves ill-equipped out into the cold winds of maturity. Thus not to allow children the experiential struggles inherent in growing up is actually a deprivation and makes the myth of happy childhood a mockery.

Allowing a child to accept the full range of his emotional life also teaches him the skills he needs in order to deal with life's emotional issues. One of the most crucial of these is learning how to be intimate with other people. Here, too, there is almost total professional agreement that a child who is not allowed to experience his real self will never be truly able to love or feel loved by someone else. Again, the myth of happiness plays its destructive role. A child who is ashamed of his feelings may believe he is not lovable as he really is. And so instead of seeking intimacy he will avoid exposing his true self, believing he would surely be rejected if he were ever really "seen." As if he were still a toddler in the playground, all his relationships take the form of a kind of "parallel play," where the people move gingerly around each other but never really touch—are always, barrenly, alone.

And, too, in excess the wish for a happy child leads children themselves to establish goals of happiness that are equally unrealistic and frequently damaging psychologically. If, as Arnold Toynbee once said, "Life is the voyage and not the harbor," being oriented only to the harbor can color the voyage dull and disappointing, with the rewards never grand enough to bring real contentment. There is a reason why Robert cries after opening his Christmas presents and why Cathy is sulky after a lavish birthday party. And the reasons are not totally related to their being overtired. Rather, the long anticipation of both occasions, the compulsion to reach ecstatic peaks while they take place, make reality (inevitably?) a letdown. Both Robert and Cathy soon become disgruntledly upset that they aren't happy "enough," and later Robert downgrades what he has been given (to localize the blame for his depression), and is already planning what "better" things he'll ask for when next Christmas comes around.

It is not cynicism but awareness of life's complexities that makes us know no gift exists that can reach the point on the happiness continuum Robert is pushing for. Happiness is not so easily manufactured, and it is perhaps this above all that should propel us to abandon a mythology that leads children to believe that it is. We must not raise children with an image of happiness that in its superficiality will ensure their being disappointed. In a sea of plenty they will then know only thirsty discontent. It is time for them to listen to and create other kinds of stories, stories grounded in real rather than fantasied experiencing, stories whose emotional tone is rich enough to grasp the intricacies of the plots life will continue to create, stories whose messages are significant enough to help them understand those other plot lines, even the ones whose narratives are upsetting.

Childhood is indeed a special time of life. But inside its special "place," a child should be allowed and helped—by his parents, his teachers—to discover his real, not his mythical self. After all, he himself is the most important element in his unfolding true-to-life story.

No one is more important in a child's life than his mother and father, but to use our unquestioned power gracefully, caringly, and to loosen our grip on it when it's appropriate, is the challenge of the parental role. At the same time, parents should rid themselves of the oppressive sense that they alone are responsible for a child's emotional pain, or that they could, if only they were better parents, get rid of those pains. Freed from the false mythology that generates such false guilt, they can help their children grow into authentically experiencing adults.